MW01193172

Baptists who embrace their histc
needed a robust and comprehensi
nuanced interpretations of the bibli.ai covenants that a baptistic hermeneutic requires. This treatment by Greg Nichols does just that and more. As a devotee of the Westminster tradition (including its chapter, "On God's Covenant with Man"), I differ here and there; sometimes significantly so. But there is so much to applaud in this volume and Baptists will do well to read this volume carefully and with much gratitude. A splendid achievement. I, for one, will insist that my Presbyterian students read it.

—Derek W. H. Thomas, Distinguished Visiting Professor of Systematic and Historical Theology, RTS, Minister of Preaching and Teaching, First Presbyterian Church, Columbia, SC, Editorial Director, Alliance of Confessing Evangelicals

There has been an urgent need for Reformed Baptists to produce a work on the covenants. I am so thankful that Greg Nichols has engaged this very weighty work. It is a very timely addition on a vitally important topic and adds much to a growing Reformed Baptist literary body.

—James R. White, Alpha and Omega Ministry, author of numerous books, including *Pulpit Crimes*, published by Solid Ground

Greg Nichols has done a wonderful job of articulating a genuinely Reformed and baptistic model of covenant theology. The fruit of decades of study and teaching on this subject, this volume should be read by all who want to understand the proper framework of divine revelation. My counsel to all ministerial students is "Tolle lege" (take up and read).

—Dr. Robert P. Martin, Emmanuel Reformed Baptist Church, Seattle, WA, Author of *A Guide to the Puritans*

The Old Testament was inspired by the Spirit of God. It is certainly a record of what is true, of creation, fall, and the promise of the Messiah. There is the whole machinery of redemptive anticipation that God set up with His old covenant people. What of family life? What of the children of believers? Their sons are no longer to be circumcised. What is the status of the sons and daughters of believers under the new covenant? Such questions are fascinating and Baptists are asking them and seeking answers. Hence the appearance of this book which comes out of many years of thought and preparation by Greg Nichols and has been eagerly anticipated by the gospel church. May it do much good. May we all look again at the Scriptures and find a new help in understanding them in this satisfying and provocative volume.

—Pastor Geoff Thomas, Alfred Place Baptist Church in Aberystwyth, Wales

I remember the very first class that I took from Pastor Nichols which was on the Doctrine of the Covenants and thinking to myself, "This material has utterly transformed the way that I look at the Bible." Until that point, I had never been taught covenant theology and so the effect of this biblical teaching on my life was nothing short of profound! Four thoughts come to mind as I think about this new book: thoroughly scriptural, historically confessional, warmly pastoral, and experientially practical. My prayer is that the publication of this work will be that which our great God uses to edify His church and to get much glory to His own holy Name.

—Pastor Rob Ventura, Grace Community Baptist Church, North Providence, RI, Co-Author of *Portrait of Paul*

As a former student of Greg's in the Trinity Ministerial Academy, I cannot say enough good about his lectures in systematic theology. In addition to playing a primary role in shaping my ministry, they have had a significant impact upon me personally. His lectures on Doctrine of the Covenants are among my favorites. I am not aware of anything in print that treats this topic as clearly and comprehensively, and from a distinctly Baptist perspective. Greg's emphasis throughout is biblical, pastoral, and practical, with a contemporary flavor.
—Pastor Jim Domm, Englewood Baptist Church, Englewood, NJ

Pastor Greg Nichols's lectures on the Biblical Covenants is a breath of fresh air among a smog of other materials available on the same subject. Presented in a plain and readily understandable way, it has revolutionized my thinking and approach to understanding God's dealing with mankind. Next to a grasp of biblical Calvinism, nothing has opened up my understanding more to the Word of God than this. It has enabled me to see the true unity that does exist in both the Old and New Testaments while at the same time enabling me to understand the differences. These lectures offer a biblical alternative to the serious Bible student without feeling they must be either Pedo-Baptist or Dispensational in their approach to the Scriptures. With nothing like them in print available, it would be a great asset to the Church of Jesus Christ to have these available in printed form.
—Pastor Martin Hoffman, Providence Baptist Church, Lecanto, FL

Greg Nichols's approach to theology is rooted in his commitment to the Word of God. He has always desired to allow the bible to speak and to sit under its revelation. Over the years I have had both the joy and the privilege to sit through his teaching on various aspects of Systematic Theology and benefited greatly from it. I can heartily recommend his writings to you. It will take you back to your Bible, deepen your understanding of God's Holy Word, and draw you closer to the Lord.
—Pastor Robert Briggs, Immanuel Baptist Church, Sacramento, CA

During the early 1980s when I was training for the Christian ministry, it was my privilege to sit under the teaching of Pastor Greg Nichols for a significant portion of my class-work. His instruction exerted a formative influence in opening up the entire Bible to me. His material on the covenants, for example, was so insightful in unveiling the framework of redemption. Reformed Baptists would benefit by having Pastor Nichols's material in print. It would help our churches to better understand our faith and better pass it on to the next generation.
—Pastor Stu Johnston, Grace Reformed Baptist Church of Mebane, NC

One of the benefits of being under the theological teachings of Greg Nichols is being able to enthusiastically recommend his lectures. His lessons enrich the soul of the Christian, and extract beautiful principles from biblical texts that fix themselves in the heart and make them unforgettable. Based on my understanding of Christ and His Word, and my Christian experience, I recommend availing yourself of the theological teachings of Greg Nichols.
—Pastor Oscar Arocha, Bautista de la Gracia, Santiago, Dominican Republic

COVENANT THEOLOGY
A Reformed and Baptistic Perspective on God's Covenants

COVENANT THEOLOGY
A Reformed and Baptistic Perspective on God's Covenants

GREG NICHOLS

Solid Ground Christian Books
Birmingham, Alabama USA

Solid Ground Christian Books
PO Box 660132
Vestavia Hills AL 35266
205-443-0311
mike.sgcb@gmail.com
www.solid-ground-books.com

COVENANT THEOLOGY
A Reformed & Baptistic Perspective on God's Covenants

Greg Nichols

First printing September 2011
First paperback edition - February 2014

This volume is the first installment in a proposed set entitled
Scriptural and Systematic Studies Series.

ISBN- 978-159925-3428 (paperback)

Foreword

My first study Bible portrayed the flow of redemptive history under the rubric of changing "dispensations." This approach helped me to appreciate the progressive nature of special revelation. But the more I studied the Scriptures, the less correspondence I sensed between the biblical text and the dispensational scheme in the accompanying notes.

Then I was introduced to an older way of viewing the flow of redemptive history that employed "covenant" as the organizing category. This approach gave me a greater appreciation for the underlying continuity of special revelation. It also seemed to follow the contours of Scripture better than the dispensational approach. Nevertheless, I couldn't reconcile certain facets of this older "covenant theology" with some of the scriptural data.

Then I had the privilege of hearing Greg Nichols lecture on the biblical covenants. Instead of simply beginning with the categories of the older covenant theology, Greg has made an inductive study of all the relevant biblical data his starting point. He has collated that data in a manner that does greater justice to both the continuity and the discontinuity of special revelation. The end result is a revised and improved version of covenant theology with a stronger exegetical foundation and more consistent theological formulation.

As one of Greg's former pupils and present colleagues, I'm delighted to see the fruit of his labors finally reach the printer's press. Greg's study doesn't merely tie up some of the loose ends left by older covenant theologians, it offers its own unique contributions. For instance, while noting an organic unity that binds all the divine-human covenants, Greg distinguishes between covenants God makes with "righteous servants" and covenants God makes with "saved communities" (i.e., the righteous servant's offspring). He also marshals exegetical evidence for a divine covenant with Christ that is distinct from the pre-temporal "covenant of redemption." This "Messianic Covenant" functions as the historical counterpart to the "New Covenant," which God makes with the Righteous Servant's (spiritual) offspring.

The reader will encounter other distinctive contributions in this study. Whether or not he finds them all equally compelling, I'm confident he'll gain a greater appreciation for God's unfolding plan of salvation as revealed in "the covenants of the promise." And I know that nothing would give Greg more joy than fostering in God's people a greater admiration for the riches of God's glorious grace.

Bob Gonzales, Dean
Reformed Baptist Seminary

Table of Contents

Acknowledgments

———◆———

I wish to express my appreciation for all who helped with this publication. I especially express gratitude to my wife, Ginger, for her unfailing love and encouragement; to my late mother, Blanche Nichols, for persistently praying for me to complete this work; to the pastors and people of Grace Immanuel, for supporting and enabling this project; and to my friend and spiritual grandson, Rob Ventura, whose vision and labor made this work a reality.

Preface

———◆———

This book stems from systematic theology lectures. Christology covers the eternal plan, solemn promise, and accomplishment of salvation. God expresses his solemn promise of salvation in his covenants. A survey of Reformed theology and the biblical testimony introduces God's covenants. The remaining lectures expound the biblical testimony. I begin with the evangelical foundation of God's covenants, the covenant of grace, which God declares in Genesis 3:15. Then I expound the Noahic, Abrahamic, Mosaic, Davidic, new, and Messianic covenants. I conclude with practical applications. I cover this material in ten lectures that morph into fifteen chapters and the conclusion of this book. Also, I append lectures on two foundational topics, the eternal counsel of redemption and the Adamic covenant. In the Christology course syllabus (Syllabus 3), I expound the eternal counsel of redemption as an aspect of God's eternal decree to save. In the anthropology course syllabus (Syllabus 2), I expound the Adamic covenant as an aspect of God's original creation. This scheme is shown below.

Chapter	Syllabus: Lecture	Course Outline: Topic
1–7	3:5	Historical Introduction: the Reformed doctrine
8	3:6	Biblical Introduction: the Biblical testimony
9	3:7	Unit 1: The Covenant of Grace
10	3:8	Unit 2: The Noahic Covenants
11	3:9	Unit 3: The Abrahamic Covenant
12	3:10	Unit 4: The Mosaic (Old) Covenant
13	3:11	Unit 5: The Davidic Covenant
14	3:12	Unit 6: The New Covenant
15	3:13	Unit 7: The Messianic Covenant
Conclusion	3:14	Conclusion: Practical Application
Appendix 1	3:4	The Eternal Counsel of Redemption
Appendix 2	2:16	The Adamic Covenant

Regarding Scripture quotations, the English reader has a rich diversity of translations from which to choose. In this book, I base quotations from Scripture on the 1901 American Standard Version and on the New American Standard Version. For the most part I use the New American Standard. However, I use my own translation on occasions when I think it enhances clarity.

My hope and prayer is that as you consider God's covenant promises, sworn in love and fulfilled in faithfulness, you will find strong encouragement and adore, praise, and glorify the triune God.

Greg Nichols
Grand Rapids, Michigan
August 2011

Abbreviations

ASV The Bible, American Standard Version. Thomas Nelson & Sons, 1901.

BAG *A Greek-English Lexicon of the New Testament.* Translation by William
F. Arndt and F. Wilbur Gingrich of Walter Bauer's *Griechisch-Deutsches
Wörterbuch.* Chicago: University of Chicago Press, 1957.

BDB *A Hebrew and English Lexicon of the Old Testament.* Francis Brown, S.R.
Driver, and Charles A. Briggs. Oxford: Oxford University Press, 1978.

BEL The Belgic Confession

CSD The Canons of the Synod of Dort

HC The Heidelberg Catechism: The version of BEL, CSD, and HC cited
is from "Doctrinal Standards of the Christian Reformed Church
consisting of the Belgic Confession, the Heidelberg Catechism, and
the Canons of Dort." In the *Psalter Hymnal.* Grand Rapids: The
Publication Committee of the Christian Reformed Church, 1959.

LCF The 1689 London Confession of Faith: The version of LCF cited is
The Baptist Confession of Faith & The Baptist Catechism. Birmingham
and Carlisle: Solid Ground Christian Books & Reformed Baptist
Publications, 2010.

LXX *The Septuagint Version of the Old Testament and Apocrypha.* Grand
Rapids: Zondervan, 1978.

WCF The Westminster Confession of Faith

WLC The Westminster Larger Catechism: The version of WCF and
WLC cited is *The Confession of Faith, The Larger and Shorter
Catechisms.* The Publications Committee of the Free Presbyterian
Church of Scotland, 1970.

Introduction

———— ❧ ————

God planned salvation in eternity. He revealed it in a framework that he himself designed and formed. Christ's person and work do not appear in a vacuum. God arranged the categories that form the backdrop, substance, and aim of his mission. Understanding these categories is essential to appreciating the significance of his person and work. Divine covenant is the broadest category in which God revealed his plan to save in Christ (Heb. 7:20–22). God structured the Bible accordingly. He divided it into two parts, the Old Testament in Hebrew and the New Testament in Greek. These correspond with his old and new covenants with his people. Since covenant is the organizing principle of Scripture, it serves as the foundation of Christ's saving work. Just as it is important to comprehend God's eternal plan to save, even so it is important to comprehend the covenantal framework in which he accomplishes, applies, and completes salvation.

In Part 1 of this book, I present God's covenants from the vantage point of dogmatic theology. I survey the Reformed doctrine. This material is too extensive to cover in class in a three-hour Christology course, since it would consume seven lectures. Yet, it is too important to neglect. Therefore, I have usually handed out these dogmatic considerations in written form, in order to devote class time to the exposition of Scripture. Now these lectures, once relegated to a handout, have been reinstated to their proper place in this book format.

God in his providence used the great religious revival known as the Reformation to give his church illumination regarding many aspects of salvation, including its covenantal framework. Our survey begins with the Westminster and London Confessions. These stem from English Puritanism. They are of fundamental importance. They summarize mature Reformed thought on God's covenantal commitments. Subsequent Reformed theologians build on their teaching and develop it. In this Puritan stream we consider the contributions of three influential men, one Baptist and two Presbyterians. We consider the contribution of John Gill, who represents Calvinistic Baptists, and the contributions of Charles Hodge and R. L. Dabney, fathers of Northern and Southern Presbyterianism respectively. Yet the Reformed tradition has two major theological streams, the waters flowing from England and the waters of Calvinism in Holland. Accordingly, we next take up the contributions of Dutch Calvinism. Having surveyed major contributions from the English Puritan and Dutch Calvinist streams, I collate and summarize the classic Reformed doctrine of divine covenant. Finally, I survey recent contributions to this doctrine from Professor Murray, Meredith Kline, O. Palmer Robertson, and others. In the interest of simplicity, I develop this topic under seven headings: the Westminster and London Confessions, John Gill on God's Covenants, Charles Hodge on God's Covenants, R. L. Dabney on God's Covenants, Dutch Calvinists on God's Covenants, a Summary of the Classic Reformed Doctrine, and Contemporary Modifications to the Reformed Doctrine. Each of these constitutes a chapter in this book.

In Part 2 of this book, having surveyed the Reformed doctrine, I expound the biblical testimony. In Chapter 8, I begin with an overview of the biblical witness to God's covenants. Then in Chapter 9, I expound the evangelical foundation of God's covenants, the covenant of grace, which God declares in Genesis 3:15. On this foundation I expound God's historical covenants as Scripture unfolds them in redemptive history. I expound the Noahic covenants in Chapter 10, the Abrahamic covenant in Chapter 11, the Mosaic covenant in Chapter 12, the Davidic covenant in Chapter 13, the new covenant in Chapter 14, and finally the Messianic covenant in Chapter 15. Then in conclusion I apply God's covenants to experiential religion.

This book thus presents a systematic study of what the Bible says about God's covenants. I do not intend to be polemical. I intend to be positive and expository. I try to set forth comprehensively what Scripture teaches, without addition or distortion. Yet, if I've heard once, I've heard a dozen times: "You can't be Reformed and Baptist," or, "There's no such thing as Reformed Baptist." Ironically, based on my study of the biblical testimony, I believe that the Bible commends a covenant theology that is both Reformed and Baptistic. I hope that after reading this book, you will know how that's possible. I also hope and pray that you will embrace what Scripture says about God's covenants, appreciate his covenant love and faithfulness, and bless his name for his wonderful grace.

— PART 1 —

THE REFORMED THEOLOGY OF GOD'S COVENANTS

1

The Westminster and London Confessions

WCF belongs to a group of documents produced by the Westminster Assembly in 1644–1647. It must be studied, therefore, in conjunction with the Larger and Shorter Catechisms. It has become the foundation of the Presbyterian doctrinal heritage. LCF was published in 1689, although it was originally adopted in 1677. It has founded Reformed Baptist doctrinal heritage. The Reformed Baptist fathers were not embarrassed to copy verbatim from the Presbyterian fathers of the previous generation when they could do so conscientiously. This is even the case with God's covenant. WCF entitles Chapter 7, "God's Covenant with Man"; LCF simply, "God's Covenant."

First, note the theological context in which both confessions present this doctrine. Both present God's covenant in their seventh chapter. Both treat the fall, sin, and the punishment thereof in Chapter 6. Both consider Christ the Mediator in Chapter 8. Thus, both discuss divine covenant subsequent to the doctrine of man and sin and prior to the doctrine of Christ's person and work. I have adopted and follow our forefathers' order. It is proper to conclude that they understood the need to study and comprehend the person and work of Christ, not in a vacuum, but in the context of divine covenant. That explains their order of presentation.

In Chapter 7 WCF has six paragraphs, LCF, three. I now conduct a paragraph-by-paragraph survey and comparison. The confessions cover three major topics: the general necessity of divine covenant (WCF 7:1, LCF 7:1), the covenant of works (WCF 7:2), and the covenant of grace (WCF 7:3–6, LCF 7:2, 3). They feature the covenant of grace. Both begin with its *focus and implementation* (WCF 7:3, LCF 7:2). Then WCF unfolds its *testamental nature* (WCF 7:4) and *dual administration* (WCF 5, 6). LCF delineates *three predominant features* (LCF 7:3). Our survey and comparison proceeds accordingly.

The General Necessity for God's Covenant (WCF 7:1, LCF 7:1)

The first paragraph of both confessions is almost identical.

> The distance between God and the creature is so great, that although reasonable creatures do owe obedience unto him as their Creator, yet they could never have any fruition of him as their blessedness and reward, but by some voluntary condescension on God's part, which he has been pleased to express by way of covenant (WCF 7:1).

> The distance between God and the creature is so great, that although reasonable creatures do owe obedience unto him as their Creator, yet they could never have attained the reward of life but by some voluntary condescension on God's part, which he has been pleased to express by way of covenant (LCF 7:1).

Both confessions begin by stressing the need for divine covenant. Almost verbatim agreement exists concerning its necessity. The only difference is that WCF says: "yet they could never have any fruition of him as their blessedness and reward," where LCF says: "yet they could never have attained the reward of life." The only difference is the manner in which they identify the reward of God's people. Complete agreement exists concerning the fundamental need for divine covenant. Both find the need for divine covenant in the Creator/creature distinction. It is important to note that sin is not their reason. It is the distance between God and the creature. The need for voluntary condescension on God's part transcends the exigencies of redemption. It pertains even to the pre-fallen state.

They appeal for support to Luke 17:5–10. If any reward at all is to be given to man, even sinless man as originally created, it must be due to voluntary divine condescension of some kind. Reward from God can only be gracious because man owes everything God demands. Man can never merit anything from God. If therefore man receives any reward, it must be an expression of voluntary divine condescension. Whatever he does right, it is only his duty. Thus Jesus says that when we have done everything required of us, we should say that we are unprofitable servants, because we have done simply what we were supposed to do. This great reality forms the foundation and introduction of their presentation of divine covenant. This informs us that above all else, God's covenantal actions express his voluntary condescension. In a covenant, God voluntarily condescends to bless man, who is an unprofitable servant, who has not merited it, even when he has walked in the path of obedience. At its very root, divine covenant displays voluntary condescension in which God blesses and rewards men in the pathway of obedience. Thus, WCF logically transitions to the pre-fall covenant of works in Paragraph 2.

The Covenant of Works (WCF 7:2)

What did the Westminster Assembly regard as the first expression of divine covenant? They write: "The first covenant made with man was a covenant of works, wherein Life was promised to Adam; and in him to his posterity, upon condition of perfect and personal obedience" (WCF 7:2). The Westminster Assembly calls the first actual and concrete expression of this voluntary condescension towards man a *covenant of works*.

Note that the Presbyterian fathers carefully couched the covenant of works in the context of God's voluntary condescension. They took pains to avoid the false notion that Adam could merit anything from God. It is a blatant caricature of their doctrine to say that the Puritan conception of the covenant of works is legalistic since it postulates reward on the basis of human merit. That is not what they taught. They taught that no creature could merit anything from God, that we are all unprofitable servants, and that any reward, including eternal life, is received as an expression of God's voluntary condescension. WCF 7:2 must be understood in the light of WCF 7:1. They did not teach that the attainment of life and blessedness before the fall was on the basis of *meritorious works*. They merely asserted that God promised life on condition of perfect, personal obedience.

It is also significant that the Baptist fathers entirely deleted WCF 7:2, so that LCF contains no explicit definition of a covenant of works. The only other place where WCF mentions the covenant of works is 19:1: "God gave to Adam a law, as a covenant of works." Again, LCF deleted the phrase. However, there is some inconsistency in LCF in this regard. In 20:1 LCF describes the covenant of works as broken. Additional difficulty arises from the fact that LCF 20 does not come from WCF (there is no equivalent to Chapter 20 in WCF) but from the Savoy Declaration of 1658. Nonetheless, it still can be said, that wherever WCF made explicit reference to a covenant of works, as something in force with Adam before the fall, the

Reformed Baptist fathers deleted it while framing LCF. One of you may someday obtain a PhD for discovering why they left it in Chapter 20 and deleted it from Chapters 7 and 19. I can't explain that. It appears mysterious and somewhat inconsistent to me. Perhaps it was an oversight. If there is a theological rationale for it, I don't perceive it.

The Covenant of Grace (WCF 7:3–6, LCF 7:2, 3)

The next four paragraphs of WCF could be entitled: "*The Covenant of Grace: The Second Expression of God's Covenant.*" Its first expression was the covenant of works. Since LCF doesn't have a "first expression," I title these paragraphs in LCF: "*The Covenant of Grace: The Redemptive Expression of God's Covenant.*" LCF only defines how God expressed his voluntary condescension in redemption. WCF establishes a parallel between its pre-fall expression in a covenant of works and its post-fall expression in a covenant of grace. In both confessions, the covenant of grace earns the lion's share of attention, whether it is viewed as the second expression of God's covenantal condescension (WCF) or as its redemptive expression (LCF). This leads to the comparison of these respective presentations.

The Focus and Implementation of the Covenant of Grace (WCF 7:3, LCF 7:2)

Both confessions begin with what I call the "*focus*" and "*implementation*" of the covenant of grace. I have chosen these words carefully, for reasons soon to be clear. LCF 7:2 and WCF 7:3 are almost identical. WCF 7:3 establishes a parallel with the covenant of works: "Man, by his fall, having made himself incapable of life by that covenant, the Lord was pleased to make a second, commonly called the Covenant of Grace." The covenant of grace arose after Adam broke the covenant of works, because it was no longer possible for man to attain life in that way. Thus, God made a second way. LCF, however, doesn't speak of a first and a second expression of God's covenant. LCF 7:2 says: "Moreover, man having brought himself under the curse of the law by his fall, it pleased the Lord to make a Covenant of Grace." They also root the covenant of grace in the fall. But they introduce God's condescension to sinners without establishing any connection between a pre-fall and a post-fall covenant. They avoid the parallelism of WCF. Once they have couched the concept differently, they describe it identically. Both confessions identify its *focus* as the application of redemption and its method of *implementation* as general and effectual gospel call:

> commonly called the Covenant of Grace; wherein he freely offers unto sinners life and salvation by Jesus Christ; requiring of them faith in him that they may be saved, and promising to give unto all those that are ordained unto eternal life his Holy Spirit, to make them willing and able to believe (WCF 7:3).

> it pleased the Lord to make a Covenant of Grace, wherein he freely offers unto sinners life and salvation by Jesus Christ, requiring of them faith in him, that they may be saved; and promising to give unto all those that are ordained unto eternal life, his Holy Spirit, to make them willing and able to believe (LCF 7:2).

LCF quotes WCF verbatim. The only difference is the reversal of a comma and a semi-colon. The gospel call by which God applies redemption is twofold. It has a universal aspect and a particular aspect. Its universal aspect is the free and indiscriminate offer of mercy to lost sinners: "Wherein he freely offers unto sinners life and salvation by Jesus Christ, requiring of them faith in him that they may be saved." Its particular aspect is the effectual call in which God enables his elect to believe by the regenerating work of the Holy Spirit: "and promising to give unto all those that are ordained unto eternal life, his Holy Spirit, to make them willing and able to believe."

Therefore, the covenant of grace in WCF and LCF focuses on redemption applied through the general and effectual call of God's gospel. God *implements* the covenant of grace by a free offer of salvation to sinners coupled to the regeneration of his elect. The Baptist and Presbyterian fathers were trying to accommodate the general call of the gospel, the effectual call of the gospel, and the covenantal form of the application of redemptive grace. We must recognize, admire, and imitate this effort. Yet we must also proceed with caution. Has their legitimate concern been expressed with precision? Closer examination reveals great potential for confusion and misunderstanding. How should we present a *"promise"* to some unconverted men, namely, the unconverted elect, that God will give them his Holy Spirit to regenerate them? Brothers, use great caution here. This could send unconverted men on a futile search to discover whether or not they are elect while they are still unconverted. How can anyone possibly know, while unconverted, whether or not God has *promised* him his Holy Spirit to enable him to believe? No one can know he is elect *before* he believes. We only know we are elect *after* we believe (Acts 13:48; 1 Thess. 1:5). We should not define the *essence* of the covenant of grace as a *promise* to the unconverted elect to regenerate them. That is one reason why I dub this its *focus* and *implementation*, not its *essence* or *substance* or *content*. If the confessions said "*determining*" rather than "*promising*," this would clarify the issue to some degree, but even that would not resolve the difficulty. This difficulty is not peculiar to Presbyterians. Our Baptist fathers copied verbatim. It confronts everyone in the English Puritan tradition who tries to define precisely the application of redemption in a covenantal form. Learn from these documents that defining God's covenant of grace is a formidable task.

Now let's think this problem through. Plainly the confessions rightly define the general and effectual call. By this gospel call, God fulfills or implements his covenant of grace and applies redemption to his elect. So then, the gospel call is the means by which God implements the covenant of grace. Its essence or substance is *God's solemn pledge to accomplish redemption by Christ and to apply it in Christ to his elect*. God pledges this in Genesis 3:15. LCF intimates as much in 7:3. WLC confirms it plainly.[1] The phrase, "*wherein he*," permits us to interpret what follows as its *focus*, the application of redemption, and its method of *implementation*, the gospel call, general and effectual. But the confessions are not as clear as WLC 31. It is understandable that some could mistakenly think that this paragraph defines the *substance* of the covenant of grace, not its *implementation*.

Now I'll illustrate the confusion that arises if we interpret this paragraph to define its essence or substance. If so, carefully note with me what its promises, parties, and conditions would be. I have taken not a few classes of students through this exercise. It is fair to say that each time the result has shocked the class. I'll try to recreate the experience for you. Suppose I write the table below on the board. I ask you to fill it in with me using the very words of this paragraph:

> a Covenant of Grace; wherein he freely offers unto sinners life and salvation by Jesus Christ; requiring of them faith in him that they may be saved, and promising to give unto all those that are ordained unto eternal life his Holy Spirit, to make them willing and able to believe.

---

1. WLC 31: "the covenant of grace was made with Christ, as the second Adam, and in him with all the elect as his seed." This unambiguously defines its human partakers as God's elect alone, not as all unconverted sinners.

FEATURES	UNIVERSAL ASPECT General Gospel Call	PARTICULAR ASPECT Effectual Gospel Call
PROMISE		
PARTAKERS		
CONDITION		

So now let's fill in the universal aspect, the general gospel call. What is the promise? And someone says, *life and salvation by Jesus Christ.* And I say, correct, very good. Now who are the partakers? To whom is this promise made? And, now another student says, *sinners.* Correct. And so I ask, what is the condition? What does God require sinners to do to be saved? And the class answers, *believe,* have *faith.* It says, "*requiring of them faith in him.*" So I say, correct, very good. Now, how does this fit together? The promise is salvation from sin, the partakers {parties} are sinners, and the condition is faith. Do we all agree? And the class all agrees. That's what it says. And then I ask, are these sinners converted or unconverted? Sometimes the class responds back almost instantaneously, *unconverted.* Sometimes they don't dare say it. Why do you say *unconverted,* I ask? Because, it says that God offers them salvation if they believe. That is the indiscriminate offer of the gospel to lost sinners: "What must I do to be saved? Believe in the Lord Jesus Christ, and you shall be saved." So then, the partakers are *lost sinners indiscriminately,* all unconverted persons who hear the gospel. Thus, if this defines the essence of the covenant of grace, then it would be a *conditional* covenant between God and *unconverted sinners.*

So now, let's complete the task, I say. Let's fill in the rest of the table. Let's look at its particular aspect, the effectual call. What is the promise? And someone quotes the confessions, "*promising to give* unto all those that are ordained unto eternal life *his Holy Spirit, to make them willing and able to believe.*" Correct, I say. And what is the word we commonly use for this work of the Holy Spirit by which he creates faith in dead sinners and makes them willing and able to believe? And someone usually says, *regeneration.* Correct, I say. And to whom does he promise regeneration? Who are the partakers, or as the old writers would say, the parties? And someone says, *God's elect.* Correct, I say, for it says, "promising to give *unto all those that are ordained unto eternal life* his Holy Spirit." And so I ask, what is the condition? And usually there is silence. So I prompt them. I ask: what does he require the elect to do in order to be regenerated by the Holy Spirit? What does it say he requires them to do? And now they get it, and they say, "*nothing.*" So I say, then it's *"unconditional?"* Well, somewhat reluctantly they say, yes. So then I ask: are the elect to whom God promises regeneration unbelievers or believers? Are they converted or unconverted? And now really the answer is obvious, it says, *"to make them willing and able to believe."* So then, someone has to admit, the elect are viewed as unconverted, and it says that God promises the unregenerate elect that he will give them his Holy Spirit to make them willing and able to believe, that is, to regenerate them. Let's sum up its particular aspect. The promise is the Spirit's work of regeneration, the partakers {parties} are the unconverted elect, and there is no condition required of them. This aspect is unconditional. Now let's put all this together in the tables below:

FEATURES	GENERAL GOSPEL CALL UNIVERSAL ASPECT	EFFECTUAL GOSPEL CALL PARTICULAR ASPECT
PROMISE	*salvation by Jesus Christ*	*his Holy Spirit, to make them willing and able to believe*
PARTAKERS	*unto sinners*	*those ordained unto eternal life...to make them able and willing to believe*
CONDITION	*requiring of them faith*	{no condition}

FEATURES	GENERAL GOSPEL CALL UNIVERSAL ASPECT	UNIVERSAL GOSPEL CALL PARTICULAR ASPECT
PROMISE	salvation from sin by Christ	regeneration by the Holy Spirit
PARTAKERS	unconverted indiscriminately	unconverted elect
CONDITION	faith	none{unconditional}

So now I say to the class, does this define *the essence* of a covenant between God and his people? Now, not reluctantly, but emphatically, and usually a little shocked, they affirm that it does not. Therefore, if this defines the *essence* of the covenant of grace, then in its essential content the covenant of grace, in both aspects, is between God and *the unconverted*. Its partakers are lost, unsaved men. The universal aspect is between God and lost sinners indiscriminately, the particular aspect between God and the unconverted elect. I conclude that this *does not* define the essence of a covenant of grace between God and his redeemed people. Generally, the response is, now what?

This is not a mere academic exercise. This imprecision of interpretation—or presentation, take your pick—has in fact engendered much confusion, as our subsequent studies shall show. Keep this in mind when we study Hodge and Dabney. To avoid this quagmire, I call this paragraph *the focus* and *implementation*, not the essence, of the covenant of grace. I attempt to define that essence precisely when I lecture on the covenant of grace. For now, let this suffice you. The covenant of grace *focuses* on the application of redemption by means of the general and effectual call. When God applies redemption by this gospel call, he *implements* or *executes* his covenant of grace. Its essence is God's solemn pledge to accomplish redemption by Christ and to apply it to his elect. The gospel call is the method by which he implements, executes, and fulfills his solemn pledge.

The Testamental Nature of the Covenant of Grace (WCF 7:4)

WCF 7:4 introduces its testamental nature. LCF completely omits WCF 7:4, which says: "This Covenant of Grace is frequently set forth in Scripture by the name of a testament in reference to the death of Christ Jesus the Testator, and to the everlasting inheritance, with all things belonging to it, therein bequeathed." Dabney says that the Westminster Assembly overstated the case when they asserted that it is "frequently" set forth in Scripture by the name testament. Dabney finds only one place in which Scripture definitely calls it a testament. The reason for deleting this paragraph from LCF is unclear.

The Dual Administration of the Covenant of Grace (WCF 7:5, 6)

WCF describes two parallel administrations. The writers of the confession obviously regarded these paragraphs as a single unit. Thus they wrote: "This covenant was differently administered in the time of the law, and in the time of the gospel." WCF 7:5 describes its administration under the law, WCF 7:6 its administration under the gospel. Thus WCF underscores the unity of the covenant of grace. God administered his one covenant of grace differently under the law and under the gospel.

Its Administration Under the Law (WCF 7:5)

WCF 7:5 defines the manner or method of its administration under the law. It was administered by "promises, prophecies, sacrifices, circumcision, the paschal lamb, and other types and ordinances." They define the people to whom it was administered: "the people of the Jews." They define the purpose for this administration: "all fore-signifying Christ to come." They define the sufficiency or efficacy of this administration: "which were, for that time, sufficient and efficacious, through the operation of the Spirit, to instruct and build up the elect in faith in the promised Messiah." They define the result of this administration: "by whom they had full remission of sins, and eternal salvation." They define the name of this administration: "and which is called the Old Testament." In sum, WCF 7:5 expounds the method, recipients, purpose, sufficiency, result, and designation of the administration of the covenant of grace under the law. They packed much truth into that brief paragraph.

Its Administration Under the Gospel (WCF 7:6)

Regarding its administration "under the gospel," they first specify its occasion: "when Christ, the substance was exhibited." Next, they identify its ordinances: "the ordinances in which this covenant is dispensed are the preaching of the Word, and the administration of the sacraments of Baptism and the Lord's Supper." Next they affirm its superiority by comparing its ordinances with the former ones: "which though fewer in number, and administered with more simplicity, and less outward glory, yet, in them, it is held forth in more fullness, evidence, and spiritual efficacy." Then they define its universal scope: "to all the nations, both Jews and Gentiles." Finally, they specify its name: "and is called the New Testament." They conclude with the unity of the covenant of grace: "There are not therefore two covenants of grace, differing in essence, or substance, but one and the same, under various dispensations." They assert plainly that God has one method of applying salvation, in both the Old and the New Testament eras, which unifies them, which involves the general and effectual call of the gospel.

Three Predominant Features of the Covenant of Grace (LCF 7:3)

LCF 7:3 corresponds to WCF 7:4–6. Where WCF unfolds its testamental nature (7:4) and dual administration (7:5, 6), LCF unfolds three predominant features:

> This covenant is revealed in the gospel first of all to Adam in the promise of salvation by the seed of the woman, and afterwards by further steps, until the full discovery thereof was completed in the New Testament; and it is founded in that eternal covenant transaction that is between the Father and the Son about the redemption of the elect; and it is alone by the grace of this covenant, that all of the posterity of fallen Adam, that ever were saved, did obtain life and blessed immortality; man being now utterly incapable of

acceptance with God upon those terms on which Adam stood in his state of innocency (LCF 7:3).

Punctuation is significant. A semi-colon separates each feature: its progressive revelation; eternal foundation; and unity and indispensability for salvation.

Its Progressive Revelation
God makes his gospel, covenant of grace, and salvation from sin known progressively. This covenant was revealed first in Genesis 3:15 and afterward by further steps. God progressively reveals the application and accomplishment of salvation with growing clarity and fullness. Its complete disclosure is in the New Testament.

Its Eternal Covenantal Foundation
The Baptist fathers assert that the covenant of grace is rooted in an eternal "covenant transaction" between the Father and the Son. LCF grounds God's covenant of grace, declared in history, in his covenantal commitment established in eternity, usually called the *"covenant of redemption."* WCF does not explicitly mention this eternal covenant.

Its Essential Unity and Indispensability for Salvation
They alter the Westminster framework of parallel administrations, yet they retain its unity. They affirm one gospel, application of redemption, and covenant of grace. LCF affirms that nobody ever has been saved, or ever will be saved, except through the covenant of grace. The gospel is a message about sin, Christ, salvation, and grace. It calls sinners to repentance and faith. It has been so from the days of Abel. It will ever be so. They say: "It is alone by the grace of this covenant that all of the posterity of fallen Adam that ever were saved, did obtain life and blessed immortality." LCF affirms the unity and indispensability of the covenant of grace. Recently some Calvinistic Baptists have rejected a covenant of grace. This has not helped the credibility of Reformed Baptists. It tends to confirm preconceived notions. It fosters division. If we challenge the existence of a covenant of grace, we will be perceived as rejecting one gospel message and way of salvation. Confessing one way of salvation doesn't inevitably lead to Paedobaptism. LCF proves this.

May God grant that we may learn from our Puritan forefathers, Baptist and Paedobaptist, imitate their graces, avoid their imprecisions, and follow them to the degree that they have followed Christ.

2

John Gill on God's Covenants

I introduce Gill's theology with a summary of his life and ministry recorded in *The History of the Baptists:*[1]

> But the man who made the deepest mark upon the Baptists of his time was John Gill, a native of Kettering, Northamptonshire, born in 1697. Very early in life he gave evidence of exceptional gifts, and his friends tried in vain to secure his admission to one of the universities; but under private teachers he became a superior scholar in Latin, Greek and logic. He was baptized when nineteen and entered the ministry at twenty-three. After the death of Benjamin Stinton, successor to Keach, in Horsleydown, John Gill was proposed as Stinton's successor, but on putting the question to vote, a majority rejected him, when his friends withdrew and formed the Church afterward located in Carter Lane, Tooley Street, March 22, 1719, and on the same day he became its pastor. Gill's party worshipped for some years in the school-room of Thomas Crosby, the historian, until Keach's Church, which they had left, built a new chapel in Unicorn Yard, when they went to the old chapel in Goat Street, which Keach's people had ceased to use. Here the doctor preached until 1757, when they built for him a new meeting-house in Carter Lane, where he continued until his death in 1771. After many years of study he became a profound scholar in Rabbinical Hebrew and a master of the Targum, Talmud, the Rabboth and the book Zohar, with their ancient commentaries. He largely assisted Dr. Kennicott in his collation, and published a dissertation concerning the antiquity of the Hebrew language, etc. He was a prolific

---

1. Thomas Armitage, *The History of the Baptists* (2 Vols.; Minneapolis: James and Klock Christian Publishing Co., 1977), 2: 560–61.

author, producing amongst many other weighty works his *Cause of God and Truth*; his *Body of Divinity*, and his learned *Commentary on the Bible*. Toplady, his intimate friend, says of him, that "if any man can be supposed to have trod the whole circle of human learning, it was Dr. Gill.... It would, perhaps try the constitutions of half the *literati* in England, only to read with care and attention the whole of what he said. As deeply as human sagacity enlightened by grace could penetrate, he went to the bottom of everything he engaged in.... Perhaps no man, since the days of St. Austin, has written so largely in defense of the system of grace, and, certainly, no man has treated that momentous subject, in all its branches, more closely, judiciously and successfully." He was also a great controversialist as well as a scholar. On this subject Toplady adds: "What was said of Edward the Black Prince, that he never fought a battle that he did not win; what has been remarked of the great Duke of Marlborough, that he never undertook a siege which he did not carry, may be justly accommodated to our great philosopher and divine."

And yet, with all his ability, he was so high a supralapsarian, that it is hard to distinguish him from an Antinomian. For example, he could not invite sinners to the Saviour, while he declared their guilt and condemnation, their need of the new birth; and held that God would convert such as he had elected to be saved, and so man must not interfere with his purpose by inviting men to Christ. Under this preaching his Church steadily declined, and after half a century's work he left but a mere handful. He did not mean to teach Antinomianism, and yet, in 1755, he republished Dr. Crisp's works, which had given rise to so much contention, with explanatory notes, defending Crisp from the charge of Antinomianism, although his doctrines had fallen like a mildew upon the Churches of the land, and none now pretend that Crisp was a safe teacher.

It is interesting to note that all was not lost in the end for Dr. Gill's congregation. John Rippon succeeded Gill as pastor. He continued in that ministry for many years, and was eventually succeeded by Charles Spurgeon.

Gill begins his treatment of the everlasting council about the salvation of men within the larger topic of God's eternal acts. He introduces the subject with this statement:[2]

---

2. John Gill, *Complete Body of Doctrinal and Practical Divinity* (2 Vols.; Grand Rapids: Baker Book House, 1978), 1: 300.

Having treated of the internal and imminent acts in the divine mind, and which are eternal; I shall consider the operations and transactions among the three divine persons when alone, before the world began, or any creature was in being; and which are chiefly, the council and covenant of God, respecting the salvation of men: these are generally blended together by divines; and indeed it is difficult to consider them distinctly with exactness and precision; but I think they are to be distinguished, and the one to be considered as leading on, and as preparatory and introductory to the other, though both of an eternal date; and shall begin with the council of God, held between the three divine persons, Father, Son, and Spirit, concerning the affair of man's salvation before the world was.

According to Gill, the divine council in eternity occasions the eternal covenant of grace. The Father, the Son, and the Holy Spirit engage in deliberation from which the covenant emerges. He first presents this eternal council. Then he expounds "The Everlasting Covenant of Grace."[3] Gill returns to this subject when he considers the historical manifestation of this covenant of grace. This uncovers a fundamental distinction in Gill's theology. *First,* we consider this fundamental distinction, *second,* the eternal establishment of the covenant of grace, and *third,* its manifestation in history.

The Fundamental Distinction in Gill's Theology

Gill first considers what he calls "the internal acts and works of God." He distinguishes these from "the acts of the grace of God toward and upon his elect in time."[4] This is his fundamental distinction. According to Gill, the covenant of grace was not made in history with men. It was made in eternity. It was only manifested in history. According to him, God cannot make a proper covenant with men. It must be made with Christ. Men are included in it only because they are viewed in Christ. This same distinction supports Gill's doctrine of eternal justification. After considering justification and adoption as imminent and eternal acts of God, he introduces the covenant

---

3. Ibid., 301–306; 306–358.

4. Gill divides his theology into Books. In Book 2 he expounds, "The internal acts and works of God, and his decrees in general." In Book 4 he expounds the "manifestation and administration of the covenant of grace." Ibid., 1: xxxii–xxxiii.

of grace.[5] With this approach, Gill departs from the perspective of WCF and LCF. For Gill, the covenant of grace is an eternal act of God in the context of eternal justification and adoption. This drives him to eliminate God's indiscriminate offer of mercy to lost sinners from God's plan of salvation. It opens the door for removing individual responsibility from God's covenantal dealings.

The Eternal Establishment of the Covenant of Grace

Gill arranges his exposition under nine headings. These are: The Covenant of Grace (pgs. 306–14), The Father's Part in the Covenant (pgs. 314–24), The Son's Part (pgs. 324–26), Christ as Covenant-head of the Elect (pgs. 326–29), Christ as Mediator (pgs. 329–40), Christ as Surety of the Covenant (pgs. 340–45), Christ as Testator (pgs. 345–50), The Concern of the Holy Spirit in the Covenant of Grace (pgs. 350–54), and The Properties of the Covenant of Grace (pgs. 354–57). I collate these nine headings into five topics. First he defines the biblical concept of the covenant of grace (Heading 1). Second, he specifies the terms of the covenant of grace. He enumerates *stipulations* on the Father's part (Heading 2) and *restipulations* on the Son's part (Heading 3). Third, he expounds the multifaceted role of the Son in this covenant. He expounds his function as Covenant-head (Heading 4), Mediator (Heading 5), Surety (Heading 6), and Testator (Heading 7). Fourth, he addresses the place of the Holy Spirit in the covenant of grace (Heading 8). Fifth, he unfolds seven distinguishing traits of the covenant of grace (Heading 9). We present now these five major topics in his order of discussion.

The Biblical Concept of the Covenant of Grace (pgs. 306–14)
Gill defines the covenant of grace as follows:[6]

> The Covenant of Grace is a compact or agreement made from all eternity among the divine Persons, more especially between the Father and the Son, concerning the salvation of the elect.

He unfolds four points: the etymology, the biblical use, the biblical names, and the contracting parties.

---

5. Ibid., 1: 288–300. Eternal justification affirms that God's elect are justified before the foundation of the world, not by faith, not as a transition from wrath to grace.

6. Ibid., 1: 306.

The Etymology of Covenant (pgs. 307–08)

The Biblical Use of Covenant (pgs. 308–09)

He develops his concept of the covenant of grace from the biblical use of covenant. He has six observations: (1) he observes that covenant is "sometimes used for an ordinance, precept, and command." (2) He observes that "Covenant, when ascribed to God, is often nothing more than a mere promise." (3) He observes a unilateral divine covenant: "we often read of covenants of God only on one side; of this kind is his covenant of the day and night… which is no other than a promise that these should always continue without requiring any condition on the part of the creature…and the covenant he made with Noah and his posterity, and with every living creature, with which latter especially there could be no restipulation." (4) He observes a *proper* human covenant: "A covenant properly made between man and man, is by stipulation and restipulation, in which they make mutual promises, or conditions, to be performed by them; whether to maintain friendship among themselves, and to strengthen themselves against their common enemies, or to do mutual services to each other, and their respective posterities; such was the confederacy between Abraham, Aner, Eschol, and Mamre; and the covenant between Abimelech and Isaac, and between David and Jonathan." (5) He concludes that no proper covenant can exist between God and man:[7]

> Such a covenant, properly speaking, cannot be made between God and man, for what can man restipulate with God, which is in his power to do or give to him, and which God has not a prior right unto? God may, indeed, condescend to promise that to man, which otherwise he is not bound to give; and he may require of man that which he has no right to refuse, and God has a right unto, without making such promise; and, therefore, properly speaking, all this cannot formally constitute a covenant, which is to be entered into of free choice on both sides; and especially such a covenant cannot take place in fallen man, who has neither inclination of will to yield the obedience required nor power to perform it.

(6) He defines the covenant of grace as a proper compact:[8]

> the Covenant of Grace made between God and Christ, and with the elect in him, as their Head and Representative, is a proper covenant,

---

7. Ibid., 1: 309.
8. Ibid.

> consisting of stipulation and restipulation; God the Father in it
> stipulates with his Son, that he shall do such and such work and
> service, on condition of which he promises to confer such and such
> honors and benefits on him, and on the elect in him; and Christ the
> Son of God restipulates and agrees to do all that is promised and
> prescribed, and, upon performance, expects and claims the fulfill-
> ment of the promises: in this compact there are mutual engagements
> each party enters into, stipulate and restipulate about, which make
> a proper formal covenant.

He builds on the idea with which WCF and LCF introduced the need
for divine covenant (WCF and LCF 7:1). He uses it to deny any "proper"
covenant between God and men. He defines the covenant of grace as a formal compact between God and Christ in eternity.

The Biblical Names for the Covenant of Grace (pgs. 310–11)
He says that Scripture uses the covenant of life or of peace, while men use
of grace or of redemption. He rejects distinguishing between a covenant of
redemption and a covenant of grace:[9]

> some divines, indeed, make them distinct covenants; the covenant
> of redemption, they say, was made with Christ in eternity; the Cov-
> enant of Grace with the elect, or with believers, in time; but this is
> very wrongly said; there is but one Covenant of Grace, and not two,
> in which the Head and Members, the Redeemer and the persons
> to be redeemed, Christ and the elect, are concerned; in which he is
> the Head and Representative of them, acts for them, and on their
> behalf. What is called a covenant of redemption, is a Covenant of
> Grace, arising from the grace of the Father, who proposed to his
> Son to be the Redeemer, and from the grace of the Son, who agreed
> to be so; and even the honors proposed to the Son in the covenant,
> redounded to the advantage of the elect…therefore, there can be no
> foundation for such a distinction between a covenant of redemption
> in eternity, and a Covenant of Grace in time.

The Contracting Parties in the Covenant of Grace (pgs. 311–14)
These he says are the Father, the Son, and the Holy Spirit. He considers
texts where the Father and Son commune with each other about salvation.
This founds an exposition of its terms and conditions.

---

9. Ibid., 1: 311.

The Terms (Stipulations) of the Covenant of Grace (pgs. 314–26)

He unfolds the commitments the Father stipulates regarding the redemption of his elect (pgs. 314–24). Then he unfolds the commitments that the Son stipulates in return (pgs. 324–26).

The Four-fold Role of Christ in the Covenant of Grace (pgs. 326–50)

Christ as Covenant-Head (pgs. 326–29)

He outlines Christ's role as Covenant-Head or Representative Head, in which he exercises a federal headship parallel to Adam's.

Christ as Mediator (pgs. 329–40)

He begins with the concept of Mediator. He moves to the fitness and the suitability of Christ to be our Mediator. He next considers the manner in which Christ was appointed as Mediator. He concludes by considering the excellence of Christ as Mediator.

Christ as Surety (pgs. 340–45)

He begins by explaining the sense in which Christ is surety of the covenant. Christ is not the surety for his Father, because the Father does not need a surety. Christ is a surety in the sense that he is engaged to pay the debt of his people. Further, Christ is also a surety in the sense that he promises absolutely to pay another's debt. He takes another's obligation and transfers it to himself. He then considers what Christ engaged to do as surety of the covenant.

Christ as Testator (pgs. 345–50)

He says that the covenant of grace is unilateral in this respect: "The Covenant of Grace having the nature of a testament, shows that there is no restipulation in it on the part of men; no more than there is restipulation of legatees in a will; what is bequeathed to them being without their knowledge and consent, and without anything being required of them, to which they give their assent. The Covenant of Grace is properly a covenant to Christ, in which he restipulates; but a testament to his people, or a pure covenant of promise" (pg. 347). He affirms that Jesus Christ is the Testator. Then he explains the import of this: "the death of Christ is necessary to put this will in force, to give strength unto it, that it may be executed according to the design of the maker of it" (pg. 349). He appeals to Hebrews 9:16, 17.

He guards this with two qualifications: (1) that the Old Testament saints received what was promised even though he had not died; and (2) that the will could not be changed even though he was still alive.

The Role of the Holy Spirit in the Covenant of Grace (pgs. 350–54)

He begins: "The third person, the Spirit, gave his approbation of, and assent unto, every article of the covenant." His second point is: "There are many things which the Holy Spirit himself undertook and engaged in covenant to do; and nothing more strongly proves this than his doing them; for had he not agreed to do them, they would not have been done by him" (pg. 352). He then enumerates various activities that the Spirit agreed to perform as the Spirit of conviction, the Spirit of regeneration, the Spirit of faith, as the Comforter, and as the Sanctifier.

Seven Distinguishing Traits of the Covenant of Grace (pgs. 354–59)

The Covenant of Grace is Eternal (pgs. 354–55)

The Covenant of Grace is Entirely Free (pg. 355)

Grace is its moving cause. God was not induced to make it from any condition found in men. The parties entered freely into it.

The Covenant of Grace is Absolute and Unconditional (pg. 356)

Faith is not a condition; it is one of the gifts that God promises and bestows in the covenant of grace.

The Covenant of Grace is Perfect and Complete (pgs. 357–58)

The Covenant of Grace is Holy (pg. 358)

The Covenant of Grace is Sure, Firm, and Immovable (pg. 358)

The Covenant of Grace is Everlasting (pg. 359)

In sum, Gill's doctrine of the covenant of grace is thorough and illuminating. God gave him many insights. His exposition of Christ's multi-faceted and central role is an important contribution. Further, his inclusion of the role of the Holy Spirit is a vital safeguard that many overlook, even today. He also labored to uncover the biblical use of covenant. He stood firm on the need for divine condescension in any covenant with men. With logical acumen he combined that need with the common notion that a proper covenant is a "formal compact between equals." Then boldly he drew the conclusion that there can be no proper covenant between God and men. His reasoning is lucid and sound. Clearly, if a proper covenant is a *"compact between equals,"* then there is no proper covenant between God and men. Rather than search out a better model, as Reformed theology still labors to do, he applied this "compact between equals" model to the eternal decree of redemption. Then he denied the existence of a *proper covenant* in history between God and his redeemed people. Possibly his great strength, his powerful logic, led him astray. I admire his bold assertion that any covenant between God and men cannot possibly be a "compact between equals." But there we must part paths, because the Bible very clearly says that God does, properly and really, enter covenantal relations in history with men.

Ironically, he was so close. As he studied the biblical use he said: "covenant, when ascribed to God, is often nothing more than a mere promise"; and, "we often read of covenants of God only on one side"; and, "the covenant he made with Noah and his posterity, and with every living creature, with which latter especially there could be no restipulation"; and, "hence we read of *covenants of promise,* or promissory covenants, Eph. 2:12; and, indeed, the covenant of grace, with respect to the elect, is nothing else but a free promise of eternal life and salvation by Jesus Christ…and which is absolute and unconditional with respect to them."[10] We should learn from Gill. We should affirm proper covenants between God and Noah's posterity, and between God and his people in Christ, because Scripture does. Clearly these are not "compacts between equals." We should try to define accurately their nature and features.

The Historical Manifestation of the Covenant of Grace

He presents this historical administration on pgs. 491–537. Notice how he introduces it: "I have considered the Covenant of Grace in the former part of this work, as it was a compact in eternity, between the three divine persons, Father, Son, and Spirit; in which each person agreed to take his part in the economy of man's salvation: and now I shall consider the administration of that covenant in the several periods of time, from the beginning of the world to the end of it."[11] According to Gill, there is only one covenant, made in eternity, which is a compact between Father, Son, and Spirit, especially the

---

10. Ibid., 1: 308–09.
11. Ibid., 1: 491.

Father and Son. He says this covenant is manifested and administered variously in history. He immediately adds:[12]

> The Covenant of Grace is but one and the same in all ages, of which
> Christ is the substance; He is the way, the truth, and the life, the
> only true way to eternal life; and there never was any other way
> made known to men since the fall of Adam; no other name under
> heaven has been given, or will be given, by which men can be saved.
> The patriarchs before the flood and after, before the law of Moses
> and under it, before the coming of Christ, and all the saints since,
> are saved in one and the same way, even by the grace of our Lord
> Jesus Christ; and that is the grace of the covenant, exhibited at different times, and in diverse manners. For though the covenant is but
> one, there are different administrations of it: particularly two, one
> before the coming of Christ, and the other after it; which lay the
> foundation for the distinction of the first and second, the old and
> the new covenant.

He develops this historical manifestation under five headings that I collate into three topics. *First*, he compares the two administrations of the covenant of grace (Heading 1). *Second*, he describes the major periods of its former administration (Headings 2–4). *Third*, he describes the transition to its new administration (Heading 5). Then he expounds the law and the gospel. This founds his exposition of Christ's person and work and the blessings of redemption. All this constitutes his detailed exposition of the new administration of the covenant of grace.

The Two Administrations of the Covenant of Grace Compared
The Agreement Between Them (pgs. 492–93)
He mentions five aspects of agreement. First, they agree in the efficient cause. God is the only author. Second, they agree in the moving cause, God's sovereign mercy and free grace. Third, they agree in the Mediator, Christ. For Gill, Christ is the only mediator. Moses, called a mediator, was only a type. Fourth, they agree in the subjects of the covenant, God's elect. Fifth, they agree in the blessings of the covenant. Salvation in Christ is held forth and enjoyed in both.

---

12. Ibid.

The Disagreement Between Them (pgs. 493–94)

He enumerates eight differences. First, under the old, believers looked forward to Christ; under the new, back to him. Second, the latter has greater clarity than the former. Third, the new has more liberty, less bondage. Fourth, the new has larger effusions of the Spirit. Fifth, the new extends to more persons, to Jew and Gentile. Sixth, the old was temporary; the new continues to the end of the world. Seventh, each has different ordinances. Eighth, they exhibit the same promises differently, the old in types, the new in plain words.

The Major Periods of its Old Administration Described (pgs. 495–513)

He does superb biblical theology. He describes the former manifestation of the covenant of grace in its three major epochs, the Patriarchal era, the Mosaic era, and the kingdom era, from David to Christ. His presentation displays rich insights.

The Transition to its New Administration Explained (pgs. 513–22)

He denominates this transition "the abrogation of the old covenant and the introduction of the new covenant." First, he says that the Mosaic administration was never intended to continue. Second, he asserts that the Mosaic administration must needs cease, because it was typical, because it was faulty, and because its rites and ceremonies were comprised by weak elements. Third, he asserts that the rending of the veil signified its abrogation, which was gradual. Fourth, he outlines the instances in which the New Testament was gradually introduced. This concludes his explicit treatment of the transition from the old to the new economy. Before he takes up the person and work of Christ, he expounds the law and the gospel (pgs. 522–37). He first expounds the law of God (pgs. 522–30). He considers the ceremonial, judicial, and moral law. He then expounds the gospel (pgs. 531–37). He discusses the name and significance of the gospel, the author and origin of the gospel, the effects of the gospel coming in power, and the properties of the gospel. He then addresses the question of whether repentance and faith belong to the law or to the gospel. He sees elements of both law and gospel in each. He never affirms or expounds the free or indiscriminate offer of the gospel.

In sum, in Gill's theology the covenant of grace unifies redemptive history. God's dealings with his people in history all grow out of his divine covenant in eternity. Truly, since God "works all things after the counsel of his own will," Gill correctly affirms that God's decision in eternity unifies history. His theology thus promotes stability. It compels one way of salvation. It enforces that there is one people of God in all ages. It supports the unity of God's permanent gospel method of saving sinners that he progressively discloses in redemptive history. Surely we must follow Gill in these concerns. However, unlike Gill, we should follow WCF and LCF when they teach that the covenant of grace, God's solemn pledge proclaimed in history (Gen. 3:15), also unites every era of redemptive history. Further, Gill insists on the existence of only one divine covenant, whereas Scripture speaks of a plurality of divine covenants with men. Yet, in spite of one structural flaw in his theology, Gill has made valuable contributions of momentous significance to the Reformed doctrine of divine covenant.

—3—

Charles Hodge on God's Covenants

Charles Hodge is the premier systematic theologian of Northern Presbyterianism. Hodge was a renowned professor of systematic theology for many years at Princeton Seminary and authored a classic work on systematic theology.[1] The Oxford Dictionary of the Christian Church says of him: "Hodge has a real claim to be considered one of the greatest of American theologians, and he had a great influence and following."[2] He lectured for fifty-six years in the Pauline Epistles, from 1822 until 1878, the year of his death. Although he was universally respected as an exegete, B. B. Warfield, one of his students, says that theology was his first love.[3] Hodge's systematic theology was first published in 1871–73. It reflects the vintage fruit of his mature thought, compiled after decades of study and analysis. His work is classic, worthy of careful consideration.

Hodge treats the covenant of grace in his soteriology. His soteriology contains twenty chapters, from the Plan of Salvation to the Means of Grace, as follows: Chapter 1, the Plan of Salvation; Chapter 2, the Covenant of Grace; Chapter 3, the Person of Christ; Chapter 4, the Mediatorial Work of Christ, etc.[4] Our concern now is with Chapter 2, The Covenant of Grace.[5] Hodge divides this chapter into seven major units of thought:

---

1. Charles Hodge, *Systematic Theology* (3 Vols.; Grand Rapids: Wm. B. Eerdmans Publishing Company, 1989 reprint).

2. *The Oxford Dictionary of the Christian Church*, edited by Frank Leslie Cross and Elizabeth A. Livingstone (Oxford: Oxford University Press, 1974), 654.

3. B. B. Warfield, *Selected Shorter Writings of Benjamin B. Warfield*, edited by John E. Meeter (2 Vols.; Nutley, NJ: Presbyterian and Reformed Publishing Company, 1970), 1: 439.

4. Hodge, *Systematic Theology*, 2: vi–viii.

5. Ibid., 2: 354–77.

1: The Plan of Salvation is a Covenant (pgs. 354–55)

2: Different Views of the Nature of that Covenant (pgs. 355–57)

3: Parties to the Covenant (pgs. 357–59)

4: Covenant of Redemption (pgs. 359–62)

5: The Covenant of Grace (pgs. 362–66)

6: The Identity of the Covenant of Grace (pgs. 366–73)

7: Different Dispensations (pgs. 373–77)

Hodge has three focal points, arranged like concentric circles. First, as a broad foundation, he expounds *the covenantal form* of God's plan of salvation (Units 1–3). He begins with the propriety of regarding the plan of salvation as covenantal (Unit 1). Next, he outlines failed efforts to depict the plan of salvation as a covenant (Unit 2). Then he presents his own view of this covenantal form (Unit 3). He uncovers the heart of his theology of God's covenant. He affirms two divine covenants, one in eternity between God and Christ, the other in history between God and his people. Second, having set this foundation, Hodge focuses on *the major features* of these two divine covenants (Units 4, 5). He delineates the eternal covenant of redemption (Unit 4) and the historical covenant of grace (Unit 5). Third, Hodge again narrows his focus. He unfolds the *administration* of the covenant of grace in redemptive history (Units 6, 7). He explains the unity and diversity in this administration. Hodge's treatment is illuminating. His development is clear and logical. We survey his seven units as we collate them with his three focal points.

The Covenantal Form of God's Plan of Salvation (pgs. 354–59)

The Plan of Salvation is a Covenant (pgs. 354–55)

Hodge starts with the propriety of viewing God's plan of salvation as a covenant. He gives two reasons: "First, from the constant use of the words בְּרִית and διαθήκη in reference to it…. Secondly, that the plan of salvation is presented in the Bible under the form of a covenant is proved not only from the signification and usage of the words above mentioned, but also and more decisively from the fact that the elements of a covenant are included in this plan. There are parties, mutual promises or stipulations, and conditions. So that it is in fact a covenant, whatever it may be called. As this is the

Scriptural mode of representation, it is of great importance that it should be retained in theology" (pgs. 354–55).

Hodge asks the crucial question: does Scripture present the plan of salvation as a covenant? He concludes it does for two reasons. His second reason is especially significant. According to Hodge a covenant has three essential elements. The plan of salvation is a covenant because it has those three elements: parties, mutual stipulations, and conditions.

Different Views of the Nature of that Covenant (pgs. 355–57)

He considers the various ways in which Universalists[6] have depicted the plan of salvation. He presents four views using a covenantal model: Pelagian, Remonstrant, Wesleyan, and Lutheran.

The Pelagian View (pg. 355)

This view is: "that there is no difference between the covenant of works under which Adam was placed, and the covenant of grace, under which men now are, except the extent of the obedience required. God promised life to Adam on the condition of perfect obedience, because he was in a condition to render such obedience. He promises salvation to men now on condition of such obedience as they are able to render, whether Jews, Pagans, or Christians. According to this view the parties to the covenant are God and man; the promise is life; the condition is obedience, such as man in the use of his natural powers is able to render" (pg. 355).

The Remonstrant Arminian View (pgs. 355–56)

Their doctrine amounts to asserting that God and all men are the parties, life is the promise, and obedience is the condition. However, they go on to say that God gives men the grace to perform this condition by the aid of the Spirit.

The Wesleyan Arminian View (pg. 356)

He says that their view "greatly exalts the work of Christ, the importance of the Spirit's influence and the grace of the gospel above the standard adopted by the Remonstrants" (pg. 356). Nevertheless, he says, in the final analysis they are essentially the same because: "The work of Christ has equal reference

---

6. The term depicts the idea that God, with a view to salvation, out of equal love for all, does the same to all men alike in their lives and for all men alike in Christ.

to all men. It secures for all the promise of salvation on the condition of evangelical obedience; and it obtains for all, Jews and Gentiles, enough measures of divine grace to render such obedience practicable. The salvation of each individual man depends upon the use which he makes of this sufficient grace" (pg. 356).

The Lutheran View (pg. 356)

He thinks their view also amounts to regarding the parties as God and all men. Men have only the power of effectual resistance. Only those who willfully resist will perish.

He summarizes these four views as follows: "According to all these views...the covenant of grace is a compact between God and fallen man, in which God promises salvation on condition of a compliance with the demands of the gospel" (pg. 356). Then he contrasts these views with the Augustinian view. He notes two essential differences. In the Augustinian view: (1) the plan of salvation has special reference to the elect, not to all mankind; and (2) God, not man, determines who will be saved (pg. 356). He closes with a survey of grace. Grace has a threefold meaning. In all three senses the plan of salvation is a covenant of grace (pg. 357). It is a covenant of grace because it: (1) grows out of unmerited love, (2) promises salvation as an unmerited benefit, and (3) has its benefits secured and applied through the supernatural influence of the Holy Spirit (pg. 357). His exposé of grace is superb. It introduces the heart of his doctrine.

Parties to the Covenant (pgs. 357–59)

Hodge calls this "parties to the covenant" because correctly identifying its partakers is the crucial issue. He begins with what he calls *"the confusion"* surrounding this issue.

The Apparent Confusion (pg. 357)

He says: "At first view there appears to be some confusion in the statement of the Scriptures respecting the parties to this covenant. Sometimes Christ is presented as one of the parties; at others He is represented not as a party, but as the mediator and surety of the covenant; while the parties are represented to be God and his people" (pg. 357). Who are the parties of this covenant of grace? Are they God and Christ, or God and his people, with Christ as mediator?

Two Solutions: One Covenant; Two Covenants (pgs. 357–58)

He presents the one covenant view: "Some theologians propose to reconcile these modes of representation by saying that as the covenant of works was formed with Adam as the representative of his race…so the covenant of grace was formed with Christ as the head and representative of his people" (pg. 357). Thus, in virtue of Christ's federal headship, both the one and the many are parties to the same covenant. This one covenant view builds on analogy between Adam and Christ, and between the covenants of works and grace. Yet this does not fully satisfy Hodge, because it does not explain Christ's role as mediator: "Still it does not remove the incongruity of Christ's being represented as at once a party and a mediator of the same covenant" (pg. 357). Surely, Hodge makes a very compelling point.

How then does Hodge propose to resolve this apparent confusion? He proposes two covenants: "There are in fact two covenants relating to the salvation of fallen man, the one between God and Christ, and the other between God and his people. These covenants differ not only in their parties, but also in their promises and conditions. Both are so clearly presented in the Bible that they should not be confounded. The latter, the covenant of grace, is founded on the former, the covenant of redemption" (pgs. 357–58). His solution is distinguishing a covenant of grace between God and his people, with Christ as Mediator, from an eternal covenant of redemption between God and Christ. Thus Hodge follows LCF 7:3. Christ is a party to the covenant of redemption, but the mediator and surety of the covenant of grace. The parties of the covenant of grace are God and his people. This distinction founds Hodge's theology.

The Difference Between the Two Solutions (pg. 358)

Although the one federal covenant view does not completely satisfy him, he is not willing utterly to divorce himself from it. He says: "This is a matter which concerns only perspicuity of statement. There is no doctrinal difference between those who prefer the one statement and those who prefer the other…. The Westminster standards seem to adopt sometimes the one and sometimes the other mode of representation" (pg. 358). What an observation! He is absolutely correct about his Westminster Standards. They use a two-covenant approach in WCF 7:3 and in WSC 20, and affirm one federal covenant in WLC 31. Listen as he proves the point: "In the Larger Catechism, however, the other view is expressly adopted. In the answer to the question,

'With whom was the Covenant of Grace made?' it is said, 'The Covenant of Grace was made with Christ as the second Adam, and in Him with all the elect as His seed'" (pg. 358). LCF 7:3 explicitly affirms two distinct covenants. But, WLC 31 is also quite clear when it affirms one federal covenant. Keep these things in mind. Ponder them. As I will attempt to show, both views express an important aspect of the truth about God's covenantal commitments with Christ and his elect people. Scripture presents the covenant of grace in Genesis 3:15 as one federal covenant in which Christ and God's elect are both parties. Yet, Scripture also presents the *Messianic* covenant with Jesus and the *new* covenant with his disciples, mediated by Jesus, as two distinct covenants. Hodge is correct. Both solutions are biblical and true.

The Best Solution: Two Covenants Distinguished (pgs. 358–59)

Hodge states his conclusion: "The apparent confusion is avoided by distinguishing between these two covenants, the covenant of redemption between the Father and the Son, and the covenant of grace between God and his people" (pg. 358). He cites Witsius and Turretin for support. Hodge quotes the Latin (pg. 359). I offer you an English translation of Turretin. Hodge quotes 12:2:12: The Covenant of Grace in Its Twofold Economy: The Nature of the Covenant of Grace: Who were the Contracting Parties? Turretin says:[7]

> And it seems superfluous to inquire here, whether this covenant is made with Christ as one of the contracting parties and in him with all his seed (as the first covenant had been made with Adam and in Adam with his whole posterity—which pleases many because the promises are said to have been made to him [Gal. 3:16]...or whether the covenant was made in Christ with all the seed so that he does not so much hold the relation of a contracting party as of Mediator, who stands between those at variance for the purpose of reconciling them.... It is superfluous, I say, to dispute about this because it amounts to the same thing. It is certain that a twofold pact must be attended to here or the two parts and degrees of one and the same pact. The former is the agreement between the Father and the Son to carry out the work of redemption. The latter is that which God makes with the elect in Christ, to save them by and on account of Christ under the conditions of faith and repentance. The former was made with the surety and head for the salvation of the

---

7. Francis Turretin, *Institutes of Elenctic Theology*, translated by George Musgrave Giger, edited by James T. Dennison, Jr. (3 Vols.; Phillipsburg, NJ: P&R Publishing, 1994) 2: 177.

members; the latter was made with the members in the head and the surety.

According to Turretin, God's covenant is a twofold pact. This pact is between God and the one, Christ, and between God and the many, his people. These are distinct but united pacts. Speaking biblically, the Messianic and new covenants are two distinct aspects of God's covenantal favor. They are united by his covenant of grace. The covenant of grace displays the evangelical unity of this divine favor; the Messianic and new covenants, its historical diversity. Following LCF and Turretin, Hodge has profoundly come to grips with the organizing principle of God's covenantal relations.

The Major Features of God's Covenants (pgs. 359–66)

The Covenant of Redemption (pgs. 359–62)

Hodge acknowledges the incomprehensibility of this subject and our dependence on God to reveal it. He reminds us that is rests on the doctrine of the Trinity. He explains how Scripture reveals it:[8]

> In order to prove that there is a covenant between the Father and the Son, formed in eternity, and revealed in time, it is not necessary that we should adduce passages of the Scripture in which this truth is expressly asserted. There are indeed passages which are equivalent to direct assertions.... The proof of the doctrine has, however, a much wider foundation. When one person assigns a stipulated work to another person with the promise of a reward upon the condition of the performance of that work, there is a covenant. Nothing can be plainer than that all this is true in relation to the Father and the Son. The Father gave the Son a work to do; He sent Him into the world to perform it, and promised Him a great reward when the work was accomplished.... We have, therefore, the contracting parties, the promise, and the condition. These are the essential elements of a covenant.

He supports the covenant of redemption, not so much from biblical assertions, but from the fact that the essential elements of a covenant are present. First, his hermeneutical method is biblical. Explicit statements are not essential. This is clearly the case with the Davidic covenant. The word covenant is not found in 2 Samuel 7. Yet the psalmist reflects on that incident

---

8. Hodge, *Systematic Theology*, 2: 360.

and says that in it God made a covenant with David (Ps. 89:28–37). Thus, Hodge provides a vital insight. It underscores the importance of defining divine covenant accurately. Else we cannot accurately discern whether or not a divine covenant is implicit in a passage.

This prompts two further questions. Does Hodge correctly identify the essential elements of a covenant? Is Hodge correct when he says that we must view the mission of Christ as a formal compact, with contracting parties, stipulations, and conditions? In my view, the answer to both questions is, no. The passages that support the eternal counsel of redemption and the Messianic covenant do not mandate a viewing Christ's redemptive mission as a formal compact. I do not deny Christ's eternal commission. I only question whether Scripture ever presents it as a formal compact. This prompts one further question. Does this imply that there is no covenant between God and Christ? It implies no such thing. What if the essence of a covenant is not a compact, but an oath-bound promise? What if Scripture presents "righteous servant" covenants between God and his righteous servants? What if God makes a righteous servant covenant in history with God the Son incarnate, Jesus Christ? If these three suppositions are true, and they are, then there is indeed a covenant between God and Christ. Further, we even discern it using the very hermeneutic that Hodge employs: "the word of the oath, which was after the law, appoints a Son, perfected forever" (Heb. 7:28). Thus, Hodge's insight, work, and contribution are of inestimable worth.

The Work Assigned to the Redeemer (pgs. 361–62)

His presentation of the work assigned to the Redeemer is lucid, comprehensive, and scriptural. Hodge asserts a threefold work assigned to the Redeemer: "(1) He was to assume our nature, humbling Himself to be born of a woman… (2) He was to be made under the law, voluntarily undertaking to fulfill all righteousness… (3) He was to bear our sins, to be a curse for us" (pgs. 361–62).

The Promises Made to the Redeemer (pg. 362)

Hodge lists eight promises made to the Son as the reward of his obedience. God promised him a body, the Spirit, his support, deliverance from death, and complete success. It is difficult to understand how giving the Son a human body could be conditioned "upon His successful and subsequent obedience in that body." In the main, however, his presentation is biblical. Keep in mind the imprecision just noted. The unconditional giving of a body to the Son is an important fact of revelation that we must account for when we describe his redemptive mission.

The Covenant of Grace (pgs. 362–66)

Hodge considers the essence, mediator, condition, and promises of this covenant of grace. He introduces this by asserting that the content of the covenant of grace follows logically from the content of the covenant of redemption. He makes no appeal to Scripture to support the existence of this covenant. Evidently he believed that his previous remarks provided sufficient support.

The Dual Essence of the Covenant of Grace (pgs. 362–64)

Hodge makes this crucial statement about its dual essence: "In virtue of what the Son of God covenanted to perform, and what in the fullness of time He actually accomplished, agreeably to the stipulations of the compact with the Father, two things follow. First, salvation is offered to all men on the condition of faith in Christ…it follows secondly, from the nature of the covenant between the Father and the Son, that the covenant of grace has also special reference to the elect. To them God has promised to give His Spirit in order that they may believe; and to them alone all the promises made to believers belong" (pgs. 362–63). Hodge defines the covenant of grace in terms of the general and effectual call of the gospel. He includes both universal and particular aspects. He builds on the confessions (WCF 7:3, LCF 7:2). Again, his contribution is invaluable.

Listen carefully as Hodge works out the implications of the universal aspect: "The gospel…is the offer of salvation upon the conditions of the covenant of grace. In this sense, the covenant of grace is formed with all mankind" (pg. 363). He says subsequently: "If this, therefore, were all that is meant by those who make the parties to the covenant of grace, God and mankind in general and all mankind equally, there would be no objection to the doctrine. For it is undoubtedly true that God offers to all and every man eternal life on condition of faith in Jesus Christ" (pg. 363). Dr. Hodge has made a valiant effort. But he has not defined precisely a covenant between God and "his elect people." The problem is that this great theologian had an impossible task. Any attempt to define a covenant between God and his elect that includes reprobate persons as parties is futile.

Do you see what Hodge did? Remember the table we filled out? Remember what happens if we assume that the confessions define the essence of the covenant of grace? Remember where that leads? We saw that it leads to a covenant of grace between God and the unconverted. Remember that I told you that this was not just an academic exercise? Here is the point. Dr. Hodge did assume that the confessions defined its essence. How natural it would be to take their words that way. Great was their potential for confusion. Then he applied his logical acumen to that interpretation and reached the only plausible conclusion. Then he stated it boldly and plainly: the covenant of grace, in one sense, is a conditional covenant between God and all unconverted men. For this we are again in his debt.

Yet we should not interpret the confessions this way. If we do we will wind up pitting them against WLC 31: "the covenant of grace was made with Christ as the second Adam, and in him with all the elect as His seed." Who are the human parties of the covenant of grace? WLC says explicitly, "all the elect," not "all unconverted men." All mankind are not in Christ, even though the general call offers Christ indiscriminately and sincerely. Hodge acknowledges that the one covenant view fosters consistent particularism: "Those who ignore the distinction between the covenants of redemption and of grace, merging the latter in the former, of course represent the parties to the covenant to be God and Christ as the head and representative of His own people. And therefore mankind, as such, are in no sense parties" (pg. 363). Then he appends the following concession: "All that is important is, that we should adopt such a mode of representation as will comprehend the various facts recognized in the Scriptures" (pg. 363). I greatly admire his theological sensitivity and honesty. Our view of divine covenant must honor the fact that God offers salvation to sinners indiscriminately. Hodge sought to honor this free offer. He recognized that this is a matter of precision, not grave doctrinal error. Thus he says: "And it is one of those facts that salvation is offered to all men on the condition of faith in Christ. And therefore to that extent, or, in a sense which accounts for that fact, the covenant of grace is made with all men. The great sin of those who hear the gospel is that they refuse to accept of that covenant, and therefore place themselves without its pale" (pgs. 363–64).

Where is the imprecision? As we saw, the confessions define its focus and implementation, not its essence. Its essence is God's solemn pledge to accomplish salvation by Christ and to apply that salvation in Christ to all his elect (Gen. 3:15). God implements this covenant when he applies redemption to his elect by means of the indiscriminate gospel call and the sovereign regenerating work of the Spirit, the effectual gospel call. Thus, WCF and LCF are in complete harmony with WLC 31. Hodge unintentionally pitted WCF against WLC. I strive to avoid this quagmire by distinguishing the essential content from the gospel implementation of the covenant of grace.

Up to this point, Hodge is lucid. From here on, however, he begins to manifest a lack of clarity. When he treats the mediator, condition, and promises of the covenant of grace, he makes no mention of which aspect of its dual essence he is discussing. Is faith the condition of the universal or particular aspect? Does Christ mediate between God and all men, or between God and his elect? Hodge doesn't apply this dual essence to these other features. This hinders clarity and precision.

Christ as the Mediator of the Covenant (pg. 364)

Hodge expounds the notion that Christ is the mediator of the covenant of grace. He asserts that Christ mediates this covenant in two senses: "(1) it was through his intervention, and solely on the ground of what He had done, or promised to do, that God entered into this new covenant with fallen men. And, (2) in the sense of a surety. He guarantees the fulfillment of all the promises and conditions of the covenant…His death…not only bound the parties to the contract, but it also secured the fulfillment of all its provisions…. His work renders certain the gifts of God's grace, and the perseverance of His people in faith and obedience" (pg. 364). Hodge says that Christ's mediation includes both intervention and guarantee. Clearly he is correct. As he says, Christ's role with respect to his elect people is rich and multi-faceted. Scripture presents him as mediator and surety of a new covenant, which is a better covenant, built on better promises. If we apply this to Hodge's definition of the human parties of the covenant of grace, then Christ would be surety of the particular aspect with the elect, but not of the universal aspect with all men. It is inconceivable that Christ could be a surety who "guarantees the fulfillment of all the promises and conditions" of any divine covenant that includes all lost men as its parties. Christ does not guarantee that all unconverted men will fulfill the condition and believe. He does not even guarantee that all unconverted men will hear the gospel. Therefore, if the general gospel call is the covenant of grace, then this covenant of grace has no surety. And, if this free offer has no surety, then it cannot be a new and better covenant, built on better promises, of which Christ is the surety. Therefore, Hodge's biblical teaching about the surety of the covenant of grace proves that the general gospel call cannot be its essence. Again, the general call is the means by which God implements the covenant of grace, not its substance.

The Condition of the Covenant (pgs. 364–65)

Hodge begins with this statement: "The condition of the covenant of grace, so far as adults are concerned, is faith in Christ" (pg. 364). Hodge does not explain what he means by "as far as adults are concerned." This seems to imply that faith is not the condition of the covenant of grace as far as some minor physical children are concerned. In the judgment of charity we should always put the best construction on ambiguous statements. It would be uncharitable on this ground to attribute to Hodge the view that God saves some minor children by sacrament without faith on their part. We should never read the works of good men like Charles Hodge with a jaundiced spirit. Nevertheless, Hodge's remark raises questions. Are all the physical children of believers included in this covenant that has only God's elect as its human parties? Does Christ act as surety for all the physical children of believers and guarantee that salvation will be applied to them? Hodge offers no answers in his soteriology to questions like these. As we shall see, our Presbyterian brothers tend to separate soteriology from ecclesiology with respect to the covenant of grace, almost as though there were two completely different covenants, one soteric, the other ecclesiastical. Dutch Calvinists pursue one cohesive definition of the covenant of grace that embraces both soteriology and ecclesiology.

Again, even "as far as adults are concerned," inconsistency is patent. As we saw when we analyzed the confessions, faith is the condition of the general gospel call. God also requires repentance. We should not forget this, especially in our day beset with Easy-Believism. However, the effectual call of the gospel is unconditional. Faith is not a condition prerequisite to regeneration. Thus inconsistency adheres to his treatment of the condition of the covenant of grace. This incongruity has occasioned endless debate about whether the covenant of grace is conditional or unconditional. As Hodge defines it, the general call is conditional, the effectual call, unconditional. Consistent definition resolves this tension.

Finally, it should be said that faith and repentance are conditions, not in the sense of meritorious acts, but in the sense of necessary means. Hodge carefully and accurately expounds this distinction as he concludes his presentation of faith as the condition.

The Promises of the Covenant (pgs. 365–66)

Hodge begins with a comprehensive statement, "The promises of this covenant are all included in the comprehensive formula...'I will be your God, and you shall be my people.' This involves the complete restoration of our normal relation to God" (pg. 365). A few lines later, he explains what it means that we are his people: "When it is said that we are to be His people, it means, (1) that we are His peculiar possession... (2) that being thus selected for the special love of God and for the highest manifestation of His glory, they are in all things fitted for this high destiny. They are justified, sanctified and glorified" (pg. 365). Again, it is difficult in the extreme to see how these promises in any way pertain to all unconverted men. In Scripture the generic promise, "you will be my people," only pertains to a community that has experienced a divine redemption. Under the Mosaic covenant this promise pertains to the nation that God redeemed from Egypt. Under the new covenant, it pertains to those redeemed from sin. This promise never pertains to all unconverted men. Clearly then, the free gospel offer to men without distinction should not be confused, commingled, and confounded with the covenantal promises that God makes to his redeemed people.

The Administration of the Covenant of Grace (pgs. 366–77)

Lastly, Hodge addresses the administration of the covenant of grace. The organizing principle is the unity and diversity found in this administration. In Unit 6 he defines the unity, in Unit 7, the diversity.

The Identity of the Covenant of Grace under all Dispensations
Hodge begins with a perspicuous statement: "By this is meant that the plan of salvation has, under all dispensations, Patriarchal, Mosaic, and the Christian, been the same" (pg. 366). He then names several groups in church history who have denied this truth. He mentions the Socinians, Remonstrants, Baptists, and Romanists. He concludes by saying: "in opposition to these different views the common doctrine of the church has ever been, that the plan of salvation has been the same from the beginning" (pg. 367). Once he has introduced the subject with this historical survey, he considers the essential aspects of this gospel unity.

Historical Survey of Diverse Opinions

✦ Socinians and Remonstrants

"Socinians say that under the old economy there was no promise of eternal life; and that the condition of salvation was not faith in Christ. The Remonstrants admitted that the patriarchs were saved and that they were saved through Christ...but they also questioned whether any direct promise of eternal life was given in the Old Testament, or whether faith in the Redeemer was the condition of acceptance with God" (pg. 366).

✦ Baptists

"The Baptists, especially those at the time of the Reformation, do not hold the common doctrine on this subject. Anabaptists not only spoke in very disparaging terms of the old economy and the state of the Jews under that dispensation, but it was necessary to their peculiar system, that they should deny that the covenant made with Abraham included the covenant of grace. Baptists hold that infants cannot be church members, and that the sign of such membership cannot properly be administered to any who have not knowledge and faith. But it cannot be denied that infants were included in the covenant made with Abraham, and that they received circumcision, its appointed seal and sign. It is therefore essential to their theory that the Abrahamic covenant should be regarded as a merely national covenant entirely distinct from the covenant of grace" (pg. 367).

✦ Romanists

"The Romanists, assuming that saving grace is communicated through the sacraments, assume a radical difference between the sacraments of the Old Testament and those of the New. The former only signified grace, the latter actually conveyed it. From this it follows that those living before the institution of the Christian sacraments were not actually saved.... At death they were not admitted into heaven, but passed into a place and state called the 'limbus patrum,' where they remained in a negative condition until the coming of Christ, who after His death descended into hell, Sheol, for their deliverance" (pg. 367).

Hodge remarks in conclusion: "In opposition to these different views the common doctrine of the Church has ever been, that the plan of salvation has been the same from the beginning. There is the same promise of deliverance from the evils of the apostasy, the same Redeemer, the same condition required for the participation in the blessings of redemption, and the same complete salvation for all who embrace the offers of divine mercy" (pg. 367). Hodge affirms the evangelical unity of the covenant of grace, God's plan of salvation, in every age and era. He points out that some have denied that eternal life was promised, some that faith in Christ was the condition of salvation, and still others that real salvation was experienced. These are the Socinians, Romanists, and Remonstrants.

Along with these, he lumps "*the Baptists.*" What do Baptists deny? "Baptists hold that infants cannot be church members.... It is therefore essential to their theory that the Abrahamic covenant should be regarded as a merely national covenant entirely distinct from the covenant of grace." Baptists do not deny the promise of eternal life, on condition of faith in Christ, or the experience of full salvation by the Old Testament saints. They merely disagree concerning the inclusion of infants in the church. Why then lump Baptists with those who reject the evangelical unity of the covenant of grace? Since you have read LCF, you know that this is not true of all Baptists. Statements like this could engender misunderstanding among brothers. But we shouldn't get all upset about it. I don't know what Hodge experienced with "Baptists." I never "walked a mile in his shoes." So if we encounter misimpressions such as these, we should simply correct them gently and graciously. In my personal experience evangelical Presbyterians are the most kind and gracious of men. We should always use due caution and restraint. We foster a climate of cordial dialogue with Presbyterian brothers when with LCF 7:2, 3 we confess the reality and unity of the covenant of grace.

Essential Aspects of Gospel Unity (pgs. 367–373)
On pages 367–68, he rightly asserts that the Old Testament saints knew more about the gospel than a casual reading of the Old Testament would suggest. Then he takes up the major strands of the unity of the covenant of grace.

• The Promise of Eternal Life before the Advent (pgs. 368–70)
Hodge has an excellent treatment of the giving of this promise prior to the incarnation. He powerfully refutes the Socinian and Roman Catholic views.

• Christ the Redeemer under both Dispensations (pgs. 370–71)

✦ Faith the Condition of Salvation from the Beginning (pgs. 371–73)
He clearly establishes this from Scripture in contrast to the Remonstrant position. He echoes the common voice of both the Westminster and London Baptist confessions.

Before Hodge moves on he draws two conclusions from the unity of the covenant of grace: "The covenant of grace, or plan of salvation, being the same in all its elements from the beginning, it follows, first, in opposition to the Anabaptists, that the people of God before Christ constituted a Church, and that the Church has been one and the same under all dispensations.... It follows from the same premises, in opposition to the Romanists, that the salvation of the people of God who died before the coming of Christ was complete" (pg. 373). Hodge states two good and necessary inferences.

Different Dispensations of the Covenant of Grace (pgs. 373–77)

The First Dispensation: From Adam to Abraham (pgs. 373–74)

The Second Dispensation: From Abraham to Moses (pg. 374)

The Third Dispensation: From Moses to Christ (pgs. 374–76)
He identifies the chief characteristics of revelation during the first two periods. These sections contain excellent biblical theology. He deals with the Mosaic dispensation in greater detail. He asserts its threefold nature. First, it was an administration of the covenant of grace. He says: "We have the direct authority of the New Testament for believing that the covenant of grace, or plan of salvation, thus underlay the whole of the institutions of the Mosaic period, and that their principle design was to teach through types and symbols what is now taught in explicit terms in the gospel" (pg. 374). This is an excellent statement of its evangelical character. He also believes it had two other aspects. Second, "it was a national covenant with the Hebrew people" (pg. 375). Third, "it contained, as does also the New Testament, a renewed proclamation of the original covenant of works" (pg. 375). He says that only this threefold view can explain the way in which Scripture describes the old covenant.

The Gospel Dispensation (pgs. 376–77)
He finishes this topic with the distinctions between the Mosaic and gospel dispensations. He addresses five: (1) the plan of salvation is not now confined to one people, but administered to all peoples; (2) it is more spiritual,

the types and ceremonies are done away; (3) it is more purely evangelical; (4) it is especially the dispensation of the Spirit; (5) the old was temporary, but it is permanent and final.

Dr. Hodge has furnished the church of Christ with a thorough, helpful, and careful treatment of this subject. We should appreciate and admire the many contributions he has made to our understanding of God's mind on this matter.

Robert Lewis Dabney on
God's Covenants

Now we consider the covenant theology of R. L. Dabney, a great light in Southern Presbyterianism. I selected Dabney for his significant influence on the development of Reformed theology on this issue. For those not familiar with Dabney, consider this brief biographical sketch by Dr. Morton H. Smith:[1]

> Dabney was a Southern Presbyterian who lived during the Nineteenth Century.... His biographer, Thomas Carey Johnson, said of him in *The Life and Letters of Robert Lewis Dabney* (1903) that he was entitled "to the first place among the theological thinkers and writers of his century." As a man who thus enjoyed such a reputation among his own contemporaries, it is no wonder that Dabney was considered the single most influential man in the Southern Presbyterian Church during the height of his ministry, 1865 through 1895...Dabney's influence was most strongly felt in the Southern Presbyterian circles. This volume...became the textbook of Systematic Theology in the Southern seminaries. He was recognized by Auguste Lecerf of France in his *Introduction to Reformed Dogmatics*, and by Herman Bavinck of the Netherlands in his *Gereformeerde Dogmatiek* as being among America's outstanding theologians.

This is why we consider Dabney's covenant theology. As Hodge's *Systematic Theology* became the textbook among Northern Presbyterians, so did Dabney's lectures among Southern Presbyterians. For that very reason,

---

1. Found in the preface to the 1972 edition of Dabney's *Lectures in Systematic Theology* (Grand Rapids: Zondervan Publishing House, 1972), 1–2.

these two men have exercised a pervasive influence on the theology of Presbyterians in the United States.

Dabney deals with the covenant of grace in Lectures 36–38.[2] His treatment has two major parts. In Lecture 36, he presents a definition of God's saving covenants. He divides this lecture into six units of thought. He presents an overview of the covenants of redemption and grace. This definition serves as the foundation and background for his second major topic, the administration of the covenant of grace, which he unfolds in Lectures 37 and 38.

A Definition of God's Saving Covenants (Lecture 36)

In his syllabus printed at the beginning of the lecture, Dabney outlines the topics he covers and suggests reading that elucidates and confirms his presentation.[3] Dabney lists six questions that he addresses in Lecture 36. These six units of thought are: (1) what are the scriptural uses of covenant, the theological uses of the covenants of redemption and grace; (2) prove the existence of the covenant of redemption, how it is related to the covenant of grace; (3) what are the identity and motives of the original parties to the covenant of redemption; (4) what is the date and the duration of the covenant of redemption; (5) what are the conditions stipulated between the parties to the covenant of redemption; and (6) are terms proposed between God and the believer in the covenant of grace? Dabney refers his students to the following works: WCF 7, WSC 20, WLC 31; Dick's Theology, Lectures 48 and 49; Turretin, which was his textbook, Topic 12, Questions 1 & 2; Witsius, Book 2, Chapter 2; and Hodge, Vol. 2 of Systematic Theology, Part 3, Chapter 2 (which we just studied). I collate these six units under three headings. He covered: (1) the terminology of God's covenants (Unit 1); (2) the covenant of redemption (Units 2–5); and (3) the covenant of grace (Unit 6).

The Terminology of God's Covenants (Unit 1)
Dabney begins with the biblical and theological context of the covenant of grace: "This remedial part of God's decree is the thing which the more recent Calvinistic divines term THE COVENANT OF GRACE—e.g., Dick."[4]

---

2. R. L. Dabney, *Lectures in Systematic Theology* (Grand Rapids: Zondervan Publishing House, 1972), 429–39, 440–52, 452–63.

3. Ibid., 429.

4. Ibid., 430.

Note that Dick uses the term the same way as Gill. Then Dabney concludes: "That being such, the Covenant of Grace must of course possess those general properties which we asserted of the Decree; and for the same reasons, viz., eternity, immutability, wisdom, freedom, absoluteness, graciousness."[5]

Then Dabney explains the biblical use of terms. He asserts that בְּרִית means an agreement or, in some instances, "an arrangement or disposition of matters determined on."[6] He says that διαθήκη means either an agreement or a last will and testament. He thinks it signifies a testament in Hebrews 9:16, 17. He asserts the essential correctness of WCF 7:4, but questions whether Scripture "often" uses the term this way. He says their assertion refers to the English translation.[7]

Then he says that *covenant* probably refers to the covenant of works in Hosea 6:7. He affirms that it describes the Abrahamic, Mosaic, and Christian dispensations. Then he makes this striking remark: "Not covenants, but dispensations; for we shall show that there is only one covenant, besides that of works." God's relations with Abraham, Israel and Christians are not distinct covenants, but dispensations. For Dabney there are only two covenants in history, the covenant of works and the covenant of grace. He says that we should not think of the Abrahamic covenant, the Mosaic covenant, and the new covenant as distinct covenants. These are merely dispensations of the one covenant, the covenant of grace. But Scripture speaks clearly and unambiguously of a plurality of divine covenants in history with his people (Jer. 31:31, 32). The new covenant is truly a covenant. The Mosaic covenant is truly a covenant. These two covenants are distinct covenants. Yet, at the same time, both are also *dispensations* of God's solemn pledge and plan of salvation, the covenant of grace (Gen. 3:15). It is not necessary to deny their distinctness as covenants in order to affirm that both administrate the covenant of grace. Scripture does not encourage us to follow Dabney when he asserts that the old and new covenants are merely dispensations of the covenant of grace. This alerts us to avoid extremes. The other extreme to avoid is the perspective that acknowledges distinct covenants but denies the unity of God's plan of salvation. We should avoid both extremes by adhering closely to the biblical use of terms.

---

5. Ibid.
6. Ibid.
7. Ibid., 431.

The Covenant of Redemption (Units 2–5)
Dabney discusses the distinct existence, original parties, date and duration, and stipulations of the covenant of redemption.

The Distinct Existence of the Covenant of Redemption (Unit 2)
He asks: "Was this part of the eternal decree in any proper sense a covenant? Has it properly the form of an eternal compact between the persons of the Trinity?" (pg. 431). As he states the question, he underlines the method by which he will answer it: "This is purely a question of revelation, to be decided not so much by finding the words covenant, compact, agreement, applied to it in Scripture, as the substance of the thing asserted" (pg. 431). Dabney employs the same method as Hodge to prove the existence of the covenant of redemption. What then, in Dabney's mind, constitutes the substance of a covenant? Does Scripture predicate that substance to the eternal decree to save and the eternal relation of the Father and Son? Dabney regarded a proper covenant to be a compact, involving contracting parties, promises, and conditions. Yet with due caution he makes an important qualification: "But here we must carefully avoid confusing the subject, by giving to this imminent transaction of the Trinity all the technical features of a 'covenant'" (pg. 431). He says that this relation involves neither prior unwillingness, nor any contingency on either part. Thus he asserts that there is no "holding the purposes of either party suspended in doubt on the promisings or doings of the other party. But it has always been certain from eternity, that the conditions would be performed; and the consequent reward would be bestowed, because there has always been an ineffable and perfect accord in the persons of the Trinity on those points: an accord possessing all the absoluteness of the other parts of the decree" (pg. 431). Then he offers specific Scripture proofs of the existence of an eternal transaction between the Father and the Son. He argues by inference from Titus 1:2. He cites Romans 5:12–19, which presents Christ in a federal relationship. He appeals to the fact that Christ is called the surety of a covenant in Hebrews 7:22. He asserts: "Many express passages describe…such an eternal agreement" (pg. 432). He cites Isaiah 42:6 and 49:8, and Psalm 40:7, 8.

    Once he has offered this scriptural proof for the existence of the covenant of redemption, he distinguishes between this eternal covenant and the historical gospel promise that he dubs the covenant of grace. His covenant theology rests on this crucial distinction.

Thus he says:[8]

> I hold that this subject cannot be treated intelligibly without dis-
> tinguishing the covenant existing from eternity between the Father
> and the Son, from the Gospel promise of salvation on terms of true
> faith offered to sinners through Christ. Many of our divines have
> agreed to retain this distinction, and to name the former covenant,
> for convenience sake, the "Covenant of Redemption," while they
> call the Gospel promise to believers, "The Covenant of Grace"....
> The Covenant of Redemption between the Father and the Son, I
> hold to be the real covenant transaction, being a free and optional
> compact between two equals, containing a stipulation which turns
> on a proper, causative condition, and bearing no relation to time, as
> it includes no mutable contingency or condition dependent on the
> uncertain will of creatures. The Covenant of Grace (so called) is a
> dispensation of promise to man, arising out of and dependent on
> the Covenant of Redemption.

Then Dabney defends his foundational distinction: "Now I repeat, the
distinction which Dick repudiates, and which so many others obscure, is
essential" (pg. 433). Then with probing questions, he challenges the adequacy
of Dick's one federal covenant: "Is Christ a party to the Covenant of Grace?
Or is man the party of the second part? Here Dr. Dick must be fatally
embarrassed. In the Covenant of Grace with man, Christ is not a party, but
Surety-True: But unless there is some party to the transaction less mutable,
feeble and guilty than believing sinners, man's prospect of deliverance is
gloomy indeed" (pg. 433). He continues: "Again: Is the Covenant conditioned
or unconditioned? Here also, Dick is fatally entangled. Will he say it is conditioned, and thus ascribe to the sinners' faith an efficient merit? Or will
he say it is unconditioned: and thus defraud us of hope with an unbought
redemption? I can answer: The Covenant of Redemption was conditioned,
on Christ's meritorious work. The Covenant of Grace is unconditioned, its
benefits are offered to believers without price" (pg. 433). Then he asserts that
Turretin has given him "his virtual support, though in a rather inconsistent
manner" (pg. 433). You will remember that Hodge also founds his covenant
theology on this distinction.

Now let's examine more carefully Dabney's crucial statement. Notice
that he calls the covenant of redemption "the real covenant transaction."

---

8. Ibid., 432.

This sounds like Gill. For Dabney, the covenant of redemption is a proper covenant, because it is an optional compact between two equals, containing a stipulation that turns on a proper, causative condition. For Dabney the covenant of grace, "so called," is not such a compact, so that it is not, strictly speaking, a proper covenant. He sees it as "a dispensation of promise to man" in history which arises out of the formal compact between the Father and Son in eternity. For Dabney, there is only one formal covenant, the eternal compact between the Father and Son, the covenant of redemption.

Let us also examine the key texts Dabney cites to support this optional compact between equals (Isa. 42:6; 49:8; Ps. 40:7, 8). In Isaiah 42:6, the prophet depicts the same person described in Isaiah 42:1: "Behold my servant whom I uphold; my chosen, in whom my soul delights." The text portrays, not the terms of an optional compact between equals, but God's disposition toward his righteous servant whom he upholds. Isaiah describes the incarnate Son in his capacity as God's servant. In Isaiah 49:8, the prophet again records a divine promise and pledge to his faithful servant. In Psalm 40:7, 8, Scripture displays a similar picture. God the Son incarnate, as God's righteous servant, says: "I delight to do your will, O my God." These passages do not portray the mission of Christ as an optional compact, containing stipulations and re-stipulations. These texts predict the coming Messiah as God's righteous servant who does the will of his God and Father. Ironically, the key texts Dabney cites do not present Christ's commission as a "formal and optional compact."

Let me be clear. I affirm the deity of the Son and his equality with the Father, and a covenant between God and Christ. I simply mean that a divine pledge does not have to be an "optional compact between equals" in order to be a "real" covenant. Therefore, there is no warrant for him to demote the covenant of grace to the rank of "so-called" covenant. If a real divine covenant is "an optional compact between equals," then neither the Messianic covenant with the God-man, Jesus, nor the covenant of grace with God's elect in Christ, is a true covenant. Dabney, to some degree, has fallen into Gill's trap. This soberly warns us that unless we use a more scriptural concept of covenant, we stand in jeopardy of overthrowing, not only the covenant of grace, but also the Messianic covenant with Christ.

Dabney, like Hodge, distinguishes the covenant of redemption from the covenant of grace. He affirms that these two covenants have distinct parties, promises, and, most pointedly, are even distinct in their nature. Dabney defines the covenant of redemption as a bilateral compact between the Father and the Son, which is conditional. But he defines the covenant of grace as a "dispensation of promise," which is "unconditioned," because it is "offered to believers without price." He identifies *"the parties"* of the covenant of grace with these phrases: "the Gospel promise of salvation on terms of true faith offered to sinners through Christ"; "the Gospel promise to believers"; "unless there is some party to the transaction less mutable, feeble and guilty than believing sinners"; "The Covenant of Grace is unconditioned, its benefits are offered to believers without price"; and "the terms proposed between God and the believer in the Covenant of Grace." So now, tell me, from Dabney's own words, who are the human parties of the covenant of grace? Are they unconverted sinners, promised salvation on condition of faith, or believers, or both? Since he embraced the Westminster Standards, in the judgment of charity, I assume that he intended to define the parties of the covenant of grace from the general and effectual call of the gospel. Yet he doesn't specify their identity with precision. We return to this in a moment.

Dabney insists on two covenants more dogmatically than Hodge. He calls it *"essential."* He acknowledges that WLC 31 poses a problem, but he stops short of asserting self-contradiction in his Westminster Standards. Dabney opened a door when he characterized the covenant of grace as a *"dispensation of promise."* Professor Murray, as we shall see shortly, walks through that door.

The Original Parties to the Covenant of Redemption (Unit 3)

+ The Identity of these Parties (pgs. 434–35)

Dabney identifies the contracting parties as the Father and the Son: "The Father, on the one part, then, acts as the representative of the Godhead; Christ as the representative of the elect.... To the question whether believers are also parties in the Covenant of Grace, no better answer can be given than that of Turretin.... In the eternal sense of the Covenant, they were not parties; in the sense of its exhibitions in time, they are parties; i.e., in their surety" (pg. 434). Dabney seems to use "Covenant of Grace" here in a broad sense that spans eternity and history. It appears to encompass the eternal divine covenantal relation and its historical manifestation. Or, it could simply be a synonym for covenant of redemption. It is not clear to me how exactly he uses it here, or why he felt it necessary to use covenant of grace in more than one way in the same lecture. If we aim at clarity, then it would seem best to explain what we mean by a term and to try to use it consistently, as much as possible.

◆ The Motivation of these Parties (pg. 435)

He says: "Having considered the Godhead (represented in the Father) and Christ, as the original parties to this covenant, the question naturally arises: What motivated them to do so?" (pg. 435). He says they were motivated by free love and mercy. He properly and ably defends the idea that love motivates the Father as well as the Son. We must be careful to underscore this in our teaching and preaching.

The Date and Duration of the Covenant of Redemption (Unit 4)[9]

He affirms that it began in the counsels of eternity past and that its administration will extend to eternity future. It is as eternal as God's decree. From this Dabney concludes: "Hence the covenant can only be one; and therefore it can only be spoken of as 'first,' 'second' (e.g. Heb. 8:7), or 'old,' 'new' (as Heb. 8:8; 12:24) with reference to its forms of manifestation" (pg. 435). Dabney's thinking develops as follows: (1) covenant strictly speaking is a compact between equals; (2) the real compact is between the Father and the Son; (3) there is thus, only one compact. It originates in eternity past and lasts to eternity; (4) the terms "old" and "new" therefore, do not depict distinct covenants in history between God and men, because, strictly speaking, there is only one covenant. Therefore "old" and "new" simply picture ways in which God manifests and administers this one eternal covenant established before the foundation of the world.

Dabney, like Gill, develops his theology on the view that real or proper covenants are voluntary compacts between equals. Dabney is very informative. Like Gill, he also shows us where this will lead if we carry out its logical implications. It will lead us to deny that God actually makes real covenants with men in history. Conversely, since God actually makes real covenants with men in history, we must conclude that a genuine covenant is not necessarily an "optional compact between equals containing mutual stipulations and causative conditions." Dabney, thankfully, states things so boldly and clearly as to lead us here. We are not alone. Where do we go from here?

---

9. Note that Unit 4, "the covenant eternal," is located on pgs. 434–35. It is sandwiched between two parts of Unit 3: "the original parties to the covenant" (pg. 434) and "motives of God to the covenant" (pg. 435).

What is a divine covenant with men? Scripture must guide our efforts to answer this basic question accurately.

The Stipulations of the Covenant of Redemption (Unit 5)

+ Stipulations (Conditions) Pledged by the Son (pgs. 435–36)

Dabney asks: "What were the conditions agreed upon by the Son to the Godhead, on behalf of His people?" (pg. 436). He asserts that the stipulations pledged by Christ are threefold: (1) obedience: the Son agreed to do exactly what and all that we should have done; (2) penalty: the Son agreed to endure the penalty that we should have endured; (3) mediation: the Son took the offices of the mediator.

+ Stipulations (Conditions) Pledged by the Father (pgs. 436–37)

He says: "Passing now to the other side of the compact…the Father… engaged to…clothe Him with humanity…to endue Christ plenteously with gifts and graces…to uphold Him under His heavy task…to give Him an elect seed, as the sure reward of His labors…and to bestow His royal exaltation, with all its features of glory" (pgs. 436–37).

The Covenant of Grace (Unit 6: pgs. 437–39)

Dabney begins: "When we consider the covenant between God and believers, however, it is evident that there are terms bargained between them" (pg. 437). Evidently he uses a figure of speech. He does not mean that the covenant of grace is a compact between equals, or that its terms were literally "bargained out." He defines the parties to this covenant as "*God and believers.*" Previously, he spoke of the covenant of grace as:

> the Gospel promise of salvation on terms of true faith offered to sinners through Christ…while they call the Gospel promise to believers, The Covenant of Grace.

Previously he associated the general call with its parties: "promise of salvation on terms of true faith offered to sinners." Now he appears to define its parties only in particular terms: "*God and believers.*" What specifically does God "bargain" with believers in the covenant? He says: "In this covenant God briefly bargains, on His part, to be reconciled to believers, and to communicate Himself to them as their guide, light, consolation, and chief good. They, on their part, are held bound to the correlative reconciliation, grounding their weapons of rebellion and exercising the spirit of adoption, to a life

of self-consecration and obedience, to separation from the world of His enemies, and conformity of the heart and life to God's will." Note carefully that
he does not define its promise as the regeneration of the unconverted elect.
He enumerates divine promises associated, not with the regeneration of the
unconverted elect, but with the Christian experience of believers. He says
they are summed up in the repeated phrase: "I will be their God, and they
shall be my people." To support this he cites Genesis 17:7 and other texts.

Then he adds a significant remark: "it is true, that the transaction of
Gen. 17th is rather ecclesiastical than spiritual; but the spiritual is always
included and represented in the outward" (pg. 437). That statement appears to
contain an implicit distinction between an *ecclesiastical* "transaction" and the
evangelical covenant of grace. Yet he doesn't explain this distinction. Who
are the parties of this ecclesiastical transaction? What are its promises? Are
there conditions? He doesn't answer these questions.

His main focus is on the condition of the covenant of grace: "The question arises, whether all the graces and duties of the Christian life may be
accounted as conditions of the Covenant of Grace." He replies: "So far it is
from being true that this holy life is in any sense a meritorious condition of
receiving grace, or a procuring cause; it is itself the fruit of grace" (pg. 438). The
next question is: "whether faith itself should be spoken of as a condition of the
covenant." He answers: "But it is most manifest that there is a sense in which
faith is the condition" (pg. 438). Then he quotes John 3:16, Acts 8:37, John
11:36, and Mark 16:16. These texts present faith as the duty of unconverted
sinners who hear the gospel. He adds: "No human wit can evade the fact,
that here God proposes to man something for him to do, which, if done, will
secure redemption; if neglected, will ensure damnation—and that something
is in one sense a condition" (pg. 438). Then, as Hodge did, he qualifies this: "In
the covenant of works, the fulfillment of the condition on man's part earned
the result, justification by its proper moral merit. In the Covenant of Grace,
the condition has no moral merit to earn the promised grace, being merely
an act of receptivity. In the covenant of works, man was required to fulfill the
condition in his own strength. In the Covenant of Grace, strength is given
to him to believe from God" (pgs. 438–39). His final question is whether or
not faith is the only condition: "The question now remains, whether, in this
instrumental sense, anything else besides faith is a condition" (pg. 439). He
replies that faith alone is the condition of the covenant of grace.

This treatment lacks the precision, clarity, and especially the penetra-
tion that are so characteristic of his theology. He offers no distinctions,

definitions, or headings. He merely raises and answers a series of questions. Remember how Dabney criticized Dr. Dick:[10]

> Again: Is the Covenant conditioned or unconditioned? Here also, Dick is fatally entangled. Will he say it is conditioned, and thus ascribe to the sinner's faith an efficient merit? Or will he say it is unconditioned: and thus defraud us of hope with an unbought redemption? I can answer: The Covenant of Redemption was conditioned, on Christ's meritorious work. The Covenant of Grace is unconditioned, its benefits are offered to believers without price.

Now it appears he was too hard on Dr. Dick. He admits that faith is *"the condition"* of his *"unconditioned"* covenant of grace. The issue of conditionality mandates a consistent application of the universal and particular aspects of the gospel call. Faith is the condition of the general gospel call, which God declares indiscriminately to lost sinners. Faith is not the condition of regeneration. Faith is the gift of God. It is one of the blessings of the covenant of grace: "to you it has been granted…to believe" (Phil. 1:29). God's commitment to give the Holy Spirit to enable his elect to believe cannot possibly be conditioned on their faith. Rather, their faith results from God fulfilling that commitment. Yet Dabney doesn't overtly employ these distinctions. This instructs us that clarity results when we state categories plainly, and carry distinctions through consistently. Otherwise there is significant potential for confusion.

Dabney, it appears, formally defines *the parties* of the covenant of grace as "God and believers," using the effectual gospel call. Yet it also seems that he formally defines *the condition* of the covenant of grace as "faith," using the general gospel call: "the Gospel promise of salvation on terms of true faith offered to sinners through Christ." It appears that he does so without stating explicitly his distinctions or assumptions. As a teacher of students, I can imagine in my mind's eye the question-and-answer session that followed this lecture. My heart goes out to Dabney. Possibly he just couldn't bring himself formally to name unconverted men indiscriminately as parties to God's covenant of grace. I don't blame him. Nor should you. I wouldn't want to walk down that road with good Dr. Hodge either. Yet, at the same time, he just can't totally divorce the covenant of grace from human responsibility to believe as defined in the general gospel call. So he combines these two major emphases of Scripture and leaves it there. God's covenant of grace

---

10. Ibid., 433.

is emphatically with his elect people, believers; and yet, God calls his elect people to himself by the general call of the gospel; he requires faith—the very faith that he himself creates and supplies. Don't undervalue Dabney as a theologian because his approach to this topic is somewhat confusing. Even here Dabney contributes something very worthwhile. He recognizes that the distinguishing trait of the new covenant community of God's people is their faith in Christ. As repentance marked John's disciples, so also faith in Christ distinguishes the new covenant community (Acts 19:4). I think Dabney perceived this truth, and for this reason singled out faith, although he didn't articulate its role clearly or precisely.

The Administration of the Covenant of Grace (Lectures 37, 38)

Lectures 37 and 38 build on the foundation he laid in Lecture 36. These two lectures expound the administration of the covenant of grace in redemptive history. He covers eight units of thought: (1) has God ever had more than one covenant with man since the fall?; (2) how many dispensations has this covenant been administered in?; (3) the revelation of the covenant to the Antediluvians; (4) the revelation of the covenant from Abraham to Moses (including proof that Abraham's covenant was also a covenant of grace); (5) the revelation of the covenant in the Mosaic economy; (6) the true nature of the Mosaic dispensation; (7) differences between the old and new dispensations; and (8) is there a *limbuspatrum*?

He covers the first four units in Lecture 37, the last four in Lecture 38. I collate these eight units under four headings. First, he presents the unity and diversity of the covenant of grace (Units 1, 2). Second, he unfolds its progressive development and disclosure (Units 3–6). Third, he compares its Mosaic and gospel dispensations (Unit 7). Fourth, as an appendix, he demonstrates the complete salvation of the Old Testament saints (Unit 8). We use these four headings to survey his exposition of the administration of the covenant of grace.

Its Unity and Diversity (Units 1, 2)

Its Unity (Unit 1: pgs. 440–43)

Has there ever been more than one way of salvation from sin since the fall? Dabney plainly affirms that there has only been one. He founds this answer on the immutability of God (pg. 441). His argument is compelling.

Since God is immutable, and since man's sin necessarily destroys communion with God, then whatever plan God adopts to reconcile one sinner must
be substantially the same plan he implements to reconcile any other sinner.
This rests on God's singularity, the nature of sin, and his immutable moral
character, especially his holiness, justice, and mercy. On this solid foundation, Dabney builds a formidable house. He musters five lines of evidence
for support: (1) the direct testimony of Scripture (pg. 442); (2) the sameness of the mediator (pg. 442); (3) the sameness of the condition (pg. 442);
(4) the sameness of the promise (pg. 442); and (5) the evangelical significance of types (pgs. 442–43). In LCF 7:3, Reformed Baptists confess hearty
affirmation of this truth.

Its Diversity (Unit 2: pg. 444)

Dabney asks how many dispensations exist. He takes a different approach
than Hodge, although the difference is only a matter of emphasis. He
answers two. For him the decisive event in redemptive history is the incarnation. He says: "There seems no adequate reason for regarding the patriarchal
age, from Adam to Moses, as essentially a different dispensation from that
of Moses." He makes two insightful comments about why the incarnation
occurs some 4,000 years after the fall (pg. 444). He says this serves to inten-
sify the expectation of God's people for the coming of Christ. He also says
by this delay God draws more attention to his Son and his glory when he
finally appears in a climactic role.

Its Progressive Development and Disclosure (Units 3–6)

Dabney next discusses the unfolding of the plan of salvation. This completes
Lecture 37 and continues into the first two headings of Lecture 38. Dabney
considers this progressive unfolding in three periods of redemptive history:
From Adam to Abraham (Unit 3); From Abraham to Moses (Unit 4); and
from Moses to Christ (Unit 5). Unit 6 is an excursus that defends the propriety of Unit 5. He outlines with great skill the strategic revelatory deposits
of each of these periods. He displays a masterful grasp of the principles of
biblical theology. Dabney follows and develops the lead of the Baptist fathers
(LCF 7:3), although perhaps not consciously or deliberately.

Its Revelation to the Antediluvians (Unit 3: pgs. 445–49)

This is an admirable example of excellent biblical theology within a systematic study. Dabney notes three things about the plan of salvation revealed to the Antediluvians: (1) that repentance was necessary, revealed by means of their sorrows (pgs. 445–46); (2) the necessity of satisfaction, revealed by the institution of bloody sacrifice (pgs. 446–47); and (3) that satanic bondage was not final, revealed by the promise of a deliverer in Genesis 3:15 (pgs. 447–49). While introducing this he says: "We must not suppose that this traditionary knowledge of God was scanty, because the hints of it given in earlier revelations are scanty; for the purpose of the revelation to us through Moses did not require that God should give us full information as to the religious knowledge of the Antediluvians." Jude underscores this truth (Jude 14, 15). This text indicates explicitly that they knew of Christ, of his coming to earth, of his deity, and of his rule as a judge.

Its Revelation to the Patriarchs (Unit 4: pgs. 449–52)

He observes several notable additions from Abraham to Moses: (1) the separation of the sons of God as a peculiar people (pg. 449); (2) the institution of the sealing ordinance, circumcision (pg. 449); (3) the additions noted in Romans 3 & 4 and Galatians 3 (pg. 449). Concerning these he says: "We are expressly taught, that the seed in whom the promise was made was Christ: that the central benefit received by Abraham, was gospel salvation through faith: that the sacrament was a gospel one, a seal of the righteousness of faith: that the promise of Canaan was typical of that of heaven: that Abraham is the exemplar and head of all gospel believers: and that the society founded in his family was, and is, the visible Church of Christ, reformed and enlarged at the new dispensation." He also says: "In that age of the world, every organized society unavoidably took the patriarchal form; hence the family, or clan of Abraham, became the visible Church: and the race-limit tended approximately to set them to be the boundary between Church and world" (pg. 449). We should distinguish this ecclesiastical development from the personal application of redemption by the covenant of grace. Nevertheless, it is true that an "ecclesiastical" community came into existence at this period. It is also true that this visible society was marked by circumcision, was associated with the implementation of the covenant of grace, and is organically related to the Christian church. Although Christ has reformed this visible community evangelically and transformed it spiritually, nevertheless, that very community is today the church of Jesus Christ. Dabney concludes Lecture 37 with an important question: "Was eternal life promised to the patriarchs?" He answers in the affirmative. He gives six good reasons for this answer (pgs. 450–51).

Its Revelation in the Mosaic Economy (Units 5–6: pgs. 452–56)
Dabney begins Lecture 38 with this consideration. He first establishes that the Mosaic covenant was not a covenant of works (pgs. 452–53). This, he correctly observes, would have been a curse rather than a blessing. He then addresses what he calls an ingenious attempt to regard it as a symbolic covenant of works. He rightly rejects this innovation. He then notes four major developments: (1) the republication of the moral law; (2) the institution of the sacrament of the passover; (3) the establishment of the theocratic church-state; and (4) the great enlargement of the sacrificial ritual associated with good standing. In conclusion, he shows these four additions are consistent with regarding the Mosaic covenant as gracious (pg. 454).

Then Dabney appends an excursus (Unit 6: pgs. 454–56). This parenthetical unit aims to prove that the Mosaic covenant is indeed gracious. He expounds in detail the positive scriptural arguments for regarding the Mosaic covenant as an administration of the plan of salvation. He calls this: "the true nature of the Mosaic dispensation." He gives seven "irresistible" arguments: (1) there are only two covenants, works and grace, works is impracticable (pgs. 454–55); (2) it would be inconsistent with the merciful character of what took place at Sinai (pg. 455); (3) the formula adopted was the formula of the covenant of grace (pg. 455); (4) fidelity to the covenant with Abraham mandates that it be gracious per Galatians 3:17 (pg. 455); (5) purification with blood reveals that it was gracious (pg. 455); (6) the fact that the law was enforced under Abraham indicates that it was gracious (pg. 456); and (7) the fact that the law is still binding in the New Testament also indicates that it was gracious (pg. 456). Then he discusses Jeremiah 31:32 (pgs. 456–57). He shows that this passage does not prove that the Mosaic covenant was a covenant of works republished. Clearly he is correct, it proves no such thing.

Comparison of its Old and New Dispensations (Unit 7: pgs. 457–62)
His comparison has five major observations: (1) the Old Testament is too much depreciated (pgs. 457–58); (2) both dispensations are two sided, containing law and gospel (pgs. 457–60); (3) Galatians 3 & 4 must be carefully interpreted (pgs. 460–61); (4) the old dispensation is inferior to the new (pg.

461); and (5) there are five real points of difference (pgs. 461–62). These are: (a) the old preceded Christ's vicarious work; (b) the old rituals were types, the new rituals commemorative symbols; (c) the old rituals were more numerous, varied, and laborious; (d) the old was limited to the Jewish nation, the new receives all nations; (e) the old was temporary, the new endures to the consummation. Although what he says is true, he does not mention the momentous change in the moral nature and spiritual composition of the covenant community that occurs when Jesus leads God's people from the old to the new covenant.

The Intermediate State of the Old Testament Saints (Unit 8: pgs. 462–63)
He refutes the Romanist doctrine of a *limbus patrum* (pgs. 462–63). He demonstrates that even prior to the first advent of Christ, the souls of believers entered into heaven immediately upon death.

Conclusion
Dabney has made some worthwhile and lasting contributions to covenant theology. Especially helpful is his grasp of the progressive unfolding of the plan of salvation in redemptive history.

— 5 —

Dutch Calvinists on God's Covenants

Herman Bavinck and Louis Berkhof illustrate for us covenant theology among Dutch Calvinists. Their contributions develop from the molding influence of the Triple Knowledge.[1]

The Triple Knowledge on God's Covenants

In 1561, Guido de Bres prepared the Belgic Confession to publish and vindicate the true doctrines of the persecuted Reformed Churches in the Netherlands. In 1563, Zacharias Ursinus and Casper Olevianus, at the request of Elector Frederick III of the Palatinate, wrote the Heidelberg Catechism, to ground believers in their faith. In 1618–19, the Reformed Synod of Dordrecht adopted the Canons of Dort, more popularly known as "the five points of Calvinism," which they wrote in response to the Arminian threat to church unity. These documents hold a place in Dutch Calvinism similar to that of the Westminster standards in English Puritanism. If anything, their influence and acceptance has been even more widespread among Dutch Calvinists than that of the Westminster standards among English Calvinists. Studying the doctrine of God's covenants in the Reformed standards is more difficult. This topic does not receive the same prominence that the Westminster standards explicitly give it.

The Belgic Confession

BEL displays the same general order as WCF. Yet it doesn't explicitly mention the covenant of grace as the bridge from the creation and fall of man to the

---

1. This denotes the doctrinal standards of Dutch Calvinism: BEL, HC, and CSD.

person and work of Christ. In BEL two articles link anthropology and soteriology: "Eternal Election" (BEL 16), and "The Recovery of Fallen Man" (BEL 17). Their chain of reasoning is like that of Hodge in his soteriology: "The Plan of Salvation" (Chapter 1), and "The Covenant of Grace" (Chapter 2).[2] Thus, BEL 17 sheds light on their covenant theology. It reads:

> We believe that our most gracious God, in His admirable wisdom and goodness, seeing that man had thus thrown himself into physical and spiritual death and made himself wholly miserable, was pleased to seek and comfort him, when he trembling fled from His presence, promising him that He would give His Son (who would be born of a woman) to bruise the head of the serpent and to make him blessed.

BEL 17 does not explicitly mention a covenant, but the generic idea of the covenant of grace is present implicitly. WCF starts with the Creator-creature distinction (WCF 7:1). BEL begins with an offended God graciously pursuing his offending creature, man, who neither wants nor seeks him. It stresses that God takes the initiative to seek and save sinners. BEL also recognizes that God seeks lost men immediately after the fall. It refers to Genesis 3:15 as the embodiment of God's plan of salvation. It stresses God's promise of certain deliverance through God the Son, announced to fallen Adam to comfort him. BEL explicitly mentions God's covenant only to defend infant baptism.[3] This gives their doctrine of the covenant a polemic thrust. Thus, it should come as no surprise to find that BEL 34 has lifted this polemic to a prominent place in Dutch Calvinist thinking. This is because BEL, which predates WLC and WCF by some 80 years, only explicitly features a polemic use.

The Heidelberg Catechism

HC is a momentous work, which develops according to its first two questions. It thus expounds three heads of doctrine: sin and misery, deliverance, and gratitude. HC does not explicitly mention God's covenant when it defines the transition from misery to deliverance. It mentions only the holy

---

2. Hodge, *Systematic Theology*, 2: vi–vii.

3. "Therefore we detest the error of the Anabaptists, who are not content with the one only baptism they have once received, and moreover condemn the baptism of the infants of believers, who we believe ought to be baptized and sealed with the sign of the covenant, as the children of Israel formerly were circumcised upon the same promises which are made unto our children" (BEL 34).

gospel as the means of this deliverance (HC 19).[4] It describes the progressive revelation of this holy gospel from Genesis 3:15 until the incarnation. Thus implicitly, when compared with BEL 17, it seems to associate the gospel with the covenant of grace. This is only an implicit association. To be completely transparent, they do not mention the covenant of grace explicitly either in BEL 17 or in HC 19. In Questions 23–58, HC expounds the content of the Christian faith, following the Apostles' Creed. Then it transitions to the ministry of the Spirit and the means of grace, which it expounds in Questions 66–85. They only explicitly mention God's covenant in this connection. God's covenant furnishes support for baptizing infants (HC 74)[5] and for keeping unbelievers from the Lord's Supper (HC 82).[6] Like BEL, HC only mentions God's covenant in reference to the sacraments. The Dutch Calvinists didn't merely seize a convenient weapon for the fray with Anabaptists. Rather, they viewed the sacraments as especially rooted in divine covenant. When their doctrine of the sacraments was challenged, they uncovered the foundation on which it rested. Therefore, to say that they invented covenant doctrine to justify a practice that was really based on tradition, would not only be uncharitable, it would also be untrue. They did not invent it for, but applied it to, the practice of infant baptism. Further, if the sacred rituals that picture God's salvation are linked with God's covenant, so also must be the spiritual realities that they signify. BEL and HC, formulated in the 16th century, do not explicitly define this connection.

The Canons of Dort

CSD responds to specific errors. It is not a systematic collation of the entire body of divinity that aims to give each doctrine its due prominence. This mandates great caution in drawing sweeping doctrinal conclusions. Thus,

---

4. "From the holy gospel, which God himself first revealed in Paradise; and afterwards published by the patriarchs and prophets, and represented by the sacrifices and other ceremonies of the law; and lastly, has fulfilled it by his only begotten Son" (HC 19).

5. "Q. Are infants also to be baptized? A. Yes; for since they, as well as adults, are included in the covenant and church of God, and since both redemption from sin and the Holy Spirit, the Author of faith, are through the blood of Christ promised no less to them than to adults, they must also by baptism, the sign of the covenant, be ingrafted into the Christian Church, and distinguished from the children of unbelievers, as was done in the Old covenant or testament by circumcision, instead of which baptism was instituted in the new covenant" (HC 74).

6. "Q. Are they also to be admitted to this supper who, by their confession and life, show themselves to be unbelieving and ungodly? A. No; for in this way the covenant of God would be profaned and His wrath kindled against the whole congregation" (HC 82).

CSD only displays how they spoke of divine covenant in their defense against the Arminian challenge.

Divine covenant first appears under the first head of doctrine, "Divine Election and Reprobation." They connect the covenant of grace, not with infant baptism, but with the delicate matter of shepherding godly parents whose beloved child dies in infancy:

> Since we are to judge of the will of God from His word, which testifies that the children of believers are holy, not by nature but in virtue of the Covenant of Grace, in which they together with the parents are comprehended, godly parents ought not to doubt the election and salvation of their children whom it pleases God to call out of this life in their infancy (Gen. 17:7; Acts 2:39; 1 Cor. 7:14) (CSD:1:17).

This use is not polemical, but pastoral. It aims to comfort grieving souls. It is sacred ground, on which all should tread with due regard for the suffering of precious saints, as anyone who has wept with and tried to comfort such parents surely knows. The covenant of grace was not just a weapon in their arsenal. It was a healing balm in their pastoral medicine chest. While administering this loving pastoral care to grieving parents, they plainly identify the partakers of the covenant of grace. They define its partakers as believers and their minor physical children.

CSD refers to divine covenant most frequently under the second head of doctrine: "The Death of Christ, and the Redemption of Men Thereby." CSD refers to the new covenant in Article 8.[7] The synod explicitly associates the new covenant with the accomplishment of particular redemption. They recognize that God enters covenantal relations with men in history. They also affirm that God confirms a new covenant when Christ sheds his blood.

Again, under the second head of doctrine, in paragraph two, the synod rejects the errors of those:

> Who teach: That it was not the purpose of the death of Christ that He should confirm the new covenant of grace through His blood, but only that He should acquire for the Father the mere right to establish with man such a covenant as He might please, whether of

---

7. "It was the will of God that Christ by the blood of the cross, whereby He confirmed the new covenant, should effectually redeem out of every people, tribe, nation, and language, all those, and those only, who were from eternity chosen to salvation and given to Him by the Father" (CSD:2:8).

grace or of works. For this is repugnant to Scripture which teaches that Christ has become the surety and mediator of a better, that is, the new covenant, and that a testament is of force where there has been death (Heb. 7:22; 9:15, 17) (CSD:2:P2).

They speak of "the new covenant of grace" that Christ confirmed by his blood. They deny that Christ died to make any covenant scheme of salvation possible. They affirm that he died to confirm that definite scheme of salvation from sin, which God ordained before the foundation of the world, and progressively revealed in history through the gospel. They seem to use Hebrews 7:22, 9:15, 17 to demonstrate that God's scheme of salvation from sin is mediated by Christ and confirmed by his blood. It is not clear how this covenantal arrangement could be in force ever since the fall and yet not be in force until Christ shed his blood. Confusion results unless the new covenant, ratified "after those days" by Christ's blood, is distinguished from the covenant of grace, enacted immediately after the fall and implemented ever since the fall.

Again, under this second head of doctrine, in the fourth paragraph, the synod rejects the errors of those:

> Who teach: That the new Covenant of Grace, which God the Father, through the mediation of the death of Christ, made with man, does not herein consist that we by faith, in as much as it accepts the merits of Christ, are justified before God and saved, but in the fact that God, having revoked the demand of perfect obedience of faith, regards faith itself and the obedience of faith, although imperfect, as the perfect obedience of the law, and does esteem it worthy of the reward of eternal life through grace. For these contradict the Scriptures: *Being justified freely by his grace through the redemption that is in Christ Jesus; whom God set forth to be a propitiation, through faith in his blood* (Rom. 3:24, 25). And these proclaim, as did the wicked Socinus, a new and strange justification of man before God, against the consensus of the whole Church (CSD:2:P4).

This demonstrates that what modern men call a "new perspective" is really the resurrection of an old error that the synod of Dort condemned as a "strange justification." It also clearly demonstrates that they call God's plan, scheme, and way of salvation from sin the "new covenant of grace." Thus, their term is virtually synonymous with the common use of "covenant of grace." The synod affirms that God, in his scheme of salvation, does not accept faith and its fruits in place of perfect obedience, but rather, accepts the perfect obedience of Christ. They affirm that God justifies Christians by faith, since faith receives and rests on Christ and his merits.

Again, under this second head of doctrine, in the fifth paragraph, the synod rejects the errors of those:

> Who teach: That all men have been accepted into the state of recon-
> ciliation and unto the grace of the covenant, so that no one is worthy
> of condemnation on account of original sin, and that no one shall be
> condemned because of it, but that all are free from the guilt of origi-
> nal sin. For this opinion is repugnant to the Scripture which teaches
> that we are *by nature children of wrath* (Eph. 2:3) (CSD:2:P5).

They condemn the error of *prevenient grace*, which alleges that God includes all men in his covenantal scheme of salvation to such an extent that he removes from all men the guilt of original sin. Thus, they use "the covenant" to refer to God's plan and way of salvation.

Summary of the Use of Divine Covenant in the Triple Knowledge
Three observations emerge from this survey. First, the Triple Knowledge asserts explicitly and repeatedly that believers and their minor physical children partake in the covenant of grace. HC and BEL base infant baptism on the participation of the physical children of believers in God's covenant (BEL 34; HC 74). CSD uses the inclusion of a believer's physical children in the covenant of grace to comfort godly parents whose child dies in infancy (CSD:1:17). Second, the Triple Knowledge affirms that divine covenant should regulate the observance of the sacraments. They use this to support both infant baptism (BEL 34; HC 74) and believer-only communion (HC 82). Third, the Triple Knowledge presents God's scheme of salvation from sin as covenantal. They affirm that God's plan of salvation, in its accomplishment by Christ and in its application to God's people, is a covenantal commitment on the part of God. They call this way of salvation the *new covenant of grace*. They affirm that this method of salvation involves particular redemption (CSD:2:P2) and justification by faith (CSD:2:P4). They deny that God's covenant is universal in the sense of prevenient grace, which they condemn as error (CSD:2:P5). They closely associate God's scheme of salvation with the new covenant (CSD:2:8), which most clearly displays its properties and essence. On this foundation Dutch Calvinism builds their theology of divine covenant.

The Triple Knowledge doctrine of divine covenant has eventuated in controversy among Dutch Calvinists over the doctrine of presumptive regeneration. The seeds of this controversy are hidden in the Triple Knowledge itself, especially in what those caring pastors said to comfort the grieving in CSD:1:17. They asserted: "godly parents ought not to doubt the election and salvation of their children." The reason for this confidence is that these children, together with their believing parents, are comprehended in the covenant of grace. It is true that they applied this parental confidence *only to one specific situation*. It is also true that their motive was compassion. Nevertheless, their stated basis for this comfort would pertain, not to that specific case alone, but to a believer's other children also. They affirm that *every* minor child of a believer is comprehended in the covenant of grace. Thus, sooner or later, someone was bound to draw the conclusion that godly parents should not doubt the election and salvation of any of their minor children, because all their minor children partake in the covenant of grace. It is conceded that the reasoning that reaches this conclusion is flawed in several respects. It is also acknowledged that not all Dutch Calvinists adopt this conclusion. Still, this is a prominent path by which the doctrine of presumptive regeneration arises logically from the Triple Knowledge.

Finally, the Triple Knowledge doctrine of divine covenant displays overt *particularism*. They affirm explicitly that believers in Christ alone, not all mankind, are parties to the covenant of grace. To this they overtly couple *organic continuity*. They affirm explicitly that the minor children of believers partake with their parents in the covenant of grace. Thus, those who build their covenant theology on the Triple Knowledge grapple to formulate one cohesive definition of the partakers of the covenant of grace that welds *particularism* to *organic continuity*. This prompts Dutch Calvinists in a sincere effort to formulate a comprehensive definition of covenant participation that spans soteriology and ecclesiology. This is a noble quest, and yet, one doomed to failure, for as we shall see, it entangles them in the insoluble dilemma of universalism.

Herman Bavinck on God's Covenants

I begin with Zylstra's sketch of the life and labors of Herman Bavinck. He says: "Those who are familiar with the history of the Reformed Churches of the Netherlands...will know that...no two names are held in such esteem as the names of Abraham Kuyper and Herman Bavinck. They were heroic figures of giant accomplishment in Christian endeavor."[8] Bavinck expounds the covenant of grace in his systematic theology, *Gereformeerde Dogmatiek*, in English, *Reformed Dogmatics*,[9] and also in an abridged compendium of his theology, *Our Reasonable Faith*.[10] For some twenty-seven years I surveyed only *Our Reasonable Faith*. Since the translation of Bavinck's Christology in 2006, I now conclude with a brief analysis of Bavinck's doctrine of divine covenant in his systematic theology.

Bavinck wrote *Our Reasonable Faith* in narrative style without headings or sub-points. This makes analysis a bit more difficult. He develops six units of thought. He begins with man's need for God's covenantal intervention (pgs. 260–64). He says that this need arises from God's righteous judgment on human sin (Unit 1) and from men's futile religious efforts to deliver themselves from evil (Unit 2). This introduces his presentation of God's intervention in history to deliver sinners. He begins with the eternal foundation of saving grace, the counsel of redemption (pgs. 266–70). After he expounds the content of God's counsel (Unit 3), he makes a pastoral application. He shows the proper and improper use of this counsel (Unit 4). This leads him to explain how God implements this counsel in history by his institution of the covenant of grace (Unit 5: pgs. 270–73). He concludes with the nature of the covenant of grace (Unit 6). He expounds and applies "three remarkable characteristics" (pgs. 273–79).

I present these six units of thought under four headings that relate them to the covenant of grace: its necessity (Units 1–2), eternal foundation (Units 3–4), institution (Unit 5), and nature (Unit 6).

The Necessity for the Covenant of Grace (Units 1–2)

Bavinck approaches man's need for God's covenant grace from two vantage points. Its necessity arises from God's righteous wrath (Unit 1) and from the futility of man-made religion (Unit 2).

---

8. Henry Zylstra, translator's preface to *Our Reasonable Faith* (Grand Rapids: Baker Book House, 1977 paperback edition), 5.

9. Herman Bavinck, *Reformed Dogmatics: Volume 3: Sin and Salvation in Christ*, edited by John Bolt, translated by John Vriend (Grand Rapids: Baker Academic, 2006), 193–232.

10. Herman Bavinck, *Our Reasonable Faith*, translated by Henry Zylstra (Grand Rapids: Baker Book House, 1977 paperback edition), 260–79.

God's Righteous Wrath Necessitates the Covenant of Grace
Bavinck ends Chapter 13, "Sin and Death," with a question: who can stand in that judgment? He begins Chapter 14, "The Covenant of Grace," with the answer: none, such as he is by nature. He reasons from God's evident quarrel with man to the presence of a redemptive idea in all religions (pgs. 260–61). The question of all religions is: "what must I do to be saved?" (pg. 262).

Man's Futile Religion Necessitates the Covenant of Grace
Bavinck addresses man's futile search for "deliverance from evil" and his effort to possess "the highest good." He notes three common denominators of all religions (pgs. 263–64). This sets the stage for God's intervention to save men.

The Eternal Foundation of the Covenant of Grace: (Units 3–4)
God's eternal counsel of redemption is the foundation of the covenant of grace. Bavinck introduces this counsel with its connection to men's futile search for deliverance:[11]

> Between the self-conceived and self-willed religions, on the one hand, and the religion based on…special revelation…there is…a difference in principle. In the first it is always man who tries to find God…but in the second, in the religion of the Holy Scriptures, it is always God who seeks man, who discloses man to himself in his guilt and impurity, but who also, makes Himself known as He is in His grace and compassion…. In the Christian religion the work of men is nothing, and it is God Himself who acts, intervenes in history, opens the way of redemption in Christ and by the power of His grace brings man into that redemption and causes him to walk in it….
>
> Immediately after the fall God already comes to man. Man has sinned and is seized upon by shame and fear. He flees his creator and hides himself…. But God does not forget him. He does not let go of him, but condescends, seeks him out, talks with him, and leads him back into fellowship with Himself (Gen. 3:7–15).
>
> And this thing that happened…immediately after the fall, continues in history from generation to generation…. That God is the first in the work of salvation is evident not only from the fact that special revelation proceeds wholly from Him, but also is clearly

---

11. Bavinck, *Our Reasonable Faith*, 265–66.

manifested in the fact that the whole of that redemptive work
depends upon an eternal counsel.

God's gracious initiative connects man's futile search to God's eternal
counsel. Divine condescension makes Christianity unique. God displays
this grace first in the garden just after man's fall. He continues to display
it from generation to generation. Did Bavinck just dream up this marvelous perspective? I think not. This perspective, which Bavinck so masterfully
embellishes, is the heart of BEL 17: "our most gracious God...was pleased to
seek and comfort him, when he trembling fled from His presence, promising him that He would give His Son." Bavinck builds his doctrine of God's
remedial covenant on BEL, especially on its clear doctrine of sovereign grace.
For Bavinck, salvation springs from God's intervention, initiative, grace, and
compassion. This is the starting point of Dutch Calvinist soteriology. The
Westminster approach is more formal, objective, and theological. BEL is
more personal, historical, and experiential.

The Content of God's Counsel (Unit 3: pgs. 266–68)
Bavinck introduces the content of God's counsel by listing the major biblical
terms for it: will, good pleasure, purpose, foreknowledge, and foreordina-
tion (pg. 266). Then he observes that this counsel contains three things. First,
it includes his decree of election: "that gracious purpose of God according to which He ordained those whom He had before known in love to be
conformed to the image of Christ" (pg. 266). Second, it includes his decree
to accomplish redemption by Christ: "the achievement of that whole salvation which God wants to grant His elect" (pg. 267). Third, God's counsel
of redemption includes his decree to apply redemption by the Spirit: "the
working out and the application of the salvation wrought by Christ" (pg. 268).
This eternal counsel is comprehensive in scope.

The Application of God's Counsel (Unit 4: pgs. 268–70)
Bavinck applies God's counsel to experiential religion. He affirms that it
should comfort God's people: "the counsel of God, consequently, is also
inexpressibly rich in comfort" (pg. 268). He calls us to embrace it gratefully,
since God intends it to soothe his saints in their trials and struggles. Bavinck
observes that some misrepresent God's counsel, as though it were a cause
of discouragement and despair. He shows how this wrests it from its true
intent. Bavinck writes pastorally. He applies his theology to the spiritual

experience and needs of God's people. This personal note and experiential flavor animate his covenant theology and make it refreshing.

The Institution of the Covenant of Grace (Unit 5: pgs. 270–73)
He says that God institutes the covenant of grace in history when he executes this counsel he determined in eternity: "the counsel of redemption itself is a work of God in eternity, but as such it is also the principle, the motivating power, and the guarantee of the work of redemption in time.... As soon as man has fallen, therefore, the counsel of redemption begins to work" (pg. 270). He expounds Genesis 3:14–15, of which he says: "In this mother-promise is contained nothing less than the announcement and institution of the covenant of grace" (pg. 271). From this he derives the content of God's remedial covenant: "promise and faith are the content of the covenant of grace" (pg. 271). Then he contrasts the covenant of grace with the pre-fall arrangement: "According to it, man immediately at the beginning receives eternal life, accepts it in childlike faith, and out of that faith proceeds to bring forth good works. The order is reversed. Before the fall the rule was: through works to eternal life. Now, after the fall, in the covenant of grace, the eternal life comes first, and out of that life the good works follow as the fruit of faith" (pg. 272). Finally, he defines the relation between the eternal counsel of redemption and the covenant of grace: "the counsel of redemption, fixed in eternity, and the covenant of grace with which man is acquainted immediately after the fall, and which is then set up, stand in the closest of relationships with each other" (pg. 272). He explains why: "We know that the election was purposed in Christ, and that the counsel of God is not merely a work of the Father but also of the Son and of the Holy Spirit. It is a Divine work of the Holy Trinity. In other words, the counsel of redemption is itself a covenant—a covenant in which each of the three Persons, so to speak, receives His own work and achieves His own task. The covenant of grace that is raised up in time and continued from generation to generation is nothing less than the working out and the impression or imprint of the covenant that is fixed in the Eternal Being" (pg. 273).

The Nature of the Covenant of Grace (Unit 6: pgs. 273–79)
He expounds three remarkable traits: "When we give our attention to this historical development of the covenant of grace, we detect a trio of remarkable characteristics in it" (pg. 274).

It has one Essence, many Forms (pgs. 274–75)

He affirms: "The covenant of grace is everywhere and at all times one in essence, but always manifests itself in new forms and goes through differing dispensations...it always has the same essential content. It is always the same Gospel" (pgs. 274–75).

It is Organic (pgs. 276–77)

He says next: "The second peculiarity or remarkable characteristic of the covenant of grace is that in all of its dispensations it has an organic character" (pg. 276). He means that those involved in it are united to one another as a community. Thus he says: "The elect, accordingly, do not stand loosely alongside one another, but are one in Christ" (pg. 276). He further says: "If the covenant of grace itself is thought of as organic in Christ then it must also be organically set up and continued. Hence we observe that in history the covenant is never concluded with one discreet individual, but always with a man and his family or generation, with Adam, Noah, Abraham, Israel, and with the church and its seed. The promise never concerns a single believer alone, but in him his house or family also" (pg. 277).

It Honors Man's Rational and Moral Nature (pgs. 277–78)

He says: "The third and final characteristic of the covenant of grace goes paired with the second, namely, that it realizes itself in a way which fully honors man's moral and rational nature" (pg. 277). He adds: "This accounts for the fact that the covenant of grace, which really makes no demands and lays down no conditions, nevertheless comes to us in the form of a commandment, admonishing us to faith and repentance (Mark 1:15). Taken by itself the covenant of grace is pure grace, and nothing else, and excludes all works. It gives what it demands, and fulfills what it prescribes. The Gospel is sheer good tidings, not demand but promise, not duty but gift" (pg. 278).

From these remarkable characteristics, Bavinck draws a profound conclusion that, in my view, makes a significant contribution to the Reformed doctrine: "Inasmuch as the covenant of grace enters into the human race in this historical and organic manner, it cannot here on earth appear in a form which fully answers to its essence" (pg. 278). Its outward appearance and visible framework can never, on earth, perfectly equal its essence. Bavinck explains why:[12]

---

12. Ibid., 278–79.

Not only does there remain much in the true believers which is diametrically opposed to a life in harmony with the demand of the covenant.... But there can also be persons who are taken up into the covenant of grace as it manifests itself to our eyes and who nevertheless on account of their unbelieving and unrepentant heart are devoid of all the spiritual benefits of the covenant. That is the case now not only, but has been so throughout all the ages....

On the basis of this conflict between essence and appearance, some have tried to make a distinction and a separation between an internal covenant, which was made exclusively with the true believers, and an external covenant, comprehending the external confessors. But such a separation and difference cannot stand in the light of the Scriptural teaching. What God has joined together, no man may put asunder. No one may take away from the demand that being and appearance answer to each other and from the demand that confessing with the mouth and believing with the heart shall correspond (Rom. 10:9). But, even though there are no two covenants standing loosely alongside each other, it can be said that there are two sides to the one covenant of grace. One of these is visible to us; the other also is perfectly visible to God, and to Him alone. We have to keep to the rule that we cannot judge of the heart, but only of the external conduct and even of that defectively.

Bavinck prudently distinguishes the appearance from the essence of the covenant of grace. This distinction explains why the covenant of grace defines God's relationship with his elect, true believers; and yet, unbelievers can wrongly infiltrate the visible society of believers. Bavinck recognizes that now, under the new covenant, its appearance ought to answer to its essence: "what God has joined together, no man may put asunder. No one may take away from the demand that being and appearance answer to each other." The unconverted have no right, under the new covenant, to be members of the visible covenant community, for its distinguishing mark is: "they shall all know me." Nevertheless, they sometimes wrongly enter, through human limitation and error: "We have to keep to the rule that we cannot judge of the heart, but only of the external conduct and even of that defectively." Scripture commends Bavinck's distinction and conclusion (Heb. 10:29). Bavinck has shown us the biblical path from soteriology to ecclesiology. The church of Christ is the visible society of the people of God, Christian Israel under the new covenant (Eph. 2:11–22). As such, it is the visible society of the covenant of grace (Eph. 2:1–10). When we apply Bavinck's distinction to ecclesiology, we speak of the church as *visible* and *invisible*. The church visible consists of *professing believers*; the church invisible, of *true believers*. Thus, the church visible constitutes *the appearance* of the covenant of grace; the church invisible, *its essence*. As Bavinck clearly realized and boldly declared, now that Christ has come, its appearance *ought to* answer to its essence. No one should be added to the church visible unless he belongs to the church invisible. Or, in other words, under the new covenant, the visible church should be composed of true believers only. We stand greatly indebted to Bavinck for his invaluable contributions to covenant theology.

Conclusion: The Covenant of Grace in Reformed Dogmatics
Bavinck's presentation in *Reformed Dogmatics* (pgs. 193–232) is extremely informative. It begins with an abstract overview (pgs. 193–96). He introduces the covenant of grace by expounding the context of Genesis 3:15, where God offers grace to fallen man in covenantal form (pgs. 196–200). He then offers an informative study of the biblical concept and terminology (pgs. 200–206). Next he lucidly surveys the historical theology of divine covenant (pgs. 206–12). He builds his exposition of God's covenants on this solid exegetical and dogmatic foundation. His exposition starts with the "Pactum Salutis," the eternal covenantal commitment of the Trinity, which founds the covenant of grace (pgs. 212–16). Then he expounds God's "Covenant with Nature," his covenant of common grace through Noah that frames and complements the covenant of grace (pgs. 216–19). Next he expounds "Covenant in OT Salvation History," focusing on God's covenant with Abraham and Israel (pgs. 219–22). He shows convincingly that the old covenant was a covenant of grace. Finally, he expounds the new covenant (pgs. 222–23). He plainly demonstrates the unity of the covenant of grace. He concludes with theological analysis of two relevant issues. He first compares the covenant of grace to the covenant of works (pgs. 224–28), then to the decree of election (pgs. 228–32). His analysis is edifying and cogent.

Louis Berkhof on God's Covenants

Berkhof expounds his theology of God's covenants in *Systematic Theology*.[13] His presentation is thorough, clear, and well organized. He does not cum-

---

13. Louis Berkhof, *Systematic Theology* (Grand Rapids: Wm. B. Eerdmans Publishing Company, 1949), 262–304.

ber the reader with endless detail, but comes straight to the point. For this reason, among others, I use his work as the primary textbook for systematic theology. He includes the covenant of grace with his Doctrine of Man. His headings are: "Man in His Original State," "Man in the State of Sin," and "Man in the Covenant of Grace." It certainly is plausible to view the doctrine of man's states this way. Any full-orbed treatment of man's states at least mentions the state of grace, in accord with Boston's classic work.[14] Thus, even though it is subsumed under Berkhof's anthropology, it still furnishes a bridge to his soteriology. Still, God's covenant of grace is essentially remedial and redemptive. If we identify it predominantly with anthropology, we become vulnerable to a man-centered soteriology. We risk giving the impression that man is the ultimate end of God's redemptive work. Scripture clearly reveals that God himself, especially the praise of his glorious grace, is the ultimate end of salvation (Eph. 1:6). To avoid this drawback I prefer Hodge's arrangement to Berkhof's. It seems more suitable to treat God's covenants as an aspect of God's work of salvation, namely, as its solemn promise and historical framework.

Berkhof has five major units, clearly named and subdivided. He presents: "The Name and Concept of the Covenant"; "The Covenant of Redemption"; "The Nature of the Covenant of Grace"; "The Dual Aspect of the Covenant"; and "The Different Dispensations of the Covenant." His theology is so well ordered that we simply review it as he presents it.

The Name and Concept of the Covenant (pgs. 262–64)
After a helpful survey of the biblical usage, he says: "A covenant is a pact or agreement between two or more parties" (pg. 264). He acknowledges that this definition could seem to undermine a "proper" divine covenant with man. Still Berkhof forges ahead. His solution is not to redefine divine covenant, but to allege that God honors man with equality:[15]

> Now we should not say that we cannot properly speak of a covenant between God and man, because the parties are too unequal, and therefore proceed on the assumption that the covenant of grace is nothing but the promise of salvation in the form of a covenant.... It is perfectly true that both the covenant of works and...the covenant

---

14. I refer to *Man's Fourfold State*, found in *Complete Works of Thomas Boston* (12 Vols.; Wheaton: Richard Owen Roberts Publishers, 1980 reprint), 8: 9–375.
15. Berkhof, *Systematic Theology*, 264.

of grace are monopleuric in origin, that they are of the nature of arrangements ordained and instituted by God, and that God has priority in both; but they are nevertheless covenants. God graciously condescended to come down to the level of man, and to honor him more or less on the footing of equality.

Berkhof and Gill show us the extremes to which this definition of covenant can lead. Consider this summary illustration: definition: a proper covenant is "a voluntary compact between equals." Extreme One: Gill: Therefore, no proper covenant exists between God and men, because Scripture says clearly that God and man are not equals. Extreme Two: Berkhof: Therefore, God and man are equals—more or less—because Scripture says clearly that God makes a proper covenant with men. Berkhof has found the extreme opposite of Gill. He posits "unequal equals." If, somehow, even until now, you were still unsure, I hope that now at last you realize that a proper divine covenant with men cannot possibly be a "compact between equals."

The Covenant of Redemption (pgs. 265–71)

Berkhof offers this definition of the covenant of redemption: "The covenant of redemption may be defined as the agreement between the Father, giving the Son as Head and Redeemer of the elect, and the Son, voluntarily taking the place of those whom the Father had given Him."[16] Berkhof's presentation is clear and concise. He follows Hodge's hermeneutic for biblical support and Bavinck's presentation of its relation to the covenant of grace.

The Nature of the Covenant of Grace (pgs. 272–83)

After a brief comparison of the covenants of works and grace, he launches a discussion of the contracting parties. God is the first party, clearly, but who is the second party? Berkhof denies a universal aspect. In no sense are all mankind parties to it. Later he underscores this: "it is particular and not universal" (pg. 278). Who then are the human parties to this particular covenant? His answer constitutes a significant contribution:[17]

> It is not easy to determine precisely who the second party is. In general it may be said that God naturally established the covenant of grace with fallen man. Historically, there is no definite indication of any limitation until we come to the time of Abraham. In course of

16. Ibid., 271.
17. Ibid., 273.

time it became perfectly evident, however, that this new covenant relation was not meant to include all men. When God formally established the covenant with Abraham, He limited it to the patriarch and his seed. Consequently, the question arises as to the exact limits of the covenant.

Reformed theologians are not unanimous in answering this question. Some simply say that God made the covenant with the sinner, but this suggests no limitation whatsoever, and therefore does not satisfy. Others assert that He established it with Abraham and his seed, that is, his natural, but especially his spiritual, descendants; or, to put it in more general form, with believers and their seed. The great majority of them, however, maintain that He entered into the covenant relationship with the elect or with the elect sinner in Christ.

This regulates his definition of the covenant of grace:[18]

> The covenant of grace may be defined as that gracious agreement between the offended God and the offending but elect sinner, in which God promises salvation through faith in Christ, and the sinner accepts this believingly, promising a life of faith and obedience.

Unlike the Westminster Presbyterians, Berkhof does not attempt to combine the universal and particular aspects of the gospel call in his definition of the covenant of grace. This highlights a notable difference between classic Presbyterian theology and Dutch Calvinism. Hodge included both universal and particular aspects, Dabney confounded them, but Berkhof defines the covenant of grace in particular terms. Then he adds: "the description, 'believers and their seed,' merely serves as a convenient practical designation of the limits of the covenant. The harmonizing of these two aspects will come up later" (pg. 277). Somehow the physical children of believers are included in the covenant of grace; yet, the parties of this covenant of grace are "the offended God and the offending but elect sinner." Berkhof recognized and felt the tension, and now seeks to resolve it.

The Dual Aspect of the Covenant (pgs. 284–89)
In my judgment, his forthright effort to address this tension is his most valuable contribution:[19]

---

18. Ibid., 277.
19. Ibid., 284.

In speaking of the contracting parties in the covenant of grace it was already intimated that the covenant may be considered from two different points of view. There are two different aspects of the covenant, and now the question arises, In what relation do these two stand to each other?

He says that some have distinguished between an external and internal covenant, others between the essence and administration of the covenant, and others between a conditional and absolute covenant (pgs. 284–85). The proper distinction, he says, is between the covenant as purely a *legal relationship* and the covenant as a *communion of life* (pgs. 286–87). He then expounds membership in the covenant as a purely legal relationship (pgs. 287–89). He says: "it should be borne in mind that the covenant in this sense is not merely a system of demands and promises…but that it also includes a reasonable expectation that the external legal relationship will carry with it the glorious reality of a life in intimate communion with the covenant God" (pg. 287). He then makes the crucial application:[20]

ADULTS IN THE COVENANT. Adults can only enter this covenant voluntarily by faith and confession. From this it follows that in their case, unless their confession be false, entrance into the covenant as a legal relationship and into the covenant as a communion of life coincide.

CHILDREN OF BELIEVERS IN THE COVENANT. With respect to the children of believers, who enter the covenant by birth, the situation is, of course, somewhat different. Experience teaches that, though by birth they enter the covenant as a legal relationship, this does not necessarily mean that they are also at once in the covenant as a communion of life. It does not even mean that the covenant relation will ever come to its full realization in their lives. Yet even in their case there must be a reasonable assurance that the covenant is not or will not remain a mere legal relationship, with external duties and privileges, pointing to that which ought to be, but is also or will in time become a living reality. This assurance is based on the promise of God, which is absolutely reliable, that He will work in the hearts of the covenant youth with His saving grace and transform them into living members of the covenant. The

---

20. Ibid., 287–88.

covenant is more than the mere offer of salvation, more even than the offer of salvation plus the promise to believe the gospel. It also carries with it the assurance, based on the promises of God, who works in the children of the covenant, when, where, and how He pleases, that saving faith will be wrought in their hearts. As long as the children of the covenant do not reveal the contrary, we shall have to proceed on the assumption that they are in possession of the covenant life. Naturally, the course of events may prove that this life is not yet present; it may even prove that it is never realized in their lives. The promises of God are given to the seed of believers collectively, and not individually.

Presbyterian theologians implicitly include the physical children of believers, while minors, in some respect, as parties to the covenant of grace. Berkhof incorporates this overtly into his covenant theology. His formal definition of the partakers of the covenant of grace is particular: "that gracious agreement between the offended God and the offending but elect sinner." Its partakers are God's elect, and God's elect alone. Yet, to his credit, he doesn't sidestep the issue of organic continuity. The Westminster Standards, Hodge, and Dabney do not overtly present this dimension of their covenant theology in their soteriology. This affords much opportunity for confusion. I admire Berkhof's straightforward effort to tackle every issue that hampers clear understanding of God's covenants.

However, as much as I admire his honesty, his formula doesn't carry my conscience or convince my judgment. Only the unpleasant facts of "experience" prevent him from declaring that all covenant children are elect. He says: "It carries the assurance...that saving faith will be wrought in their hearts." Why isn't faith wrought in all their hearts? He answers that this assurance has reference "to the seed of believers collectively, and not individually." Berkhof thus injects a universal element into his particular definition of God's covenant of grace. His position is particularist with respect to everyone else, and universalist with respect to the minor children of believers. Berkhof is a particularist, but his formula for organic continuity is inconsistent with his particularism. His universalist tenet is subsidiary, and, in the judgment of charity, unintentional. Nevertheless, it entangles Berkhof in the inescapable dilemma of universalism.

Nonetheless, we should recognize the important element of truth in Berkhof's noble effort. Hodge rightly saw that the indiscriminate gospel call was somehow bound to the covenant of grace. This occasioned imprecision when he included all the unconverted as its parties. Similarly, Berkhof rightly saw that parental nurture is also closely bound to the covenant of grace. He recognizes that God is often, even normally, pleased to use this nurture as the instrumental means of our children's salvation. Although he does not explicitly name them as parties in his definition, nevertheless, he includes them as parties to the covenant. Like Hodge, he has confused *the means* by which God implements his solemn commitment to save, with *the substance* of that commitment. Thus, our presentation of the covenant of grace should address this instrumental role of parental nurture and of the general gospel call.

Finally Berkhof misapplies the distinction that Bavinck observed between appearance and essence. Berkhof prefers *legal relationship* and *communion of life.* This distinction does not convey on any non-elect persons the right to belong to the visible church. Adult hypocrites who profess faith may in fact join the visible church. Yet they have no right to be members. If their true state is discovered, they should be removed. This distinction therefore offers no biblical ground for including, by right, any non-elect persons in the church. So it boils down to this. Is birth into a Christian family the equivalent of a credible profession of faith? How can we discern if someone is elect? Paul tells us: "knowing your election, how our gospel came to you with power" (1 Thess. 1:5). He did not say: "knowing your election, how you were born to Christian parents." When, through parental nurture, the gospel comes with power to our physical children, then God implements his covenant of grace and makes them partakers. When they are grown, we may with joy behold them in its visible society, the Christian church.

What then, don't we care for the souls of our children? Of course we care! God ordinarily uses parental training as a means of grace. But we do not have "assurance" that they will be saved. Their salvation is not "guaranteed." As painful as it may be, even for particularists to admit, the salvation of our dear children still remains in the hand of a sovereign God. He hardens or has mercy on whomever he wills. I can only speak personally now (Rom. 10:1–3). I love my children. I will always love them. From their conception I longed and prayed that they would be saved. As they grew, I prayed with them, catechized them, directed them, and molded them in Christian nurture as God gave me grace. I pleaded that he would save them early in life so they wouldn't scar their lives. God ordinarily and often uses these means. But brothers, we can make no demand of God. We still must submit to his sovereign electing love. We should wait until they confess faith and manifest the fruits of conversion before we affirm them to be God's elect.

The Different Dispensations of the Covenant (pgs. 290–304)

Berkhof concludes with a survey of these dispensations. He begins with a helpful and convincing refutation of the fundamental premise of Dispensationalism. This was no doubt necessary because he wrote in 1949 in America. His exposition of the old dispensation features the historic covenants. Like Hodge and Dabney, he contrasts the new and old dispensations.

In sum, Berkhof reflects the cream of three centuries of Reformed thinking on the covenant of grace. He presents a formidable doctrine with an admirable effort to state and support it thoroughly and clearly.

— 6 —
Summary of the Classic Reformed Doctrine

The Reformers and their spiritual children in English Puritanism and Dutch Calvinism set forth the classic Reformed doctrine of God's covenantal relations and commitments. Their doctrine of divine covenant provides cohesion to their doctrine of Christ, of the Christian life, of the church, and of the completion of salvation.[1] In light of our survey, I now summarize this classic doctrine. I begin with a summary of how they expound the *nature* of God's covenants. On this foundation, I review how they define human *participation* in divine covenant.

The Classic Doctrine of the Nature of God's Covenants

In eternity God commits to save sinners. In history he promises to effect this salvation. In the fullness of time he sends Christ to accomplish this salvation in fulfillment of this eternal commitment and historical promise. The root of the classic Reformed doctrine of divine covenant is that *this eternal commitment and historical promise are covenantal* in form. Some regard God's eternal commitment and historical promise to be one covenant, enacted in eternity, executed in history.[2] Others regard this eternal commitment and

---

1. Witsius illustrates this. He uses divine covenant to organize his anthropology, Christology, soteriology, and ecclesiology. Herman Witsius, *The Economy of the Covenants Between God and Man* (2 Vols.; Phillipsburg, NJ: Presbyterian and Reformed Publishing Company, 1990), 1: vii–viii; 2: iii–iv.

2. For example: John Dick, *Lectures on Theology* (Xenia, OH: The Board of Calvinistic Book Concern, 1846), 258; John Gill, *Body of Divinity*, 1: 354–55; Herman Hoeksema, *Reformed Dogmatics* (Grand Rapids: Reformed Free Publishing Association, 1976), 330; G. H. Kersten, *Reformed Dogmatics* (Translated by Joel R. Beeke: 2 Vols.; Netherlands Reformed Book and Publishing Committee, 1980), 1: 233, 234, 237.

historical promise as two distinct covenants. Such present God's eternal commitment to redeem as a divine covenant. They present God's historical promise to redeem as a divine-human covenant.[3] Shedd presents them as distinct covenants united in one covenant of mercy.[4] Similarly, Turretin calls God's covenant a twofold pact, in which Christ is partaker in eternity, mediator in history.[5]

God's Eternal Commitment to Redeem

Reformed theologians designate this eternal commitment in various ways, most commonly as the *covenant of redemption*.[6] Gill and Dick call it the *covenant of grace*.[7] Classic Reformed theology regards this eternal commitment as a proper covenant that consists in a formal agreement or compact.[8] Most Reformed theologians assign a preeminent role to the Father and the Son.[9] Some also include the role of the Holy Spirit.[10] I expound the biblical testimony and summarize the biblical teaching on this eternal counsel of redemption in Appendix 1.

God's Historical Promise to Redeem

Most Reformed theologians call God's historical promise to redeem *the covenant of grace*. God first announces this promise in Genesis 3:15. He enhances and enlarges this promise throughout the Old Testament. He fully discloses it in the New Testament with the bright light of the apostolic gospel.[11] Thus, the covenant of grace is a dispensation of gospel promise to fallen man, founded on God's eternal commitment to redeem his elect in

---

3. For example: R. L. Dabney, *Lectures in Systematic Theology*, 432–33; Charles Hodge, *Systematic Theology*, 2: 358–59; Louis Berkhof, *Systematic Theology*, 265.

4. W. G. T. Shedd, *Dogmatic Theology* (2 Vols.; Grand Rapids: Zondervan Publishing House, n. d.), 2: 359–60.

5. Francis Turretin, *Institutes of Elenctic Theology*, 2: 177.

6. For example: Berkhof, *Systematic Theology*, 271; Hodge, *Systematic Theology*, 2: 359; Dabney, *Lectures in Systematic Theology*, 432.

7. Dick, *Lectures on Theology*, 254; Gill, *Body of Divinity*, 1: 306–07.

8. For example: Gill, *Body of Divinity*, 1: 309; Dabney, *Lectures in Systematic Theology*, 432.

9. For example: LCF 7:3; Dick, *Lectures on Theology*, 254–58; Dabney, *Lectures in Systematic Theology*, 431–32; Berkhof, *Systematic Theology*, 267–271.

10. For example: Gill, *Body of Divinity*, 1: 311, 350–354; Herman Bavinck, *Our Reasonable Faith*, 273.

11. Speaking of the covenant of grace, LCF affirms: "This covenant is revealed in the gospel; first of all to Adam in the promise of salvation by the seed of the woman, and afterwards by farther steps, until the full discovery thereof was completed in the New Testament" (7:3).

Christ. Reformed theologians on this point stand in agreement. Harmony also exists regarding the singularity and substance of the covenant of grace. Presbyterians and Reformed Baptists confess in unison that God has only one method and message of salvation from sin. They confess that God dispenses salvation only through Christ's mediation. They confess verbatim that in this gospel message God promises eternal life to sinners and requires faith of them. They confess verbatim that God in sovereign grace enables elect sinners to believe by the power of the Holy Spirit.[12] They affirm in harmony that there is only one method of salvation, which God dispenses by his covenant of grace in every era of redemptive history.[13] The Dutch Calvinist theologians echo these historical confessions.[14] Harmony also exists regarding diversity in the administration and revelation of the covenant of grace. WCF stresses diversity in dispensation; LCF diversity in disclosure (WCF 7:5; LCF 7:3).

In Chapter 9, I expound the biblical testimony to the covenant of grace, beginning with Genesis 3:15, and summarize what Scripture teaches about its foundation, features, fulfillment, form, and functions.

The Classic Doctrine of Participation in Divine Covenant

The very soul of the Reformed doctrine of covenant participation is unveiled in the question: "With whom was the covenant of grace made?" The Reformed doctrinal standards have shaped the classic answer to this question. I arrange this summary accordingly. I review the identity of its human parties or partakers in the camp of the Westminster standards, Triple Knowledge, and LCF.

---

12. WCF and LCF affirm verbatim: "the covenant of grace; wherein He freely offers unto sinners life and salvation by Jesus Christ; requiring of them faith in Him, that they may be saved, and promising to give unto all those that are ordained unto eternal life His Holy Spirit, to make them willing, and able to believe" (WCF 7:3, LCF 7:2).

13. LCF affirms: "it is alone by the grace of this covenant that all the posterity of fallen Adam that ever were saved did obtain life and blessed immortality, man being now utterly incapable of acceptance with God upon those terms on which Adam stood in his state of innocency" (7:3). Similarly, WCF says: "This covenant was differently administered in the time of the law, and in the time of the Gospel…. There are not therefore two covenants of grace, differing in substance, but one and the same, under various dispensations" (7:5, 6).

14. For example: Bavinck, *Our Reasonable Faith*, 275–76; Kersten, *Reformed Dogmatics*, 1: 238–47; Berkhof, *Systematic Theology*, 279–80.

The Westminster Doctrine of Participation in Divine Covenant
WLC 31 epitomizes the Westminster doctrine of participation in the covenant of grace.[15] They confess that only Christ, as the second Adam, and God's elect in Christ, as his posterity, participate in the covenant of grace. The Westminster Standards in WCF 7:3 associate participation in the covenant of grace with the gospel.[16] These two statements frame subsequent Presbyterian thinking on covenant participation. No little stir has arisen about how to reconcile WLC 31 and WCF 7:3.[17] As we saw, some who use WCF 7:3 to define covenant participation actually affirm that not only God's elect, but also all unconverted sinners are parties to the covenant of grace.[18]

Yet if the intent of WCF 7:3 really was to include all lost men as partakers in the covenant of grace, then truly it would contradict WLC 31. We should afford the Westminster divines the benefit of the doubt. Surely they did not intend to define participation in God's covenant *universally* and *particularly* in WCF 7:3 and *particularly* in WLC 31. Rather, they intended to say that God implements covenant grace and fulfills his covenant of grace by means of the general and effectual call of the gospel. The general and effectual call should not be regarded as distinct expressions of divine covenant. Rather, God, in his inscrutable wisdom, has determined to fulfill his covenant of grace, his pledge to apply redemption to his elect, through the general and effectual call of the gospel, not in isolation, but in combination. Thus, it is not the hearers of the gospel who partake in this divine covenant, but the receivers and doers of the gospel, who obey the gospel in repentance and faith.

In the covenant of grace, God does not say: "if you believe, I will apply redemption." Rather, God applies redemption by creating the very faith he requires in the gospel. He creates faith when in the effectual call his Holy Spirit enables his elect to believe. This is exactly what WCF 7:3 asserts. Thus, it doesn't contradict the particularism of WLC 31. Rather, it enhances it. If there is any contradiction, it is not in these two statements in the

---

15. "The covenant of grace was made with Christ, as the second Adam, and in him with all the elect as his seed" (WLC 31).

16. "The covenant of grace; wherein He freely offers unto sinners life and salvation by Jesus Christ; requiring of them faith in Him, that they may be saved, and promising to give unto all those that are ordained unto eternal life His Holy Spirit, to make them willing, and able to believe" (WCF 7:3).

17. Dabney acknowledges that these two statements seem to define the covenant of grace from different vantage points (*Lectures in Systematic Theology*, 433).

18. For example, Hodge, *Systematic Theology*, 2: 363–64.

Westminster standards. Rather, it is the seeming—not real—contradiction between sovereign grace and the free offer of the gospel. This tension leads to the fence around the mystery, the insoluble problem of God's revealed will and decretive will appearing, from one limited point of view, to be at odds with each other. The Westminster standards confess both sovereign grace and the free offer of the gospel. Thus, they highlight this tension. Clearly, they define participation in the covenant of grace particularly. They limit its partakers to Christ and his posterity, God's elect (WLC 31). They affirm that in his covenant of grace, God calls his elect to himself through the general and effectual gospel call (WCF 7:3).

Reformed Baptists do well to pay careful attention to this issue, rather than shrug it off as a "Presbyterian quagmire." When LCF copied verbatim from WCF 7:3, it became a Reformed Baptist quagmire too. Thus Reformed Baptists need the explicit and clear statement of WLC 31 to wade safely through this theological swamp. The correct principle of interpretation is to interpret what is unclear with the light of the clear, and what is dubious, with Christian charity.

Yet charity does not forbid straightforward transparency. It seems that the Westminster standards do use two incompatible definitions of covenant participation. The quest to reconcile them is a large hurdle that challenges the beloved brothers who champion the Westminster teaching. When the Westminster Assembly confesses the doctrine of salvation, they define participation in divine covenant particularly. As we have seen, they affirm repeatedly, plainly, and overtly that only Christ and God's elect, called to him through the gospel, are the partakers of the covenant of grace. Yet, when they confess their doctrine of the church, they employ a different definition. They define the partakers of the covenant of grace as believers and their minor children. They affirm that the minor children of believers have the right to membership in Christ's church, the covenant community, because, along with their believing parents, they participate in God's covenant. They explicitly affirm this when they define baptism. They depict baptism as the ordinance of admission into the visible church and as a sign and seal of the covenant of grace. Thus, in WLC they overtly assert that all physical infants of a believing parent should be baptized because they partake in the covenant of grace.[19]

---

19. "Baptism is not to be administered to any that are out of the visible church, and so strangers from the covenant of promise, till they profess their faith in Christ, and obedience

In their ecclesiology (WLC 166), they affirm that all the physical children born to believers are "within the covenant." Yet in their soteriology (WLC 31), they define the partakers of this very covenant as Christ and God's elect. This prompts the question, "Are all the physical children of believers God's elect?" If so, no contradiction exists. Yet, most don't go this far. Rather, they struggle to solve the dilemma that typically plagues universalism: (1) the partakers of the covenant of grace are God's elect alone; (2) all the minor physical children of believers partake in the covenant of grace; (3) not all the minor physical children of believers are elect. When faced with patent inconsistency of this stripe, the judgment of conscience trumps the judgment of charity. Warfield exposes this insoluble problem that stifles every effort to wed supernaturalism, universalism, and reprobation.[20] Supernaturalism insists that only God's elect partake in the covenant of grace. Universalism alleges that *all* the physical children of believers partake in the covenant of grace. Reprobation unveils that some of these physical children are not elect.

The Triple Knowledge Doctrine of Participation in Divine Covenant
In the Westminster standards the organic aspect of covenant participation is more implicit and limited to ecclesiology. However, the Triple Knowledge asserts overtly and consistently that believers and their minor physical children partake in the covenant of grace. HC and BEL base infant baptism on the participation of the physical children of believers in God's covenant (BEL 34; HC 74). CSD uses the inclusion of a believer's physical children in the covenant of grace to comfort godly parents whose child dies in infancy (CSD:1:17). Thus, the Triple Knowledge doctrine of the partakers in divine covenant weds overt *particularism* and *organic continuity*. This combination, and the tension inherent in it, has prompted a noble effort to formulate a comprehensive definition of covenant participation that bridges soteriology and ecclesiology. Unlike the Westminster camp, with two incompatible definitions of the partakers—a particular definition for soteriology, an organic definition for ecclesiology—the Dutch Calvinists strive to find one cohesive definition of its partakers. As we saw, Berkhof patently illustrates this quest.

---

to him, but infants descending from parents, either both, or but one of them, professing faith in Christ, and obedience to him, are in that respect within the covenant, and to be baptized" (WLC 166).

20. B. B. Warfield, *The Plan of Salvation* (Grand Rapids: Wm. B. Eerdmans Publishing Company, 1977), 74–75.

Accordingly, he defines its partakers particularly as God and his elect: "The covenant of grace may be defined as that gracious agreement between the offended God and the offending but elect sinner."[21] Yet he overtly affirms that all the physical children of believers partake in this covenant between God and his elect. He proposes a "dual aspect" of the covenant to resolve this tension.[22] He pursues an impossible quest when he adds a universal definition of organic continuity that includes *all* the physical children of believers. This inconsistency, which in the judgment of charity was not intentional, entangles him too in the inescapable dilemma of universalism.

The biblical solution is that the organic continuity of the covenant of grace is particular and spiritual. Only a believer's spiritual children, an elect remnant of the physical children, partake in the covenant of grace.[23] Hodge and Berkhof rightly perceived that gospel preaching and Christian nurture are primary means by which God implements his covenant of grace. Yet the partakers of the covenant of grace are not all the hearers of the gospel, nor all who have the privilege of Christian nurture. The partakers of the covenant of grace are God's elect, who obey the gospel, who by faith are the spiritual children of believers, of Abraham, and of Jesus.

The LCF Doctrine of Participation in Divine Covenant
Some who adhere to covenant theology confess a thoroughly particular doctrine of covenant participation. LCF affirms the eternal predestination of the Redeemer and identifies the elect as his seed.[24] LCF 7:3 asserts that Scripture first discloses the covenant of grace in Genesis 3:15, which reveals God's solemn pledge to accomplish redemption by Christ and to apply it to his elect in Christ. This text affirms that the organic continuity of the covenant of grace is particular and spiritual. Eve's seed are believers; the devil's seed, the wicked (Gen. 4:25; 1 John 3:8–10). Thus, LCF implicitly recognizes the truth confessed in WLC 31. Thus, it also implicitly identifies as partakers: Christ, the Conqueror of Satan, and God's elect in Christ, as

---

21. Berkhof, *Systematic Theology*, 277.
22. Ibid., 284.
23. This does not clash with the pastoral comfort for grieving parents expressed in CSD:1:17. It could well be that this elect remnant includes not only those children who come to confess faith, but also those whom the Lord takes to himself in infancy (LCF:10:3).
24. "Unto whom he did from all eternity give a people to be his seed and to be by him in time redeemed, called, justified, sanctified, and glorified" (LCF:8:1).

his seed.[25] Accordingly, following WCF verbatim, LCF affirms that God implements this solemn pledge to apply redemption to his elect through the general and effectual call of the gospel.[26] Further, LCF uses this same definition of covenant participation when it confesses the doctrine of the church. It affirms that only visible saints should be admitted to local churches. They regard visible saints as those who confess faith credibly.[27]

Thus, LCF distinguishes between *God's elect* and *visible saints*. As God's elect alone partake in the covenant of grace (LCF 7:2), so visible saints alone should comprise the membership of local churches (LCF 26:2). This vital distinction is variously named. It goes back at least as far as Turretin.[28] Bavinck uses *appearance* and *essence* to depict it. He applies it prudently. He affirms that faith in the heart (God's elect) should correspond with confession of faith with the mouth (visible saints).[29] This distinction pertains to the *visible society* of Christ's *spiritual posterity*. Christ organized evangelically the visible community of believers. Moral tension adheres to this organized society, since no man can infallibly discern the heart. The church may receive visible saints who profess faith credibly, who do not have saving faith in their hearts. As Berkhof points out, hypocrites may as adults credibly profess faith and join the church. Such are members of the church in fact, *de facto*, but not by right, *de jure*. LCF defines *particularly* the right to join the church. That right belongs only to God's elect, true believers. LCF perceives that the *visible society* of the covenant of grace—*visible saints, confessing believers*—can never in this life perfectly correspond with its *partakers*—God's elect, true believers—due to the limits of human discernment. This anomaly does not convey to any child of Satan the right to belong to the visible community of Jesus' children. It does not confer on any reprobate person the right to belong to a local church.

---

25. Spurgeon, who embraced and published LCF, affirms this identification in his exposition of Genesis 3:15: "the carnal seed of the man and the woman are not meant, but the spiritual seed, even Christ Jesus and those who are in him." Charles Spurgeon, "Christ the Conqueror of Satan," in *The Metropolitan Tabernacle Pulpit* (63 Vols.; Pasadena, TX: Pilgrim Publications, 1971), 22: 664.

26. LCF:7:2, WCF 7:3.

27. "All persons throughout the world, professing the faith of the gospel, and obedience unto God by Christ according unto it, not destroying their own profession by any errors everting the foundation, or unholiness of conversation, are and may be called visible saints; and of such ought all particular congregations to be constituted" (LCF:26:2).

28. Turretin, *Elenctic Theology*, 2: 207–08, expounds this distinction between internal essence and external dispensation in 12:6:5, 6.

29. Bavinck, *Our Reasonable Faith*, 278.

When LCF defines the partakers of the covenant of grace particularly, it unlocks the mystery of how Scripture combines particularism with organic continuity. The organic continuity of the covenant of grace is particular because it is *spiritual*. In Genesis 3:15 Scripture depicts Christ's seed as the "seed of the woman." Christ's spiritual children are her spiritual children. Plainly, the covenant of grace manifests organic continuity. Just as plainly, this organic continuity is with Eve's spiritual seed, not with all of her physical children. Cain was Eve's physical child. Yet he was a spiritual child of the devil. He was not elect, or a partaker of the covenant of grace, even though he had the privilege of godly nurture from his believing mother. Abel was God's elect, Eve's spiritual seed, and a partaker of the covenant of grace. Similarly, in every generation Eve's spiritual seed, a gospel remnant of her physical seed, partakes in the covenant of grace. In this very same way, the organic perpetuity of the visible community of the covenant of grace is spiritual. This community is the visible society of Christ's spiritual seed. Thus, in every generation it propagates by spiritual generation. God calls this elect remnant to himself through the general and effectual call of the gospel. The covenant of grace insures that in every generation God will create a spiritual seed. He has pledged to apply redemption in every generation. He will perpetuate the spiritual enmity he initiated between Eve and Satan, and between Eve's spiritual seed and Satan's spiritual seed. In this way LCF honors the organic continuity of the covenant of grace without becoming mired in universalism.

Herman Hoeksema also warns God's people to avoid "injecting Arminianism." He cogently observes that the organic continuity of the covenant pertains to the *spiritual seed* of believers. Yet, he employs what he calls "the organic idea" to justify including all the physical children of believers in the visible community of God's covenant. He says that Scripture describes the entire community in terms of its elect kernel.[30] Yet only this elect kernel has the right to belong to the visible community of Christ's posterity.

Conclusion

The classic Reformed doctrine of divine covenant has confessional prominence in the Westminster standards, Triple Knowledge, and LCF. This classic doctrine focuses on the covenant of grace. It affirms that it is founded on God's eternal counsel of redemption (LCF 7:3). It affirms that Scripture

---

30. Herman Hoeksema, *Believers and Their Seed* (Grand Rapids: Reformed Free Publishing Association, 1977), 108, 114, 117–135.

first unveils this covenant of grace in Genesis 3:15 (LCF 7:3). It affirms that it is one and the same in every generation and indispensible for salvation (WCF 7:5, 6; LCF 7:3). It affirms that the covenant of grace is particular. It defines its partakers as Christ and God's elect (WLC 31). It affirms that God implements the covenant of grace through his gospel (WCF 7:2; LCF 7:3). It also affirms that the covenant of grace is organic. Its partakers connect organically from generation to generation. Here the creeds diverge. The Westminster and Triple Knowledge affirm that this organic continuity is physical (CSD 1:17; WLC 166). This entangles them unwittingly in the insoluble dilemma of universalism. LCF does not confess physical organic continuity. It implies that the organic continuity of the covenant of grace is spiritual (LCF 7:3).

This classic Reformed doctrine stands well fabricated. Yet some shingles on the roof need replacing. Next we take up these contemporary improvements.

—7—

Contemporary Modifications

We have seen that the classic Reformed doctrine of divine covenant is of confessional prominence. However, these Reformed creeds never explicitly define the generic concept of divine covenant. Nor do they define God's distinct historical covenants with men. Thus, contemporary Reformed theologians continue to build on the Westminster standards, Triple Knowledge, and LCF. Their modifications aim to align this classic doctrine more closely with the biblical testimony. They try to clarify confusion arising from imprecisions and inconsistencies, without abandoning the great light shining from this classic teaching. Their work especially focuses on the *generic concept* and *historical plurality* of God's covenants. Further, contemporary theologians who build on LCF focus on how *sacramental tokens* of God's covenants relate to organic continuity.

The Generic Concept of God's Covenants

Most teachers of this classic doctrine assume that a proper covenant is a *formal compact*, a voluntary agreement between equals that involves contracting parties, mutual stipulations, and conditions. Thus Gill concludes that God never makes a proper covenant with men, because God and man are not equal. Similarly, Dabney concludes that the covenant of redemption is the proper covenant transaction, while the covenant of grace is merely a dispensation of promise to man, not a proper covenant between God and man.[1] At the other extreme, Berkhof, working with this same notion, concludes that

---

1. Gill, *Body of Divinity*, 1: 309; Dabney, *Lectures in Systematic Theology*, 432–33.

when God enters covenant with men he stoops in kindness to treat man more or less on the footing of equality.[2]

Contemporary theologians face this difficulty and labor to correct the imprecision that occasioned it. For example, Robertson and Kline propose revised definitions of the generic concept of divine covenant.[3] Both of their insights convey important aspects of biblical truth. Robertson rightly observes that divine covenant establishes a personal relationship, a bond between God and his people. Kline judiciously discerns that divine covenant expresses divine sovereignty, the will of the King for his people. John Murray, however, most clearly uncovers the path toward a biblical solution. Based on careful exegesis, he defines covenant as "sworn fidelity," rather than "mutual contract." This also pertains to men's covenants.[4] The tremendous importance of his insight can hardly be overestimated. With this cogent modification Murray unlocks the continuity between human and divine-human covenants. The common denominator is sworn fidelity. He defines a divine covenant as: "oath-bound, oath-certified assurance of irrevocable grace and promise," "oath-bound promise," and "a sovereign administration of grace and promise."[5] This comports with the equally valid insight of Robert Gonzales. He defines covenant as: "a formal commitment or obligation that is self-imposed or imposed upon another party or parties."[6]

The Historical Plurality of God's Covenants

The teachers of classic covenant theology all affirm only one divine covenant in history with various administrations or dispensations. They recognize development and diversity in the disclosure and dispensation of this covenant of grace. Most see two major periods, one before and one after the

---

2. Berkhof, *Systematic Theology*, 264.

3. O. Palmer Robertson defines divine covenant as a "bond in blood sovereignly administered," *The Christ of the Covenants* (Grand Rapids: Baker Book House, 1980), 3–15. Meredith Kline defines a divine-human covenant as a "sovereign administration of the kingdom of God," *By Oath Consigned: A Reinterpretation of the Covenant Signs of Circumcision and Baptism* (Grand Rapids: Wm. B. Eerdmans Publishing Company, 1975), 15–16.

4. John Murray, *The Covenant of Grace* (London: The Tyndale Press, 1954), 10.

5. Ibid., 25, 28, 29.

6. Robert Gonzales, Jr., "The Covenantal Context of the Fall: Did God Make a Primeval Covenant with Adam?" in *Reformed Baptist Theological Review* (IV:2 July 2007), 8. The Mosaic covenant features a conditional promise by which God imposes obligation both on himself and on Israel (Exod. 19:3–5).

advent of Christ. All try to honor the progressive unfolding of the gospel in history. Yet none spoke of a plurality of divine covenants in history.

While maintaining the unity of the covenant of grace, contemporary theologians now affirm plurality in God's covenantal relations in history. Smith defines this plurality boldly, specifically, and with much precision:[7]

> The term "Covenant of Grace" is used to refer to the gracious plan of salvation which God has given us in Christ. It may be a misleading term, if we are led to believe that there is just one gracious covenant. Actually, the Bible presents a series of covenants that may be described as gracious in character. They are all part of the progressive revelation of the ultimate Covenant of Grace. Specifically, we find the following gracious covenants: 1) the pre-diluvian Noahic covenant, 2) the post-diluvian Noahic covenant of common grace, 3) the Abrahamic Covenant, 4) the Mosaic Covenant, 5) the Davidic Covenant, 6) the New Covenant that is associated with the coming of Christ, and that was ratified in his blood. We may thus think of the grace of God coming in progressive revelations in a series of gracious covenants. They climax in the New Covenant.

To Smith's list of six covenants Scripture adds a seventh, the Messianic, ratified with Christ upon his session and coronation (Heb. 7:21, 28). Smith's astute observation has profound implications. A plurality of divine covenants opens the door to a plurality of covenant promises and covenant partakers. Does the postdiluvian Noahic covenant have the same promise and partakers as the new covenant? A cursory reading of the texts Smith cites to support this plurality unveils that these covenants have different partakers and different promises (Gen. 9:9–17; Heb. 8:8–12). Again, the Mosaic and new covenants cannot have identical promises, because the new covenant has been enacted on "better promises" (Heb. 8:6). Again, a plurality of covenants opens the door to different types or categories of divine covenants. Is the Mosaic covenant the same type of covenant as the Abrahamic covenant or the Davidic covenant? Again, a plurality of covenants raises the issue of how the partakers and promises of each of these divine covenants relate to the partakers and promises of the covenant of grace. The answers to these questions must come from careful and fresh exegesis of the Scriptures.

---

7. Morton Smith, *Systematic Theology* (2 Vols.; Greenville: Greenville Seminary Press, 1994), 1: 333.

Two Categories of Divine Covenants
Accordingly, contemporary theologians have undertaken the challenge of categorizing God's historical covenants. Like Murray, Kline also recognizes the importance of an oath for defining divine covenant. He distinguishes two types of covenants accordingly, based on who swears the oath. He says that God swears the oath in a promise covenant, man in a law covenant. He calls the Abrahamic covenant a promise covenant, the Mosaic, a law covenant. He argues for the priority of law covenant in defining God's covenantal relation to his people.[8] Delbert Hillers, like Kline, rightly observes that the Abrahamic and Davidic covenants do not have the same format as the Mosaic. God alone is bound in the former, says Hillers, while the people are bound in the latter.[9] Thus, Hillers and Kline correctly recognize that Scripture reveals two distinct types of divine covenants. They also correctly categorize the Abrahamic and Davidic as one type of covenant, the Mosaic as another type. Relationally, these two types of divine covenants are *righteous servant* covenants and *saved community* covenants. Yet, Hillers and Kline minimize the fact that in every divine covenant, even the Mosaic covenant, God swears an oath-bound promise to its partakers. Although the solemn promise of the Mosaic covenant is conditional—and thus inferior to the unconditional promises of the new covenant (Exod. 19:3–6; Jer. 31:33, 34)—nevertheless, the Mosaic promise is still God's solemn pledge of peace and blessing to Hebrew Israel.

The Form and Interrelations of Divine Covenants
Further, contemporary theologians labor better to understand the form of the Mosaic and new covenants and the interrelations of God's covenants. Following the trail blazed by Mendenhall,[10] Kline attempts to show that the Ten Commandments and Deuteronomy mirror the structure of Hittite treaties.[11] Campbell takes this further. Building on the work of Hillers, he elaborates six characteristics of Hittite treaties: Preamble, Prologue, Stipulations, Future Provisions, Witnesses, and Sanctions. Then Campbell tries to

---

8. Kline, *By Oath Consigned*, 16, 24, 25, 29–35.

9. Delbert Hillers, *Covenant: The History of a Biblical Idea* (Baltimore: John Hopkins University Press, 1969), 104, 105, 112.

10. George E. Mendenhall, *Law and Covenant in Israel and The Ancient Near East* (Pittsburgh: The Biblical Colloquium, 1955).

11. Meredith G. Kline, *Treaty of the Great King: The Covenant Structure of Deuteronomy* (Grand Rapids: Wm. B. Eerdmans Publishing Company, 1963), 14, 20, 48, 49.

squeeze into this Hittite mold, not only the Mosaic covenant, but even the Noahic, Abrahamic, and Davidic covenants.[12] Campbell presses whatever truth is found in the Hittite analogy to an extreme. The fact that God, before the Hittites even existed, made the Noahic community covenant with those he rescued from the flood, should serve as a warning not to follow Campbell too far down this path. Murray, based on the principle of first mention and the exegesis of Isaiah 54:9, 10, rightly affirms that the Noahic community covenant reflects the nature of the new covenant. Kline, based on the priority of law in man's original relation with God and the exegesis of Jeremiah 31:31–34, rightly affirms that Mosaic covenant also reflects the nature of the new covenant. Robertson judiciously observes the validity of these insights of both Murray and Kline.[13] Thus, contemporary theologians have demonstrated that both the Mosaic economy and the Noahic economy portray the form of the Christian economy of divine covenants.

The Sacramental Tokens of God's Covenants

Consider one further development. LCF does not explicitly associate the covenant of grace with the ordinances of baptism or the Lord's Supper. It deletes statements to this effect from WCF and the Savoy Declaration.[14] When Christ ratifies the new covenant, he institutes the Lord's Supper as its token. Neither WCF, nor SD, nor LCF, explicitly mentions this connection of the Lord's Supper to the new covenant. Contemporary theologians who build on LCF recognize and expound this covenantal connection of baptism and the Lord's Supper.[15] They show that only genuine believers, who partake in the covenant of grace, should partake in these covenant symbols. They ground this on the fact that the organic continuity of the covenant of

---

12. K. M. Campbell, *God's Covenant* (Nutley, NJ: Presbyterian and Reformed Publishing Company, 1974), 28, 29, 33.

13. O. Palmer Robertson, "Current Reformed Thinking on the Nature of the Divine Covenants," in *The Westminster Theological Journal* (XL:1: Fall 1977), 63 ff.

14. Compare LCF 28:1, 2, 29:1 with WCF 27:1, 28:1 and with SD 28:1, 29:1.

15. For example: P. K. Jewett, *Infant Baptism and the Covenant of Grace* (Grand Rapids: Wm. B. Eerdmans Publishing Company, 1978), 75–137, 233–243; David Kingdon, *Children of Abraham* (Worthing and Haywards Heath: Henry Walter Ltd. and Carey Publications Ltd., 1973), 15–67; Fred A. Malone, *The Baptism of Disciples Alone* (Cape Coral, FL: Founders Press, 2003), 51–125; and Samuel E. Waldron, *Biblical Baptism*, (Grand Rapids: Truth for Eternity Ministries, 1998), 27–39, and, *A Modern Exposition of the 1689 Baptist Confession of Faith* (Darlington: Evangelical Press, 1989), 347–356, 364, 367.

grace is spiritual, rather than physical. They develop explicitly and overtly what was only implicit in LCF.

Summary and Conclusion

Now to summarize: first, regarding the *generic concept*, contemporary Reformed theologians have demonstrated that a divine covenant is an oath-bound promise, a solemn pledge. God's covenants always obligate God. These obligations are self-imposed and voluntary. In the case of the Mosaic covenant, God the King also imposes obligation on his theocratic people, since his solemn promise to bless them is conditional (Exod. 19:3–5). Second, regarding *historical plurality*, contemporary theologians have shown that God fulfills the covenant of grace, not only by means of his gospel, but also in a framework of historical covenants. God has successively ratified seven covenants, arranged in three covenantal economies, Noahic, Mosaic, and Christian. Through careful exegesis of Scripture we must now labor to identify the partakers and promises of each of these seven covenants, and to define how each relates to the partakers and promises of the covenant of grace. Third, regarding *sacramental tokens*, contemporary theologians who build on LCF have shown that the organic continuity of the covenant of grace is spiritual, and thus supports believer-only communion and baptism, which are visible tokens of God's covenantal favor to his people in Christ.

In closing, this summarizes the Reformed doctrine of God's covenantal commitments. God has given much light to his servants. We have a goodly heritage. Dogmatic theology sets the stage; yet it is only the vestibule of systematic theology. Scripture is our ultimate teacher and guide. Let us follow Reformed theologians only as far as they follow Scripture. Thus, we now focus directly on the Scriptures.

— PART 2 —

A BIBLICAL EXPOSITION
OF GOD'S COVENANTS

—8—

An Overview of the Biblical Testimony

"I will establish my covenant with you"; "this is my blood of the covenant."

—GENESIS 6:18; MATTHEW 26:28

Introduction: Biblical Texts and Terms

God's covenants furnish perspective, the big picture. A better grasp of God's covenants fosters deeper confidence and peace. After reading more than a few Reformed theologians, I felt confused, until I applied to this topic the method I use for every other topic. I studied every use of the Hebrew word for covenant, בְּרִית, beginning at Genesis 6:18, and every use of the corresponding Greek word, διαθηκη, beginning in Matthew 26:28. This led to a study of closely related terms and texts. I offer on the next page, not detailed study notes, but a complete list of these terms and texts. If you desire you can more readily survey this entire biblical testimony for yourselves. I have tried to study it objectively just as I was trained to analyze data as a chemical engineer. I entreat you to consider the Word of God on this topic with an open mind, willing to go wherever Scripture plainly leads. It fosters confusion to study the Bible with preconceived ideas and then try to squeeze its witness into that mold.

As we study this testimony keep in mind questions that emerged from reading Reformed theologians. What is a covenant? What is a divine covenant? Does God make "proper" covenants with men? Has he made only one covenant, or more than one, with men? Who are the partakers of these divine covenants? What are their promises? How do God's gospel, his eternal plan of salvation, and his historical promise of salvation relate to these divine covenants?

OLD TESTAMENT TERMS

בְּרִית: translated "covenant," "confederate," 'league"; major Old Testament term for divine covenant; also describes human covenants. Used 287 times: Gen. 6:18, 9:9, 11, 12, 13, 15, 16, 17, 14:13, 15:18, 17:2, 4, 7(2), 9, 10, 11, 13(2), 14, 19(2), 21, 21:27, 32, 26:28, 31:44; Exod. 2:24, 6:4, 5, 19:5, 23:32, 24:7, 8, 31:16, 34:10, 12, 15, 27, 28; Lev. 2:13, 24:8, 26:9, 15, 25, 42(3), 44, 45; Num. 10:33, 14:44, 18:19, 25:12, 13; Deut. 4:13, 23, 31, 5:2, 3, 7:2, 9, 12, 8:18, 9:9, 11, 15, 10:8, 17:2, 29:1(2), 9, 12, 14, 21, 25, 31:9, 16, 20, 25, 26, 33:9; Josh. 3:3, 6(2), 8, 11, 14, 17, 4:7, 9, 18, 6:6, 8, 7:11, 15, 8:33, 9:6, 7, 11, 15, 16, 23:16, 24:25; Judg. 2:1, 2, 20, 20:27; 1 Sam. 4:3, 4(2), 5, 11:1, 18:3, 20:8, 16, 23:18; 2 Sam. 3:12, 13, 21, 5:3, 15:24, 23:5; 1 Kings 3:15, 5:12, 6:19, 8:1, 6, 21, 23, 11:11, 15:19(2), 19:10, 14, 20:34(2); 2 Kings 11:4, 17, 13:23, 17:15, 35, 38, 18:12, 23:2, 3(3), 21; 1 Chron. 11:3, 15:25, 26, 28, 29, 16:6, 15, 16, 17, 37, 17:1, 22:19, 28:2, 18 2 Chron. 5:2, 7, 6:11, 14, 13:5, 15:12, 16:3(2), 21:7, 23:1, 3, 16, 29:10, 34:30, 31(2), 32; Ezra 10:3; Neh. 1:5, 9:8, 32, 13:29; Job 5:23, 31:1, 41:4; Pss. 25:10 14, 44:17, 50:5, 16, 55:20, 74:20, 78:10, 37, 83:5, 89;3, 28, 34, 39, 103:18, 105:8, 9, 10, 106:45, 111:5, 9, 132:12; Prov. 2:17; Isa. 24:5, 28:15, 18, 33:8, 42:6, 49:8, 54:10, 55:3, 56:4, 6, 59:21, 61:8; Jer. 3:16, 11:2, 3, 6, 8, 10, 14:21, 22:9, 31:31, 32(2), 33, 32:40, 33:20(2), 21, 25, 34:8, 10, 13, 15, 18(2), 50:5; Ezek. 16:8, 59, 60(2), 61, 62, 17:13, 14, 15, 16, 18, 19, 20:37, 30:5, 34:25, 37:26(2), 44:7; Dan. 9:4, 27, 11:22, 28, 30(2), 32; Hos. 2:18, 6:7, 8:1, 10:4, 12:1; Amos 1:9; Obad. 1:7; Zech. 9:11, 11:10; Mal. 2:4, 5, 8, 10, 14, 3:1.

כָּרַת: translated "to cut," "to covenant," "make covenant," "to make" {with בְּרִית} refers to divine or human covenants at least 14 times: Deut. 29:12, 14; Josh. 9:15; 1 Sam. 11:2, 20:16; 1 Kings 8:9; 1 Chron. 7:18, 16:16; 2 Chron. 5:10; Neh. 9:38; Ps. 105:9; Isa. 57:8; Ezek. 17:13; Hag. 2:5.

אָלָה: translated "oath," "curse'; used of both divine and human covenants these 10 times: Gen. 26:28; Deut. 29:12, 14; Neh. 10:29; Ezek. 16:59, 17:13, 16, 18, 19; Dan. 9:11.

שְׁבוּעָה: translated "oath'; used of divine and human oaths at least these 10 times: Gen. 26:3; Deut. 7:8; Josh. 9:20; 2 Sam. 21:7; 1 Kings 2:43; 1 Chron. 16:16; Neh. 10:29; Ps. 105:9; Jer. 11:5; Dan. 9:11.

שָׁבַע: translated "to swear'; used of swearing an oath in reference to divine and human covenants at least these 55 times: Gen. 21:31, 22:16, 26:3, 31, 31:53, 50:24; Exod. 13:5, 11, 32:13, 33:1; Num. 14:16, 23, 32:11; Deut. 1:8, 35, 4:31, 6:10, 18, 23, 7:8, 12, 13, 8:1, 18, 9:5, 10:11, 11:9, 21, 19:8, 26:3, 15, 28:9, 11, 29:13, 30:20, 31:20, 31:7, 21, 23; Josh. 1:6, 5:6, 21:43, 44; Judg. 2:1; 2 Sam. 3:9; Pss. 89:3, 35, 49, 110:4, 132:11; Isa. 54:9(2); Jer. 32:32; Ezek. 16:8; Mic. 7:20.

יָד נָשָׂא: literal translation, "to raise a hand." Used as an expression for making a covenant by taking an oath at least these 3 times: Exod. 6:8; Num. 14:30; Neh. 9:15.

NEW TESTAMENT TERMS

διαθηκη: translated "covenant," "testament." Used 31 times: Matt. 26:28; Mark 14:24; Luke 1:72, 22:30; Acts 3:25, 7:8; Rom. 9:4, 11:27; 1 Cor. 11:25; 2 Cor. 3:6, 3:14; Gal. 3:15, 4:24; Eph. 2:12; Heb. 7:22, 8:6, 8:8, 8:9(2), 8:10, 9:4(2), 9:15(2), 9:16, 9:17, 10:17, 10:29, 12:24, 13:20; Rev. 11:19.

διατιθεμαι: translated "to appoint"; "to make a covenant"; "testator." Used 6 times: Luke 22:29 (2); Acts 3:25; Heb. 8:10, 9:16, 17, 10:16.

ὀμνυω: translated "to swear." Used in reference to divine covenant at least these 6 times: Luke 1:73; Acts 2:30; Heb. 6:13(2), 6:16, 7:21.

ὁρκος: "oath." Used of divine covenant 4 times: Luke 1:73; Acts 2:30; Heb. 6:16, 17.

ὁρκωμοσια: "oath." Used of divine covenant 4 times: Heb. 7:20, 21(2), 28.

In the Old Testament בְּרִית appears 287 times. In the New Testament the corresponding word διαθηκη occurs only 31 times, 16 of them in Hebrews. This wide variation in usage could in part be due to the relatively large size and time period (about 1500 years) of Old Testament revelation, compared to the short period (the apostolic generation) of New Testament revelation. It could also in part be due to the transformation of the people of God. It is not surprising, therefore, that over half of the New Testament uses are in Hebrews, which expounds in detail the significance and nature of the new covenant in contrast to the old covenant. The use of these Old and New Testament terms reveals both continuity and development. For example, in Luke 1:72, 73 διαθηκη is clearly synonymous with בְּרִית. Similar examples of continuity are Acts 3:25 and Hebrews 8:8, 10:16, where the writer quotes Jeremiah 31:31–34. There also appears to be development. In Hebrews 9:15–20 διαθηκη probably signifies last will and testament. In both Testaments, other terms and phrases for swearing an oath depict God's covenantal relations. Scripture plainly affirms that an oath is an essential aspect of covenant: "to remember his holy *covenant, the oath which he swore* to Abraham" (Luke 1:72, 73). In sum, this biblical testimony has 379 uses in the Old Testament, 51 in the New, a total of 430 in Scripture.

In these passages the Bible tells a wonderful story of divine love and faithfulness displayed in divine covenants. I begin with this inspired story. Once we have listened to this story, we examine these divine pledges. In this overview we unfold their remarkable form, distinctive features, and practical functions.

The Inspired Story of God's Covenants

Redemptive history has one chief character and hero, Christ the Redeemer: "and he shall bruise your head, and you shall bruise his heel" (Gen. 3:15). Yet God doesn't send him immediately after the fall. He first sets up a framework for his appearance. Over some four thousand years he enhances this proclamation of emancipation. He builds anticipation and expectation. As God builds this framework of solemn promises, he progressively discloses the Redeemer's person and work. This covenantal framework includes saved societies and righteous servants organically joined.

Select Societies Supernaturally Rescued

To construct this promissory framework, God intervenes in history on three momentous occasions to save with supernatural power a select society of men. Scripture records with marked emphasis these marvelous rescues. They shape human history. The first two are symbolic. They provide colorful previews of Christ's saving work and greater light about salvation in Christ. They prepare for God's final intervention, when he fulfills this remarkable promise to accomplish redemption and sends the Redeemer to save his people from their sins.

The first monumental rescue occurred at the time of the flood. God saved Noah's family and the animals through the ark. The rest of humanity perished under floods of divine wrath that destroyed the world that then was (2 Pet. 3:6, 7). Only eight escaped through the supernatural initiative of the living God. Scripture says that men were *saved* from the flood: "By faith Noah, being warned *by God* about things not yet seen, in reverence prepared an ark for the salvation of his household" (Heb. 11:7). God saved Noah's family and the animals, not from sin, but from drowning in the flood. God saved them from the worldwide flood that destroyed every other creature living on the dry land.

The second divine intrusion into history to save men occurred when the God of grace redeemed the Hebrew nation from slavery in Egypt and made them his own special people. Moved with compassion, he manifested his omnipotence, broke the yoke of their oppressor, and set them free. Scripture says that God *saved* the Israelites. In Exodus 3:8 the Lord says that he has "come down to deliver them from the power of the Egyptians, and to bring them up from that land to a good and spacious land." This divine rescue includes both emancipation from slavery in Egypt and endowment with an inheritance, the land of Canaan. Exodus 14:30 says, "Thus the LORD saved Israel that day from the hand of the Egyptians, and Israel saw the Egyptians dead on the seashore." Again, Jude 5 says, "The Lord, after saving a people out of the land of Egypt, subsequently destroyed those who did not believe." Clearly God saved the Hebrew nation, not from sin and wrath, but from slavery in Egypt.

The third, and most momentous deliverance, occurred when God the Son became human and saved his people from their sins (Matt. 1:21). He accomplished their salvation through the blood of his cross (Heb. 9:12) and the power of his resurrection (Rom. 4:25). He will complete their salvation when he returns to earth in glory (Rom. 5:9). In each of these supernatural interventions the Supreme Being himself intrudes into history and saves. He rescues supernaturally from a flood, from bondage in Egypt, and from sin.

How does this support covenant theology? What does it have to do with God's covenants? When God intervened to save on these three occasions, he made a covenant with the entire community that experienced his deliverance. These are the Noahic community, old, and new covenants. It is not accidental that בְּרִית translated *covenant* first appears in Scripture when God saves Noah's family from the flood (Gen. 6:18) and afterward makes a covenant with the men and animals that emerged from the ark (Gen. 9:8–17). The next two divine rescues, or redemptions of his people, are even more strategic. Through them God first formed then re-formed his people, Israel. When he redeemed Israel from Egypt he formed them into his people under the old covenant. When he redeemed Israel from sin he re-formed them as his people under a new covenant (Jer. 31:31–34; Rom. 9:6). God gave his people two bodies of special revelation in conjunction with these covenants. The Bible has a covenantal form.

The Redeemer Pledged to God's Righteous Servants
The New Testament focuses on the Redeemer. God at last, in the fullness of time, fulfills his remarkable promise to send a Redeemer. The first line of the New Testament puts this fulfillment into perspective: "The book

of the genealogy of Jesus Christ, the son of David, the son of Abraham" (Matt. 1:1). These words would be incomprehensible without the Old Testament. The Redeemer does not appear in a vacuum. Jesus, in his humanity, descends from Abraham and David (Matt. 1:2–16). God promised each of them, with an oath, that their heir would be the Redeemer.[1] God fulfills these solemn promises to Abraham and David through the incarnation and resurrection of God the Son.[2] These promises about Christ unify the Testaments (Mal. 4:4–6; Matt. 17:10–13).

What does this have to do with divine covenant? Scripture calls these very promises to Abraham and David divine covenants: "the covenant which God made with your fathers, saying to Abraham, And in your seed all the families of the earth shall be blessed" (Acts 3:25); "I have made a covenant with my chosen; I have sworn to David my servant, I will establish your seed forever, and build up your throne to all generations" (Ps. 89:3, 4). God keeps these solemn pledges to Abraham and David when he sends Christ to save his people from their sins.

Righteous Servants and Saved Societies Organically Joined
How does this fit together? The diagram to the right illustrates how servant and community covenants relate in a covenantal economy.

God pledges to bless his righteous servants and their posterity. Each saved society is the posterity of a righteous servant. God perpetuates each covenant with a saved society. God makes covenants with the societies he saved from the flood, Egypt, and sin. He makes the Noahic community covenant with Noah's posterity, the old covenant with the Patriarch's physical posterity, and the new covenant with Jesus' spiritual posterity.[3] The table on page 110 illustrates three corresponding economies:

---

1. Gen. 22:16–18; Ps. 89:3, 29, 35, 36.
2. Acts 2:29–31, 3:25, 26; Gal. 3:16, 19.
3. Isa. 53:10, 11; Heb. 2:12–17, 7:21, 22, 8:6–8.

A COVENANTAL ECONOMY

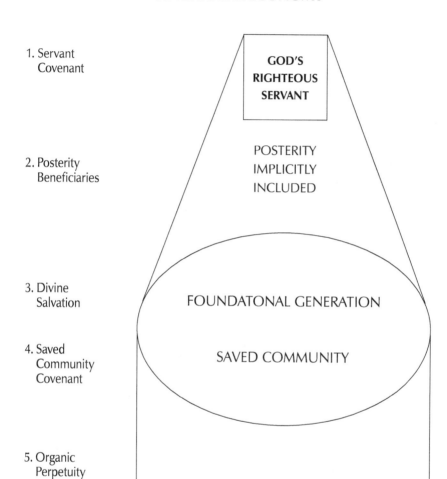

1. Servant
Covenant

**GOD'S
RIGHTEOUS
SERVANT**

2. Posterity
Beneficiaries

POSTERITY
IMPLICITLY
INCLUDED

3. Divine
Salvation

FOUNDATONAL GENERATION

4. Saved
Community
Covenant

SAVED COMMUNITY

5. Organic
Perpetuity

FEATURE	Noahic Economy	Mosaic Economy	Christian Economy
Righteous servant Servant covenant	Noah Noahic servant	Patriarchs Abrahamic	Jesus Messianic
Posterity beneficiaries	Noah's family	Patriarch's physical children	Jesus' children (Abraham's spiritual children)
Divine salvation	from flood	from Egypt	from sin
Saved society Community covenant	Ark dwellers Noahic community	Hebrew Israel old	Christian Israel new
Organic perpetuity	physical posterity of Ark dwellers	physical children of Patriarchs, Hebrew Israel	spiritual children of Jesus, Christian Israel

God's covenant with David is unique. It crowns the Mosaic economy and organically binds it to the Christian economy (Jer. 33:15, 17). God's covenant with Jesus, David's heir, fulfills the Davidic covenant.[4] Similarly, God's old covenant with Hebrew Israel (Exod. 6:2–8; Deut. 29:12, 13) and new covenant with Christian Israel (Luke 1:72; Acts 3:25, 26) both fulfill the Abrahamic covenant.[5] Finally, the Noahic community covenant pictures the new covenant (Isa. 54:9, 10).

The diagram on the next page depicts these seven divine covenants and their relations in three covenantal economies.

The Remarkable Form of God's Covenants

The Supreme Designer, Artist, and Engineer of the universe arranges his pledges in a form that is beautiful, intricate, orderly, and revelatory; in a word, it is remarkable. These seven covenants have a *benevolent framework* that consists in the Noahic economy. They have a *redemptive focus* comprised of the Mosaic and Christian economies. They culminate with a *Messianic fulfillment* in the Christian economy. This entire house of pledges rests on an *evangelical foundation*, the mother-promise, the covenant of grace.

---

4. Acts 2:29–31; Ps. 110:1, 4; Heb. 7:20–22, 28.

5. Jer. 31:31–34; Heb. 8:6–13; Rom. 9:6, 7: Christian Israel is Abraham's spiritual posterity; Hebrew Israel his physical posterity.

GOD'S SEVEN HISTORICAL COVENANTS

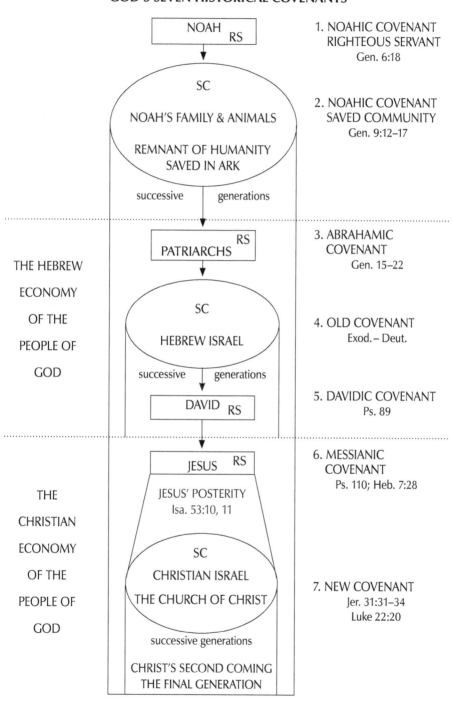

NOAH RS

1. NOAHIC COVENANT
RIGHTEOUS SERVANT
Gen. 6:18

SC

NOAH'S FAMILY & ANIMALS

REMNANT OF HUMANITY
SAVED IN ARK

2. NOAHIC COVENANT
SAVED COMMUNITY
Gen. 9:12–17

successive   generations

THE HEBREW

ECONOMY

OF THE

PEOPLE OF

GOD

RS
PATRIARCHS

3. ABRAHAMIC
COVENANT
Gen. 15–22

SC

HEBREW ISRAEL

4. OLD COVENANT
Exod. – Deut.

successive   generations

DAVID RS

5. DAVIDIC COVENANT
Ps. 89

THE

CHRISTIAN

ECONOMY

OF THE

PEOPLE OF

GOD

JESUS RS

JESUS' POSTERITY
Isa. 53:10, 11

6. MESSIANIC
COVENANT
Ps. 110; Heb. 7:28

SC

CHRISTIAN ISRAEL
THE CHURCH OF CHRIST

7. NEW COVENANT
Jer. 31:31–34
Luke 22:20

successive generations

CHRIST'S SECOND COMING
THE FINAL GENERATION

The Benevolent Framework of God's Covenants

"I will establish my covenant with you"; "the everlasting covenant between God and every living creature" (Gen. 6:18, 9:16).

The Noahic economy frames God's covenants. God first enters covenant with his righteous servant Noah (Gen. 6:18), who alone finds favor in his eyes in a world slated for destruction by the flood (Gen. 6:8–17). He fulfills this pledge to Noah supernaturally and personally (Gen. 7:1, 16) when he saves Noah's family and the animals in the ark (Gen. 8:15; 1 Pet. 3:20). God then blesses Noah and his family, a new humanity, with a new rule for life in the post-flood world (Gen. 9:1–7). Then he makes a covenant with this community that he rescued from the flood (Gen. 9:8–17). Thus, every man and animal living on earth today is in covenant with God. Thus, God has given the Noahic economy an important role in redemptive history. It forms a benevolent framework of common grace in which he works the redemption of his people. Accordingly, the Noahic community covenant pictures his covenant with those he rescues from sin: "for this is as the waters of Noah to me; for as I have sworn that the waters of Noah shall no more go over the earth, so have I sworn that I will not be wroth with thee" (Isa. 54:9, 10).

The Redemptive Focus of God's Covenants

"The covenants of the promise" (Eph. 2:12).

Within this benevolent framework, God works redemption for his people. This redemptive work encompasses the Mosaic and Christian economies. Thus, God's covenants focus on Christ the Redeemer and spotlight his commitment to his redeemed people: "I will be their God, and they shall be my people" (2 Cor. 6:16). In Ephesians 2:12 Paul sums up this divine commitment to his people: "the covenants of the promise."[6] He affirms the reality, plurality, and unity of these divine covenants. First, proper divine covenants with his people truly exist in reality. Second, God has made more than one covenant with his people, *"the covenants."* God enters not merely one but a plurality of distinct covenants with his people in history. Accordingly, Morton Smith rightly observes, "Actually, the Bible presents a series of covenants that may be described as gracious in character."[7] Third, God's distinct covenants with his people relate to the same divine promise of the Redeemer

---

6. The Greek contains the article: "the promise."
7. Morton Smith, *Systematic Theology* (2 Vols.; Greenville: Greenville Seminary Press, 1994), 1: 33.

to save them from sin, "the covenants *of the promise.*"[8] God's covenants are symphonious, not atomistic. They display spiritual harmony and evangelical unity. Every major misconception of God's covenants distorts or denies one of these fundamentals. Some insist that a proper covenant is a contract between equals that involves stipulation and restipulation. Then they affirm that God makes a "proper" covenant only with Christ, not with his people, since God and man are not equal.[9] Others insist that God has made only one covenant with his people. They deny that the old and new covenants are distinct covenants.[10] Others deny that one gospel promise of salvation unites God's distinct covenants with his people.[11] In Ephesians 2:12, Paul dispels these misconceptions and guides along the razor's edge of truth. Gentile Christians once were strangers from these covenants of the promise. Now in Christ they are included in the commonwealth of God's people Israel (Eph. 2:11–22). Scripture closely associates five covenants with God's redemptive favor to his people. These are his pledges with Abraham, Hebrew Israel, David, Jesus, and Christian Israel. These pledges are the core of his covenant promises. The New Testament begins with an organizing perspective on this redemptive favor: "Jesus Christ, the son of David, the son of Abraham" (Matt. 1:1). The inception of God's redemptive favor to his people is his covenantal blessing of Abraham the patriarch. Its fulcrum is his covenantal blessing of David the king. Its culmination is his covenantal blessing of Jesus the Messiah.

The Inception: Abraham the Patriarch

God in sovereign grace selects Abraham to be the father of his people. He solemnly promises the patriarchs that Christ will be their son and heir: "in your seed all the nations of the earth shall be blessed."[12] This promise unifies

---

8. Accordingly, Hodge comments: "That the promise meant is that great promise of a redeemer made to Abraham, and so often afterwards repeated, is plain." Charles Hodge, A Commentary on the *Epistle to the Ephesians* (Grand Rapids: Wm. B. Eerdmans Publishing Company, 1966), 127.

9. For example, John Gill, *Complete Body of Doctrinal and Practical Divinity* (2 Vols.; Grand Rapids: Baker Book House, 1978), 1: 309.

10. For example, R. L. Dabney, *Lectures in Systematic Theology* (Grand Rapids: Zondervan Publishing House, 1976), 435.

11. Bass documents this tendency in Dispensational Theology, though he concedes that Dispensationalists do not want to admit that their teaching has this tendency. Clarence B. Bass, *Backgrounds to Dispensationalism* (Grand Rapids: Baker Book House, 1978), 33–35.

12. Gen. 22:18. God repeats this promise to Isaac (Gen. 26:4) and Jacob (Gen. 28:14).

God's people and his redemptive dealings with them. God also promises the patriarchs that their posterity will grow into a great nation, that he will take that nation to himself for his people, and that he will give them the land of Canaan as their inheritance.[13] God also pledged to Abraham that his unique identity would be as the father of a multitude of nations.[14] All subsequent redemptive history occurs in fulfillment of these promises.

The Fulcrum: David the King

God in sovereign grace chooses his righteous servant David to be king over the society of his people. God pledges to perpetuate his kingdom (Ps. 89:3, 4). He pledges this blessing to David,[15] to his royal posterity,[16] and to his ultimate heir, the Messiah.[17] In fulfillment of that promise Solomon rules over Israel and builds God's temple. Further, David's dynasty of heirs reigns in Jerusalem over Judea until the captivity. Then the psalmist laments that David's crown has been thrown to the ground. He wonders when God will fulfill his pledge and restore David's kingdom (Ps. 89:38–52). Thus, God's people were waiting for their promised Messiah and king, the heir of Abraham and David, the Redeemer. Jesus is the ultimate fulfillment of this promise. God sets him on David's throne by his resurrection from the dead and session at God's right hand.

The Culmination: Jesus the Messiah

Since Jesus is the covenantal heir of Abraham and David, God culminates his redemptive favor to his people through Jesus and his posterity. This is its ultimate fulfillment.

The Messianic Fulfillment of God's Covenants

"This cup is the new covenant in my blood" (Luke 22:20).
"The word of the oath…appoints a Son perfected forever" (Heb. 7:28).

God fulfills his redemptive favor to his people in the Christian economy. It is the ultimate set of God's covenants with his people. He makes the Messianic covenant with Jesus and the new covenant with his people, Jesus' posterity,

---

13. Gen. 15:18, 17:7–14, 26:3, 4, 28:4, 13.
14. Gen. 17:4–6; Rom. 4:9–18.
15. 2 Sam. 7:8–11, 23:5; 1 Chron. 17:7–10; Ps. 89:3, 34–36, 132:11; Acts 2:29, 30.
16. 2 Sam. 7:12–15; 1 Chron. 17:11–13; Ps. 89:4, 29–33.
17. 2 Sam. 7:16; 1 Chron. 17:14; Ps. 89:36; Luke 1:31–33; Acts 2:29–31.

through the mediation of Jesus. In this prophetic mediation Christ evangelically reforms and spiritually transforms God's people. The Abrahamic covenant also provides the framework for this Messianic transformation. By gospel reformation Christ spiritually transforms God's people from Hebrew Israel under the old covenant to Christian Israel under the new. As God's people under the old covenant were Abraham's patriarchal posterity, so under the new they are his Messianic posterity. This displays their organic unity and covenantal diversity. Christ's reformation has a profound impact on the life of God's people.

When Jesus reforms and transforms Hebrew Israel into Christian Israel, he accomplishes their redemption from sin. They are his children, his spiritual posterity. Upon Christ's resurrection and coronation, God perpetuates his royal priesthood by means of the Messianic covenant. Thus, the Messianic covenant relates to the new covenant in a remarkable way. In one sense, it reflects the relation of the Abrahamic covenant to the old covenant. In another sense, it reflects the relation of the Davidic covenant to the old covenant. Jesus is both the patriarch and the king of Christian Israel. The new covenant community is both his spiritual posterity and his theocratic kingdom.

The diagram on the next page illustrates God's redemptive favor to his people, the core of covenant theology.

THE CORE OF COVENANT THEOLOGY
GOD'S COVENANTS WITH HIS PEOPLE

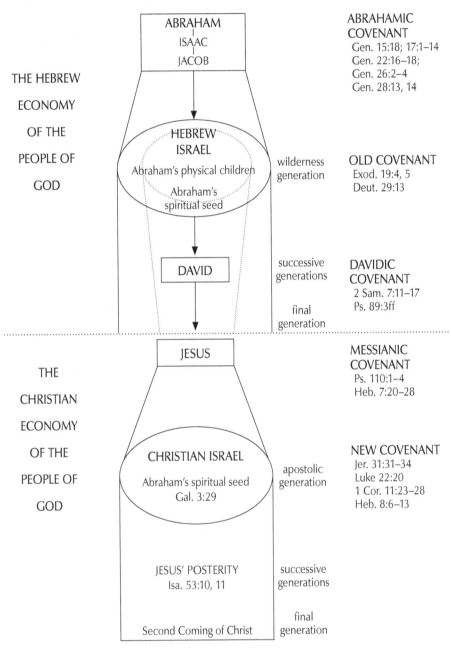

THE HEBREW

ECONOMY

OF THE

PEOPLE OF

GOD

ABRAHAM
ISAAC
JACOB

ABRAHAMIC
COVENANT
Gen. 15:18; 17:1–14
Gen. 22:16–18;
Gen. 26:2–4
Gen. 28:13, 14

HEBREW
ISRAEL
Abraham's physical children
Abraham's
spiritual seed

wilderness
generation

OLD COVENANT
Exod. 19:4, 5
Deut. 29:13

DAVID

successive
generations

final
generation

DAVIDIC
COVENANT
2 Sam. 7:11–17
Ps. 89:3ff

THE

CHRISTIAN

ECONOMY

OF THE

PEOPLE OF

GOD

JESUS

MESSIANIC
COVENANT
Ps. 110:1–4
Heb. 7:20–28

CHRISTIAN ISRAEL

Abraham's spiritual seed
Gal. 3:29

apostolic
generation

NEW COVENANT
Jer. 31:31–34
Luke 22:20
1 Cor. 11:23–28
Heb. 8:6–13

JESUS' POSTERITY
Isa. 53:10, 11

successive
generations

Second Coming of Christ

final
generation

The Evangelical Foundation of God's Covenants

"I will put enmity between you and the woman, and between your seed and her seed: he shall bruise your head, and you shall bruise his heel" (Gen. 3:15).

All God's pledges rest on the greatest promise ever made. They have a solid gospel foundation. God starts to apply salvation even before he enters covenant with Noah (Gen. 3:15; Heb. 11:4–6). This *"proto evangelicum"* unifies God's covenants and establishes their common design and focus. In this covenant of grace God declares war on the devil. He pledges both the application of salvation from sin to God's elect, Eve and her spiritual children, and its accomplishment through her victorious son, the Redeemer. He fulfills this promise when he applies redemption by *the gospel* and when he accomplishes redemption by Christ within *his covenants.*

The Distinctive Features of God's Covenants

Scripture highlights three distinguishing features. It delineates the generic concept, distinguishing characteristics, and specific content of God's covenants.

The Generic Concept of God's Covenants

God's covenants are verbal promises, spoken to men in human language.[18] They are more than bare promises; they are solemn promises, confirmed and sworn with an oath.[19] Even men's covenants are sworn commitments.[20] God's covenants express, as men's do, his favor or goodwill, the opposite of hostility and wrath.[21] This favor may involve friendship, or a grant given as inheritance, or an alliance or peace treaty. In sum, Scripture presents God's covenants as his sworn, verbal promises of favor. They are God's solemn pledges of friendship, donation, or peace. Through them God obligates himself, solemnly and voluntarily, to keep his Word.

---

18. Gen. 15:18; Exod. 19:5, 34:28; Deut. 4:13; 1 Chron. 16:15; 2 Chron. 34:31; Ps. 89:34.
19. Deut. 4:31, 8:18, 29:12, 14; 1 Chron. 16:15, 16; Ps. 89:3, 34, 35; Isa. 54:9, 10; Ezek. 17:16–19; Luke 1:72; Acts 3:25 with Gen. 22:16–18.
20. Gen. 21:27, 31, 32; Ezek. 16:59, 17:13, 16; Hos. 10:4.
21. Gen. 6:8, 18; Exod. 34:12; Deut. 7:2; 1 Sam. 11:1; Ps. 25:14; Isa. 54:9, 10; Ezek. 37:25, 26.

Five Distinguishing Characteristics of God's Covenants
First, God's covenants display solemnity. God makes formal commitments. He places himself under solemn obligation to perform what he has promised to do. Each is confirmed with an oath.[22] Sometimes a solemn ceremony accompanies this oath.[23] God seals his pledges to the three saved communities that he supernaturally rescues with a token or reminder.[24]

Second, God's covenants display numerical plurality. They are different pledges with distinct persons. They have distinct parties, or partakers, and distinct promises.[25]

Third, God's covenants display temporal historicity. They are ratified at different times and places in history.[26]

Fourth, God's covenants display organic perpetuity. They always involve, at least implicitly, the posterity of God's righteous servants whom he pledges to bless.[27] His covenants with saved communities all explicitly include their posterity.[28] The Messianic and new covenants include a spiritual posterity (Isa. 53:10, 11; Gal. 3:29).

Fifth, God's covenants display evangelical unity. The same gospel promise of salvation from sin in Christ unites them all. God's solemn pledge to accomplish and apply redemption, the covenant of grace, founds this gospel unity.[29]

The Specific Content of God's Covenants
The table below summarizes the content of God's covenants. Then follows a collation of the biblical testimony in these categories.

---

22. Gen. 6:18; Ps. 89:3; Heb. 7:28; Gal. 3:15, 17.
23. Gen. 15:17, 18 with Jer. 34:18; Gen. 17:9–14; Exod. 24:8.
24. Gen. 9:12; Exod. 31:16, with 31:12–17; Luke 22:20.
25. Deut. 5:2, 3; Ps. 89:3; Jer. 31:32; Heb. 7:22, 28, 8:6, 9:1.
26. Gen. 6:18, 9:10, 15:18; Deut. 5:2, 3, 29:1; 1 Kings 8:9; Jer. 31:31, 33; Heb. 7:28.
27. Gen. 6:18; 17:7; Ps. 89:4, 36; Isa. 53:10, 11; Ps. 110:1, 4; Heb. 7:28.
28. Gen. 9:9, 12; Exod. 31:16, 17; Deut. 29:25, 29 with Acts 3:25; Isa. 59:21; Jer. 32:39, 40; Ezek. 16:60; Heb. 12:22–24, 13:20.
29. Gen. 3:15, 22:18; Acts 3:25, 26; Rom. 4:5, 6; Gal. 3:7, 8, 14, 16, 29; Eph. 2:12.

THE CONTENT AND FEATURES OF GOD'S COVENANTS

Covenant Name	Partakers principal {dependent}	Promises	Token explicit {implicit}
1. Noahic RS	Noah {his family} Gen. 6:18	Enter ark Gen. 6:18	None
2. Noahic SC	Ark dwellers & physical posterity Gen. 9:8–10	No more flood to destroy whole earth Gen. 9:11; Isa. 54:9, 10	Rainbow Gen. 9:12–17
3. Abrahamic	(1) Abraham {his posterity} Gen. 15:18, 17:1–8; 22:16–18	(1) Be the father of many nations Gen. 17:4–6	Physical circumcision Gen. 17:9–14
	(2) Patriarchs, A,I,J {their posterity} Gen. 26:3, 4, 28:13, 14	(2) Be God's people, inherit Canaan; all nations blessed through Christ their heir Gen.17:7, 8, 22:16–18, 26:3, 4, 28:13, 14	
	(3) Jesus {his posterity} Gal. 3:7, 16, 19, 29	(3) Give, receive gospel blessing; be God's people, inherit new universe Acts 3:26; Rom. 4:13; Gal. 3:8, 14, Eph. 1:13, 14	{Heart circumcision} Col. 2:11
4. Old	Wilderness gen. of Hebrew Israel & physical posterity Exod. 24:8; Deut. 29:12, 13	If keep 10c, will be royal priests, remain God's people forever Exod. 19:4, 5; Jer. 31:31, 32	{Circumcision} Jewish Sabbath Exod. 31:16, 17
5. Davidic	David {his royal heirs, Jesus} 2 Sam. 7:11–16; Acts 2:29–31	Perpetual rule over God's people Ps. 89:3, 4; Luke 1:31–33	None
6. Messianic	Glorified Christ Jesus {his posterity} Heb. 7:20, 21, 28; Isa. 53:10, 11; 1 Pet. 2:9; Rev. 3:21	Perpetual, royal priesthood Ps. 110:1, 4; Heb. 7:20, 21, 28	{Baptism, communion} John 4:1, 2; Heb. 2:13; Gen. 14:18
7. New	On earth: apostolic gen. of Christian Israel & spiritual posterity 1 Cor. 11:23–25; Eph. 2:12–22, 3:21 In heaven: all the righteous Heb. 12:22–24	Every spiritual blessing, theocracy, preservation in Christ Isa. 59:20, 21; Jer. 32:40; Heb. 8:6–13	{Baptism} John 4:1, 2; Acts 2:38, 3:22, 10:47 Communion Luke 22:20

COLLATION OF THE BIBLICAL TESTIMONY

General or Unclassified: Exod. 34:10; Neh. 13:29; Dan. 9:27, 11:22; Hos. 6:7; Amos 1:9.

Human Covenants: Gen. 14:13, 21:27, 32, 26:28, 31:44; Exod. 23:32, 34:12, 15; Deut. 7:2; Josh. 9:6, 7, 11, 15, 16, 24:25; Judg. 2:2; 1 Sam. 11:1, 18:3, 20:8, 16, 23:18; 2 Sam. 3:21, 5:3; 1 Kings 20:34(2); 2 Kings 11:4, 17, 23:3(2); 1 Chron. 11:3; 2 Chron. 15:12, 23:1, 3, 16, 29:10, 34:31; Ezra 10:3; Neh. 9:38; Job 5:23, 31:1, 41:4; Pss. 50:5, 55:20, 83:5; Isa. 28:15, 18, 33:8; Jer. 34:8, 10, 15, 18; Ezek. 17:13, 14, 15, 16, 18; Hos. 12:1; Mal. 2:14.

Divine Covenants: (1) Abstract: Exod. 34:10; Jer. 33:20(2), 25; Hos. 2:18; Zech. 11:10; (2) Generic: Deut. 7:9; 1 Kings 8:23; 2 Chron. 6:14; Neh. 1:5, 9:32; Ps. 25:14; Dan. 9:4; (3) specific personal: Num. 25:12, 13.

Noahic RS: Gen. 6:18.

Noahic SC: Gen. 9:9, 11, 12, 13, 15, 16, 17; Isa. 54:9.

Abrahamic: Gen. 15:18, 17:2, 4, 7(2), 9, 10, 11, 13(2), 14, 19(2), 21, 22:16; Exod. 2:24, 6:4, 5; Lev. 26:42(3); Deut. 7:12, 8:18, 29:13; 2 Kings 13:23; 1 Chron. 16:15, 16, 17; Neh. 9:8; Ps. 105:8, 9, 10; Luke 1:72; Acts 3:25, 7:8; Gal. 3:15, 17.

Mosaic: (old): Exod. 19:5, 24:7, 8, 31:16, 34:27, 28; Lev. 2:13, 24:8, 26:9, 15, 25, 44, 45; Num. 10:33, 14:44, 18:19, 25:12, 13; Deut. 4:13, 23, 31, 5:2, 3, 9:9, 11, 15, 10:8, 17:2, 29:1(2), 9, 12, 14, 21, 25, 31:9, 16, 20, 25, 26, 33:9; Josh. 3:3, 6(2), 8, 11, 14, 17, 4:7, 9, 18, 6:6, 8, 7:11, 15, 8:33, 23:16; Judg. 2:1, 20, 20:27; 1 Sam. 4:3, 4(2), 5; 2 Sam. 15:24; 1 Kings 3:15, 6:19, 8:1, 6, 9, 21, 23, 11:11, 19:10, 14; 2 Kings 17:15, 35, 38, 18:12, 23:2, 3, 21; 1 Chron. 15:25, 26, 28, 29, 16:6, 37, 17:1, 22:19, 28:2, 18; 2 Chron. 5:2, 7, 10, 6:11, 14, 34:30, 31, 32; Pss. 25:10, 44:17, 50:16, 74:20, 78:10, 37, 103:18, 106:45, 111:5, 9, 132:12; Prov. 2:17; Isa. 24:5, 56:4, 6, 57:8; Jer. 3:16, 11:2, 3, 6, 8, 10, 14:21, 22:9, 31:32(2), 34:13, 18; Ezek. 16:8, 59, 60, 61, 17:19, 20:37, 44:7; Dan. 11:28, 30(2), 32; Hos. 8:1; Mal. 2:4, 5, 8, 10; 2 Cor. 3:14; Heb. 8:7, 9(2), 9:1, 4(2), 9:15, 18, 20; Rev. 11:19.

Davidic: 2 Sam. 23:5; 1 Kings 11:11; 2 Chron. 13:5, 21:7; Pss. 89:3, 28, 34, 39, 132:12; Isa. 55:3; Jer. 33:21; Acts 2:30.

Messianic: Ps. 110:4; Isa. 42:6, 49:8; Heb. 7:20, 21, 28.

New: Isa. 54:10, 59:21, 61:8; Jer. 31:31, 33, 32:40, 50:5; Ezek. 16:60, 62, 34:25, 37:26(2); Zech. 9:11; Mal. 3:1; Matt. 26:28; Mark 14:24; Luke 22:20; Rom. 11:27; 1 Cor. 11:25; 2 Cor. 3:6; Heb. 7:22, 8:6, 8, 10, 13, 9:15, 10:16, 29, 12:24, 13:20.

The Practical Functions of God's Covenants

This scriptural testimony to God's covenants has momentous practical ramifications. God's covenants with his people, forged by lovingkindness, kept by faithfulness, frame Messianic redemption and fashion special revelation.

God's Covenants with His People Configure Christ's Person and Work
In the Abrahamic covenant, he is the anointed, who receives and bestows the blessing of the Holy Spirit (Acts 2:33; Gal. 3:14). In the Davidic covenant, he is the king, who rules God's people on David's throne (Luke 1:31–33; Acts 2:29–36). In the Messianic covenant, he is the priest, who atones and intercedes for God's people (Heb. 7:20–28, 9:11). In the new covenant, he is the prophet, who reveals God's will and mediates the new covenant with his people (Acts 3:22, 23; Heb. 8:6). Thus, Hugh Martin judiciously observes that divine covenant is:

> the largest category of Christology that is either necessary or possible. We find it embracing all Christ's work, and all inspired expositions of it. It accounts for all the phenomena which it professes to explain. It explains all Christ's history, as the incarnate Son of God; all His interposition, as the Saviour of men. It embraces alike the impetration of redemption and the application of it. It expounds Christ's complete office.[30]

God's Covenants with His People Configure Scripture
The Bible has a covenantal form and structure because God gave his people two bodies of special revelation in conjunction with the old and new covenants. Under the Mosaic covenant God gave his people the Old Testament. It began to be written through Moses in Hebrew. Under the new covenant he gave his people the New Testament. It was written through the apostles of Jesus in Greek. Thus, the Bible has two parts that correspond to the two redemptions of God's people and his two covenants with them. Nothing is more fundamental to the form of written revelation than this. When God made the new covenant, he rearranged the Old Testament accordingly: first, the formation and history of Hebrew Israel (Genesis – Esther); second, the religious experience of Hebrew Israel (Job – Song of Solomon); and third, the eschatological perspective of Hebrew Israel (Isaiah – Malachi).

---

30. Hugh Martin, *The Atonement* (Edinburgh: Knox Press, 1976), 36–37.

Similarly, God organized the New Testament around its connection to the community to whom he gave it. Again, these emphases, though not iron-clad, are clearly discernible: first, the formation of Christian Israel (Matthew – Acts); second, the apostolic direction of Christian Israel (Romans – Jude); and third, the eschatological perspective of Christian Israel (Revelation).

This does not imply that the New Testament alone is the canon or rule-book for the church of Christ. The New Testament does not replace the Old, but supplements it and defines its multi-faceted relation to Christian Israel. The New Testament itself permits no other attitude toward the Old (1 Cor. 10:6–11). God gave the church the whole Bible because the whole Bible is its canon. This is due to the intimate and organic connection of Hebrew and Christian Israel (Jer. 31:31–34).

Thus, there are two redemptions of God's people, two divine covenants with them, and two Testaments of Scripture. Yet, there are not two peoples of God, but one; not two Bibles, but one; not two redemptions from sin, but one; not two ways of salvation, but one, by grace through faith in Christ. God divided the Bible not into seven parts but two. Each Testament cor-responds to a redemptive act of God and the community that experienced it. Thus duality in unity characterizes God's progressive revelation of the gospel of his grace. God's covenants constitute the framework of salvation from sin and determine the structure of the Bible. These stark facts trumpet the importance of divine covenant for understanding the person and work of Christ, the identity of the Christian church, and the relevance of the whole Bible. These compelling facts also commend Reformed theology for embrac-ing the covenantal framework of special revelation and of divine redemption and for building on this foundation.

The remaining lectures expound God's covenants in the order in which God ratifies them in redemptive history. We begin with their evangelical foundation, the covenant of grace.

— 9 —

The Covenant of Grace

*"I will put enmity between you and the woman and between your seed
and her seed; he shall bruise your head, and you will bruise his heel."*

—GENESIS 3:15

Introduction

We begin with an exposition of the greatest promise ever made. This glorious promise unifies God's covenants and defines their common design and focus. This declaration of war on the devil has historically been termed *"the covenant of grace."* It seems prudent to retain and use this term, as long as we duly qualify it. It is true that the term *covenant* does not appear in this text and that Scripture never explicitly calls this promise a covenant. For two reasons this declaration does not fit the pattern of God's other covenants. First, God addresses his other covenants directly to his righteous servants or to societies that he rescued. Here God addresses, not Eve and her seed, but rather Satan: "and God said to the serpent." Second, God's other covenants are solemn pledges of his favor and blessing. Here God pronounces his judgment, curse, and condemnation. He declares war on the devil, not peace. This is the antithesis of covenant (Exod. 34:12, 13; Deut. 7:2). These qualifications notwithstanding, this declaration is unconditional, perpetual, and inviolable. Even though it is implicit, not explicit, it still has all the force of a solemn pledge to redeem Eve and her seed. Further, God declares its general substance with an oath to Abraham: "in your seed shall all the families of the earth be blessed" (Gen. 22:18). I call it *"the emancipation proclamation,"* since in it God pledges to Eve and her seed divine emancipation from bondage to the devil. I also retain covenant of grace, because implicitly it is God's solemn pledge to rescue Eve and her seed from sin. LCF also retains it. Speaking of the covenant of grace, it says: "this covenant is revealed in the gospel; first of all to Adam in the promise of salvation by the seed of the woman" (LCF 7:3). Now consider with me its foundation, features, fulfillment, form, and functions.

The Foundation of the Covenant of Grace

Consider the setting of this fantastic promise. God has created man. Adam has rebelled against God (Gen. 2:16, 17, 3:6, 7). By his fall he has trapped himself and his posterity in sin and its consequences (Rom. 5:12–19). God pronounces judgment on all involved in the fall, first the serpent, then Eve, then Adam. In Genesis 3:14–15, God condemns first the animal (3:14), then the spiritual being, the devil, who used the animal for his evil plan (3:15). He speaks to the devil in picturesque language as though he is talking to a serpent. Thus, when God utters this promise, fallen mankind is spiritually dead in sin, slated for destruction, and under the wrath and curse of God. Fallen man cannot rescue himself from sin, and would not if he could. If there is any deliverance or hope for fallen man, God must take the initiative.

The wonder and glory of the Bible, the very soul of its message, is that God shines his grace against the backdrop of sin. God proclaims his plan of salvation implicitly as he condemns the devil. Compassionately, he promises a Redeemer to crush the devil's head and to rescue a remnant of mankind from sin. This is the greatest promise ever made. It displays grace, mercy, and hope to sinners.

The covenant of grace has two deeper roots. First, the breaking of the Adamic covenant founds and occasions it (Gen. 2:16, 17). Second, God's predestination of the redeemed and of the Redeemer also founds it: "it is founded in that eternal covenant transaction that was between the Father and the Son about the redemption of the elect" (LCF 7:3). God declares war on the devil in history because he decided to do so in eternity (Eph. 1:11). I have appended an exposition of each. Appendix 1 expounds the eternal counsel of redemption; Appendix 2, the Adamic covenant.

The Features of the Covenant of Grace

The exposition of Genesis 3:15 uncovers two essential features, its promises and partakers, and five distinguishing features. It is unconditional, perpetual, immutable, inscrutable, and historical. From this exposition, I derive a definition of the covenant of grace.

The Promises of the Covenant of Grace

First, God pledges that he himself will establish enmity between the devil and Eve: "I will put enmity between you and the woman." This means that Eve will be spiritually at war with the devil and fight against him. God himself will cause and sustain this spiritual hostility. This implies necessarily that God will redeem her from sin. This salvation from sin must be comprehensive and permanent. It must, therefore, include the moral renewal of her heart, the legal clearing of her record, and her personal reconciliation to God. And, the power of God must preserve her all her life in this enmity with the devil, must after death bring her to heaven, and must in the consummation deliver her from death itself. Furthermore, the Lord adds that he will perpetuate and establish this very same spiritual warfare between Satan's seed and Eve's seed: "And between your seed and her seed." As her spiritual children, they will walk in the footsteps of her spiritual warfare with the devil. Her seed will resist and overcome the devil's spiritual children. In this way they will carry on her warfare with the devil. Thus, they too must be saved from sin. God will apply to Eve's seed the very salvation from sin that he applies to Eve.

Second, God pledges that Eve's son will destroy the devil: "He shall bruise your head, and you shall bruise his heel." God now speaks of Eve's seed individually. This final promise has primary reference to her victorious son. God assures the devil that a son of Eve will do battle with him, defeat him, and destroy him, even though the devil will wound him in this conflict. Thus God here promises the accomplishment of redemption from sin and death through Eve's son.

In sum, in this emancipation proclamation God explicitly declares war on the devil. Implicitly, he pledges to apply redemption from sin to Eve and her seed and to accomplish it through her son.

The Partakers of the Covenant of Grace

First, who are Eve's "seed"? After the death of Abel, Eve says of Seth: "God has appointed me another offspring in place of Abel; for Cain killed him" (Gen. 4:25). Abel was her seed. Seth was her seed. Cain was not her seed. John says that Cain was of the evil one (1 John 3:10–12). Cain was a son of the devil, one of his spiritual children. Thus Jesus says of his wicked countrymen: "You are of your father the devil" (John 8:44). All wicked men who walk in the footsteps of the devil's hate and lies are his spiritual seed. They are of the evil one. Thus, Eve's seed are the righteous; the devil's seed, the wicked. Since Eve is the mother of the whole human race, her seed are all God's elect, whom he chose in Christ for salvation before the foundation of the world. The devil's seed are all wicked men, who are by nature children of wrath. Second, who is Eve's son that shall bruise the devil's head and destroy his works? John says that Christ was manifested for this very purpose (1 John 3:8). Clearly, the son of Eve who will crush the serpent's head is Jesus Christ. This final aspect of this promise focuses on Christ's person and work.

The Unconditionality of this Pledge

God says: "I will put enmity" and "he shall bruise your head." These promises to apply and accomplish redemption contain no "ifs." They depend on God alone. God here enlists no cooperation whatsoever from fallen men. Rather, redemption is his work, accomplished and applied by divine power. God stands committed supernaturally to establish and perpetuate this spiritual war in the devil's house. Christ is God the Son incarnate, sent from God the Father to save his people from their sins. Christ's work can never fail. Its success is certain. Its success does not rest on any decision of fallen men, any more than the application of redemption does (Rom. 8:31–39). Therefore, this divine pledge is unilateral and efficacious.

The Organic Perpetuity of this Pledge

God says: "between you and the woman, and between your seed and her seed." God pledges to perpetuate this spiritual enmity from generation to generation between Eve's seed and the devil's seed. Clearly the covenant of grace displays organic continuity and perpetuity. Just as clearly, its principle of perpetuity is spiritual, not merely physical. Wicked men like Cain are Eve's physical children, but they are not her seed. They are neither partakers of this promise, nor parties of the covenant of grace. God does not apply redemption to them. This momentous text that first mentions God's solemn pledge to save his elect testifies plainly that its participants connect organically to Eve spiritually, not just physically. Jesus applies this principle of spiritual generation to Abraham and his children (John 8:36–44). God perpetuates this covenant of grace when he supernaturally generates Eve's spiritual seed. He stands committed to apply redemption to some of the devil's children in every generation, and thus to perpetuate Eve's seed. Otherwise all men would remain dead in sin permanently. Here is solid hope for every generation of sinners. God has pledged to emancipate some.

The Immutability of this Pledge

This grows necessarily out of its organic perpetuity: "And between your seed and her seed." God pledges to perpetuate this same enmity in every generation. This is the only way that he will ever rescue any person from sin. This means that his covenant of grace abides the same before and after the incarnation of Christ. God only saves sinners in one way. He implements this covenant of grace. He applies to his elect this redemption he accomplishes by Christ.

The Inscrutability of this Pledge

This also stems from its organic continuity: "And between your seed and her seed." Cain, Abel, and Seth were all Eve's physical children, brothers. Abel and Seth were her spiritual children. Cain was the devil's spiritual child. How could Eve tell the difference? How could she discern that God had applied redemption to Abel and Seth, but not to Cain? The manifest difference was that Abel, not Cain, had saving faith: "By faith Abel offered to God a better sacrifice than Cain" (Heb. 11:4). From Seth's days men began to confess that faith: "Then *men* began to call on the name of the LORD" (Gen. 4:26). As Paul says, "Whoever will call upon the name of the LORD will be saved" (Rom. 10:13); and, "if you confess with your mouth Jesus *as* Lord, and believe in your heart that God raised Him from the dead, you shall be saved" (Rom. 10:9). Faith in the heart, confessed with the mouth, distinguishes Eve's spiritual seed. This displays the limitation inherent in identifying the partakers of this pledge. Men can discern if a person has faith, but human discernment is not infallible. God alone sees the heart. Plainly, some who profess faith with their mouth do not really have faith in their hearts. Sometimes their hypocrisy is evident. Sometimes it is far from evident. Therefore, when God names a spiritual seed, he ordains the inscrutability of his covenant of grace.

The Historicity of this Pledge

The passage begins: "The LORD God said to the serpent." God enacted the covenant of grace in Eden immediately after the fall. Although it rests on

God's eternal decree, it is distinct from it. In sum, these observations support the following definition:

> The covenant of grace is God's solemn pledge to accomplish redemption by Jesus Christ and to apply redemption to all his elect in Christ.

The following table displays its promises and partakers, the two essential features of the covenant of grace:

ESSENTIAL FEATURES	THE REDEEMED	THE REDEEMER
Partakers named	**All God's elect** Eve and her spiritual children	**Jesus Christ** Eve's victorious son
Promises made	**Apply redemption** Create enmity with the devil and his spiritual children, the wicked	**Accomplish redemption** Crush the devil's head

The covenant of grace is dual and representative. It features Christ, the one, who accomplishes redemption, and God's elect in Christ, the many to whom God applies redemption. It closely binds its participants and promises. It unites the Redeemer and the redeemed. It binds redemption accomplished and applied. Since this pledge contains two promises, both Christ and God's elect are its parties or partakers. Plainly the covenant of grace is particular. All men in Adam do not partake of it. The elect are the focus of the promise to apply redemption in union with Christ. Christ is the focus of the promise to accomplish redemption for the benefit of his elect.

This comports with the Larger Catechism: "the covenant of grace was made with Christ as the second Adam, and in him with all the elect as his seed."[1] Christ's seed, patently, are not his physical children, but his spiritual children (Isa. 53:10, 11). Christ is their Representative Head. They are God's elect and Eve's seed. How can this be? Jesus tells the Jews the answer, but they won't hear it: "Before Abraham was born, I am" (John 8:58). The Father gives them to his Son in the eternal counsel of redemption. He designates him as their Representative Head and Redeemer before he creates the world.[2]

Accordingly, this remarkable divine pledge binds Christology and soteriology.[3] Since the Holy Spirit unites the Christian life to the Christian

---

1. WLC 31.
2. John 17:5, 6, 24.
3. Soteriology refers to the doctrine of the Christian life, salvation in the fullest sense.

church, this very definition of the covenant of grace should also be employed in ecclesiology. Biblical ecclesiology and soteriology together stand on this definition of the covenant of grace.

The Fulfillment of the Covenant of Grace

God himself in the Bible tells the amazing story of how he keeps this promise. That story is redemptive history. It is as remarkable as the pledge itself. Scripture associates two prominent themes with this story: *God's gospel* and *God's covenants*. God implements his promise to apply redemption to his elect through his gospel. He implements his promise to accomplish redemption by the Redeemer within his gracious covenants.

Redemption Applied through God's Gospel

God's gospel is his message about salvation from sin in his Son (Rom. 1:1, 2). Through it he transforms sinners into saints, emancipates some of the devil's spiritual children, powerfully creates Eve's spiritual seed, and implements this solemn pledge. Scripture patently connects election, the application of redemption, and the gospel: "knowing, brethren beloved of God, your election; for our gospel did not come to you in word only, but also in power and in the Holy Spirit and with full conviction" (1 Thess. 1:4, 5); and, "God has chosen you from the beginning for salvation through sanctification by the Spirit and faith in the truth. And it was for this he called you through our gospel" (2 Thess. 2:13, 14). It has always been so (Gal. 3:8). It could not be otherwise due to the unchanging nature of man's sin and God's grace. All of Adam's descendants are conceived in sin (Ps. 51:5; Rom. 5:12–19). All by nature are slaves to sin, totally depraved, and children of wrath.[4] All fallen men by nature are sons of the devil. If it were left to men, all would perish, for no fallen man could rescue himself from sin or God's wrath. God, rich in mercy, transforms dead sinners into Eve's seed (Eph. 2:4–10).

He begins to apply redemption, to establish this spiritual war, immediately after the fall. He transforms Abel into Eve's spiritual child, while leaving Cain a child of the devil. After Abel's murder, he perpetuates this war and saves Seth (Gen. 4:25). From the fall to the incarnation he applies redemption to sinners. He transforms the wicked into righteous sons of Eve. He saves such as Enoch, Noah, Job, Melchizedek, Lot, Abraham, Moses,

---

4. Rom. 3:9–18, 8:7, 8; Eph. 2:1–3, 4:22; Titus 3:3–5; 1 Pet. 4:2–4.

Samuel, David, and the prophets (Heb. 11:5–32). When Christ comes, God continues to apply redemption with the bright light of the apostolic gospel (2 Thess. 2:13–15). In every generation until the second coming, he transforms sinners from every kindred and tongue into Eve's spiritual children.[5] Then he eternally punishes the devil and all the wicked in the lake of fire and dwells with his saints in glory forever.[6]

We now unfold God's method by which he implements the covenant of grace with his gospel. We consider the twofold call of God's gospel, its progressive disclosure, and its means of conveyance.

The Twofold Call of God's Gospel

WCF and LCF judiciously define this twofold call and affirm its connection with the implementation of the covenant of grace.[7] Both aspects of this gospel call, general and effectual, should be considered together. Otherwise, confusion inevitably results.

✦ The General Gospel Call

In the free offer of the gospel God indiscriminately and sincerely offers lost sinners pardon, mercy, and life in his Son. The general call proclaims the message of God's gospel, the Word of God (1 Thess. 2:13). That message has always been the same. It is a message about God, about sin, about Christ, and about repentance and faith. This message is all about grace and of grace. It is good news to lost sinners. In this inspired message God commands and pleads with lost men to repent. He sincerely offers to them Christ, his provision sufficient for any sinner, and urges them to come to Christ in faith for salvation. With compassion he calls them to repentance and solemnly warns them to flee from the wrath to come. Scripture plainly affirms this indiscriminate gospel call.[8] The gospel presses on lost men their responsibility to repent and believe. If men repent and believe, they obey the gospel.

Thus, some call faith (let none forget repentance) the "condition" of the covenant of grace. Assuredly, no unbelieving and impenitent person is ever

---

5. Eph. 2:3–5, 6:10–20; Rev. 7:9, 10, 12:9, 17.

6. Rev. 20:10, 15; 21:1, 7, 8.

7. "It pleased the Lord to make a covenant of grace, wherein he freely offers unto sinners life and salvation by Jesus Christ, requiring of them faith in him, that they may be saved; and promising to give unto all those that are ordained to eternal life, his Holy Spirit, to make them willing and able to believe" (WCF 7:3, LCF 7:2).

8. Isa. 45:22; Ezek. 33:11, 18; Matt. 11:28–30; John 5:34, 40, 6:37; Acts 2:38–40; Rev. 22:17.

saved from sin. Yet, God didn't say in Genesis 3:15: "*if men believe* I will put enmity," or "*if men repent* he will bruise your head." How can this be? This leads to the rest of the story.

+ The Effectual Gospel Call
In the effectual call of the gospel, God by his Spirit, in conjunction with the general call, regenerates elect sinners, draws them to Christ, and creates in them repentance and faith. Scripture just as plainly affirms this sovereign and effectual call.[9] Remarkably, God creates and gives the very faith and repentance he requires in the gospel. Otherwise, no fallen man would ever repent or believe. God does not implement the covenant of grace through the general call in isolation. That would be futile, no fulfillment at all. Rather, he fulfills this pledge by the general and effectual call combined. His effectual call is completely unconditional. It is a supernatural work, a moral renewal that the Spirit performs in the secret recesses of the human soul. It is not conditioned upon faith or repentance, but rather is the cause of both. Thus, God creates spiritual enmity with Satan when he gives spiritual life to dead sinners, creates faith and repentance in their hearts, and morally renews their souls. In his inscrutable wisdom, he calls his elect effectually in conjunction with the general call of the gospel to sinners indiscriminately (James 1:18; 1 Pet. 1:23). How to reconcile sovereign grace and the sincere gospel offer is God's affair. He alone can fully comprehend his decrees, judgments, and ways. Again we stand at the fence around the mystery, designed to guard God's treasure from the hands of men. Man's place is simply to believe his Word and to convey what it says accurately and clearly.

The Progressive Disclosure of God's Gospel
LCF adds: "This covenant is revealed in the gospel; first of all to Adam in the promise of salvation by the seed of the woman, and afterward by farther steps, until the full discovery thereof was completed in the New Testament" (LCF 7:3). God's gospel message is always the same. Yet God reveals it progressively with ever increasing clarity and fullness until he completes its disclosure in the New Testament.[10] As Dabney reminds us, we should not assume that the Old Testament narrative tells us everything that men living in those days

---

9. Rom. 8:29, 30; 2 Cor. 1:9; Eph. 2:1–10; Phil. 1:29; 2 Thess. 2:13, 14; 2 Tim. 1:9; Titus 3:5; James 1:18; 1 Pet. 1:23, 2:9.
10. Gen. 12:3, 22:18 with Gal. 3:7, 16; Luke 24:27; John 5:39.

knew of the gospel. The New Testament posts this warning (Jude 14, 15). God also connects this progressive revelation to his redemptive work. He also connects it with his covenants with Noah, Abraham, Israel, and David. As he makes and keeps these solemn obligations, he further reveals his gospel and his method of grace.

The Means of Conveying God's Gospel

The God who ordains the ends also appoints the means; and he uses the means he appointed to accomplish his ends. God associates instrumental means with the gospel method by which he implements his covenant of grace. These appointed means display continuity and diversity. The permanent means that God has always used are preachers, parents, and prayer. God also uses diverse means of grace that comport with his distinct covenants.

✦ The Permanent Means of Grace: preachers, parents, and prayer

God always associates his gospel method with these means. Eve nurtured Abel and Seth; Noah was a preacher of righteousness; and God answered Abraham's prayers. He blesses the preaching of his appointed preachers, owns the nurture of godly parents, and answers the prayers of his redeemed people. God uses the preaching of men he equips for the work: "they repented at the preaching of Jonah" (Matt. 12:41); and, "they so spoke that a great multitude both of Jews and Greeks believed" (Acts 14:1); and, "how shall they hear without a preacher" (Rom. 10:14, 15). God also uses the training, teaching, and example of godly parents: "he may command his children, and his household after him, that they may keep the way of Jehovah" (Gen. 18:19); and, "the rod of correction will drive it far from him" (Prov. 22:15); and, "the unfeigned faith that is in you; which dwelt first in your grandmother Lois, and your mother Eunice" (2 Tim. 1:5). Finally, God answers prayer. He saves sinners in response to the intercessory prayers of his redeemed people (Rom. 10:1; 1 Tim. 2:1, 4). So it is now, so it always was, and so it shall ever remain while the earth lasts.

Now, has God so connected the means to the ends that these means are in every instance effectual? Is every hearer of the gospel converted? Does every child nurtured by godly parents inherit his parents' faith? Does every sinner for whom the redeemed intercede repent and believe? I could wish the answer to these questions was yes, but it is not (Luke 8:11–15, 18, 21; 2 Cor. 2:15, 4:1–6). God makes these means effective as it pleases him. As it is said, the best of means are means at best. The means of grace are great privileges. Yet, the partakers of the covenant of grace are all the elect, not all the privileged. All hearers of the gospel are not elect. All children raised in godly homes are not elect. All sinners for whom saints pray are not elect (Rom. 9:10–13). We should not confound being privileged by the means of grace with being a partaker of the covenant of grace.

♦ The Diverse Means of Grace
As there are abiding means associated with God's gospel, so also there are additional means. WCF enumerates these when it unfolds the administration of the covenant of grace. Under the old covenant God administered his covenant of grace by "promises, prophecies, sacrifices, circumcision, the paschal lamb, and other types and ordinances." In New Testament times "the ordinances in which this covenant is dispensed are the preaching of the Word, and the administration of the sacraments of Baptism and the Lord's Supper" (WCF 7:5, 6). God appoints different means, at different times, by which he implements his solemn pledge to apply redemption through his gospel. WCF also properly affirms the effectiveness of these means, even under the old covenant: "which were, for that time, sufficient and efficacious, through the operation of the Spirit, to instruct and build up the elect in faith in the promised Messiah, by whom they had full remission of sins, and eternal salvation" (WCF 7:5). WCF also rightly affirms the superiority of the means of grace under the new covenant: "which though fewer in number, and administered with more simplicity, and less outward glory, yet, in them, it is held forth in more fullness, evidence, and spiritual efficacy" (WCF 7:6). Behold here both continuity and diversity in the means of grace. God regulates this diversity in accord with his covenants.

Redemption accomplished within God's covenants.
Within a covenantal framework God fulfills this pledge to accomplish redemption. This framework consists of the seven divine covenants of the Noahic, Mosaic, and Christian economies. The two symbolic rescues from the flood and Egypt disclose his gospel progressively. In his infinite wisdom they provide colorful previews of Christ's saving work and greater light about salvation in Christ. Thus, the remaining lectures expound this framework of covenants in which God fulfills his promise to accomplish redemption in Christ.

The Remarkable Form of the Covenant of Grace

I borrow *remarkable* from Bavinck. By *form* I mean its nature and distinguishing traits. We derived five characteristics from Genesis 3:15. It is unconditional, immutable, perpetual, inscrutable, and historical. It seemed best to examine these after unfolding its fulfillment through God's gospel and God's covenants.

The Conditionality of Covenant of Grace

The substance or essence of the covenant of grace is *unconditional*. Yet its fulfillment has both conditional and unconditional aspects. This is the reason I waited. I said clarity requires consistency. Thus I myself must labor to present its conditionality consistently. God implements his unconditional promise to apply redemption, "I will put enmity," through the gospel call. Yet that gospel call, as we saw when we analyzed LCF 7:2, has a conditional dimension, the general call, and an unconditional dimension, the effectual call. Further, God fulfills his unconditional promise to accomplish redemption, "he will bruise your head," within a framework of gracious covenants, especially the old and new covenants. Yet, remarkably, the old covenant is conditional, the new unconditional. Thus, God fulfills his unconditional pledge in a manner that has both conditional and unconditional aspects.

The Conditionality of the Pledge to Apply Redemption

In its essence God's solemn pledge to apply redemption is patently *unconditional*. However, God implements this unconditional pledge through the gospel call. The general call of the gospel is *conditional*. It offers salvation indiscriminately *on condition* of repentance and faith. But effectual gospel call is unconditional. God unconditionally gives to his elect the very faith and repentance he openly requires in the general call. In regenerating grace he creates faith and repentance (Acts 11:18; Eph. 2:1–4, 8, 9; Phil. 1:29). God, by his power alone, regenerates some of the devil's children and creates Eve's spiritual seed. The devil's children, in and by their own moral strength, cannot and do not cooperate, or even not resist (John 6:44; Rom. 8:7). Thus, the general call presents salvation conditionally; but in fact, to fulfill this unconditional pledge, God unconditionally produces compliance with the conditions he requires! Oh the depth, who can fathom it! We beheld this tension when we analyzed LCF 7:2. This remarkable trait displays the riches of

God's kindness. It also displays the hardness of men's hearts. It evicts human pride, all man's works, and gives all glory and praise to God.

Now let's apply this and think it through. Is faith the condition of salvation? The answer is *yes*. Is repentance too? The answer is *yes* (Mark 1:15; Acts 20:21).[11] Is God's solemn pledge to apply salvation to his elect, in its essence, conditioned on their faith? The answer is *no*. God applies salvation to all his elect unilaterally. He does so when he gives them, for nothing done by them, the very faith and repentance that he requires as conditions of salvation. Therefore, faith and repentance *are* conditions of conversion, but *not* of the covenant of grace.

Furthermore, we should not misconstrue the role of faith. Is faith *alone* the condition of salvation? The answer is *no*. To avoid "Easy-Believism," we must affirm that repentance also is necessary for salvation from sin. Another question: is faith alone the instrumental means of justification? The answer is, *yes*. Another question: is perseverance in faith necessary for final salvation? The answer is *yes* (Heb. 3:12–14, 10:39). Yet, the God who requires perseverance in faith and holiness gives the very perseverance he requires. He preserves all his elect by his power (Phil. 1:6). Therefore, perseverance *is* a condition of final salvation, but *not* of the covenant of grace. God himself supplies, and that not for any condition met by his elect, everything he requires. For initial salvation, he unconditionally gives repentance and faith; and for final salvation, perseverance in faith. It's all of God, all of grace, from beginning to end. That's why it's a covenant *of grace*. If we ask precise questions, and give precise answers, we hopefully avoid confusion. Already there is mystery enough!

Good men speak of the covenant of grace as *conditional* to avoid errors and dangers. Indeed we must avoid the error of *eternal justification*. Gill called the covenant of grace unconditional and fell into that error. How do we avoid his mistake? We affirm with Paul that God's elect were "by nature children of wrath, even as the rest" (Eph. 2:1–3). Thus I spoke of God transforming the devil's children, children of wrath even as the rest, into Eve's spiritual seed. The tension in that terminology conveys that conversion is not superfluous. Further, when we say that the covenant of grace is unconditional in essence, we must take care to avoid *fatalism*. A fatalistic mentality would say, if God will certainly apply redemption to his elect, then why pray, why preach, why parent? Rather, we affirm, preach, pray, and parent,

---

11. I am not addressing exceptional situations like infants dying in infancy.

because God uses means. Unconditional in essence doesn't equal *absolute*, without means, in fulfillment! Should we teach that the eternal decree of election is conditional to avoid eternal justification and fatalism? I surely hope not! We stand committed to teach unconditional election, even if men abuse the doctrine. The covenant of grace reflects and rests on this unconditional decree. Did God decree in eternity to require faith and repentance for initial salvation and perseverance in faith for final salvation? The answer is, yes. Does that make his decree conditional? The answer is, no, because God also decrees to supply all he requires, and that not for anything done by his elect. So also is his covenant of grace.

Why do good men like Dabney, Hodge, and Smith call faith, and faith alone, the condition of the covenant of grace? I think this reflects their sensitivity to redemptive history. In conjunction with the accomplishment of redemption, Jesus forms a visible society of disciples. He gathers his seed (Eve's seed, Abraham's spiritual children) into that visible society. With this society God makes the new covenant, mediated by Christ, ratified in his blood, and symbolized by the Lord's Supper. The distinguishing trait of this visible society is its faith in Christ. John the Baptist formed a similar society of disciples, whose distinguishing trait was their repentance (Acts 19:4). Possibly, when these good men single out faith, they are thinking of its unique covenantal role in redemptive history. What spiritual trait distinguishes the society of the new covenant that Jesus formed in history? The answer is their faith in Christ. I think that they endeavored to express this truth.

The Conditionality of the Pledge to Accomplish Redemption

God's solemn pledge to accomplish redemption is also patently unconditional. However, God implements this unconditional pledge through his gracious covenants with his people. The old covenant was conditional, "If you obey my voice and keep my covenant, then you shall be" my special people and a kingdom of priests (Exod. 19:4–6). The new covenant is unconditional: "I will write my law on their hearts..." (Jer. 31:31–34). It is a better covenant, built on better promises. Thus the covenantal framework in which God accomplishes redemption has both conditional and unconditional aspects.

Thus, the application of redemption by the gospel pictures its accomplishment in the domain of these gracious covenants. The conditional promise of the old covenant reflects the general call of the gospel. Similarly, the unconditional promises of the new covenant reflect the effectual call of the gospel. When Christ accomplishes redemption, the new covenant pledge, "I will write my law on their hearts," is the very image of the pledge to apply redemption, "I will put enmity." Thus, the society of the new covenant, the Christian church, distinguished by its faith in Christ, is the very image of the society of the covenant of grace, Eve's spiritual seed, to whom God applies redemption.

The Immutability of the Covenant of Grace

The covenant of grace has one immutable essence. Yet it has diverse administration and progressive disclosure. God's solemn pledge to accomplish and apply redemption is, and ever shall remain, one and the same. Its fulfillment through God's gospel and covenants supports its essential unity and immutability. Yet it is revealed progressively and administrated diversely under the old and new covenants. Both Confessions state this truth from different vantage points. LCF 7:3 unfolds its progressive disclosure and indispensability. WCF 7:5, 6 affirms its essential unity and diverse administration under old and new covenants. We should retain both perspectives since clearly both are biblical.

The Organic Perpetuity of the Covenant of Grace

The organic continuity of the covenant of grace is essentially spiritual, not merely physical. It perpetually connects from generation to generation with Eve's spiritual seed, a spiritual remnant of her physical children. The enmity that God creates disrupts the devil's spiritual house and divides the human family. It divides Cain and Abel (1 John 3:10–12), Jacob and Esau (Rom. 9:10–13), faithful homes (Matt. 10:34–36), and Christian marriages (1 Cor. 7:12–16). Genesis 3:15 introduces a remnant according to the election of grace. God transforms a remnant of Eve's physical children into her spiritual seed, not all of them. To all her physical children he graciously grants religious privileges. Eve nurtures both Cain and Abel alike. Yet God selects only Abel, not Cain, as her spiritual seed, in a sovereign manner, in his eternal decree. Only God can create a spiritual seed. Thus, the fulfillment of the covenant of grace ever depends totally on God alone.

The Bible also presents this organic continuity of the covenant of grace when it speaks of Jesus' seed (Isa. 53:10, 11). Jesus' seed are not his physical children. He has no physical children or grandchildren. The organic perpetuity of Jesus' posterity is patently not essentially physical, but spiritual. Again, Jesus says that the Jews who rejected Christ were not Eve's seed, but the devil's children (John 8:44). He says that even though they were Abraham's physical descendants, they were not his spiritual children. Paul adds that Gentiles who believe in Christ are Abraham's spiritual children, even though they are not his physical descendants (Gal. 3:29). Abraham's spiritual seed are a believing remnant of his physical children plus believing Gentiles who are not his physical children. This displays that the perpetuity of spiritual seed is essentially spiritual, even when the spiritual seed are also physical children. The spiritual posterities of Eve, Jesus, and Abraham have an organic perpetuity that is spiritual. This is the organic continuity of the covenant of grace.

Similarly, Christians are Eve's and Abraham's spiritual children. The physical children of Christians thus enjoy great religious privileges. They enjoy these religious privileges in their final and finest form. God often uses the nurture of Christian parents, gospel preaching, and intercessory prayer to apply redemption to our physical children. Yet sadly, not a few of them, in spite of all their privileges, remain, like Cain, the devil's children. And patently, the devil's children, however privileged, are not partakers of the covenant of grace. God's gospel method and message pertain to all Eve's physical descendants. God always implements the covenant of grace by the general and effectual gospel call.

In this light Christians should evaluate our views of our physical children. God made the covenant of grace with Eve {the believer} and her seed {spiritual children}. Ask some plain questions. First question, was total inability removed from all her physical children because God made the covenant of grace with her? Second question, did God remove the guilt of Adam's sin from all her physical children? Third question, did God assure Eve that he would work faith in all her physical children's hearts? Fourth question, were all her physical children, collectively, God's elect? Fifth and final question, were all her physical children partakers of the covenant of grace? The answer to all these questions is, no. Ask the same questions about Noah and his physical children. Even ask these questions about Abraham and his physical children. The answers are all the same, no. We should apply these answers conscientiously to our doctrines and practices. Conscience in submission to Scripture, not parental longing, should govern our theology.

The Inscrutability of the Covenant of Grace
Although the covenant of grace is discernible and visible in appearance, yet it is inscrutable in its essence. This trait stems from organic perpetuity of

spiritual seed. Can men discern God's creation of spiritual seed, the fulfillment of this solemn pledge? The answer is yes (1 Thess. 1:5). Can men *infallibly* discern God's creation of spiritual seed? The answer is no. Man looks on what appears to be genuine conversion in a credible profession of faith; but only God sees the real spiritual state of every heart. Thus Bavinck most cogently distinguishes *appearance* from *essence*.[12]

Its fulfillment is discernible, but not infallibly so. We must judge with due care and discrimination, yet also with charity. We discern genuine conversion by its moral, doctrinal, and experiential fruits. Yet, "we cannot judge of the heart, but only of the external conduct and even of that defectively." This human limitation does not furnish any just ground knowingly to admit, tolerate, or retain the devil's children in any visible society of Eve's spiritual seed. As Bavinck warned: "what God has joined together, no man may put asunder." Outward profession should always coincide with inward experience. Now, in the new covenant era, this ethical tension that has always pertained to individuals also pertains to the covenant community. Only Eve's seed should be admitted to the visible community of the new covenant. Church leaders lack infallible discernment. Some hypocrites make a credible confession of faith and are admitted to the churches (Acts 5:1–11, 8:13–24, 20:30). Some, usually during persecution, renounce their profession of faith, cease to assemble with the church, and return to the world (Luke 8:13; Heb. 10:29). Others remain in church pews and pulpits sowing discord and controversy and corrupting the ways of the just (3 John 9, 10). These satanic implants do much harm to saints and churches. Yet Bavinck is right: "it can not appear in a form which fully answers to its essence," at least not here on earth in this age. Nevertheless, we should not throw up our hands in fatalistic despair. Rather, we should watch carefully and pray fervently to prevent the hardening of all who profess faith (Heb. 3:12–15). Whenever we discern wickedness in our churches, we should use God's means for its curtailing and removal, church discipline (1 Cor. 5:1–13).

The Historicity of the Covenant of Grace

God declared, ratified, and instituted the covenant of grace in the Garden of Eden, immediately after the fall. Yet he founded it eternally and he will fulfill it unendingly. God spoke this solemn pledge verbally in history, but resolved it in eternity in the counsel of redemption and decree of election.

---

12. Herman Bavinck, *Our Reasonable Faith*, 278–79.

He fulfills it in every era of redemptive history and in the world to come forever in glory.

The Functions of the Covenant of Grace

We conclude with a summary of benefits and responsibilities connected with the covenant of grace. We feature five functions: it guarantees victory, bestows hope, commends the means of grace, certifies divine love, and honors the church of Christ.

The Covenant of Grace Guarantees Victory

The covenant of grace assures us of spiritual war. God stands committed to initiate and perpetuate this war. He pledges complete victory in Christ, "he shall bruise your head." Christ will defeat the devil and all the evil associated with him. Christ will defeat sin, suffering, and death. In the covenant of grace, God guarantees complete victory over every foe. This gives his people confidence.

The Covenant of Grace Bestows Hope

The covenant of grace gives us hope for the salvation of sinners in every generation, "and between your seed and her seed." The declaration of perpetual war assures us that God will save some in every generation until Jesus comes again.

The Covenant of Grace Commends the Means of Grace

God implements his pledge to apply redemption through his gospel, "whereunto he called you through our gospel," "knowing your election, how our gospel came to you in power." Therefore, since God uses means, the covenant of grace calls us diligently and prayerfully to use the divine means of grace. It calls us to pray for the conversion of sinners (1 Tim. 2:1–5). It calls us to nurture our children in Christianity. It calls us to proclaim the gospel to sinners. God will certainly save some—so preach, parent, pray—knowing that your labor is never in vain in the Lord.

The Covenant of Grace Certifies God's Love

The covenant of grace flows from divine grace, mercy, and love for sinners who deserve to go to hell. It assures us that he loved us, even when we were dead in our trespasses and sins. It assures us that his love and grace made us alive spiritually and called us out of darkness into the marvelous light of fellowship with his Son. It demonstrates God's abiding favor and love for his people in Christ.

The Covenant of Grace Honors the Church
The covenant of grace calls us to appreciate and love the church of Christ, its visible society: "knowing brothers, beloved of God, your election." The church is the visible society of God's elect, of Jesus' spiritual children. This calls us to a lofty ecclesiology. We should not disparage the church, but rather value and appreciate it, because it is the visible society of partakers in the covenant of grace.

Conclusion: the Covenant of Grace and God's Covenants

To conclude we consider how partakers in the covenant of grace relate to the partakers of the historical covenants in whose domain Christ accomplishes redemption. Eve's spiritual children form a remnant within the original humanity and within Noah's posterity. This remnant includes men like Abel, Seth, Enoch, Melchizedek, and Lot. Scripture calls Noah a preacher of righteousness, but gives little information about how effective his witness was, or how long that gospel light lasted among his descendants. We know that by the time of the exodus the nations were steeped in false religion. During the old covenant era for the most part God restricted gospel light to Israel. One notable exception was the men of Nineveh, who repented at the preaching of Jonah. Even within Israel, most were the devil's spiritual children. The wilderness generation with only two exceptions perished in their unbelief (Ps. 95:8–11). Isaiah calls Hebrew Israel a disobedient and gainsaying people (Rom. 10:20, 21). Jeremiah says that most were uncircumcised in heart (Jer. 9:25, 26). So they remained until their final generation (Acts 7:51). Nevertheless, within Hebrew Israel, stiff-necked and unbelieving, God in every generation preserved a remnant that did not bow the knee to Baal (Rom. 11:4, 5). These were Abraham's spiritual children, and Eve's seed, to whom the Lord applied redemption. That "invisible" society within Hebrew Israel had no unique ordinances, even though they, as individuals, possessed every spiritual blessing in Christ. They experienced forgiveness of sins (Ps. 32:1, 2). God wrote his law in their hearts (Pss. 37:31, 40:8). They knew the Lord (Ps. 36:10; 1 Sam. 2:12, 3:7).

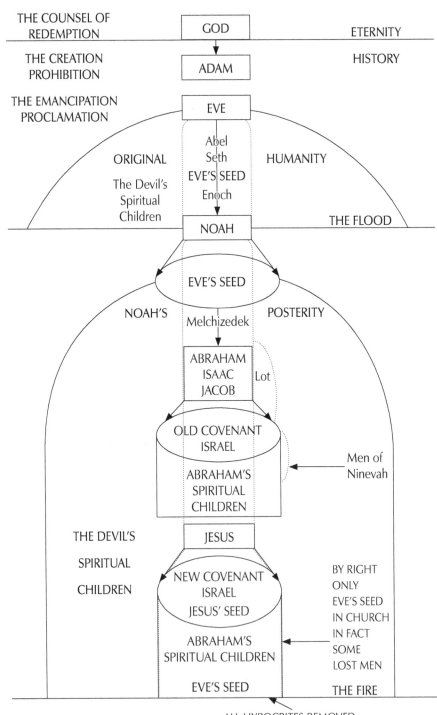

THE COUNSEL OF
REDEMPTION   GOD   ETERNITY

THE CREATION   HISTORY
PROHIBITION   ADAM

THE EMANCIPATION   EVE
PROCLAMATION

                             Abel
ORIGINAL   Seth   HUMANITY
                         EVE'S SEED
The Devil's
Spiritual   Enoch
Children   NOAH   THE FLOOD

                         EVE'S SEED

NOAH'S   Melchizedek   POSTERITY

                         ABRAHAM
                         ISAAC   Lot
                         JACOB

                     OLD COVENANT
                        ISRAEL
                                              Men of
                     ABRAHAM'S   Ninevah
                     SPIRITUAL
                     CHILDREN

THE DEVIL'S   JESUS

SPIRITUAL   BY RIGHT
                     NEW COVENANT   ONLY
CHILDREN   ISRAEL   EVE'S SEED
                     JESUS' SEED   IN CHURCH
                                             IN FACT
                     ABRAHAM'S   SOME
                 SPIRITUAL CHILDREN   LOST MEN

                     EVE'S SEED   THE FIRE

                 ALL HYPOCRITES REMOVED

When Christ appears, he gathers this "invisible" society of Abraham's spiritual children into a "visible" body of believers, the organized society of his disciples. He makes the new covenant with them, and gives them their own ordinances of baptism and the Lord's Supper. Then he incorporates Gentile believers into that same society and transforms his people into Christian Israel. The distinguishing trait of this new covenant community is that God has applied redemption to them (1 Thess. 1:1, 4, 5). Thus the devil's children have no right to belong to God's people under the new covenant (Matt. 18:15–18; 1 Cor. 5:13). Only Eve's seed, the partakers of the covenant of grace, have that right. Nevertheless, on earth, false disciples still manage to infiltrate this visible society of the saints (Heb. 10:29). The Lord will end this anomaly when he comes to present his church to himself in glory without spot, or wrinkle, or any such thing (Eph. 5:26, 27). The diagram to the left illustrates how Eve's spiritual children, God's elect, believers, relate to each of the saved societies with which God made the Noahic, old, and new covenants.

As we now study these covenants and covenantal economies, keep in mind their vital relation to the covenant of grace.

The Noahic Covenants

"I will establish my covenant with you," "the everlasting covenant between God and every living creature of all flesh."

—GENESIS 6:18, 9:16

Introduction

The first two passages where *covenant* appears in Scripture display a set of divine pledges. First, God enters covenant with Noah himself before the flood. After the flood, he enters covenant with every living creature that he rescued in the ark. We consider these divine pledges together since they stand organically connected as the Noahic covenantal economy.

The Noahic Righteous Servant Covenant (Gen. 6:18, 19, 7:1)

The Bible first uses *covenant* in Gen. 6:18: "I will establish *my covenant*." The first covenant in Scripture is a divine covenant, not a human covenant. We consider first its *features*, which are its principal partaker and its promise, and then its *fulfillment*.

The Features

The Principal Partaker: Noah, God's Righteous Servant

I call this the *"Noahic"* servant covenant because God made it with Noah, personally: "But I will establish my covenant *with thee*." I retain the archaic, *"thee,"* to highlight that the Hebrew clearly uses the second person singular pronoun. Notice that this divine covenant explicitly names Noah, and Noah alone, as the principal human party or partaker. It doesn't name Jesus, or all God's elect as the "parties." As soon as we turn from the writings of men to the Word of God, this stark fact confronts us. What are we to do with it? We should simply accept it because God has revealed it to us. What then does the Bible tell us about this man, Noah, with whom God made this covenant? Scripture records that Noah found favor, or grace, in the eyes of the Lord (Gen. 6:8). Then it says: "This is the history of Noah. Noah was a righteous man, and perfect in his generations. Noah walked with God" (Gen. 6:9). Noah had already been saved from sin. He was already one of Eve's spiritual seed. God didn't make this covenant to save Noah from sin. Noah was already right with God and faithfully served him before God made this covenant with him. So then, God made this covenant with his righteous servant, Noah.

The Promise: "enter the ark" (Gen. 6:18, 19–21)

God thus expresses the substance of his pledge to Noah:

> I will establish my covenant with you; and you shall come into the ark, you, and your sons, and your wife, and your sons' wives with you. And of every living thing of all flesh, two of every sort shall you bring into the ark to keep them alive with you; they shall be male and female. Of the birds after their kind, and of the cattle after their kind, of every creeping thing of the ground after its kind, two of every sort shall come unto you, to keep them alive (Gen. 6:19–21).

God promises Noah that he will enter the ark with his family and with pairs of animals. God pledges to spare him and his family from the destruction that he intends to bring on the rest of mankind and the whole earth. The destruction will take the form of a flood. The means of deliverance will be "the ark," a large seaworthy vessel of wood that God commands Noah to build.

Scripture records this revelation to Noah beginning in Genesis 6:13. God discloses that he intends to destroy all flesh with the earth. In Genesis 6:14–16 Scripture records God's commandment to Noah to construct the ark. In 6:17 God describes the manner in which he will destroy all flesh. In contrast with them he says to Noah: "But I will establish my covenant with thee." God's covenant distinguishes and separates Noah from those God intends to destroy. God by this covenant specifically contrasts those who suffer his vengeance from the partaker of his deliverance. The wider context bristles with the anger of an aggrieved God: "And Jehovah saw that the wickedness of man was great in the earth, and that every imagination of the thoughts of his heart was only evil continually. And it repented the Lord that he had made man on the earth, and it grieved him at his heart. And Jehovah said, I will destroy man whom I have created from the face of the ground; both man, and beast, and creeping things, and birds of the heavens; for it repents me that I have made them" (Gen. 6:5–7). The whole human race was abiding under the wrath of God with one exception: "But Noah found favor" (Gen. 6:8). God expressed that favor when he disclosed to Noah his intention to destroy everyone but him. This is how God told him he was different: "but I will establish my covenant with thee." It is important to notice that even though God names Noah alone as principal partaker, the promise includes Noah's family as *beneficiaries*. They too enter the ark with Noah. They partake of the promise along with God's righteous servant. Thus, the family of God's righteous servant benefits from God's pledge to him, even though God does not name his posterity explicitly as principal parties. Subsequent studies shall show that this kind of solidarity also pertains to God's covenants with Abraham, David, and Jesus. For now, simply note this fact well.

The Fulfillment (Gen. 7:1, 4, 9, 13–16, 8:14, 15)
In gospel obedience Noah built the ark in accordance with God's specifications (Gen. 6:22). To keep this solemn pledge, God first sent the animals to Noah (Gen. 6:20). Then, as he was about to send the flood, he told Noah to enter the ark and personally "shut them in" (Gen. 7:1, 4, 9, 13–16). In faithfulness to this promise God also kept them alive in the ark while the floodwaters prevailed over the earth. Then he revealed to Noah exactly when he could safely disembark from the ark (Gen. 8:14, 15).

The Noahic Saved Community Covenant (Gen. 9:8–17)
The second passage in Scripture where *covenant* appears is Genesis 9:8–17. Professor Murray makes this text his paradigm for understanding the essence of a divine covenant. We consider the foundations, features, fulfillment, and functions of this divine pledge.

The Foundations
This covenant rests on the fulfillment of God's servant covenant with Noah by rescuing all the "ark-dwellers" and on the renewed creation mandate and blessing (Gen. 9:1–7).

Divine Salvation of the Ark-Dwellers[1]

The Noahic community covenant rests on divine deliverance. When Noah, his family, and the animals enter the ark, and Jehovah shuts them in, the flood comes and destroys everyone but them. Then Genesis 8:15 records how God tells Noah to leave the ark: "And God spoke to Noah saying, Go forth from the ark; you and your wife and your sons and your sons' wives with you. Bring forth with you every living thing that is with you of all flesh. And Noah went forth." Thus God makes this covenant with the entire community that he personally rescued by his supernatural power in his common grace.

Renewed Creation Blessing and Mandate (Gen. 9:1–7)

This covenant also rests on divine blessing with a renewed creation mandate. Noah's family is the sole surviving remnant of the human race. After they left the ark, the Creator who saved them from the flood gave them his prescription for living on earth. Prior to the fall the Creator spoke the creation blessing to Adam and Eve (Gen. 1:27–30). They were to be fruitful, to multiply, to subdue the earth, and to eat a diet of fruit and vegetables. God's renewed mandate parallels his original one: "And God blessed Noah and his sons and said to them, Be fruitful and multiply and replenish the earth." Yet God changes some aspects. He enlarges their diet to include meat: "Every moving thing that lives shall be food for you; as the green herb I have given you all." He provides additional protection: "And the fear of you and the dread of you shall be upon every beast of the earth and upon every bird of the heavens withal wherewith the ground teems and all the fishes of the sea, into your hand they are delivered." He institutes capital punishment for murder: "And surely the blood of your lives will I require at the hand of every beast and at the hand of man will I require it. Even at the hand of every man's brother will I require the life of man. Whoso sheds man's blood, by man shall his blood be shed. For in the image of God made he man." Capital punishment originates, not in Mosaic civil law, but in this renewed creation mandate. Finally, he concludes the blessing as it began: "And you, be ye fruitful and multiply, and bring forth abundantly in the earth and multiply therein." This divine blessing displays the general categories in which God dispenses common grace in this new world. Thus, after the flood even common grace is covenant grace.

---

1. Gen. 6:13–15; 7:1, 16, 8:1, 15–17; 1 Pet. 3:20.

The Features: the Partakers, Promise, and Token

The Partakers: Ark-dwellers and their Physical Posterity

> And God spoke to Noah and to his sons with him, saying, And behold, I establish my covenant with you and with your seed after you, and with every living creature that is with you, the birds, the cattle, and every beast of the earth with you; of all that go out of the ark, even every beast of the earth (Gen. 9:8–10).

✦ The Foundational Generation: The Ark-Dwellers

God made the *ante-diluvian* covenant with Noah alone. He makes this *post-diluvian* covenant, not with Noah alone, but with the entire community that came out of the ark: "And God spoke to Noah and to his sons with him, saying, And behold, I establish my covenant with *you…all that go out of the ark*." In the Hebrew it is patently "*you*" plural. God entered this covenant with every creature in the ark that experienced firsthand deliverance from the flood of divine wrath. Thus I call this the "*Noahic community*" covenant, since the "*parties*" to this covenant are Noah, his family, and the animals, not all God's elect. What do Noah, his family, and the animals have in common? One thing distinguished them as a group. God saved them in the ark: "Wherein eight souls were saved." What were they saved from? Were they saved from sin and hell? Clearly not. Noah was saved from sin and hell before the flood. Salvation from sin and hell doesn't pertain to animals. Rather, God saved the ark-dwellers from drowning in that worldwide flood by which he poured his wrath on a fallen world. God regarded the human branch of this saved society as a new humanity, making a new beginning in the new world (Gen. 9:1–7).

✦ Successive Generations: The Physical Posterity of Ark-Dwellers

God established this covenant not only with that saved society but also with their physical posterity while the earth remains. Every living creature that descends from Noah, from his sons, and from the animals participates in this covenant. We who live on earth today are its partakers or parties: "And I, behold, I establish my covenant with you, *and with your seed after you*" (Gen. 9:9). The context stresses this fact: "the covenant which I make between me and you and every living creature that is with you, *for perpetual generations*" (9:12), "my covenant, which is between me and you and *every living creature of all flesh*" (9:15), "*the everlasting covenant* between God and every living creature of all flesh that is upon the earth" (9:16). This covenant community has organic continuity throughout its successive generations. Remember that Bavinck rightly observed this trait of God's covenants. Here the principle of organic continuity is natural or physical procreation. Successive generations of animals demonstrate this beyond doubt. Each generation of this Noahic community arises from the former by natural generation and physical birth. Its organic continuity is purely natural, not spiritual like the covenant of grace. Noah's natural descendants remain partakers and parties of this covenant from birth until death. They don't grow out of it when they cease to be minors. This reveals tension between this covenant with Noah's race and God's covenant of grace with Christ and his elect. Both have organic continuity. The Noahic community covenant has organic continuity of a physical seed, in common grace, by natural procreation; the covenant of grace of a spiritual seed, in special grace, by supernatural regeneration. This physical organic continuity pictures the spiritual organic continuity of the covenant of grace.

The Promise: No More Flood (Gen. 9:11; Isa. 54:9, 10)

> And I will establish my covenant with you; neither shall all flesh be cut off any more by the waters of the flood; neither shall there any more be a flood to destroy the earth (Gen. 9:11).

What promise constitutes the substance or content of this covenant? What did God promise, with an oath, to the ark-dwellers and their posterity? He promised that he would never send another flood to destroy the entire earth and everything living on it. Scripture confirms that God solemnized this promise with an oath:

> For this is as the waters of Noah to me, for as I have sworn that the waters of Noah shall no more go over the earth, so I have sworn that I will not be wroth with you nor rebuke you. For the mountains may depart and the hills may be removed, but my lovingkindness shall not depart from you, neither shall my covenant of peace be removed, says the Lord who has mercy on you (Isa. 54:9, 10).

Thus, God has made a solemn pledge to everyone alive on earth that he will never again destroy the whole earth with a flood. In this respect God is in covenant with everyone living on earth. Yet, this doesn't mean that all Noah's descendants are Eve's seed, or saved from sin, or parties of the covenant of grace. Rather, it means that they are partakers of the Noahic community covenant.

The Token: the Rainbow

> And God said, this is the token of the covenant which I make between me and you and every living creature with you for perpetual generations. I do set my bow in the cloud. It shall be for a token of a covenant between me and the earth. And it shall come to pass, when I bring a cloud over the earth, that the bow shall be seen in the cloud, and I will remember my covenant which is between me and you and every living creature of all flesh. And the waters shall no more become a flood to destroy all flesh. And the bow shall be in the cloud and I will look upon it that I may remember the everlasting covenant between God and every living creature of all flesh that is upon the earth. And God said to Noah, this is the token of the covenant which I have established between me and all flesh that is upon the earth (Gen. 9:12–17).

When God perceives rainbows he remembers his promise. This token is a visible symbol and reminder of God's personal pledge. It tangibly demonstrates the sincerity of his pledge, much like wedding rings. The token highlights God's sincerity, reliability, and credibility. This emblem of God's solemn pledge sparkles in the limelight. Whenever it rains men might think it could mean another flood. God gives us visible assurance that it will never happen again. He sees his token and remembers his promise. What kindness and condescension! Whenever you see a rainbow, remember, "No more flood." Remember that God keeps his covenant never again to destroy every living thing on earth with a flood. That's the message of the rainbow.

The Fulfillment (Gen. 8:21, 22)

> And Noah built an altar unto the Lord and took of every clean beast and of every clean bird, and offered burnt offerings on the altar. And Jehovah smelled the sweet savor, and Jehovah said in his heart, I will not again curse the ground any more for man's sake, for that the imagination of man's heart is evil from his youth. Neither will I again smite any more everything living as I have done. While the earth remains, seed time and harvest, cold and heat, summer and winter, day and night shall not cease (Gen. 8:20–22).

The Lord conveys his intention to fulfill this pledge to the ark-dwellers and their physical posterity. This fulfillment continues from the flood to the fire. It lasts until the return of Christ (2 Pet. 3:6–13).

The Functions
It Provides Stability (Gen. 8:21, 22; 9:1–6, 11, 15)
This divine pledge gives everyone everywhere order and security. It lets all mankind know what to expect from God as long as the earth remains. It provides a benevolent framework of divine kindness and common grace in which God works his saving purpose and fulfills his covenant of grace.

It Displays Salvation (Isa. 54:9–10; Matt. 24:37; 1 Pet. 3:19–21)
The symbolism of these events is self-evident. Nevertheless, Peter puts an inspired imprimatur on the propriety of drawing a parallel between this symbolic deliverance and the deliverance accomplished by Christ (1 Pet. 3:18–19). In this Noahic community covenant God paints a picture of salvation from sin: "This is as the waters of Noah to me. As I have sworn, that the waters of Noah will never become a flood to go over the earth, so I have sworn that I will not be wroth with thee" (Isa. 54:9–10). God himself connects this promise to the ark-dwellers to his promise to heavenly Zion, those who believe in Jesus Christ. Again, just as God judged the whole world with the flood, even so God will judge the whole world with fire when Christ returns. Jesus makes this connection:

> And as were the days of Noah, so shall be the coming of the Son of man. For as in those days which were before the flood, they were eating and drinking, marrying and giving in marriage, until the day that Noah entered into the ark, and they knew not until the flood came and took them all away; so shall the coming of the Son of man be (Matt. 24:37–39).

So does Peter:

> Knowing this first, that in the last days mockers shall come with mockery, walking after their own lusts and saying, where is the promise of his coming. For, from the day that the fathers fell asleep, all things continue as they were from the beginning of the creation. For this they willfully forget, that there were heavens of old and an earth compacted out of water and amidst water, by the word of God, by which means the world that then was, being overflowed

with water perished. But the heavens that now are and the earth by the same word, have been stored up for fire, being reserved against the day of judgment and destruction of ungodly men.... Seeing that these things are all thus to be dissolved, what manner of persons ought ye to be in all holy living and godliness, looking for and earnestly desiring the coming of the day of God (2 Pet. 3:3–12).

In Noah's day the whole human race was eating and drinking, marrying, and giving in marriage. They had no idea that sudden judgment was coming on them until the day that Noah entered the ark. Swift destruction by the flood came upon the wicked and destroyed them all. So shall it be when Christ returns.

It Gives Opportunity and Incentive to Repent

The goodness of God leads you to repentance (Rom. 2:4); the Lord is not slack concerning his promise, as some count slackness; but is longsuffering to you-ward, not wishing that any should perish, but that all should come to repentance (2 Pet. 3:9).

Common grace complements and fosters saving grace. The kindness of God in the Noahic community covenant calls all who participate in it to repentance and faith. This incentive alone is not sufficient to save anyone from sin. Yet it gently nudges all Noah's descendants to walk in the faith of our father Noah. It also provides the exclusive sphere in which God, after the flood, implements his covenant of grace. In every generation from the flood to the fire God creates Eve's seed from Noah's posterity. God brings each of his elect to repentance in fulfillment of his covenant of grace in the orbit of Noahic grace.

Conclusion: Lessons from the Noahic Economy

The Noahic economy includes two divine covenants and the supernatural rescue from the flood bound up with them. The table below summarizes its features.

COVENANT NAME	COVENANT FORM	PARTAKERS	PROMISES	TOKEN
Noahic Servant (Gen. 6:18)	Righteous Servant	Principal: Noah Beneficiaries: his family	Enter the ark	
Noahic Community (Gen. 9:8–17)	Saved Community	Ark-dwellers & Physical Posterity (Gen. 9:8–10)	No more flood (Gen. 9:11; Isa. 54:9,10)	Rainbow (Gen. 9:12–17)

This Noahic economy teaches valuable lessons about the general idea of a divine covenant, the general nature of the Christian economy, and the compatibility of common and saving grace.

First, the Noahic economy furnishes a valuable lesson about the general idea of a "proper" divine covenant. Observe how Scripture presents divine covenant in these passages. God speaks of "my" covenant: "I will establish my covenant with thee"; and "I will establish my covenant with you and with your seed after you." Then he says: "this is the token of the covenant which I make between me and you and every living creature that is with you for perpetual generations"; and "the everlasting covenant between God and every living creature of all flesh"; and "the covenant which I have established between me and all flesh."

This way of speaking delimits the concept of divine covenant. A correct construction must fit this usage. It must be compatible with what God discloses here. As with Cinderella's slipper, only the right idea fits. The notion that a divine covenant is a compact between equals simply doesn't fit. These divine covenants evidently were not optional compacts entered voluntarily with mutual stipulations and conditions. Animals didn't agree to anything, or "re-stipulate" anything, or even grasp the significance of God's words. No biblical principle of exegesis justifies eliminating these passages from the process of determining the concept of a "proper" divine covenant. Further, the Hittite treaty model doesn't fit either. When God entered covenant with Noah, his family, and the animals, the Hittites were yet unborn. How did God borrow the essential format for his covenants from a Hittite society that didn't yet exist? Whatever truth may be found in Hittite analogies, we must avoid the trap of trying to force every divine covenant into a Hittite treaty mold. The Noahic economy of genuine divine covenants predates any such treaties.

It may be difficult to find one English synonym for covenant that fits every expression in these passages. Robertson's definition, a "bond in blood sovereignly administered" doesn't fit well. Nor does Hendriksen's: "a legal relation which purposes a true friendship."[2]

What does fit? I submit that *pledge* seems to fit well. What is a pledge? It is a "solemn promise," a sworn promise, one confirmed with an oath. When God gives his pledge, he gives his Word. He obligates himself and establishes a verbal and solemn commitment to his creatures. This fits every use of covenant in these passages and comports well with the analogy of Scripture. For example: "I will establish my *pledge* with thee"; and "I will establish my *pledge* with you and with your seed after you"; and "this is the token of the *pledge* which I make between me and you and every living creature that is with you for perpetual generations"; and "the everlasting *pledge* between God and every living creature of all flesh"; and "the *pledge* which I have established between me and all flesh." In this case God's pledge is unilateral, not bilateral. These promises express his goodwill and favor to Noah and his posterity. This favor has a limited scope and focus. God pledges that he will temporarily restrain his wrath so that while the earth remains he will never display that wrath in a worldwide flood again. He pledges this much, and no more, to every living creature—whether they appreciate it or not—whether they understand it or not.

Someone may observe that God nowhere in these passages explicitly affirms that these are solemn or oath-bound promises. God's inspired reflection does explicitly affirm it: "This is as the waters of Noah to me. As I have *sworn*, that the waters of Noah will never become a flood to go over the earth, so I have *sworn* that I will not be wroth with thee" (Isa. 54:9, 10). God himself says that his promise to the ark-dwellers was solemn and oath-bound. He says it is just as "proper" a covenant as his covenant with heavenly Zion: "this is as the waters of Noah to me." Thus, it serves as a genuine model that accurately reveals the nature of salvation from sin in Christ.

Second, the Noahic economy furnishes a valuable lesson about the general nature of the Christian economy. God formed this entire complex of Noahic covenants to picture salvation in Christ. First, God established a covenant with Noah, his righteous servant, personally before the flood. Then God supernaturally in the ark saved his family, his beneficiaries, from the flood of divine wrath. This divine wrath destroyed the "then" world and everyone in it. Then after the flood God established a covenant with the

---

2. William Hendriksen, *The Covenant of Grace* (Grand Rapids: Wm. B. Eerdmans Publishing Company, 1932), 21–22.

entire society he rescued and with their physical posterity until the end of the world. God gave his righteous servant a task (Gen. 6:14–16). The result of his labors, the ark, is the vehicle for the rescue of his beneficiaries (Gen. 6:22, 7:5, 9). In sum, Noah is God's righteous servant who by his obedience and work delivers his posterity, a renewed humanity, from eschatological judgment and wrath. This displays the nature of the Christian economy. Jesus Christ is God's righteous servant who by his obedience delivers his posterity, a renewed humanity, from the wrath to come. God makes a covenant with Jesus and then with his posterity, the community rescued from sin through Jesus' work.

The Noahic economy displays generic categories in which God saves from sin in Jesus Christ. First, the covenant with Noah corresponds to the Messianic covenant with Jesus. Second, as Noah's family members are beneficiaries of this pledge to Noah, so Jesus' posterity, as royal priests, are beneficiaries of God's pledge to Jesus. Third, as God saves Noah's posterity from the flood, so he saves Jesus' posterity from sin and from the wrath to come. Fourth, as God made the Noahic community covenant with Noah's beneficiaries, the society he saved by Noah, even so he made the new covenant with Jesus' beneficiaries, the society he saved by Jesus. Fifth, as the Noahic community covenant involves organic perpetuity of Noah's posterity, so the new covenant of Jesus' posterity.

Third, the Noahic economy furnishes a valuable lesson about the compatibility of common grace and saving grace. I do not intend to repeat here my lecture on common grace, the final lecture in my anthropology syllabus. As I close I simply want to stress one thing about divine grace. Note well the beautiful harmony of all God's favor and kindness to men in this fallen world. Noah was God's righteous servant, saved by grace. He found "grace" with God. And in that grace God blessed his posterity as long as the world remains. We call that blessing "common" grace, because it is common to men and creatures alike. Yet never forget, that those men and creatures all descended from the ark-dwellers, so that all God's favor after the flood is covenantal, even common grace. Note well that this favor complements and fosters God's saving grace. Common grace in Noah and saving grace in Jesus are not adversaries. Rather, both display the covenantal lovingkindness and faithfulness of our great God and Savior.

— 11 —

The Abrahamic Covenant

"In that day Jehovah made a covenant with Abram,"
"I will establish my covenant between me and thee and thy seed after thee,"
"in thy seed shall all the families of the earth be blessed."
—GENESIS 15:18, 17:7, 22:18

Introduction: Overview of the Biblical Testimony

It would be desirable, if practical, to begin with a survey of 30 texts.[1] Since this testimony is so extensive, I summarize its major emphases. From study-ing this testimony I observe three major categories of thought in which Scripture presents this divine pledge: its essential features, historical fulfill-ment, and practical functions.

In texts 1–10, Scripture presents its essential features. Two texts epito-mize this witness (Gen. 15:1–21, 17:1–14). These reveal four features: its partakers (Gen. 15:18, 17:2–6, 17:7, 8), promises (Gen. 15:18, 17:2–6, 17:7, 8), ratification (Gen. 15:8–17), and token (Gen. 17:9–14). This pledge focuses on Abraham (Gen. 17:2–6), the Patriarchs (Gen. 15:18, 17:8), and the Messiah (Gen. 22:18).

---

1. (1) Gen. 12:1–3; (2) Gen. 15:1–21; (3) Gen. 17:1–14; (4) Gen. 17:18–21; (5) Gen. 18:18; (6) Gen. 22:15–18; (7) Gen. 26:3–5; (8) Gen. 28:13, 14; (9) Gen. 35:9–12; (10) Gen. 48:3, 4; (11) Exod. 2:24; (12) Exod. 6:3–8; (13) Lev. 26:42; (14) Deut. 7:12, 13; (15) Deut. 8:18; (16) Josh. 21:43–45; (17) 2 Kings 13:23; (18) 1 Chron. 16:8–22; (19) Neh. 9:7, 8, 23, 24, 32–38; (20) Ps. 105:1–15; (21) Luke 1:68–75; (22) John 8:37–39, 44; (23) Acts 3:25, 26; (24) Rom. 4:11–17; (25) Rom. 9:6, 7; (26) Gal. 3:6–9; (27) Gal. 3:14–19, 29; (28) Col. 2:11–13; (29) Heb. 2:13–17; (30) Heb. 6:13–18.

Scripture also presents its historical fulfillment. In texts 11–20, it highlights how God fulfills this pledge through the Patriarchs and their posterity.[2]

In texts 21–30, it highlights how God fulfills this pledge through the Messiah and his posterity.[3]

Scripture also stresses its practical functions for the redemption, reformation, and devotion of God's people.[4]

The Essential Features of the Abrahamic Covenant

We consider four features: its partakers, Abraham and his posterity; its promises, the blessing of Abraham's posterity; its ratification, ceremony with prophecy; and its token, circumcision.

The Partakers of the Abrahamic Covenant

We collate this biblical testimony around three focal points: (1) Abraham and his posterity; (2) the Patriarchs, Isaac and Jacob, and their posterity; and (3) the Messiah, Jesus, and his posterity.

Abraham and his Posterity (Gen. 12:1–3, 15:18, 17:1–8, 22:16–18)

God reveals this covenant progressively during major events in Abram's life. God discloses it initially at his call (Gen. 12), then when he promises him an heir (Gen. 15), then just prior to his heir's birth (Gen. 17). It reaches its

---

2. "You are Jehovah the God, who chose Abram, and brought him forth out of Ur of the Chaldees, and gave him the name of Abraham, and found his heart faithful before you, and made a covenant with him to give the land of the Canaanite, the Hittite, the Amorite, and the Perizzite, and the Jebusite, and the Girgashite, to give it unto his seed, and have performed your words; for you are righteous" (Neh. 9:7, 8).

3. Two texts epitomize this testimony: "Ye are the sons of the prophets, and of the covenant which God made with your fathers, saying unto Abraham, And in thy seed shall all the families of the earth be blessed. Unto you first God, having raised up his Servant, sent him to bless you, in turning away every one of you from your iniquities" (Acts 3:25–26); "Now to Abraham were the promises spoken, and to his seed. He says not, and to seeds, as of many; but as of one, and to thy seed, which is Christ.... What then is the law? It was added because of transgressions, till the seed should come to whom the promise has been made...if ye are Christ's, then are ye Abraham's seed, heirs according to promise" (Gal. 3:16, 19, 29).

4. One text epitomizes this testimony: "For when God made promise to Abraham, since he could swear by none greater, he swore by himself.... Wherein God, being minded to show more abundantly unto the heirs of the promise the immutability of his counsel, interposed with an oath; that by two immutable things, in which it is impossible for God to lie, we may have a strong encouragement, who have fled for refuge to lay hold of the hope set before us" (Heb. 6:13, 17–18).

apex when Abraham is willing to offer Isaac to God (Gen. 22). The first passage tells how God calls Abram and promises him gospel favor. The other three focus on Abraham's heir. God explicitly pledges covenantal blessing to Abram on the occasions of the promise, birth, and offering of his heir.

✦ The Gospel Call of Abraham (Gen. 12:1–3)[5]

This uncovers the evangelical foundation of the Abrahamic covenant. When God calls Abram at age 75, he promises to make him a great nation and give him a great name (12:2). He promises to befriend and defend him, to curse his enemies and bless his friends (12:3). According to Paul's inspired interpretation,[6] he promises to make him the means of global spiritual blessing through the gospel (12:3). Abram embraces this promise in faith.[7] It regulates his life. Thus, God makes this covenant with his righteous servant, who walks with him by faith, whom he calls out of darkness and idolatry (Josh. 24:2, 3, 14, 15). In Genesis 18:18 God cites this promise as his reason for treating Abraham as a friend.

✦ The Promise of Abraham's Heir (Gen. 15:1–21)

Abram, now between 75 and 86 years of age, longs for a natural heir. Although God is his shield and reward, he struggles with being childless (15:1–3). God grants the desire of his heart (15:4, 5).[8] Abram trusts in the Lord and believes his promise of a natural heir. God blesses his faith and

---

5. "Now Jehovah said unto Abram, Get thee out of thy country, and from thy kindred, and from thy father's house, unto the land that I will show thee: and I will make of thee a great nation, and I will bless thee, and make thy name great; and be thou a blessing; and I will bless them that bless thee, and him that curses thee will I curse: and in thee shall all the families of the earth be blessed" (Gen. 12:1–3).

6. "And the scripture, foreseeing that God would justify the Gentiles by faith, preached the gospel beforehand unto Abraham, saying, In thee shall all the nations be blessed" (Gal. 3:8).

7. "By faith Abraham, when he was called, obeyed to go out unto a place which he was to receive for an inheritance; and he went out, not knowing whither he went. By faith he became a sojourner in the land of promise, as in a land not his own, dwelling in tents, with Isaac and Jacob, the heirs with him of the same promise" (Heb. 11:8–9).

8. "After these things the word of Jehovah came unto Abram in a vision, saying, Fear not, Abram: I am thy shield, and thy exceeding great reward. And Abram said, O Lord Jehovah, what will you give me, seeing I go childless, and he that shall be possessor of my house is Eliezer of Damascus? And Abram said, Behold, to me you have given no seed: and, lo, one born in my house is mine heir. And, behold, the word of Jehovah came unto him, saying, This man shall not be your heir; But he that shall come forth out of your own bowels shall be your heir. And he brought him forth abroad, and said, Look now toward heaven, and number the stars, if you are able to number them: and he said unto him, So shall thy seed be. (Gen. 15:1–5).

promises to give him Canaan as an inheritance. He identifies the land that his descendants, issued through his heir, will occupy (15:6, 7).[9] Then Abram asks the decisive question. He asks for confirmation regarding this promise of Canaan: "And he said, O Lord Jehovah, whereby shall I know that I shall inherit it?" (15:8). God responds graciously to Abraham's request for reassurance. He confirms his promise with an oath, that is, he makes a covenant with Abram. He ratifies this covenant with a ceremony and prophecy (15:9–17). Then he states explicitly the substance of this covenant:

> In that day Jehovah made a covenant with Abram, saying, Unto thy seed have I given this land, from the river of Egypt unto the great river, the river Euphrates (Gen. 15:18).

Thus, this key text epitomizes its features. Jehovah is its sole author: "*Jehovah* made a covenant." He ratifies it, not in eternity, or in Eden, but in Abram's life: "*In that day* Jehovah made a covenant." Abram is its principal partaker: "Jehovah made a covenant *with Abram*." Its promise or substance is that his posterity will inherit Canaan: "Jehovah made a covenant with Abraham saying, *Unto thy seed I have given this land*." Like Noah's posterity, Abram's posterity benefits from this divine pledge to Abram.

+ The Birth of Abraham's Heir (Gen. 17:1–21)

Abram is now 99 years old. Ishmael, born when he was 86, is at puberty. His heir, Isaac, is about to be born.[10] God prepares him for his birth. He confirms and enhances this pledge (17:1-8), then commemorates it with a token (17:9–14).

First God confirms and enhances this covenant with Abraham personally.[11] This pledge so defines Abram's unique identity that God changes his name to Abraham.

---

9. "And he believed in Jehovah; and he reckoned it to him for righteousness. And he said unto him, I am Jehovah that brought thee out of Ur of the Chaldees, to give thee this land to inherit it" (Gen. 15:6, 7).

10. "But my covenant will I establish with Isaac, whom Sarah shall bear unto thee at this set time in the next year" (Gen. 17:21).

11. "And I will make my covenant between me and thee, and will multiply thee exceedingly.... As for me, behold, my covenant is with thee, and thou shalt be the father of a multitude of nations. Neither shall thy name any more be called Abram, but thy name shall be Abraham; for the father of a multitude of nations have I made thee. And I will make thee exceeding fruitful, and I will make nations of thee, and kings shall come out of thee" (Gen. 17:2, 4–6).

Second, God perpetuates this covenant. He explicitly includes Abraham's posterity as partakers.[12] He promises that throughout their generations Abraham's posterity will be his people. This defines their unique place among the nations (Amos 3:1, 2). He connects their identity as God's people with their inheritance of Canaan. When they inherit Canaan, he takes them to himself for his special people.

✦ The Offering of Abraham's Heir (Gen. 22:1–18)

Now Isaac is a lad. God proves Abraham.[13] Abraham obeys God. He is ready, by faith, to offer his heir and only son as a sacrifice to God (22:3–10). Then God intervenes. He vindicates Abraham's religion, *"now I know that you fear God,"* and provides an animal for the sacrifice (22:11–14). Then God further enhances his pledge to Abraham. Here it reaches its zenith. With an oath, he applies to Abraham's heir, Jesus, the gospel promise he made to Abraham:

> By myself have I sworn, says Jehovah, because thou hast done this thing, and hast not withheld thy son, thine only son, that in blessing I will bless thee, and in multiplying I will multiply thy seed as the stars of the heavens, and as the sand which is upon the seashore; and thy seed shall possess the gate of his enemies; and in thy seed shall all the families of the earth be blessed; because thou hast obeyed my voice (Gen. 22:16–18).

Although the word, *covenant*, does not occur, God says explicitly that he solemnizes this promise with an oath: "by myself have I sworn." Peter by inspiration affirms explicitly that this promise is a divine covenant with Abraham:

> "Ye are the sons of the prophets, and of the covenant which God made with your fathers, saying unto Abraham, And in thy seed shall all the families of the earth be blessed" (Acts 3:25).

---

12. "And I will establish my covenant between me and thee and thy seed after thee throughout their generations for an everlasting covenant, to be a God unto thee and to thy seed after thee. And I will give unto thee, and to thy seed after thee, the land of thy sojournings, all the land of Canaan, for an everlasting possession; and I will be their God" (Gen. 17:7–8).

13. And it came to pass after these things, that God did prove Abraham, and said unto him, Abraham. And he said, Here am I. And he said, Take now thy son, thine only son, whom thou lovest, even Isaac, and get thee into the land of Moriah. And offer him there for a burnt-offering upon one of the mountains which I will tell thee of (Gen. 22:1–2).

The Patriarchs: Isaac and Jacob, and their posterity

God confirms this pledge to Isaac and Jacob, so that in one sense, it is a patriarchal covenant:

> Then will I remember my covenant with Jacob; and also my covenant with Isaac, and also my covenant with Abraham will I remember; and I will remember the land (Lev. 26:42);

> The covenant which he made with Abraham, And his oath unto Isaac, And confirmed the same unto Jacob for a statute, To Israel for an everlasting covenant, Saying, Unto thee will I give the land of Canaan, The lot of your inheritance (Ps. 105:9–11).

We consider now the confirmation of the Abrahamic covenant with the patriarchs, Isaac and Jacob.

♦ Isaac, the Heir of Abraham[14]

God promises Abraham that he will establish his covenant with his heir, Isaac (17:19, 21). Scripture records how God pledges to Isaac the very covenant promises that he first established with Abraham. He promises Isaac that his posterity will inherit Canaan (26:3–4). He also promises Isaac that his heir will be the means of global spiritual blessing (26:4). Thus, God confirms to Isaac the solemn promises of inheriting Canaan and of instrumentality in global gospel blessing.

♦ Jacob, or Israel, the Heir of Abraham and Isaac

God confirms to Jacob his solemn promises to Abraham and Isaac. He confirms to Jacob that his posterity will inherit Canaan (28:13, 35:12, 48:4). He also confirms to Jacob that through his heir spiritual blessing will come to every branch of the human family (28:14). In conjunction with this confirmation, he reiterates that he has changed his name from Jacob to Israel (35:10). God first gave him this name when he faced the crisis of reunion with Esau. This name Israel is a compound of the verb שָׂרָה, to strive, contend, persevere,

---

14. "And God said, Nay, but Sarah thy wife shall bear thee a son; and thou shalt call his name Isaac: and I will establish my covenant with him for an everlasting covenant for his seed after him" (Gen. 17:19); "But my covenant will I establish with Isaac, whom Sarah shall bear unto thee at this set time in the next year" (Gen. 17:21); "I will be with thee, and will bless thee; for unto thee, and unto thy seed, will I give all these lands; and I will establish the oath that I swore unto Abraham thy father; and I will multiply thy seed as the stars of heaven; and in thy seed shall all the nations of the earth be blessed" (Gen. 26:3–4).

persist, and אֵל, the shortened form of God's name. Thus, Israel means, "one who strives and prevails with God."[15] It also intimates that Israel prevails with men, precisely because he has prevailed with God. Now God connects Israel's identity with this pledge. When Israel inherits this promise, he strives and prevails with God and men.[16]

The Messiah, Jesus, and his Posterity

The promises of Genesis 22:16–18 focus on the Messiah and his posterity, even as the promises of Genesis 15 and 17 focus on the Patriarchs and their posterity. Abraham's "*seed*" refers both to Christ personally (22:18) and to his spiritual posterity collectively (22:17). As with the covenant of grace (Gen. 3:15), these promises unite the one, Jesus Christ, to the many that God chose to save in Christ. Jesus has no physical children, but a multitude of spiritual children: "he shall see his seed" (Isa. 53:10).

In Acts 3:25–26 Peter says explicitly that the Messiah is the focus of Gen. 22:18. In Galatians 3:16 Paul says that God spoke these promises "to Abraham and his seed." He explicitly identifies Abraham's seed as the Messiah: "and to thy seed which is Christ." In Galatians 3:19 he adds that God made this promise to the Messiah, even as he made it to Abraham: "until the seed should come to whom the promise has been made." In Galatians 3:29, he says that Christians too partake in the Abrahamic covenant. Since Jesus is Abraham's heir, Christ's spiritual children are Abraham's spiritual children: "and if you are Christ's, you are Abraham's seed, heirs according to promise" (Gal. 3:29). Scripture confirms repeatedly that Abraham has not only a physical posterity but also a spiritual posterity that walks in the

---

15. "And he said unto him, What is thy name? And he said, Jacob. And he said, Thy name shall be called no more Jacob, but Israel: for thou hast striven with God and with men, and hast prevailed" (Gen. 32:27–28).

16. "I am Jehovah, the God of Abraham thy father, and the God of Isaac: the land on which you lie, to thee will I give it, and to thy seed; and thy seed shall be as the dust of the earth, and you shall spread abroad to the west, and to east, and to the north, and to the south; and in thee and in thy seed shall all the families of the earth be blessed" (Gen. 28:13–14); "And God said to him, Thy name is Jacob: thy name shall not be called any more Jacob, but Israel shall be thy name: and he called his name Israel. And God said unto him, I am God Almighty: be fruitful and multiply; a nation and a company of nations shall be of thee, and kings shall come out of thy loins; and the land which I gave unto Abraham and Isaac, to thee will I give it, and to thy seed after thee will I give the land." (Gen. 35:10–12); "God Almighty appeared unto me at Luz, in the land of Canaan, and blessed me, and said unto me, Behold I will make thee fruitful, and multiply thee, and I will make of thee a company of peoples, and will give this land to thy seed after thee for an everlasting possession" (Gen. 48:3–4).

footsteps of his faith (John 8:39; Rom. 4:11, 12, 16, 9:6–7). Clearly then, Messiah and his spiritual children, Christians, Gentile and Hebrew believers, are partakers of the Abrahamic covenant.[17]

The Promises of the Abrahamic Covenant

Now I collate and try to elucidate what Scripture teaches about the content of the solemn promises of the Abrahamic covenant. These promises all relate to Abraham's posterity. They have three focal points: Abraham, the Patriarchs, and the Messiah. Abraham has physical descendants issued to him through the Patriarchs. He also has spiritual descendants issued to him through the Messiah. We collate these promises accordingly.

A Promise to Abraham's Posterity (Gen. 17:2–6)

God promises that Abraham's posterity will become many nations (17:4). When God fulfills this promise Abram becomes exceedingly fruitful. He becomes "Abraham," a "father of a multitude." It so defines his personal identity that it redefines his name (17:5). He is not just the father of the nation of Israel, but many nations and kings come from him. His posterity will develop into many distinct nations (17:6). This promise pertains uniquely to Abraham. Accordingly, it defines his unique role in redemptive history (Rom. 4:11–16).

Promises to Abraham's Patriarchal Posterity

God promises that his patriarchal posterity will be his people, with homeland, fecundity, and victory (Gen. 17:7–8, 26:3, 28:13).

---

17. "By myself have I sworn, says Jehovah, because you have done this thing, and have not withheld your son, your only son, that in blessing I will bless thee, and in multiplying I will multiply thy seed as the stars of the heavens, and as the sand which is upon the seashore; and thy seed shall possess the gate of his enemies; and in thy seed shall all the families of the earth be blessed; because thou hast obeyed my voice" (Gen. 22:16–18); "Ye are the sons of the prophets, and of the covenant which God made with your fathers, saying unto Abraham, And in thy seed shall all the families of the earth be blessed. Unto you first God, having raised up his Servant, sent him to bless you, in turning away every one of you from your iniquities" (Acts 3:25, 26); " Now to Abraham were the promises spoken, and to his seed. He says not, And to seeds, as of many; but as of one, And to thy seed, which is Christ. Now this I say: A covenant confirmed beforehand by God, the law, which came four hundred and thirty years after, doth not disannul, so as to make the promise of none effect. For if the inheritance is of the law, it is no more of promise: but God hath granted it to Abraham by promise. What then is the law? It was added because of transgressions, till the seed should come to whom the promise has been made…. And if ye are Christ's, then are ye Abraham's seed, heirs according to promise" (Gal. 3:16–19, 29).

✦ The Foundational Promise: Theocratic Society (Gen. 17:7–8)
This promise plainly pertains to Abraham's patriarchal posterity. God promises that "throughout their generations" they will be the people of God: "I will be their God." Their relationship with God will be unique. No other nation will be his theocratic society.

✦ The Promise of Divine Inheritance: A Homeland, Canaan[18]
God repeatedly affirms that he will give Canaan to the physical posterity of Abraham, Isaac, and Jacob. He specifies the nations that he will dislodge in order to bestow this homeland on his people. Canaan is a divine inheritance (1 Chron. 16:18). They receive it as his people (Gen. 17:8). It remains their possession as long as they remain God's theocratic nation (Gen. 17:8, 48:4; 1 Chron. 16:17).

✦ The Promise of Fecundity in Canaan
This promise rests on the foundational promise of a homeland inherited from God. God repeatedly promises the patriarchs that their physical posterity will be more numerous than men can number, like the stars of heaven (Gen. 26:4) and as the dust of the earth (Gen. 28:14). He promises them that their posterity will include royal dynasties (Gen. 35:11) and multiple societies (Gen. 35:11, 48:4).[19]

---

18. "In that day Jehovah made a covenant with Abram, saying, Unto thy seed have I given this land, from the river of Egypt unto the great river, the river Euphrates: the Kenite, and the Kenizzite, and the Kadmonite, and the Hittite, and the Perizzite, and the Rephaim, and the Amorite, and the Canaanite, and the Girgashite, and the Jebusite" (Gen. 15:18–21); "And I will give unto thee, and to thy seed after thee, the land of thy sojournings, all the land of Canaan, for an everlasting possession; and I will be their God" (Gen. 17:8); "For unto thee, and unto thy seed, I will give all these lands, and I will establish the oath which I swore unto Abraham thy father...and will give unto thy seed all these lands (Gen. 26:3, 4); "The land whereon thou liest, to thee will I give it, and to thy seed" (Gen. 28:13); "the land which I gave unto Abraham and Isaac, to thee I will give it, and to thy seed after thee will I give the land" (Gen. 35:12); "and will give this land to thy seed after thee for an everlasting possession" (Gen. 48:4); "The covenant which he made with Abraham, And his oath unto Isaac, And confirmed the same unto Jacob for a statute, To Israel for an everlasting covenant, Saying, Unto thee will I give the land of Canaan, The lot of your inheritance" (1 Chron. 16:16–18); "and made a covenant with him to give the land of the Canaanite, the Hittite, the Amorite, and the Perizzite, and the Jebusite, and the Girgashite, to give it unto his seed" (Neh. 9:8).

19. "And I will multiply thy seed as the stars of heaven" (Gen. 26:4); "And thy seed shall be as the dust of the earth, and thou shalt spread abroad to the west, and to the east, and to the north, and to the south" (Gen. 28:14); "be fruitful and multiply; a nation and a company of nations shall be of thee, and kings shall come out of thy loins" (Gen. 35:11); "Behold, I will make thee fruitful, and multiply thee, and I will make of thee a company of peoples" (Gen. 48:4).

✦ The Promise of Peace and Victory in Canaan[20]

God promises rest and victory to Abraham's patriarchal posterity, not just his Messianic posterity (Gen. 22:17). He associates that victory and rest with their redemption from slavery (Gen. 15:13–14) and with their conquest of their homeland (Josh. 21:43–44).

Promises to Abraham's Messianic Posterity (Gen. 22:16–18)

The promises of Genesis 22:16–18 especially pertain to Christ and his posterity. He does not reiterate the promise of Canaan. Rather, he promises three blessings through Christ: (1) fecundity, "I will multiply thy seed as the stars of the heavens, and as the sand which is upon the seashore" (22:17); (2) victory, "thy seed shall possess the gate of his enemies" (22:17); and (3) global spiritual prosperity, "and in thy seed shall all the families of the earth be blessed" (22:18). These promises also rest on the promise of theocracy.

✦ The Foundational Promise: Theocratic Society[21]

The promise in Genesis 17:7 pertains to Abraham's Messianic posterity, not only to his patriarchal posterity. They too become his theocratic society in fulfillment of this promise (2 Cor. 6:16).

✦ The Promise of Divine Inheritance[22]

God promises spiritual blessing through the gospel by means of Messiah (Gen. 22:18; Acts 3:25–26; Gal. 3:7, 8, 14). This spiritual blessing is an

---

20. "And he said unto Abram, Know of a surety that thy seed shall be sojourners in a land that is not theirs, and shall serve them; and they shall afflict them four hundred years; and also that nation, whom they shall serve, will I judge: and afterward shall they come out with great substance" (Gen. 15:13–14); "thy seed shall possess the gate of his enemies" (Gen. 22:17); "Jehovah gave them rest round about, according to all that he sware unto their fathers: and there stood not a man of all their enemies before them; Jehovah delivered all their enemies into their hand" (Josh. 21:44).

21. "For an everlasting covenant, to be a God unto thee and to thy seed after thee" (Gen. 17:7); "what agreement has a temple of God with idols? for we are a temple of the living God; even as God said, I will dwell in them, and walk in them; and I will be their God, and they shall be my people" (2 Cor. 6:16).

22. "And in thy seed shall all the nations of the earth be blessed" (Gen. 22:18, 26:4, 28:14); "In thy seed shall all the families of the earth be blessed" (Acts 3:25); "For not through the law was the promise to Abraham or to his seed that he should be heir of the world" (Rom. 4:13); "Scripture...preached the gospel beforehand unto Abraham, saying, In thee shall all the nations be blessed" (Gal. 3:8); "That upon the Gentiles might come the blessing of Abraham in Christ Jesus; that we might receive the promise of the Spirit through faith" (Gal. 3:14).

aspect of their divine inheritance (Eph. 1:13–14). This blessing is global. Eventually, Jesus and his posterity will be divine heirs of the entire world (Rom. 4:13).

✦ The Promise of Fecundity[23]

Abraham's spiritual posterity through Messiah will be as the stars of heaven (Gen. 22:17). Upon his resurrection, Jesus begets spiritual children through the gospel. He justifies many (Isa. 53:10–11). All Christ's children are Abraham's spiritual children and heirs of this promise (Gal. 3:29; Heb. 2:13, 14, 16). These are a great multitude that no man can number (Rev. 7:9–10).

✦ The Promise of Peace and Victory[24]

God promises to Messiah and his posterity divine deliverance from all their enemies (Luke 1:68–75). The gates of hell will not prevail against the church of Christ (Matt. 16:18). God will deliver Jesus' posterity from the devil, sin, suffering, and death. The rest and victory that God promises to Jesus' posterity is complete, final, ultimate, and irreversible (Rom. 8:35, 37; 1 Cor. 15:55, 57).

The Ratification of the Abrahamic Covenant (Gen. 15:8–17; Jer. 34:18)[25]

God solemnized this pledge to Abram by a ceremony (Gen. 15:9–17) with a prophecy (Gen. 15:12–16). It is difficult to grasp the nuances of this

---

23. "In blessing I will bless thee, and in multiplying I will multiply thy seed as the stars of the heavens, and as the sand which is upon the seashore" (Gen. 22:17); "Yet it pleased Jehovah to bruise him; he hath put him to grief: when thou shalt make his soul an offering for sin, he shall see his seed, he shall prolong his days, and the pleasure of Jehovah shall prosper in his hand. He shall see of the travail of his soul, and shall be satisfied: by the knowledge of himself shall my righteous servant justify many; and he shall bear their iniquities" (Isa. 53:10–11); "And if ye are Christ's, then are ye Abraham's seed, heirs according to promise" (Gal. 3:29).

24. "And thy seed shall possess the gate of his enemies" (Gen. 22:17); "Blessed be the Lord, the God of Israel; For he hath visited and wrought redemption for his people.... Salvation from our enemies, and from the hand of all that hate us; To show mercy towards, our fathers, And to remember his holy covenant; The oath which he spoke unto Abraham our father, To grant unto us that we being delivered out of the hand of our enemies Should serve him without fear, In holiness and righteousness before him all our days" (Luke 1:68, 71–75).

25. "And he said, O Lord Jehovah, whereby shall I know that I shall inherit it? And he said unto him, Take me a heifer three years old, and a she-goat three years old, and a ram three years old, and a turtle-dove, and a young pigeon. And he took him all these, and divided them in the midst, and laid each half over against the other: but the birds divided he not. And the birds of prey came down upon the carcasses, and Abram drove them away. And when the sun was going down, a deep sleep fell upon Abram; and, lo, a horror of great darkness fell upon him. And he

covenantal ritual. It involves ancient practices associated with that culture and era. What is the significance of a flaming torch passing between cut pieces of animals? What is the significance of cut pieces of animals? Commentators and theologians differ in their interpretations. Yet most agree that this ritual confirms God's commitment to be faithful to his promise to Abram. God's rationale for this ritual was to assure Abram that he would keep his word (Gen. 15:8, 9). Thus, this ceremony certifies God's promise. Scripture sheds further light on this ritual:

> And I will give the men that have transgressed my covenant, that have not performed the words of the covenant which they made before me, when they cut the calf in twain and passed between the parts thereof (Jer. 34:18).

When the princes of the land passed through the pieces of the calf, they solemnly affirmed the covenant they were making. Similarly, the flaming torch, representing God, passed through the animal pieces to solemnize God's covenant with Abram.

In Genesis 15:12–16 God connects a prophecy with this ratification ceremony. The prophetic word of God further assures Abram by showing him the history of his descendants. Abram's posterity, the children of Israel, will go down to Egypt, sojourn there, and return to the land of Canaan to inherit it. Thus, this prophecy also underscores the absolute certainty of God's pledge to Abram that his descendants will inherit Canaan.

The Token of the Abrahamic Covenant: Circumcision[26]

God adds a visible reminder or token. As the rainbow was the token of the Noahic community covenant, so circumcision is the token of this

---

said unto Abram, Know of a surety that thy seed shall be sojourners in a land that is not theirs, and shall serve them; and they shall afflict them four hundred years; and also that nation, whom they shall serve, will I judge: and afterward shall they come out with great substance. But thou shalt go to thy fathers in peace; thou shalt be buried in a good old age. And in the fourth generation they shall come hither again; for the iniquity of the Amorite is not yet full. And it came to pass, that, when the sun went down, and it was dark, behold, a smoking furnace, and a flaming torch that passed between these pieces" (Gen. 15:7–17).

26. "And God said unto Abraham, And as for thee, thou shalt keep my covenant, thou, and thy seed after thee throughout their generations. This is my covenant, which ye shall keep, between me and you and thy seed after thee: every male among you shall be circumcised. And ye shall be circumcised in the flesh of your foreskin; and it shall be a token of a covenant betwixt me and you. And he that is eight days old shall be circumcised among you, every male throughout your generations, he that is born in the house, or bought with money of any foreigner that is not

covenant with Abraham and his descendants. We consider its distinguishing traits, unique significance for Abraham, and remarkable relation to Messiah's posterity.

Five Distinguishing Traits of Circumcision

✦ Circumcision is Symbolic: "it is a token" (17:11)

The word translated *"token"* in Genesis 17:11 is אוֹת, which means *"sign," "symbol,"* or *"distinguishing mark."* The token symbolizes God's pledge. It is the visible reminder of God's pledge. Thus, God equates his pledge with its token: "This is my covenant which ye shall keep.... Every male among you shall be circumcised" (Gen. 17:10). Jesus speaks the same way of the cup as the token of the new covenant: "This cup *is* the new covenant in my blood." Stephen confirms the symbolic nature of circumcision: "And he gave him *the covenant of circumcision*: and so Abraham begat Isaac, and circumcised him the eighth day" (Acts 7:8). He speaks of "the covenant of circumcision," a genitive of apposition, which means, "the covenant that is circumcision." Further, in Romans 4:11 Paul calls circumcision a sign, σημειον, which means *"token,"* or *"symbol."* He also uses a genitive of apposition, the *"sign of circumcision,"* the *"sign that is circumcision."* Thus Paul confirms its symbolic nature.

✦ Circumcision is Obligatory: "which you shall keep" (17:10)

This is notably different from the rainbow. Both are tokens of divine pledges. Yet God produces the rainbow without human agency, whereas men perform circumcision in obedience to God. God's token comes into existence only through human hands. God intimately combines a *certain* divine pledge with *necessary* human compliance. Thus, the human partakers can incur guilt and judgment in connection with God's pledge: "And the uncircumcised male who is not circumcised in the flesh of his foreskin, that soul shall be cut off from his people, *he has broken my covenant*" (Gen. 17:14). Men can *"keep"* or *"break"* God's pledge, because the token requires human obedience and because the token is identified with the pledge.

---

of thy seed. He that is born in thy house, and he that is bought with thy money, must needs be circumcised: and my covenant shall be in your flesh for an everlasting covenant. And the uncircumcised male who is not circumcised in the flesh of his foreskin, that soul shall be cut off from his people; he hath broken my covenant" (Gen. 17:9–14).

✦ Circumcision is Personal: "in the flesh of your foreskin" (17:11)

Abraham's physical posterity carry the token of God's pledge on their bodies, on their privy member, in a secret place, hidden from the gaze of the world at large. The token of this pledge is not external to them, like the rainbow, but part of them. In comparison with the partakers of the Noahic covenant, this heightens their personal attachment to God's pledge. Possibly God locates this token on the procreative faculties of Abraham and his descendants because the promises of this pledge focus on the blessing of his posterity.

✦ Circumcision is Indispensable: "that soul shall be cut off" (17:14)

Thus, unless a physical descendant of the patriarchs is circumcised, he has no right or title to the promises of this covenant, but will be cut off from the society of its partakers. Failure to bear the token of God's pledge is grounds for disinheritance and banishment from the community of this covenant. The descendants are passive (eight days old) as far as bearing this token is concerned. Yet without it, they will be "cut off" from the community of heirs.

✦ Circumcision is Commemorative: "this is my covenant" (17:10)

As the rainbow visibly reminded God of his promise, "no more flood" (Gen. 9:14–16), so circumcision reminds him of his promises to bless Abraham and his posterity. Abraham's circumcision commemorated God's promise to make him the father of a multitude of nations. The circumcision of the Patriarch's physical posterity reminded God of his promises to make them his people, give them Canaan as their inheritance, and bless them with fecundity and victory.

The Unique Significance of Circumcision for Abraham[27]

God designs this token to suit Abraham for his unique role in redemptive history as the father of all believers, whether Gentile of Jew. Paul affirms that this token has a special significance for Abraham. It was a "seal of the righteousness of faith" that he had while still uncircumcised. The word translated "seal" is σφραγις, which means an "authenticating mark." Thus,

---

27. "And he received the sign of circumcision, a seal of the righteousness of the faith which he had while he was in uncircumcision; that he might be the father of all them that believe, though they be in uncircumcision, that righteousness might be reckoned unto them; and the father of circumcision to them who not only are of the circumcision, but who also walk in the steps of that faith of our father Abraham which he had in uncircumcision" (Rom. 4:11–12).

Abraham's circumcision confirmed Abraham's already extant faith. Plainly this significance does not pertain to his physical posterity. Many physical descendants never have faith. Elect descendants confess faith after their circumcision, not before.

The Relation of Circumcision to Messiah's Posterity

As the physical descendant of the Patriarchs, Jesus was circumcised (Luke 2:21). His circumcision was a visible reminder to God of his promise to make him the means of global spiritual blessing through the gospel. But he had no physical children to circumcise. How does circumcision relate to Jesus' spiritual posterity? In light of its indispensability (Gen. 17:14), how can Gentile believers be Abraham's heirs unless they are circumcised? Such questions occasioned significant controversy in the apostolic church (Acts 15:1, 24). The apostles plainly declared that it was not necessary to circumcise Gentile believers in order to include them in the society of Abraham's spiritual children, Christian Israel.

Christian Israel is a spiritual posterity, and as such, is marked by a spiritual circumcision. Jesus' spiritual children have all been spiritually circumcised in their souls. Their circumcision is not made with human hands. Their circumcision involves "putting off the body of the flesh," the regeneration of their hearts. Their circumcision is the work of Christ, by his Holy Spirit.[28] The society of those with circumcised hearts, not circumcised bodies, is the society that pleases God and hears his commendation.[29] Yet, the concept of heart circumcision did not originate with the apostles. God promised that one day he would make heart circumcision the distinguishing trait of his people.[30] God fulfills this promise through the new covenant with Jesus' posterity. The Lord also warns Hebrew Israel that they need to have

---

28. "In whom ye were also circumcised with a circumcision not made with hands, in the putting off of the body of the flesh, in the circumcision of Christ; having been buried with him in baptism, wherein ye were also raised with him through faith in the working of God, who raised him from the dead. And you, being dead through your trespasses and the uncircumcision of your flesh, you, I say, did he make alive together with him, having forgiven us all our trespasses" (Col. 2:11–13).

29. "For he is not a Jew who is one outwardly; neither is that circumcision which is outward in the flesh: but he is a Jew who is one inwardly; and circumcision is that of the heart, in the spirit, not in the letter; whose praise is not of men, but of God" (Rom. 2:28–29); "For we are the circumcision, which worship God in the Spirit, and rejoice in Christ Jesus, and have no confidence in the flesh" (Phil. 3:3).

30. "And Jehovah thy God will circumcise thine heart, and the heart of thy seed, to love Jehovah thy God with all thine heart, and with all thy soul, that thou mayest live" (Deut. 30:6).

their hearts circumcised, not just their bodies. He threatens to punish all of Abraham's physical posterity who live and die with uncircumcised hearts.[31]

Conclusion: Two Circumcisions, Two Posterities
Circumcision is a covenantal sign and initiatory rite that distinguishes Abraham and his posterity from the rest of mankind. It consists of a change in the secret place. Scripture presents two circumcisions: physical circumcision, a change in the secret place of the body, and spiritual circumcision, a change in the secret place within, the heart. It also presents two posterities. Abraham has a physical posterity, issued to him through the Patriarchs, composed of his physical descendants. He also has a spiritual posterity, issued to him through the Messiah, composed of his spiritual children. His patriarchal posterity is circumcised in body, his Messianic posterity in heart. Paul calls each posterity, *Israel*. Abraham's physical seed are *Hebrew* Israel; his spiritual children *Christian* or *Messianic* Israel:

> "But it is not as though the word of God hath come to naught. For they are not all Israel, that are of Israel: neither, because they are Abraham's seed (σπερμα), are they all children (τεκνα)" (Rom. 9:6–7).

All of his physical seed are not his spiritual children (Rom. 9:7). All of his spiritual children are not his physical seed (Gal. 3:29). God elected a remnant of his physical seed to be his spiritual children (Rom. 11:5, 7). God made the Mosaic (old) covenant with Hebrew Israel, the new covenant with Christian Israel. These circumcisions are related symbolically. Circumcision of body pictures circumcision in heart. Thus, this token points Hebrew Israel to the spiritual reality that their hearts must morally change in order to receive the gospel blessing of Abraham. Sometimes heart circumcision depicts the divine agency in moral renewal, regeneration (Deut. 30:6), sometimes the human agency, repentance and faith (Deut. 10:16; Jer. 4:4). Thus God promises that he will circumcise the hearts of his people, and yet, calls unconverted Jews to circumcise their stiff-necked hearts by repenting of their sins and believing in Jehovah.

---

31. "Behold, the days come, says Jehovah, that I will punish all them which are circumcised in their uncircumcision; Egypt, and Judah, and Edom, and the children of Ammon, and Moab, and all that are in the utmost corners, that dwell in the wilderness: for all these nations are uncircumcised, and all the house of Israel are uncircumcised in the heart" (Jer. 9:25–26).

The Historical Fulfillment of the Abrahamic Covenant

The promises of this covenant focus on Abraham, the Patriarchs, and the Messiah. We present their fulfillment accordingly.

The Fulfillment of the Pledge to Abraham: Father of a Multitude

God fulfills this pledge to Abraham through Hagar, Keturah, and Sarah. Scripture affirms that God fulfills this promise through Ishmael, the sons of Keturah, Esau, Jacob, and Jesus.

Ishmael (Gen. 17:20, 21:13, 25:12–18)[32]

God fulfills this promise through Ishmael, his twelve princes, and the nation descended from him. This explains why Ishmael was circumcised. His circumcision was a visible reminder of God's pledge to make him a great nation because he was Abraham's descendant.

Sons of Keturah: Midianites

> And Abraham took another wife, and her name was Keturah. And she bare him Zimran, and Jokshan, and Medan, and Midian, and Ishbak, and Shuah. And Jokshan begat Sheba, and Dedan. And the sons of Dedan were Asshurim, and Letushim, and Leummim. And the sons of Midian: Ephah, and Epher, and Hanoch, and Abida, and Eldaah. All these were the children of Keturah. And Abraham gave all that he had unto Isaac. But unto the sons of the concubines, that Abraham had, Abraham gave gifts. And he sent them away from Isaac his son, while he yet lived, eastward, unto the east country (Gen. 25:1–6).

> And the children of Israel did evil in the sight of the LORD: and the LORD delivered them into the hand of Midian seven years.... And the Midianites and the Amalekites and all the children of the east lay along in the valley like grasshoppers for multitude; and their camels were without number, as the sand by the sea side for multitude (Judg. 6:1, 7:12).

---

32. "And Abraham said unto God, Oh that Ishmael might live before thee!... And as for Ishmael, I have heard thee: behold, I have blessed him, and will make him fruitful, and will multiply him exceedingly; twelve princes shall he beget, and I will make him a great nation" (Gen. 17:18, 20); "And also of the son of the handmaid will I make a nation, because he is thy seed" (Gen. 21:13).

Moses provides further details about the posterity of Jokshan (Gen. 25:3) and Midian (Gen. 25:4). Jokshan's posterity, Sheba and Dedan, seem to attain to a national identity (Job 6:19; Ps. 72:10; 1 Kings 10:1; Isa. 60:6; Ezek. 38:13). Scripture also speaks of Midian as a powerful nation, with a large army, princes, and kings that both tempted and oppressed Israel (Num. 25:18, 31:8; Judg. 6:1, 7:12). Thus, God also fulfilled this promise to Abraham though the sons of Keturah and the nations descended from them.

Esau or Edom (Gen. 36:1–43)

> Now these are the generations of Esau (the same is Edom).... And Esau took his wives, and his sons, and his daughters, and all the souls of his house, and his cattle, and all his beasts, and all his possessions, which he had gathered in the land of Canaan; and went into a land away from his brother Jacob. For their substance was too great for them to dwell together; and the land of their sojournings could not bear them because of their cattle. And Esau dwelt in mount Seir: Esau is Edom. And these are the generations of Esau the father of the Edomites in mount Seir.... And these are the kings that reigned in the land of Edom, before there reigned any king over the children of Israel...these are the chiefs of Edom, according to their habitations in the land of their possession. This is Esau, the father of the Edomites (Gen. 36:1, 6–9, 31, 43).

God also fulfills this promise when Esau develops into the nation of Edom.

Jacob: Israel and Judah

Plainly, God fulfills this promise when Jacob develops into the nations of Israel and Judah.

Jesus: Spiritual Nation of Believers

> the sign of circumcision, a seal of the righteousness of the faith which he had while he was in uncircumcision; that he might be the father of all them that believe, though they be in uncircumcision, that righteousness might be reckoned unto them.... For this cause it is of faith, that it may be according to grace; to the end that the promise may be sure to all the seed; not to that only which is of the law, but to that also which is of the faith of Abraham, who is the father of us all (as it is written, A father of many nations have I made thee) (Rom. 4:11, 16–17).

Paul states explicitly that Abraham is the father of all who believe in Christ (Rom. 4:11, 16). Further, Christ's posterity is a great nation (1 Pet. 2:9, 10). Paul says explicitly that this nation of believers fulfills the promise made to Abraham that he would be the father of many nations (Rom. 4:17).

The Fulfillment of the Pledge to the Patriarchs

The Promise of Theocracy (Gen. 17:7, 8)[33]

Scripture affirms clearly that God fulfills the promise of theocracy when he redeems Israel from Egypt, enters the Mosaic covenant with them, and gives them Canaan (Exod. 6:6–8; Deut. 29:12–13). The Mosaic covenant founds the theocratic society of Hebrew Israel.

The Promise of Canaan (Gen. 15:18–21)

In Exodus 6:6–8 Scripture says explicitly that God fulfills this promise when Israel enters the land of Canaan.[34] This fulfillment sheds light on the prophecy of Genesis 15:13–14. As predicted, they sojourned in a foreign land. That land was Egypt. As predicted, they were afflicted in that land. They endured the many rigors and horrors of slavery. As predicted, God emancipated them with judgments. He brought ten plagues on the Egyptians and overthrew their army in the Red Sea. As·predicted, they went out with great substance. They despoiled the Egyptians. As predicted, the time of their affliction in Egypt was some four centuries. In Joshua 21:43 Scripture confirms that God fulfilled this promise in Joshua's conquest and allotment of Canaan.[35] Yet, Joshua did not completely remove the Canaanites from the

---

33. "Wherefore say unto the children of Israel, I am Jehovah, and I will bring you out from under the burdens of the Egyptians, and I will rid you out of their bondage, and I will redeem you with an outstretched arm, and with great judgments: and I will take you to me for a people, and I will be to you a God; and ye shall know that I am Jehovah your God, who brings you out from under the burdens of the Egyptians. And I will bring you in unto the land which I swore to give to Abraham, to Isaac, and to Jacob; and I will give it you for a heritage: I am Jehovah" (Exod. 6:6–8); "that you may enter into the covenant of Jehovah thy God, and into his oath, which Jehovah thy God makes with thee this day; that he may establish thee this day unto himself for a people, and that he may be unto thee a God, as he spoke unto thee, and as he swore unto thy fathers, to Abraham, to Isaac, and to Jacob" (Deut. 29:12–13).

34. "And I have also established my covenant with them, to give them the land of Canaan, the land of their sojournings, wherein they sojourned…and I will take you to me for a people, and I will be to you a God; and ye shall know that I am Jehovah your God, who brings you out from under the burdens of the Egyptians. And I will bring you in unto the land which I swore to give to Abraham, to Isaac, and to Jacob; and I will give it you for a heritage: I am Jehovah" (Exod. 6:4, 7–8).

35. "So Jehovah gave unto Israel all the land which he swore to give unto their fathers; and they possessed it, and dwelt therein" (Josh. 21:43).

land. The process of subduing the land continued until the days of David and Solomon, when the conquest was completed (1 Kings 4:21).[36] Solomon ruled over all the land that God promised Abraham, from the river of Egypt to the river Euphrates. Thus Nehemiah looks back on this entire panorama and says that God faithfully fulfilled his promise to give Canaan to Israel (Neh. 9:8).[37] In 2 Kings 13:23 God says that he bears patiently with their many provocations and keeps them in their land because he remembers this pledge to their fathers.[38] In Leviticus 26:41-45 Scripture contemplates Israel in captivity. God promises that in fulfillment of this pledge he will bring a remnant of Israel back to Canaan. God kept his promise. After seventy years of exile he restored his people to Canaan.[39]

Psalm 105 is an inspired meditation on the fulfillment of this promise of Canaan. It tells the story in detail. It calls God's people to remember God's glorious work in fulfilling this promise, to talk of it, to sing praise to him, to glory in his holy name, and to seek the Lord and his strength forever (Ps. 105:1–45).[40]

---

36. "And Solomon ruled over all the kingdoms from the River unto the land of the Philistines, and unto the border of Egypt: they brought tribute, and served Solomon all the days of his life" (1 Kings 4:21).

37. "You are Jehovah the God, who did choose Abram, and brought him forth out of Ur of the Chaldees, and gave him the name of Abraham, and found his heart faithful before you, and made a covenant with him to give the land of the Canaanite, the Hittite, the Amorite, and the Perizzite, and the Jebusite, and the Girgashite, to give it unto his seed, and have performed your words; for you are righteous" (Neh. 9:7, 8).

38. "Jehovah was gracious unto them, and had compassion on them, and had respect unto them, because of his covenant with Abraham, Isaac, and Jacob, and would not destroy them, neither cast he them from his presence as yet" (2 Kings 13:23).

39. "Brought them into the land of their enemies: if then their uncircumcised heart be humbled, and they then accept of the punishment of their iniquity; then will I remember my covenant with Jacob; and also my covenant with Isaac, and also my covenant with Abraham will I remember; and I will remember the land. And yet for all that, when they are in the land of their enemies, I will not reject them, neither will I abhor them, to destroy them utterly, and to break my covenant with them; for I am Jehovah their God; but I will for their sakes remember the covenant of their ancestors, whom I brought forth out of the land of Egypt in the sight of the nations, that I might be their God: I am Jehovah" (Lev. 26:41–45).

40. "He has remembered his covenant for ever, The word which he commanded to a thousand generations, The covenant which he made with Abraham, And his oath unto Isaac, And confirmed the same unto Jacob for a statute, To Israel for an everlasting covenant, Saying, Unto thee will I give the land of Canaan, The lot of your inheritance.... And he brought forth his people with joy, And his chosen with singing. And he gave them the lands of the nations; And they took the labor of the peoples in possession" (Ps. 105:8–11, 43–44).

The Promise of Fecundity (Gen. 26:4, 28:14)

Scripture affirms that God fulfills this promise in the days of Joshua (Deut. 10:22; Neh. 9:23) and Solomon (1 Kings 4:20).[41] The Lord associates material prosperity with this fecundity. Great fecundity coupled with poverty would be an affliction rather than a blessing (Deut. 7:12, 13, 8:18).[42]

The Promise of Victory (Gen. 22:17)

Again, Scripture says explicitly that God fulfilled this promise in Joshua's conquest of Canaan (Josh. 21:44; Neh. 9:24)[43] and in the victories of David that eventuated in the rest Israel enjoyed in the reign of Solomon (1 Kings 4:24, 25, 5:4).[44]

The Fulfillment of the Pledge to the Messiah

The Promise of Theocracy (Gen. 17:7)

As God fulfilled this foundational promise to Abraham's patriarchal posterity by entering the Mosaic covenant with them, so he fulfilled it to his Messianic posterity by entering the new covenant with them. Like he established Hebrew Israel as his people through Moses, so he established Christian Israel as his people through Jesus. When he made the new covenant he transformed

---

41. "Thy fathers went down into Egypt with threescore and ten persons; and now Jehovah thy God hath made thee as the stars of heaven for multitude" (Deut. 10:22); "Their children also you multiplied as the stars of heaven" (Neh. 9:23); "Judah and Israel were many as the sand which is by the sea in multitude, eating and drinking and making merry" (1 Kings 4:20).

42. "Because ye hearken to these ordinances, and keep and do them, that Jehovah thy God will keep with thee the covenant and the lovingkindness which he swore unto thy fathers: and he will love thee, and bless thee, and multiply thee; he will also bless the fruit of thy body and the fruit of thy ground, thy grain and thy new wine and thine oil, the increase of thy cattle and the young of thy flock, in the land which he swore unto thy fathers to give thee" (Deut. 7:12–13); "But thou shalt remember Jehovah thy God, for it is he that gives thee power to get wealth; that he may establish his covenant which he swore unto thy fathers, as at this day" (Deut. 8:18).

43. "And Jehovah gave them rest round about, according to all that he swore unto their fathers: and there stood not a man of all their enemies before them; Jehovah delivered all their enemies into their hand" (Josh. 21:44); "Their children also you multiplied as the stars of heaven, and brought them into the land concerning which you did say to their fathers, that they should go in to possess it. So the children went in and possessed the land, and you subdued before them the inhabitants of the land, the Canaanites, and gave them into their hands, with their kings, and the peoples of the land, that they might do with them as they would" (Neh. 9:23–24).

44. "For he had dominion over all the region on this side the River, from Tiphsah even to Gaza, over all the kings on this side the River: and he had peace on all sides round about him. And Judah and Israel dwelt safely, every man under his vine and under his fig-tree, from Dan even to Beer-sheba, all the days of Solomon…. But now Jehovah my God hath given me rest on every side; there is neither adversary, nor evil occurrence" (1 Kings 4:24–25, 5:4).

his people and transferred the privilege of theocratic society from Hebrew Israel to Christian Israel.[45] Jesus preached the gospel to Hebrew Israel and culled from them a society who listened to him, learned from him, and believed in him. The unbelievers in Hebrew Israel, who would not become disciples of Jesus, were cut off from God's people.[46] Jehovah Jesus instituted the new covenant with this believing remnant of Israel (Rom. 9:6–7; Heb. 8:8, 13). He thus established his disciples, his spiritual children, as God's people. Then he blessed Christian Israel with the Holy Spirit, gave them the Lord's Day, and grafted Gentile believers into this theocratic society of the new covenant. In this way God took the theocracy away from Hebrew Israel and made Messiah's posterity the people of God.[47]

The Promise of Divine Inheritance (Gen. 22:18)

Scripture tells us explicitly that God fulfills this promise when he blesses Gentiles and Jews spiritually through the gospel, granting to them repentance toward God and faith in Christ (Acts 3:25–26, 11:18; Phil. 1:29).[48] When they believe in Christ, God imputes to them the virtue of Christ (Gal. 3:8) and imparts to them the Spirit of Christ (Gal. 3:14).[49] In fulfillment of the Abrahamic covenant, God in Christ lavishes on believers every spiritual blessing as a first installment of their divine inheritance (Eph. 1:3, 13–14).[50] In its ultimate fulfillment God will give to Jesus and his posterity,

45. "Therefore say I unto you, The kingdom of God shall be taken away from you, and shall be given to a nation bringing forth the fruits thereof" (Matt. 21:43).

46. "Moses indeed said, A prophet shall the Lord God raise up unto you from among your brethren, like unto me. To him shall ye hearken in all things whatsoever he shall speak unto you. And it shall be, that every soul that shall not hearken to that prophet, shall be utterly destroyed from among the people" (Acts 3:22–23).

47. "But ye are an elect race, a royal priesthood, a holy nation, a people for God's own possession, that ye may show forth the excellences of him who called you out of darkness into his marvelous light: who in time past were no people, but now are the people of God: who had not obtained mercy, but now have obtained mercy" (1 Pet. 2:9–10).

48. "Unto you first God, having raised up his Servant, sent him to bless you, in turning away every one of you from your iniquities" (Acts 3:26).

49. "And the scripture, foreseeing that God would justify the Gentiles by faith, preached the gospel beforehand unto Abraham, saying, In thee shall all the nations be blessed" (Gal. 3:8); "that upon the Gentiles might come the blessing of Abraham in Christ Jesus; that we might receive the promise of the Spirit through faith" (Gal. 3:14).

50. "In whom ye also, having heard the word of the truth, the gospel of your salvation,— in whom, having also believed, ye were sealed with the Holy Spirit of promise, 14 which is an earnest of our inheritance, unto the redemption of God's own possession, unto the praise of his glory" (Eph. 1:13–14).

believers from every kindred, tribe, and tongue, his new heavens and earth as their eternal inheritance.[51]

The Promise of Fecundity (Gen. 22:17)

The posterity of Jesus will be innumerable, out of every nation, tribe, people, and tongue.[52] In every generation God will bring to faith and repentance many sinners from around the globe, and will guard them by faith unto complete salvation (1 Pet. 1:5). The gospel can never fail. Christ will see his seed. He will surely see fruit from his cross and be satisfied. He will justify many, not few (Isa. 53:10–11). He will continue to build his church, Christian Israel, in every generation until he returns (Matt. 16:18; Eph. 3:21).

The Promise of Victory (Gen. 22:17)

God grants victory and triumph to Jesus and his posterity through the gospel (2 Cor. 2:14–15).[53] Jesus reigns at God's right hand on David's throne with all authority in heaven and earth. Jesus and his posterity fight against sin, evil, suffering, death, and the devil. Jesus and his posterity will overcome all these enemies (Rom. 8:35–37; Rev. 17:14, 19:13–16). By faith Christians overcome the world (1 John 5:4–5). In heaven they overcome sin and suffering. By resurrection and transformation they overcome death (1 Cor. 15:55–57; 1 Thess. 4:13–17). In the new heavens and earth Christ and his posterity will totally vanquish every enemy. They will reign forever, permanently free from sin, suffering, temptation, evil, and death, in the ultimate fulfillment of the Abrahamic covenant.[54]

---

51. "For not through the law was the promise to Abraham or to his seed that he should be heir of the world, but through the righteousness of faith" (Rom. 4:13).

52. "After these things I saw, and behold, a great multitude, which no man could number, out of every nation and of all tribes and peoples and tongues, standing before the throne and before the Lamb, arrayed in white robes, and palms in their hands; and they cry with a great voice, saying, Salvation unto our God who sits on the throne, and unto the Lamb" (Rev. 7:9–10).

53. "But thanks be unto God, who always leads us in triumph in Christ, and makes manifest through us the savor of his knowledge in every place. For we are a sweet savor of Christ unto God, in them that are saved, and in them that perish" (2 Cor. 2:14–15).

54. "To show mercy towards our fathers, And to remember his holy covenant; The oath which he spoke unto Abraham our father, To grant unto us that we being delivered out of the hand of our enemies Should serve him without fear, In holiness and righteousness before him all our days" (Luke 1:72–75); "Who shall separate us from the love of Christ? shall tribulation, or anguish, or persecution, or famine, or nakedness, or peril, or sword?... Nay, in all these things we are more than conquerors through him that loved us" (Rom. 8:35, 37); "O death, where is thy victory? O death, where is thy sting? The sting of death is sin; and the power of

The diagram that follows illustrates this manifold fulfillment of the Abrahamic covenant.

FULFILLMENT OF THE ABRAHAMIC COVENANT

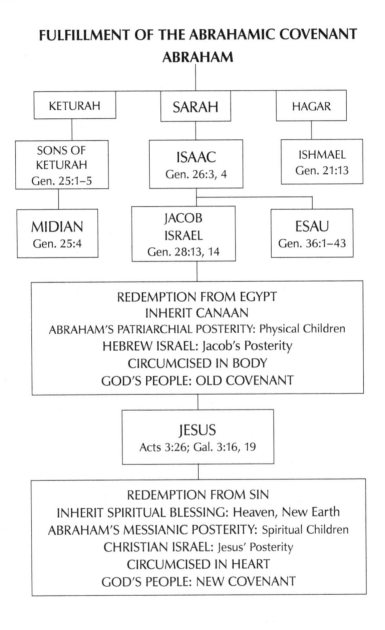

ABRAHAM

KETURAH	SARAH	HAGAR

SONS OF KETURAH Gen. 25:1–5	ISAAC Gen. 26:3, 4	ISHMAEL Gen. 21:13

MIDIAN Gen. 25:4	JACOB ISRAEL Gen. 28:13, 14	ESAU Gen. 36:1–43

REDEMPTION FROM EGYPT
INHERIT CANAAN
ABRAHAM'S PATRIARCHIAL POSTERITY: Physical Children
HEBREW ISRAEL: Jacob's Posterity
CIRCUMCISED IN BODY
GOD'S PEOPLE: OLD COVENANT

JESUS
Acts 3:26; Gal. 3:16, 19

REDEMPTION FROM SIN
INHERIT SPIRITUAL BLESSING: Heaven, New Earth
ABRAHAM'S MESSIANIC POSTERITY: Spiritual Children
CHRISTIAN ISRAEL: Jesus' Posterity
CIRCUMCISED IN HEART
GOD'S PEOPLE: NEW COVENANT

Practical Functions of the Abrahamic Covenant

First, it unifies and connects the divine redemptions of God's people. Second, it frames Christ's gospel reformation of God's people. Third, it strengthens the religious devotion of God's people. We now consider these important functions of the Abrahamic covenant for God's people.

The Abrahamic Covenant Unifies the Redemptions of God's People

All God does to redeem his people from Egypt and from sin he does in fulfillment of this covenant. There is only one people of God. Abraham is their father. They are Abraham's covenantal posterity. This posterity experiences two divine redemptions because it has two aspects, physical and spiritual. Thus, it displays duality and unity. We now consider Abraham's covenantal posterity. We unfold its identity, distinctive features, and redeemed societies.

The Identity of Abraham's Covenantal Posterity

One generic definition applies to both the physical and spiritual aspects of his covenantal posterity. Abraham's covenantal posterity is:

> Abraham's circumcised descendants issued to him through his God-given and elected heir, throughout successive generations.

This general definition applies to both Patriarchal and Messianic aspects of Abraham's covenantal posterity. Accordingly, we identify each aspect. Abraham's Patriarchal posterity consists in:

> Abraham's physical descendants, circumcised in body, issued to him through his patriarchal heirs, Isaac and Jacob, propagated by natural generation.

---

sin is the law: but thanks be to God, who gives us the victory through our Lord Jesus Christ" (1 Cor. 15:55–57); "For whatsoever is begotten of God overcomes the world: and this is the victory that hath overcome the world, even our faith. 5 And who is he that overcomes the world, but he that believeth that Jesus is the Son of God?" (1 John 5:4, 5); "These shall make war with the Lamb, and the Lamb shall overcome them: for he is Lord of lords, and King of kings: and they that are with him are called, and chosen, and faithful" (Rev. 17:14); "And he was clothed with a vesture dipped in blood: and his name is called The Word of God. And the armies which were in heaven followed him upon white horses, clothed in fine linen, white and clean. And out of his mouth goes a sharp sword, that with it he should smite the nations: and he shall rule them with a rod of iron: and he treads the winepress of the fierceness and wrath of Almighty God. And he hath on his vesture and on his thigh a name written, KING OF KINGS, AND LORD OF LORDS" (Rev. 19:13–16).

Abraham's Messianic posterity consists in:

Abraham's spiritual children, circumcised in heart, issued to him through his Messianic heir, Jesus, propagated by spiritual generation.

Three Distinctive Features of Abraham's Covenantal Posterity

First, God limits the covenantal inheritance to Abraham's circumcised descendants. Anyone not circumcised in body must be removed from the visible society of his patriarchal posterity (Gen. 17:14). Anyone not circumcised in heart must be removed from the visible society of his Messianic posterity (1 Cor. 5:1–13).

Second, God limits the covenantal inheritance to Abraham's circumcised descendants that issue to him through his God-given and elected heir. The patriarchal inheritance pertains to his God-given heir, Isaac, but not to Ishmael (Gen. 17:20–21). It pertains to his elected heir, Jacob, but not his twin brother Esau (Gen. 15:12–16). The Messianic inheritance pertains to one heir, the Messiah, who is both God-given and elect.

Third, God perpetuates the covenantal inheritance throughout successive generations. The patriarchal posterity propagates by natural generation, the Messianic by spiritual generation. Spiritual generation occurs through the gospel. Men procreate natural descendants. Only God creates spiritual descendants.

Two Redeemed Societies of Abraham's Covenantal Posterity

Each aspect successively becomes God's redeemed society, his theocratic nation in covenant with him. First, God redeemed from Egypt the patriarchal posterity, Hebrew Israel, and entered the Mosaic covenant with them. He thus gave them visible organization and form as the old covenant community. To them he revealed and entrusted the Old Testament. When Christ came, God redeemed from sin the Messianic posterity, Christian Israel (Gal. 3:29; 1 Cor. 11:23–26). He entered the new covenant with them and gave them visible organization and form as the new covenant community. To them he revealed the New Testament and entrusted the whole Bible.

Therefore, the Abrahamic covenant unifies the two redemptions of God's people and the two covenants God made with them when he redeemed them from Egypt and from sin. Thus, the two aspects of Abraham's covenantal posterity are connected symbolically. The patriarchal posterity pictures the

Messianic. They also stand connected organically. This organic connection is manifest in Christ's gospel reformation that spiritually transformed God's people.

The table below illustrates the symbolic connection of these two redeemed communities:

Corresponding Feature	Patriarchal Posterity	Messianic Posterity
Heir: God-given, elect:	Isaac, Jacob	Jesus
Circumcision	Physical, in body	Spiritual, in heart
Organic Perpetuation	Natural generation	Spiritual generation
Visible Covenantal Form	Old Covenant	New Covenant
Theocratic Nation	Hebrew Israel	Christian Israel

This unity in duality also characterizes the promises of the Abrahamic covenant. God couched promises in language suited to comprehend both aspects of Abraham's posterity. This perspective should keep us from undervaluing the religion of true believers under the Mosaic economy. Hebrew believers in Christ, during the old covenant era, not only received its patriarchal fulfillment, by faith they saw in that fulfillment the emblem of its Messianic fulfillment. The Spirit illuminated its significance to their faith, so that they not only enjoyed the natural inheritance, they also experienced the spiritual realities it signified. Their sins were forgiven, the law written on their hearts, and they knew the Lord.

The Abrahamic Covenant Frames Christ's Gospel Reformation

The Abrahamic covenant provides the framework for the spiritual transformation of God's people from Patriarchal Israel to Messianic Israel. There is one covenant with Abraham and his posterity, one gospel, one people of God, and one father of God's people, Abraham. Yet there are two covenants with God's people, old and new. By gospel reformation Christ spiritually transforms God's people from Hebrew Israel under the old covenant to Christian Israel under the new. He thus displays their organic unity and covenantal diversity. Some tend to stress diversity at the expense of unity, others unity at the expense of diversity. Let's walk the razor's edge of truth.

Christ's spiritual transformation of God's people is a threefold process that involves pruning, instituting, and engrafting. We introduce our study of this process with an *overview* of this gospel reformation and conclude with its *impact* on the life of God's people.

Introduction: An Overview of Christ's Gospel Reformation
We survey and summarize the witness of five texts.

First, in Matthew 21:43[55] Jesus speaks to the leaders of Hebrew Israel. They did not believe in him, listen to him, or learn from him as disciples. They rejected his claim to be their promised Savior and King, the Messiah. He told them that God would take his kingdom away from Hebrew Israel. God's people have the unique privilege, among all the nations of the earth, of having God as their King, Lawgiver, and Judge. This unique form of national government is *theocracy*, a kingdom in which God is King. There is only one theocracy, the society of God's people. When Jesus says that God will take his kingdom, the theocracy, away from Hebrew Israel, he means that they will no longer be his people. He also says that God will give his theocracy to another nation that will appreciate it. When God takes the theocracy from Hebrew Israel, he gives it to Christian Israel, the nation composed of Abraham's spiritual children circumcised in heart. Only such a nation can bear fruit worthy of the theocracy. Only such a nation can evangelically obey and please God.

Second, in Matthew 24:1–2, 34[56] Jesus foretells the destruction of the Jewish temple. He says it will happen in "this generation." His prediction came true. In that very generation Jerusalem was surrounded with armies, besieged, and destroyed. Their temple was demolished. The altar was desecrated. The priests after the order of Aaron and the sacrificial system associated with them have disappeared from the earth. It all happened in that generation, almost 2000 years ago, just as Jesus said.

Third, in Galatians 3:18–19[57] Paul says that God designed the old covenant, and all the institutions associated with it, to be temporary. He intended the entire Mosaic economy to end when the Messiah came. When

---

55. "Therefore say I unto you, The kingdom of God shall be taken away from you, and shall be given to a nation bringing forth the fruits thereof" (Matt. 21:43).

56. "His disciples came to him to show him the buildings of the temple. But he answered and said unto them, See ye not all these things? Verily I say unto you, There shall not be left here one stone upon another, that shall not be thrown down.... Verily I say unto you, This generation shall not pass away, till all these things be accomplished" (Matt. 24:1–2, 34).

57. "If the inheritance is of the law, it is no more of promise: but God granted it to Abraham by promise. What then is the law? It was added because of transgressions, till the seed should come to whom the promise has been made" (Gal. 3:18–19).

Messiah came, then God fulfilled the promise of Genesis 22:18. Then all nations began to experience spiritual blessing through the gospel. In the same generation God terminated the old covenant and its institutions.

Fourth, in Hebrews 8:13[58] the ratification of the new covenant makes the Mosaic covenant and its institutions old or obsolete. The writer says that the old covenant is close to disappearing from the earth. He confirms Jesus' words. He tries to persuade Hebrew Christians not to forsake the superior institutions of the new covenant in order to return inferior ones that were already almost gone.

Fifth, in Heb. 9:7–10[59] the writer says that God instituted the Aaronic priesthood, day of atonement, sacrificial system, Jewish tabernacle, and levitical requirements as earthly ordinances of limited duration. When Christ reformed theocratic society, he altered their worship accordingly.

In sum, Scripture teaches that Christ spiritually transforms his people by gospel reformation in the apostolic generation. His people under the old covenant were Abraham's patriarchal posterity. Under the new they are his Messianic posterity. Christ's coming signals the time of the new covenant and gospel reformation.

Jesus Prunes Hebrew Israel into Christian Israel[60]

As Moses mediated the old covenant, so Jesus mediates the new. John and Jesus preached to Hebrew Israel repentance and faith. God ordained that anyone who would not listen to Jesus and learn from him as his disciple should be removed from the society of his people. Jesus did not remove them by trying unbelieving Hebrews one by one and casting them out. Rather, he reorganized the theocratic society. From the ranks of Hebrew Israel, he called out Abraham's spiritual children and formed them into a visible

---

58. "In that he says, A new covenant he has made the first old. But that which is becoming old and waxes aged is nigh unto vanishing away" (Heb. 8:13).

59. "But into the second the high priest alone, once in the year, not without blood, which he offers for himself, and for the errors of the people: the Holy Spirit this signifying, that the way into the holy place has not yet been made manifest, while the first tabernacle is yet standing; which is a figure for the time present; according to which are offered both gifts and sacrifices that cannot, as touching the conscience, make the worshipper perfect, being only (with meats and drinks and divers washings) carnal ordinances, imposed until a time of reformation" (Heb. 9:7–10).

60. "Moses indeed said, A prophet shall the Lord God raise up unto you from among your brethren, like unto me. To him shall ye hearken in all things whatsoever he shall speak unto you. And it shall be, that every soul that shall not hearken to that prophet, shall be utterly destroyed from among the people" (Acts 3:22–23).

society that they alone had the right to join. That visible society of believing Hebrews is Abraham's Messianic posterity, circumcised in heart.

Jesus formed a visible society composed by right of a spiritual posterity. This introduced tension. Abraham's spiritual children are circumcised in heart. Yet only God can see the heart. Man looks on a credible profession of faith. Only God can infallibly discern genuine faith and heart circumcision. Therefore, this society has in it by right, only Abraham's spiritual children, but may have in it, at times, in fact, some of the devil's spiritual children, even though they don't belong.

John the Baptist formed a society of disciples marked by their repentance from sin.[61] He warned Hebrew Israel that simply being Abraham's physical descendant was not enough. He would only receive into his visible community of disciples those who brought forth fruits indicative of genuine gospel repentance. This is the very image of what Jesus does with a view to reforming and transforming Israel. He only admits into Christian Israel those who bring forth fruits indicative of genuine gospel repentance and faith.

John and Jesus both employed the same gospel method.[62] Jesus' reformation of Israel is evangelical. He preached the gospel, made disciples, and openly identified them with the society of his disciples. He instituted an ordinance closely bound to making disciples, Christian baptism. For this reason Scripture closely identifies Christian baptism with circumcision of heart (Col. 2:11–13). Only Abraham's spiritual posterity, circumcised in heart, has the right to enter the community of Jesus' disciples. When new disciples enter that society, they should be baptized. Therefore, no one should be baptized unless they have been circumcised in heart. This is why Paul assumes, in the judgment of charity, that the society of disciples in Colossae had experienced both circumcision of heart and Christian baptism: "you were circumcised with a circumcision not made with hands... having been buried with him in baptism."

In sum, all unbelievers in Hebrew Israel who would not hearken to Jesus' gospel ministry were broken off from God's people (Rom. 11:19). All that remained of Israel was a believing remnant circumcised both in body,

---

61. "They were baptized of him in the river Jordan, confessing their sins. But when he saw many of the Pharisees and Sadducees coming to his baptism, he said unto them, Ye offspring of vipers, who warned you to flee from the wrath to come? Bring forth therefore fruit worthy of repentance: and think not to say within yourselves, We have Abraham to our father: for I say unto you, that God is able of these stones to raise up children unto Abraham" (Matt. 3:6–9).

62. "Jesus was making and baptizing more disciples than John" (John 4:1).

and, by right, in heart. Thus, when Jesus reformed Israel, he organized a spiritual posterity into a visible society. Thus, like a magnet, he gathered Abraham's spiritual children into a visible society of disciples. He instituted an ordinance, Christian baptism, for entering that visible society (John 4:1–2). Thus Scripture intimately connects circumcision of heart with Christian baptism (Col. 2:11–13). Only those circumcised in heart should be admitted to Christian Israel. Yet men cannot discern the heart infallibly. Sometimes the devil's children may infiltrate this society of Christ's disciples. This anomaly must continue until Jesus glorifies his church and removes from it all hypocrites at his coming.

Christ Institutes the New Covenant with Christian Israel[63]
God promised he would make a new covenant with "the house of Israel" (Jer. 31:31). On the night before his death Jesus instituted this new covenant with Christian Israel, in fulfillment of this promise and the promise of Genesis 17:7. In this way he constituted Abraham's spiritual children, his Messianic posterity, as God's people and gave them the privilege of theocracy. Then he ratified the new covenant by shedding his own blood on the cross. Thus he accomplished the redemption of Christian Israel from their sins.

When God glorified Jesus he gave him the promised Spirit, the blessing promised to Abraham (Gal. 3:14).[64] In turn, Christ poured out this blessing on Christian Israel as the down payment of their inheritance under the new covenant (Rom. 4:13; Eph. 1:13-14).

In sum, God constituted Hebrew Israel as his people when he redeemed them from Egypt, made the old covenant with them, and gave them Canaan as their inheritance. Even so, Jehovah Jesus constituted Christian Israel as his people when he made the new covenant with them, redeemed them from sin, and gave them the Spirit as their inheritance. Thus, Christian Israel under the new covenant was—for a time—composed only of those circumcised in body and, by right, in heart. They multiplied evangelically as God added to them day by day those that were being saved (Acts 2:47).

This displays the organic unity of the people of God. Messiah did not form his posterity independently. Rather, he formed them as a remnant of Hebrew Israel according to the election of grace (Rom. 11:5, 7). Thus, God

---

63. "And the cup in like manner after supper, saying, This cup is the new covenant in my blood, even that which is poured out for you" (Luke 22:20).
64. "Being therefore by the right hand of God exalted, and having received of the Father the promise of the Holy Spirit, he has poured forth this, which you see and hear" (Acts 2:33).

does not simultaneously have two independent and separate peoples, one descended from the Patriarchs physically, and the other from the Messiah spiritually. God removed unbelievers from Hebrew Israel when they refused to become Jesus' disciples. They were no longer included in God's people under the new covenant even though they still participated in the institutions of the old covenant.

God in Christ Engrafts Gentile Believers into Christian Israel

We again survey and summarize the testimony of five texts.

First, in Acts 15:5, 24[65] Luke records that the gospel conversion of Gentiles caused controversy in Christian Israel. Some erroneously said it was necessary to Judaize them in order to incorporate them into the society of God's people under the new covenant. The apostles deliberated the issue and concluded that Gentile Christians did not need to be circumcised and keep the book of the law in order to belong to Christian Israel.

Second, in Romans 11:19–20, 23[66] Paul affirms that God incorporated believing Gentiles into the people of God, Christian Israel under the new covenant. Conversely, he removed unbelieving Hebrews from his people. Yet, when Hebrew Israelites repent and believe the gospel, God reunites them with his people under the new covenant (11:23).

Third, in 1 Corinthians 11:26, Paul instructs the church in Corinth about the Lord's Supper: "For as often as ye eat this bread, and drink the cup, you proclaim the Lord's death till he come." That local church was composed largely of Gentile Christians. Yet that church clearly participated in the token of the new covenant, which Jesus instituted with Christian Israel. Thus, that church belonged to Christian Israel. What pertained to that local church also pertains to every local church. All genuine churches belong to Christian Israel under the new covenant. Thus, all genuine Christian churches may and should partake of the Lord's Supper.

---

65. "Certain of the sect of the Pharisees who believed, saying, It is needful to circumcise them, and to charge them to keep the law of Moses.... Forasmuch as we have heard that certain who went out from us have troubled you with words, subverting your souls; to whom we gave no commandment" (Acts 15:5, 24).

66. "You will say then, Branches were broken off, that I might be grafted in. Well; by their unbelief they were broken off, and you stand by your faith. Be not highminded, but fear.... And they also, if they continue not in their unbelief, shall be grafted in: for God is able to graft them in again" (Rom. 11:19–20, 23).

Fourth, in Ephesians 2:11–13, 19,[67] Paul says explicitly that Gentile Christians were once separate from the covenants and the commonwealth of Israel. That was before they heard and believed the gospel. Now they are no longer afar off. Now they are near to God through Christ's blood. Now they are no longer strangers but fellow citizens of the theocratic society, Christian Israel.

Fifth, in 1 Peter 2:9–10[68] Peter tells Gentile believers that now they are God's people. Once they were no people at all. Now they are a holy nation consecrated to God's glory. A spiritual transformation has taken place. Now they are God's special possession, designed as a people to display God's excellence.

The following diagram illustrates the evangelical reformation and spiritual transformation of God's people:

PRUNING	INSTITUTING	ENGRAFTING
Hebrew Israel	Christian Israel: Abraham's Messianic Posterity	
Old Covenant	New Covenant	

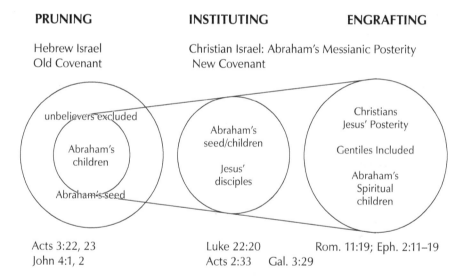

| Acts 3:22, 23 | Luke 22:20 | Rom. 11:19; Eph. 2:11–19 |
| John 4:1, 2 | Acts 2:33   Gal. 3:29 | |

---

67. "Remember that once you, the Gentiles in the flesh, who are called Uncircumcision by that which is called Circumcision, in the flesh, made by hands; that you were at that time separate from Christ, alienated from the commonwealth of Israel, and strangers from the covenants of the promise, having no hope and without God in the world. But now in Christ Jesus you that once were far off are made nigh in the blood of Christ.... So then you are no more strangers and sojourners, but you are fellow-citizens with the saints, and of the household of God" (Eph. 2:11–13, 19).

68. "You are an elect race, a royal priesthood, a holy nation, a people for God's own possession...who in time past were no people, but now are the people of God: who had not obtained mercy, but now have obtained mercy" (1 Pet. 2:9–10).

In sum, Christian Israel is the society of Abraham's spiritual children. It is now composed of an elect remnant of his physical descendants joined with his other spiritual children who are not his physical seed (Acts 15:5; Gal. 3:29; Eph. 2:11–19; 1 Pet. 2:9, 10). In this way God spiritually transforms his people in fulfillment of the promises of the Abrahamic covenant. Thus he took his theocracy away from Hebrew Israel and gave it to Christian Israel (Matt. 21:43).

Conclusion: The Impact of Christ's Gospel Reformation

Thus, in the apostolic generation God's old covenant with his people passed away with its features, regulation, and institutions (Matt. 24:1–3, 34; Gal. 3:16–19; Heb. 8:13). These include: (1) its religious service and devotion: the priesthood (Heb. 7:11–12), the day of atonement (Heb. 9:7–10), the temple (Matt. 24:1–3, 34), the set feasts (Col. 2:16–17), and the sacrifices (Heb. 10:18); (2) its theocratic constitution, the book of the law, with its ceremonial and civil statutes (Heb. 7:11–12); (3) its covenantal tokens, the Jewish Sabbath (Col. 2:16–17) and physical circumcision (Gal. 6:15–16); and (4) its covenantal inheritance, the land of Canaan.

In that very generation Jehovah Jesus ratified his new covenant with his people with its features, regulation, and institutions. These include: (1) its religious service and devotion: the royal priesthood (Heb. 7:1–28; 1 Pet. 2:5), the spiritual sacrifices of praise and giving (Heb. 13:15–16), its appointed place of worship, the spiritual temple, the Christian church (Eph. 2:19–22), and appointed time of worship, the Lord's Day (1 Cor. 16:1–2); (2) its theocratic constitution, the New Testament, the Bible; (3) its covenantal tokens, baptism and the Lord's Supper (John 4:1–2; 1 Cor. 11:23–25); and (4) its covenantal inheritance, the Holy Spirit (Gal. 3:14; Eph. 1:13–14), heaven, and the new heavens and earth (Rom. 4:13).

The table on the following page sums and illustrates the impact of Christ's gospel reformation and spiritual transformation of God's people:

COVENANTAL DISTINCTIVE	Abraham's Patriarchal Posterity Hebrew Israel	Abraham's Messianic Posterity Christian Israel
1 Divine Redemption	From Egypt	From sin
2 Saved Community Covenant	Mosaic (old) covenant	New covenant
3 Divine Inheritance	Canaan	Spirit, heaven, new heaven and earth
4 Covenantal Worship		
Who: priesthood	Aaronic priests: high, other priests	Royal priests: Jesus, believers
What: sacrifices	Day of atonement, levitical sacrifices	Christ's atonement, spiritual sacrifices
When: appointed time	Set feasts	Lord's Day
Where: appointed place	Tabernacle, temple	Christian church
5 Covenantal tokens		
Abrahamic {Messianic}	Physical circumcision	{Heart circumcision, baptism, Lord's Supper}
Mosaic / New	Jewish Sabbath	Lord's Supper
6 Theocratic Constitution	Book of Law	New Testament, Bible
7 Organic Perpetuation	Physical descendants and generation	Spiritual descendants and generation

One dimension of this impact calls for special attention. I refer to the perpetual possession of Canaan as a divine inheritance:

"I will give unto thee and to thy seed after thee the land of their sojournings, all the land of Canaan for an everlasting possession; and I will be their God" (Gen. 17:8).

In light of this testimony of Scripture, the question arises: Is the land of Canaan the perpetual inheritance of God's people? I offer five considerations in answer to this question.

First, God has already given to Hebrew Israel all the land that he promised to give them (1 Kings 4:21; Neh. 9:8).

Second, Hebrew Israel, as a society, is no longer God's theocratic nation (Matt. 21:43). In Genesis 17:8, Scripture explicitly connects possessing Canaan with being God's people. They possessed it as God's people. Yet they are no longer the theocratic nation of God's people. Possessing Canaan as divine inheritance lasted only as long as Hebrew Israel, as a society, remained God's theocratic nation.

Third, the old covenant inheritance, Canaan, was inseparably joined to the book of the law (Lev. 25:10). Joshua allotted Canaan to Hebrew Israel by tribes. They were to retain their possession by genealogical records. The year of jubilee recognizes and perpetuates this allocation of Canaan (Lev. 25:10). It is impossible to keep the year of Jubilee in Germany, or the United States, or in any other land. Canaan is the land of the book of the law. Conversely, the book of the law is the law of the land of Canaan. Plainly, God's people are no longer under the book of the law as their theocratic constitution. Therefore, the land of Canaan is no longer the divine inheritance of God's people under the new covenant.

Fourth, God has already given his people the down payment of their better, new covenant inheritance (Eph. 1:13–14).

Fifth, its description as "everlasting" was also applied to other temporary institutions. The word, עוֹלָם, translated "everlasting" in Genesis 17:8, literally means, "until the distant future." Often it does signify forever and ever (Deut. 33:27; Ps. 90:2), but not always. Context must determine its duration. Scripture uses this very word to describe the duration of the Day of Atonement (Lev. 16:34) and of the Aaronic priesthood (Exod. 29:28, 40:15).[69] Scripture indicates explicitly that these other old covenant institutions terminate with the coming of Messiah. His coming is their vanishing point, the end of the age. Similarly, in Genesis 17:8, עוֹלָם signifies "until the distant future, throughout the entire era of Hebrew Israel's theocracy." That era lasted a very long time, some fifteen-hundred years, until the promised Messiah came to institute the new covenant.

In conclusion, Scripture does not teach that the land of Canaan is the perpetual inheritance of God's people. I neither assert nor deny the right of Hebrew Israel to possess Canaan today. If they retain any right to Canaan, that right does not rest on theocracy, since they are no longer God's theocratic society. Rather, any such right would grow out of the general principles of justice that apply to all territorial disputes among nations.

---

69. "And thou shalt anoint them, as thou didst anoint their father, that they may minister unto me in the priest's office: for their anointing shall surely be an everlasting (עוֹלָם) priesthood throughout their generations" (Exod. 40:15); "And this shall be an everlasting (עוֹלָם) statute unto you, to make an atonement for the children of Israel for all their sins once a year. And he did as the LORD commanded Moses" (Lev. 16:34).

The Abrahamic Covenant Strengthens Religious Devotion

I use religious devotion in a broad sense to refer to faith and religious service. We consider five ways that it strengthens God's people in their experiential religion. The Abrahamic covenant enhances religious devotion because it portrays Christ and his saving work, commends faith, identifies and encourages the church, incites praise to God, and assures of God's love and fidelity.

The Abrahamic Covenant Portrays Christ and His Work

It reveals that the Christ is Abraham's descendant, who conveys global spiritual blessing through the gospel (Gen. 22:18). It thus declares that redemption is spiritual and evangelical. Further, God remarkably designed the lives of the Patriarchs, Abraham, Isaac, and Jacob, so that each would furnish a picture of their heir, Jesus Christ. This patriarchal collage reveals at least five characteristics of Christ's person and work. Christ's redemptive commission is: global (Abraham), supernatural and sacrificial (Isaac), and sovereign and organic (Jacob).

Like Abraham, Christ is the father of a multi-national posterity that is innumerable. Abraham's posterity includes physical and spiritual descendants. His physical descendants formed the nations of Ishmael, Midian, Edom, Israel, and Judah. His spiritual descendants are the nation of believers. So also Christ is the father of a great multitude of spiritual descendants from every nation. Thus, redemption is global.

Like Isaac, Christ is Abraham's supernaturally conceived heir, offered by his Father. Isaac was supernaturally conceived when God restored procreative ability to his parents in their old age. His father offered him when he was willing to sacrifice him in obedience to God. So also Christ was miraculously conceived in the womb of a virgin. Thus, redemption is supernatural, because Christ was conceived supernaturally. So also Christ's Father offered him as a sacrifice to atone for sin. Thus, redemption is sacrificial. Christ accomplished redemption from sin by the blood of his cross.

Like Jacob, Christ is the chosen heir of Abraham, whose posterity becomes theocratic society, Israel. God elected Jacob to be Abraham's covenantal heir, not his twin brother Esau (Rom. 9:13). So also Christ is God's chosen, his elect, in whom his soul delights (Isa. 42:1). Thus also Jesus' spiritual children are God's elect, chosen in Christ before the foundation of the world. Thus, redemption is sovereign. Further, Jacob became Israel, God's theocracy. Jacob's posterity became Hebrew Israel under the old covenant.

So also Christ became God's theocratic nation and his posterity became Christian Israel under the new covenant.[70] Thus, redemption is organic. In every generation God redeems Christ's spiritual descendants propagated by spiritual generation. Their spiritual generation occurs through the general and effectual gospel call.

In sum, the first way the Abrahamic covenant enhances religious devotion is by revealing to God's people Christ and his redemptive work. It displays that redemption in Christ is spiritual, evangelical, global, supernatural, sacrificial, sovereign, and organic. It calls God's people to fix their gaze on Christ and his work. In this way it strengthens them in their faith and religious service.

The Abrahamic Covenant Commends Faith in Christ

It portrays faith in Christ as the distinctive trait of Abraham's gospel heirs. God ordered Abraham's life to make him the father of all believers, who walk in the footsteps of his faith. Abraham exercised faith when God called him (Gen. 12:1–3),[71] promised him his heir (Gen. 15:1–21),[72] gave him his heir (Gen. 17:1–21),[73] and proved him regarding his heir (Gen. 22:1–18).[74] As faith in Christ distinguished Abraham, so also it uniquely marks his spiritual children, whether Hebrew or Gentile (Rom. 4:11–12; Gal. 3:6–7).

---

70. "Behold, my servant, whom I uphold; my chosen, in whom my soul delights: I have put my Spirit upon him; he will bring forth justice to the Gentiles" (Isa. 42:1); "and he said unto me, Thou art my servant; Israel, in whom I will be glorified" (Isa. 49:3); "When Israel was a child, then I loved him, and called my son out of Egypt" (Hos. 11:1); "And he arose and took the young child and his mother by night, and departed into Egypt; and was there until the death of Herod: that it might be fulfilled which was spoken by the Lord through the prophet, saying, Out of Egypt did I call my son" (Matt. 2:14–15).

71. "By faith Abraham, when he was called, obeyed to go out unto a place which he was to receive for an inheritance; and he went out, not knowing whither he went" (Heb. 11:8).

72. "For what says the scripture? And Abraham believed God, and it was reckoned unto him for righteousness" (Rom. 4:3).

73. "Who in hope believed against hope, to the end that he might become a father of many nations, according to that which had been spoken, So shall thy seed be. And without being weakened in faith he considered his own body now as good as dead (he being about a hundred years old), and the deadness of Sarah's womb; yet, looking unto the promise of God, he wavered not through unbelief, but waxed strong through faith, giving glory to God, and being fully assured that what he had promised, he was able also to perform" (Rom. 4:18–21).

74. "By faith Abraham, being tried, offered up Isaac: yea, he that had gladly received the promises was offering up his only begotten son; even he to whom it was said, In Isaac shall thy seed be called: accounting that God is able to raise up, even from the dead; from whence he did also in a figure receive him back" (Heb. 11:17–19).

Like their father Abraham, his spiritual children by faith respond to their gospel call, receive justification, inherit promises, and endure proving.

+ Abraham's Spiritual Children Respond to their Gospel Call by Faith
As Abraham by faith obeyed when he was called, so do his spiritual children, when Christ calls them through the gospel. Jesus states plainly that when some Hebrews respond in unbelief to his ministry, they display that they are not Abraham's children, but the devil's children. Abraham's children act like Abraham. They obey Christ by faith. They receive Christ by faith. Christ's words have free course in them. They rejoice to see Christ's day, just like Abraham.[75]

+ Abraham's Spiritual Children Experience Justification by Faith
As God justified Abraham by faith alone, so also he justifies his spiritual children by faith alone, whether Gentile or Hebrew. By faith alone, God accepts them, pardons them, and imputes righteousness to them, just as he did to Abraham.[76]

+ Abraham's Spiritual Children Inherit Promises by Faith
Abraham inherited and received the promise of his heir by faith (Rom. 4:18–21). So also, his spiritual children inherit their promises by faith. Paul affirms that Abraham's gospel heirs at their conversion receive the promise of the Spirit by faith.[77] The writer of Hebrews exhorts professing Christians to follow Abraham's example of inheriting promises by faith.[78] Peter

---

75. "I know that ye are Abraham's seed: yet ye seek to kill me, because my word has not free course in you. I speak the things which I have seen with my Father: and ye also do the things which ye heard from your father. They answered and said unto him, Our father is Abraham. Jesus says unto them, If ye were Abraham's children, ye would do the works of Abraham.... You are of your father the devil, and the lusts of your father it is your will to do" (John 8:37–39, 44).

76. "And the scripture, foreseeing that God would justify the Gentiles by faith, preached the gospel beforehand unto Abraham, saying, In thee shall all the nations be blessed. So then they that are of faith are blessed with the faithful Abraham" (Gal. 3:8–9); "And be found in him, not having mine own righteousness, which is of the law, but that which is through the faith of Christ, the righteousness which is of God by faith" (Phil. 3:9).

77. "That the blessing of Abraham might come on the Gentiles through Jesus Christ; that we might receive the promise of the Spirit through faith" (Gal. 3:14).

78. "That ye be not slothful, but followers of them who through faith and patience inherit the promises" (Heb. 6:12).

affirms that by faith Christians inherit the complete salvation in heaven and at Christ's return.[79]

◆ Abraham's Spiritual Children Endure Proving by Faith

As God proved Abraham so he proves his spiritual children. As Abraham endured his proving by faith, so also do his spiritual children. By faith they remain steadfast in their afflictions and persecutions (2 Thess. 1:4). By faith they hold fast their confession of Christ until the end of their lives (Heb. 10:38–39). By faith their tribulations and temptations produce steadfastness rather than bitterness in their hearts (James 1:3). By faith they endure all their trials and receive honor at Christ's return (1 Pet. 1:7).[80]

In sum, the second way the Abrahamic covenant enhances devotion is by commending faith to God's people. It calls them to trust God and Christ, not their own works. It calls them to wait on God. It encourages them to look to God to fulfill their hope and grant the desire of their hearts. Thus, it strengthens faith and devotion.

The Abrahamic Covenant Identifies and Comforts the Church

◆ The Abrahamic Covenant Identifies the Church

Paul says to the churches of Galatia: "and if you are Christ's, then you are Abraham's seed." Most of the Christians in Galatia were Gentiles, not Hebrews. Clearly they were not Abraham's physical descendants. Yet, since they belong to Christ, Abraham's heir, they are Abraham's spiritual children. Thus, the churches of Galatia, viewed collectively (Gal. 1:13, 22), were the visible society of Abraham's spiritual children.[81] What was true of them is true of all genuine churches. Thus, the churches of Christ in every generation and location constitute the visible society of a spiritual posterity, of Abraham's spiritual children. Thus, Paul says of the church in Philippi: "we are

---

79. "Receiving the end of your faith, even the salvation of your souls" (1 Pet. 1:9).

80. "So that we ourselves glory in you in the churches of God for your patience and faith in all your persecutions and tribulations that ye endure" (2 Thess. 1:4); "But my righteous one shall live by faith: And if he shrink back, my soul hath no pleasure in him. But we are not of them that shrink back unto perdition; but of them that have faith unto the saving of the soul" (Heb. 10:38–39); "Knowing this, that the trying of your faith works patience" (James 1:3); "That the trial of your faith, being much more precious than of gold that perishes, though it be tried with fire, might be found unto praise and honor and glory at the appearing of Jesus Christ" (1 Pet. 1:7).

81. "Paul…and all the brethren that are with me, unto the churches of Galatia…. And if you are Christ's, then you are Abraham's seed, heirs according to promise" (Gal. 1:1, 2, 3:29).

the circumcision."[82] Most Christians in Philippi were Gentiles and never were physically circumcised. How can they be *the circumcision?* They were circumcised, not in their bodies, but in their hearts. Thus, they were the visible society of Abraham's spiritual children, circumcised in heart. Again, Paul says of the church in Colossae: "you were also circumcised with a circumcision not made with hands." He tells them that once they were dead in the uncircumcision of their flesh, but God made them alive. When Christ circumcised their hearts he resurrected them from spiritual death and gave them spiritual life. Christ regenerated them by the Holy Spirit and put off the body of the flesh. Thus, the church in Colossae was a society of Abraham's spiritual children, circumcised in heart.[83]

Now consider how the church, which is Messianic Israel under the new covenant, differs radically from Hebrew Israel. God exhorted Hebrew Israel to "circumcise their hearts" (Deut. 10:16; Jer. 4:4). Why? The majority of them were "uncircumcised in heart" (Jer. 9:26). So Stephen reproved Hebrew Israel: "You stiff-necked and uncircumcised in heart and ears, you do always resist the Holy Spirit: as your fathers did, so do you" (Acts 7:51). Paul does not exhort these churches to "circumcise their hearts." Rather, he says that their hearts "have been circumcised." Under the old covenant, God's people were the visible society of Abraham's physical children circumcised in body. Under the new covenant, they are the visible society of his spiritual children, circumcised in heart. Thus the Abrahamic covenant discloses the lofty identity of the church.

Now if the church is the visible society of Abraham's spiritual children, and, if his spiritual children walk in the footsteps of his faith, then the church must be the visible society of those who believe in Christ. Scripture declares explicitly and repeatedly that this is so. The apostles exhorted Christ's disciples to "continue in the faith." They organized them into churches and commended those churches to the Lord on "whom they

---

82. "Paul and Timothy, servants of Christ Jesus, to all the saints in Christ Jesus that are at Philippi, with the bishops and deacons.... For we are the circumcision, which worship God in the Spirit, and rejoice in Christ Jesus, and have no confidence in the flesh" (Phil. 1:1, 3:3).

83. "In whom ye were also circumcised with a circumcision not made with hands, in the putting off of the body of the flesh, in the circumcision of Christ; having been buried with him in baptism, wherein ye were also raised with him through faith in the working of God, who raised him from the dead. And you, being dead through your trespasses and the uncircumcision of your flesh, you, I say, did he make alive together with him, having forgiven us all our trespasses" (Col. 2:11–13).

believed." Thus, those churches were visible societies of believers.[84] In Acts 16:5 Luke writes: "And thus were the churches established in the faith, and increased in number daily." Thus, those churches were visible societies of believers. Again, Paul tells the church in Philippi that God granted them "on behalf of Christ" to believe.[85] Clearly that church was a visible society of believers. He also tells the church of the Thessalonians that he remembers their "work of faith" constantly. He even declares that he has confidence in their eternal election because the gospel came to them powerfully.[86] Thus, faith in Christ distinguishes the church of Christ, because it is the visible society of Abraham's spiritual children.

◆ The Abrahamic Covenant Comforts the Church

Now that we have seen the lofty way that the Abrahamic covenant identifies the church, consider with me how this encourages God's people in their faith and devotion. Paul says that since the church is the society of Abraham's spiritual children, it is the society of "heirs according to the promise" (Gal. 3:29). He says that the visible society of those circumcised in heart worships by God's Spirit, rejoices in Christ, and has no confidence in the flesh (Phil. 3:3). He says that they have been forgiven all their trespasses (Col. 2:13). He says that God, on behalf of Christ, has granted them the privileges of believing in Christ and of suffering as Christians (Phil. 1:29). He says that God has chosen them for salvation in Christ before the foundation of the world (1 Thess. 1:4). Surely, these realities encourage God's people and comfort them in their earthly trials and struggles.

In sum, the third way the Abrahamic covenant enhances religious devotion is by identifying and comforting the church. It displays that the church is the visible society of Abraham's spiritual children who believe in Christ. It calls God's people to value and appreciate their lofty identity and its

---

84. "Confirming the souls of the disciples, exhorting them to continue in the faith, and that through many tribulations we must enter into the kingdom of God. And when they had appointed for them elders in every church, and had prayed with fasting, they commended them to the Lord, on whom they had believed" (Acts 14:22–23).

85. "Paul and Timothy, servants of Christ Jesus, to all the saints in Christ Jesus that are at Philippi, with the bishops and deacons...because to you it has been granted in the behalf of Christ...to believe on him" (Phil. 1:1, 29).

86. "Paul, and Silvanus, and Timothy, unto the church of the Thessalonians in God the Father and the Lord Jesus Christ...remembering without ceasing your work of faith...knowing, brethren beloved of God, your election, how that our gospel came not unto you in word only, but also in power, and in the Holy Spirit, and in much assurance" (1 Thess. 1:1, 3–5).

benefits. It calls them to consider how their identity enhances their fellow-ship with God and with each other. In this way it strengthens their faith and religious service.

The Abrahamic Covenant Incites Praise to the Lord

Scripture exhorts God's people under the old covenant to consider how God fulfilled the Abrahamic covenant. It encourages them to tell of the marvel-ous works by which God fulfilled this covenant and gave them Canaan as their inheritance. It incites them to rejoice in God, praise God, sing to God, boast in God and his work, and to seek God's face always (1 Chron. 16:7–18; Ps. 105:1–11).[87]

Now if Abraham's physical posterity should thank and praise God for blessing them with Canaan, how much more should his spiritual children praise him, rejoice and boast in him, seek him, and declare his glorious work among the nations? If Hebrew Israel should bless him for Canaan, how much more should Christian Israel bless him for the spiritual blessing of Abraham in Christ, and for our hope of heaven and eternal glory? David looked forward to such a time:

> Declare his glory among the nations, his marvelous works among all the peoples.... Let the heavens be glad, and let the earth rejoice; And let them say among the nations, Jehovah reigns.... And say ye, Save us, O God of our salvation, And gather us together and deliver us from the nations, To give thanks unto thy holy name, And to triumph in thy praise (1 Chron. 16:24, 31, 35).

In sum, the Abrahamic covenant also enhances religious devotion by inciting God's people to consider its fulfillment and respond in love, praise, joy, prayer, proclamation, and grateful service.

---

87. "Then on that day did David first ordain to give thanks unto Jehovah, by the hand of Asaph and his brethren. O give thanks unto Jehovah, call upon his name; Make known his doings among the peoples. Sing unto him, sing praises unto him; Talk ye of all his marvelous works. Glory ye in his holy name; Let the heart of them rejoice that seek Jehovah. Seek ye Jehovah and his strength; Seek his face evermore. Remember his marvelous works that he hath done, His wonders, and the judgments of his mouth, O ye seed of Israel his servant, Ye children of Jacob, his chosen ones. He is Jehovah our God; His judgments are in all the earth. Remember his covenant for ever, The word which he commanded to a thousand generations, The covenant which he made with Abraham, And his oath unto Isaac, And confirmed the same unto Jacob for a statute, To Israel for an everlasting covenant, Saying, Unto thee will I give the land of Canaan, The lot of your inheritance" (1 Chron. 16:7–18).

The Abrahamic Covenant Assures of God's Love and Fidelity
Finally, this divine pledge assures its heirs of God's love and faithfulness. The writer of Hebrews focuses on the Messiah and the spiritual blessing that he dispenses to believers from every nation. He says that God made this pledge in order to show its heirs, Abraham's spiritual children, the immutability of his plan of salvation. He did this to give them "strong encouragement." This oath gives to Christians the strongest possible assurance of God's infinite love that designed salvation and impeccable faithfulness that performs it.[88]

We have considered the essential features, historical fulfillment, and practical functions of the Abrahamic covenant. Everything else we study rests on this remarkable divine pledge. We consider God's covenantal commitments with Abraham's patriarchal posterity in the Mosaic and Davidic covenants. We consider his covenantal obligations to his Messianic posterity in the new and Messianic covenants. May God be pleased to bless this study for his glory and for the good of his people.

---

88. "For when God made promise to Abraham, since he could swear by none greater, he swore by himself, saying, Surely blessing I will bless thee, and multiplying I will multiply thee. And thus, having patiently endured, he obtained the promise. For men swear by the greater: and in every dispute of theirs the oath is final for confirmation. Wherein God, being minded to show more abundantly unto the heirs of the promise the immutability of his counsel, interposed with an oath; that by two immutable things, in which it is impossible for God to lie, we may have a strong encouragement, who have fled for refuge to lay hold of the hope set before us" (Heb. 6:13–18).

The Mosaic Covenant

"If ye will obey my voice indeed, and keep my covenant, then ye shall be mine own possession from among all peoples…a kingdom of priests, and a holy nation."
—EXODUS 19:5–6

Introduction: Overview of the Biblical Testimony

As with the Abrahamic covenant, the witness of Scripture to the Mosaic covenant is massive. Further, it involves large sections of Scripture, as well as individual verses. For these reasons, to present this material clearly and concisely poses a significant challenge. Scripture discloses five major categories of thought: its biblical foundations, essential features, historical fruition, distinctive form, and practical functions. One text epitomizes this testimony:

> And Moses went up unto God, and Jehovah called unto him out of the mountain, saying, Thus shalt thou say to the house of Jacob, and tell the children of Israel: Ye have seen what I did unto the Egyptians, and how I bare you on eagles' wings, and brought you unto myself. Now therefore, if ye will obey my voice indeed, and keep my covenant, then ye shall be mine own possession from among all peoples: for all the earth is mine: and ye shall be unto me a kingdom of priests, and a holy nation. These are the words that you shall speak unto the children of Israel (Exod. 19:3–6).

First, this text presents its biblical foundation, divine redemption from Egypt: "Ye have seen what I did unto the Egyptians, and how I bare you on eagles' wings, and brought you unto myself. *Now therefore*, if you will obey."

Second, it introduces its essential features: its mediator, Moses, "These are the words *that you shall speak*"; its partakers, Hebrew Israel, "speak unto *the children of Israel*"; its promise, theocracy, "*then you shall be mine own possession* from among all peoples...and you shall be unto me a kingdom of priests, and a holy nation"; and its condition, gospel obedience to God's voice, "*if you will obey my voice indeed,* and keep my covenant." The context further unfolds its initial institution at Sinai in five large sections of Scripture: (1) Exod. 20:3–17; (2) Exod. 21:1–23:33; (3) Exod. 24:1–12; (4) Exod. 25:1–30:34; (5) Exod. 31:12–18. These passages enlarge its condition and disclose its ratification, religious service, and token.

Thus, from Exodus 19:3–6 and its larger context, I observe seven features of the Mosaic covenant: (1) its mediator, Moses (Exod. 19:3, 6); (2) its partakers, Hebrew Israel (Exod. 19:3, 6); (3) its promise, theocracy (Exod. 19:5, 6); (4) its condition, obey God's voice (Exod. 19:5, 20:3–17) and keep the book of ordinances (Exod. 21:1–23:33, 24:8); (5) its ratification with blood, affirmation, communion meal, and attestation (Exod. 24:1–12; 31:18); (6) its religious service in the tabernacle (Exod. 25:1–27:21) and the priesthood (Exod. 28:1–30:34); and (7) its token, the Hebrew Sabbath (Exod. 31:12–17).

Third, this text discloses its distinctive form: "*if ye will obey my voice indeed,* and keep my covenant, *then ye shall be mine own possession.*" The Mosaic covenant was *conditional.* Thus, we consider its conditional form and resultant characteristics.

Fourth, Scripture reveals the historical fruition of this conditional pledge. This massive witness includes at least fifty texts.[1] These texts tell a remarkable story of divine blessing, judgment, restoration, rejection, and transformation. We consider this fruition before we take up its conditional form.

Fifth, Scripture reveals its practical functions: Ps. 103:17–18; Rom. 3:1–2, 19–20, 9:4–5; 1 Cor. 5:8, 9:9–11, 10:1–11. These texts highlight its role in redemptive history and for religious experience.

We now unfold the foundations, features, fruition, form, and functions of the Mosaic covenant.

---

1. OT: (1) Deut. 30:1–6; (2) Josh. 7:10–12, 15; (3) 23:15, 16; (4) Judg. 2:1–3; (5) 2:18–23; (6) 1 Kings 8:9, 21; (7) 11:11; (8) 19:9–10; (9) 2 Kings 17:15; (10) 18:11–12; (11) 23:2–3, 21; (12) 2 Chron. 34:30–32; (13) Ezra 1:2–4; (14) Pss. 25:10; (15) 44:17–22; (16) 78:8–10, 37–38; (17) 103:17–18; (18) Jer. 11:1–11; (19) 14:19–22; (20) 22:8–9; (21) 31:32; (22) 34:13–22; (23) Ezek. 17:16–19; (24) Hos. 8:1; (25) Mal. 2:10, 11: NT: (1) Matt. 21:43; (2) 23:34–38; (3) 27:25; (4) 27:37; (5) John 1:11–12; (6) Acts 7:51–53; (7) Rom. 2:14–15; (8) 3:1,2; (9) 3:19–20; (10) 3:31; (11) 4:13–15; (12) 5:13–14, 20; (13) 9:4–5; (14) 10:3–4; (15) 13:8–10; (16) Gal. 3:17–19; (17) 3:23–24; (18) 1 Thess. 2:14–16; (19) Heb. 7:11–12; (20) 8:7–10; (21) 8:13, 9:1; (22) 9:4; (23) 9:10; (24) 9:15–20; (25) 10:1–4.

The Biblical Foundations of the Mosaic Covenant

Introduction: the Overarching Foundation

We begin with God's redemptive acts on which this covenant rests. God acts with supernatural power on behalf of Israel in fulfillment of his covenant with Abraham, Isaac, and Jacob. This is the overarching foundation of the Mosaic covenant.[2] In faithfulness God redeems Israel from Egypt. In faithfulness he makes them his people. He does so through this Mosaic covenant, beginning at Sinai, concluding at Moab (Deut. 29:12–13). In faithfulness God preserves his people in the wilderness and brings them to Canaan. In faithfulness God bequeaths Canaan to his people for their inheritance. Thus, this covenant rests on the foundation of divine redemption, preservation, and inheritance, all in divine faithfulness.

The Mosaic Covenant Rests on Divine Redemption from Egypt

Out of compassion God redeems them from slavery and oppression and enters this covenant with them (Exod. 19:4). Thus God's love for them should motivate them to comply. God calls for gospel obedience, out of gratitude to their Redeemer. This underscores the evangelical nature of the Mosaic covenant. God enters this covenant with a redeemed people that he rescued, not from bondage to sin and wrath, but from bondage to slavery in Egypt. Thus their response of ingratitude and disobedience displays the hardness of the human heart. It proclaims that men despise even the richest blessings of God's common grace.

The Mosaic Covenant Rests on Divine Preservation in the Wilderness

Out of love, like that of a father for his children, God preserved them in the wilderness for forty years by his supernatural power.[3] He fed them with

---

2. "And I appeared unto Abraham, unto Isaac, and unto Jacob, as God Almighty; but by my name Jehovah I was not known to them. And I have also established my covenant with them, to give them the land of Canaan, the land of their sojournings, wherein they sojourned. And moreover I have heard the groaning of the children of Israel, whom the Egyptians keep in bondage; and I have remembered my covenant. Wherefore say unto the children of Israel, I am Jehovah, and I will bring you out from under the burdens of the Egyptians, and I will rid you out of their bondage, and I will redeem you with an outstretched arm, and with great judgments: and I will take you to me for a people, and I will be to you a God; and ye shall know that I am Jehovah your God, who brings you out from under the burdens of the Egyptians. And I will bring you in unto the land which I swore to give to Abraham, to Isaac, and to Jacob; and I will give it you for a heritage: I am Jehovah" (Exod. 6:3–8).

3. "And thou shalt remember all the way which Jehovah thy God hath led thee these forty years in the wilderness, that he might humble thee, to prove thee, to know what was in thy

manna. He gave them water from rock in a barren land. He miraculously preserved their clothing. He did this to teach them their complete dependence on him. He did this to prepare them for living in Canaan, with food, flocks and vineyards. He preserved them in want to protect them from pride when they lived in prosperity. He warned them never to forget that God gave them all their wealth, and that they always depend on God for life, breath, and everything.

The Mosaic Covenant Rests on Divine Inheritance of Canaan
When God bestows on Hebrew Israel the land of Canaan, he enters this covenant with them.[4] God gives to his people generously. They inherit divine blessings that they never earned or merited. Thus, this covenant rests on his favor, generosity, and unmerited provision. This underscores its graciousness.

In sum, we should never wrench the Mosaic covenant from its biblical foundations, or portray it as an evil advocate of works religion. Its foundations reveal that it was evangelical, beneficial, and gracious.

The Essential Features of the Mosaic Covenant

Introduction
God instituted this pledge with the wilderness generations of Hebrew Israel. Its institution began at Mount Sinai soon after they entered the wilderness, with those that experienced firsthand divine redemption from Egypt (Exod. 19–31). While they abode at Sinai, God enlarged this pledge. From the

---

heart, whether thou wouldest keep his commandments, or not And he humbled thee, and suffered thee to hunger, and fed thee with manna, which thou knewest not, neither did thy fathers know; that he might make thee know that man doth not live by bread only, but by everything that proceeds out of the mouth of Jehovah does man live. Thy raiment waxed not old upon thee, neither did thy foot swell, these forty years. And thou shalt consider in thy heart, that, as a man chastens his son, so Jehovah thy God chastens thee. And thou shalt keep the commandments of Jehovah thy God, to walk in his ways, and to fear him" (Deut. 8:2–6); "who led thee through the great and terrible wilderness, wherein were fiery serpents and scorpions, and thirsty ground where was no water; who brought thee forth water out of the rock of flint; who fed thee in the wilderness with manna, which thy fathers knew not; that he might humble thee, and that he might prove thee, to do thee good at thy latter end" (Deut. 8:15–16).

4. "And it shall be on the day when ye shall pass over the Jordan unto the land which Jehovah thy God giveth thee, that thou shalt set thee up great stones, and plaster them with plaster: and thou shalt write upon them all the words of this law, when thou art passed over; that thou mayest go in unto the land which Jehovah thy God giveth thee, a land flowing with milk and honey, as Jehovah, the God of thy fathers, has promised thee" (Deut. 27:2–3).

tabernacle he spoke additional ordinances, blessings, and curses. In Leviticus Scripture records this enlargement. These statutes and ordinances further define its religious service and condition (Lev. 1–25, 27). The blessings and curses in Leviticus 26 enhance its conditional promise. God further enlarged the book of the covenant as they journeyed in the wilderness for forty years. In Numbers Scripture records quite a few additions to its condition and religious service. God concluded institution in Moab with those that received firsthand divine inheritance in Canaan.[5] In Deuteronomy 29:1, Moses reflects on all he has written. He describes the content of Deuteronomy as: "the words of the covenant." He distinguishes divine covenanting at Moab from the covenant he made forty years earlier at Horeb with the "emancipation generation." This is because God ratified the Mosaic covenant anew with the "inheritance generation." Yet these two ratifications do not dedicate radically different covenants, because the essential features of this covenant remain unchanged. These ratifications have the same partakers, mediator, promise, condition, religious service, and token. In Moab God reiterated, enlarged, re-dedicated, and perpetuated the covenant he first ratified at Sinai. He provided additions, especially to its theocratic laws and dedication rites, but not a radically different covenant. Similarly, when our founding fathers added the Bill of Rights, they did not invalidate our Constitution, but added to it.

Seven large sections of Scripture unfold its completed institution at Moab: (1) Deut. 4:1–11:32; (2) Deut. 12:1–26:19; (3) Deut. 27:1–26; (4) Deut. 28:1–68; (5) Deut. 29:9–29; (6) Deut. 30:1–10; (7) Deut. 31:19–32:43. These passages enhance this pledge in various ways: (1) Moses confirms the covenant at Sinai with its condition, the Decalogue, and motivates them to gospel obedience (4:1–11:32); (2) he completes its condition, the book of the law (12:1–26:15) and confirms its foundational promise of theocracy (26:16–19); (3) he commands its final ratification in Canaan with a commemoration (27:1–13) and sanctions (27:14–26); (4) he enlarges its conditional promise with blessings (28:1–14) and curses (28:15–68); (5) he highlights that its partakers are successive generations of Hebrew Israel (29:9–29); and he concludes its ratification in Moab with (6) a prophecy (30:1-10) and with (7) two additional witnesses, the book of the law (31:24–26) and the song of Moses (31:19, 22 , 30, 32:1–44).

---

5. "These are the words of the covenant which Jehovah commanded Moses to make with the children of Israel in the land of Moab, besides the covenant which he made with them in Horeb" (Deut. 29:1).

As we expound each essential feature of this pledge, we consider the contribution of the initial institution at Sinai recorded in Exodus and Leviticus, of the ongoing institution in the wilderness recorded in Numbers, and of the completed institution at Moab recorded in Deuteronomy. We now expound its mediator, partakers, promises, condition, ratification, religious service, and token.

The Mediator of the Mosaic Covenant: Moses, with angels
When God covenanted with Abraham, he spoke to him directly. Yet he spoke directly to Moses and sent Moses to convey his covenantal promise to Israel (Exod. 19:3, 6).[6] When God spoke the Ten Commandments with his own voice to Israel, they requested that Moses would speak with them on God's behalf (Exod. 20:19; Deut. 5:5).[7] Thus, God spoke to Moses the content of his book of ordinances, and Moses told them what God required (Exod. 24:4–7). God also told Moses to inform Israel that the weekly Sabbath was the token of his pledge with them (Exod. 31:13).[8] God also gave Moses the witness to this covenant, the tables of stone, to dispense on his behalf to Israel (Exod. 24:12, 31:18). In these ways Moses acted as a mediator between God and Israel. Thus, God instituted the old covenant with his people through the mediation of Moses (John 1:17). As the mediator of this divine covenant, Moses acted as a very special prophet (Num. 12:6–8; Acts 7:37–38).[9] God spoke to him, not in dreams or visions, but plainly: "And Jehovah spoke unto Moses face to face, as a man speaks to his friend" (Exod. 33:11).

---

6. "Thus shalt thou say to the house of Jacob.... These are the words which thou shalt speak unto the children of Israel" (Exod. 19:3, 6).

7. "And they said unto Moses, Speak thou with us, and we will hear; but let not God speak with us, lest we die" (Exod. 20:19); "I stood between Jehovah and you at that time, to show you the word of Jehovah: for ye were afraid because of the fire, and went not up into the mount" (Deut. 5:5).

8. "Speak thou also unto the children of Israel, saying, Verily ye shall keep my sabbaths: for it is a sign between me and you throughout your generations" (Exod. 31:13).

9. "And he said, Hear now my words: if there be a prophet among you, I Jehovah will make myself known unto him in a vision, I will speak with him in a dream. My servant Moses is not so; he is faithful in all my house: with him will I speak mouth to mouth, even manifestly, and not in dark speeches; and the form of Jehovah shall he behold: wherefore then were ye not afraid to speak against my servant, against Moses?" (Num. 12:6–8); "For the law was given through Moses; grace and truth came through Jesus Christ" (John 1:17); "This is that Moses, who said unto the children of Israel, A prophet shall God raise up unto you from among your brethren, like unto me. This is he that was in the church in the wilderness with the angel that spoke to him in the Mount Sinai, and with our fathers: who received living oracles to give unto us" (Acts 7:37–38).

In Galatians 3:19 Paul indicates that angels were also involved in this ordination of the law.[10] Several texts confirm and underscore this angelic role.[11] When the Old Testament records the institution of this pledge in Exodus 19–20, it does not explicitly mention angels. Yet in Exodus 3:2, Scripture connects the angel of Jehovah with God's communications to Moses in Sinai: "And the angel of Jehovah appeared unto him in a flame of fire out of the midst of a bush: and he looked, and, behold, the bush burned with fire, and the bush was not consumed." The rest of the passage mentions only that Jehovah appeared to him and repeatedly spoke to him (Exod. 3:3–4:17). Yet Scripture indicates plainly that the angel "spoke to him" on Sinai (Acts 7:38). How do we put this together? One fact helps, namely, that the angel of Jehovah is Jehovah. He is the divine messenger, Jehovah, sent from Jehovah, to bring the Word of Jehovah. This divine Person himself eventually came to earth and became human in order to save his people from their sins (Matt. 1:21; John 1:1, 14). Thus, even the Mosaic covenant was mediated through God the Word, who appeared to Moses as the angel of Jehovah and spoke the words of the old covenant to him.

Scripture also speaks of a plurality of angels (Acts 7:53; Gal. 3:19; Heb. 3:2). The angel of Jehovah appeared in such a way that Moses saw a bush burning but not consumed. Similarly, when God spoke the Decalogue directly to Israel, supernatural signs accompanied his words: "And all the people perceived the thunderings, and the lightnings, and the voice of the trumpet, and the mountain smoking: and when the people saw it, they trembled, and stood afar off" (Exod. 20:18). This similarity directs us to attribute these miraculous signs to the activity of angels. Scripture contrasts the old covenant spoken with the activity of angels with the new covenant spoken by God the Son (Heb. 2:2–3). Angels attested God's law by supernatural sights and sounds. The Son incarnate attests God's gospel with a display of his supernatural power over creation, demons, and death itself.

---

10. "What then is the law? It was added because of transgressions, till the seed should come to whom the promise hath been made; and it was ordained through angels by the hand of a mediator" (Gal. 3:19).

11. "This is he that was in the assembly in the wilderness with the angel that spoke to him in the Mount Sinai, and with our fathers: who received living oracles to give unto us" (Acts 7:38); "ye who received the law as it was ordained by angels, and kept it not" (Acts 7:53); "if the word spoken through angels proved steadfast, and every transgression and disobedience received a just recompense of reward; how shall we escape, if we neglect so great a salvation? which having at the first been spoken through the Lord" (Heb. 2:2–3).

The Partakers of the Mosaic Covenant: Hebrew Israel
Its partakers are the physical children of the Patriarchs, circumcised in body. They are God's redeemed heirs, redeemed from slavery in Egypt, heirs of the homeland of Canaan. They are God's special people, the only theocratic society. We consider their original generation, successive generations, and the final generation.

The Original Partakers: The Wilderness Generation(s)
The wilderness generation, due to its rebellion, displays both continuity and diversity. There is continuity in Joshua and Caleb. They experienced first-hand both divine redemption from Egypt and divine inheritance in Canaan. There is also diversity. Most of the men that God redeemed from Egypt perished in their unbelief in the wilderness. Their children, who inherited Canaan, were either minors or yet unborn when God redeemed their fathers from Egypt. As God instituted the Abrahamic covenant at various seasons of his life, so he instituted the Mosaic covenant throughout their wilderness wanderings (Jer. 31:32). He began its institution at Sinai (Exod. 19:3, 6; Deut. 5:2–3) and concluded it in Moab (Deut. 26:17–19, 29:1, 9–13). Thus its original partakers are the wilderness generations of Hebrew Israel.[12]

---

12. "And Moses went up unto God, and Jehovah called unto him out of the mountain, saying, Thus shalt thou say to the house of Jacob, and tell the children of Israel.... These are the words which thou shalt speak unto the children of Israel" (Exod. 19:3, 6); "Jehovah our God made a covenant with us in Horeb. Jehovah made not this covenant with our fathers, but with us, even us, who are all of us here alive this day" (Deut. 5:2–3); "Thou hast avouched Jehovah this day to be thy God, and that thou wouldest walk in his ways, and keep his statutes, and his commandments, and his ordinances, and hearken unto his voice: and Jehovah has avouched thee this day to be a people for his own possession, as he has promised thee, and that thou shouldest keep all his commandments; and to make thee high above all nations that he has made, in praise, and in name, and in honor; and that thou mayest be a holy people unto Jehovah thy God, as he has spoken" (Deut. 26:17–19); "These are the words of the covenant which Jehovah commanded Moses to make with the children of Israel in the land of Moab, besides the covenant which he made with them in Horeb" (Deut. 29:1); "Keep therefore the words of this covenant, and do them, that ye may prosper in all that ye do. Ye stand this day all of you before Jehovah your God; your heads, your tribes, your elders, and your officers, even all the men of Israel, your little ones, your wives, and thy sojourner that is in the midst of thy camps, from the hewer of thy wood unto the drawer of thy water; that thou mayest enter into the covenant of Jehovah thy God, and into his oath, which Jehovah thy God makes with thee this day; that he may establish thee this day unto himself for a people, and that he may be unto thee a God, as he spoke unto thee, and as he swore unto thy fathers, to Abraham, to Isaac, and to Jacob" (Deut. 29:9–13); "not according to the covenant that I made with their fathers in the day that I took them by the hand to bring them out of the land of Egypt; which my covenant they brake, although I was a husband unto them, says Jehovah" (Jer. 31:32).

Successive Generations

God perpetuated this pledge with successive generations of Hebrew Israel, descended from the original partakers by natural generation (Deut. 29:14–15, 29).[13] If the descendants of the original partakers break this covenant, God inflicts on them its curses and judgments. Eventually, if they persist in this disobedience, even after God afflicts and judges them severely, he removes them from their inheritance in the land of Canaan and sends them into captivity in a foreign land (Deut. 29:24–28).[14] This confirms that God perpetuates this covenant with successive generations of Hebrew Israel.

The Final Generation: The Messianic Generation

These passages teach that the Mosaic covenant becomes old and vanishes away when God institutes a new covenant with his people Israel (Jer. 31:31; Heb. 8:7-9, 13). They also teach plainly that the coming of the Messiah, Abraham's heir, occasions the institution of this new covenant (Gal. 3:19).[15]

The Promises of the Mosaic Covenant

Introduction

Through Moses God promised Israel theocracy. Yet the promise had a condition. They must comply with gospel obedience to his voice. Accordingly,

---

13. "Neither with you only do I make this covenant and this oath, but with him that stands here with us this day before Jehovah our God, and also with him that is not here with us this day.... "for us and for our children" (Deut. 29:14–15, 29).

14. "The nations shall say, Wherefore has Jehovah done thus unto this land? what means the heat of this great anger? Then men shall say, Because they forsook the covenant of Jehovah, the God of their fathers, which he made with them when he brought them forth out of the land of Egypt, and went and served other gods, and worshipped them, gods that they knew not, and that he had not given unto them: therefore the anger of Jehovah was kindled against this land, to bring upon it all the curse that is written in this book; and Jehovah rooted them out of their land in anger, and in wrath, and in great indignation, and cast them into another land, as at this day" (Deut. 29:24–28).

15. "The days come, says Jehovah, that I will make a new covenant with the house of Israel, and with the house of Judah" (Jer. 31:31); "For if that first covenant had been faultless, then would no place have been sought for a second. For finding fault with them, he says, Behold, the days come, says the Lord, That I will make a new covenant with the house of Israel and with the house of Judah; Not according to the covenant that I made with their fathers in the day that I took them by the hand to lead them forth out of the land of Egypt; For they continued not in my covenant, And I regarded them not, says the Lord.... In that he says, A new covenant he has made the first old. But that which is becoming old and waxes aged is nigh unto vanishing away" (Heb. 8:7–9, 13); "What then is the law? It was added because of transgressions, till the seed should come to whom the promise has been made; and it was ordained through angels by the hand of a mediator" (Gal. 3:19).

God enhanced it by promising blessings if they complied with his law, and judgments if they disobeyed it. Accordingly, we first consider the foundational promise of theocracy. Then we consider the conditional promises of blessing and of cursing with which God enhances and enlarges this foundational promise.

The Foundational Promise: Theocracy[16]
God promised Israel that as long as they walked in gospel compliance with his voice that spoke the Decalogue, they would retain the privilege of being his special people from among all the nations, the privilege of theocracy (Exod. 19:5; Lev. 26:11–12; Deut. 26:18–19). This means that he would provide for them and protect them. It also means that he would manifest his special presence with them. It means that he would fellowship with them and commune with them by his Word. It means that he would rule over them as their King. In conjunction with this, he promised that they would be a "holy nation" (Exod. 19:6; Deut. 26:19). This means that they would be a nation consecrated to God, dedicated supremely to his glory and honor. He also promised that they would be a "kingdom of priests" (Exod. 19:6). If they walk in gospel obedience, they will be priests and kings, a holy community of royal priests who worship him acceptably and reign with him perpetually.

Blessings Promised upon Gospel Obedience[17]
God also promised them that as long as they walked in gospel obedience to the book of the law (Lev. 26:3; Deut. 28:1), then he would continually give

---

16. "Then ye shall be mine own possession from among all peoples from among all peoples: for all the earth is mine: and ye shall be unto me a kingdom of priests, and a holy nation" (Exod. 19:5, 6); "And I will have respect unto you, and make you fruitful, and multiply you, and will establish my covenant with you.... And I will set my tabernacle among you: and my soul shall not abhor you. And I will walk among you, and will be your God, and ye shall be my people. I am Jehovah your God, who brought you forth out of the land of Egypt, that ye should not be their bondmen; and I have broken the bars of your yoke, and made you go upright" (Lev. 26:9, 11–13); "and Jehovah hath avouched thee this day to be a people for his own possession, as he hath promised thee, and that thou shouldest keep all his commandments; and to make thee high above all nations that he hath made, in praise, and in name, and in honor; and that thou mayest be a holy people unto Jehovah thy God, as he has spoken" (Deut. 26:18–19).

17. "If ye walk in my statutes, and keep my commandments, and do them; then I will give your rains in their season, and the land shall yield its increase, and the trees of the field shall yield their fruit" (Lev. 26:3–4); "And it shall come to pass, if thou shalt hearken diligently unto the voice of Jehovah thy God, to observe to do all his commandments which I command thee this day, that Jehovah thy God will set thee on high above all the nations of the earth: and all

them the manifold blessings of prosperity and victory in the land of Canaan. He delineated these blessings both when he initiated the book of the law at Sinai (Lev. 26:3–13) and when he competed it in Moab (Deut. 28:1–14).

Judgments Promised upon Disobedience: Covenant Curses[18]
God also solemnly warned them that if they rejected him, served other gods, and refused to live by his ordinances contained in the book of the law, then he would punish and judge them. These *"curses of the covenant"* involve the gradual removal of their prosperity and victory. Ultimately, this judgment means their exile from Canaan and the revocation of their theocracy. He delineated these judgments when he initiated the book of the law at Sinai (Lev. 26:14–39) and when he completed it in Moab (Deut. 28:15–68).

The Condition of the Mosaic Covenant: Gospel Obedience
The Mosaic covenant was conditional. God required gospel compliance with the voice of God that spoke the Decalogue (Exod. 19:5) and with the book of the law (Exod. 24:8). The context and analogy of Scripture insist that God wanted gospel obedience, not legalistic works righteousness. God addressed this condition to Israel as a nation, as a community. It did not focus on how individual sinners get right with God. Rather, it focused on how Hebrew Israel as a society would sustain theocracy (Exod. 19:6) and all the blessings of peace and prosperity associated with it.

God's Voice: The Decalogue, God's Moral Law
God's voice spoke the Ten Commandments (Exod. 20:3–17; Deut. 4:10–12). God identifies this voice with his covenant (Exod. 19:5, 34:27–28; Deut. 4:13). He engraved the words he spoke on two tables of stone (Deut. 4:13, 5:22, 10:4). These act as a witness to this pledge. They attest the very words that God spoke with his voice directly to Israel (Exod. 31:18, 32:15). He told Moses to place them in the ark, in the most holy place in his special presence

---

these blessings shall come upon thee, and overtake thee, if thou shalt hearken unto the voice of Jehovah thy God" (Deut. 28:1–2).
　　18. "But if ye will not hearken unto me, and will not do all these commandments; and if ye shall reject my statutes, and if your soul abhor mine ordinances, so that ye will not do all my commandments, but break my covenant; I also will do this unto you" (Lev. 26:14–16); "But it shall come to pass, if thou wilt not hearken unto the voice of Jehovah thy God, to observe to do all his commandments and his statutes which I command thee this day, that all these curses shall come upon thee, and overtake thee" (Deut. 28:15).

(Deut. 10:1–2).[19] Thus, it is called, "the ark of the covenant," because it contains the tables that attest its substance. These tables of stone contain the "law and the commandment," God's abiding moral law, the voice of conscience amplified, codified, and purified.[20]

Since this remarkable divine pledge is a conditional promise, it obligates both God and his people. Thus, when they "obey his voice" in gospel obedience, they "keep" his pledge.[21]

The Book of the Law: Theocratic Law for Canaan and Religion

Moses wrote in the book of the covenant, also called the book of the law, ordinances and statutes that the divine Lawgiver ordained for his people to observe in Canaan. At Sinai God added ceremonial and civil ordinances that regulated their religious service through the Aaronic priesthood

---

19. "At that time Jehovah said unto me, Hew thee two tables of stone like unto the first, and come up unto me into the mount, and make thee an ark of wood. And I will write on the tables the words that were on the first tables which you broke, and thou shalt put them in the ark. So I made an ark of acacia wood, and hewed two tables of stone like unto the first, and went up into the mount, having the two tables in my hand. And he wrote on the tables, according to the first writing, the ten commandments, which Jehovah spoke unto you in the mount out of the midst of the fire in the day of the assembly: and Jehovah gave them unto me" (Deut. 10:1–4).

20. "Jehovah said unto Moses, Come up to me into the mount, and be there: and I will give thee the tables of stone, and the law and the commandment, which I have written, that thou mayest teach them" (Exod. 24:12); "he gave unto Moses, when he had made an end of communing with him upon mount Sinai, the two tables of the testimony, tables of stone, written with the finger of God" (Exod. 31:18); "And Moses turned, and went down from the mount, with the two tables of the testimony in his hand; tables that were written on both their sides; on the one side and on the other were they written. And the tables were the work of God, and the writing was the writing of God, graven upon the tables" (Exod. 32:15–16); "Jehovah said unto Moses, Hew thee two tables of stone like unto the first: and I will write upon the tables the words that were on the first tables, which you broke" (Exod. 34:1).

21. "If ye will obey my voice indeed, and keep my covenant" (Exod. 19:5); "Jehovah said unto Moses, Write thou these words: for after the tenor of these words I have made a covenant with thee and with Israel. And he was there with Jehovah forty days and forty nights; he did neither eat bread, nor drink water. And he wrote upon the tables the words of the covenant, the ten commandments. And it came to pass, when Moses came down from mount Sinai with the two tables of the testimony in Moses' hand" (Exod. 34:27–29); "the day that you stood before Jehovah thy God in Horeb, when Jehovah said unto me, Assemble me the people, and I will make them hear my words, that they may learn to fear me all the days that they live upon the earth, and that they may teach their children. And ye came near and stood under the mountain; and the mountain burned with fire unto the heart of heaven, with darkness, cloud, and thick darkness. And Jehovah spoke unto you out of the midst of the fire: ye heard the voice of words, but ye saw no form; only ye heard a voice. And he declared unto you his covenant, which he commanded you to perform, even the ten commandments; and he wrote them upon two tables of stone" (Deut. 4:10–13).

and the tabernacle. At Moab Moses completed this book of the law. We consider this biblical testimony to its substance and formation in the wilderness generations.

✦ The Inaugural Book of the Covenant at Sinai (Exod. 21:1–23:33)

> Now these are the ordinances which thou shalt set before them (Exod. 21:1); And Moses came and told the people all the words of Jehovah, and all the ordinances: and all the people answered with one voice, and said, All the words which Jehovah hath spoken will we do. And Moses wrote all the words of Jehovah (Exod. 24:3–4); And he took the book of the covenant, and read in the audience of the people: and they said, All that Jehovah has spoken will we do, and be obedient. And Moses took the blood, and sprinkled it on the people, and said, Behold the blood of the covenant, which Jehovah hath made with you concerning all these words (Exod. 24:7–8).

> And Jehovah commanded me at that time to teach you statutes and ordinances, that ye might do them in the land whither ye go over to possess it (Deut. 4:14).

When God first disclosed his Book of Law for Israel in Canaan, he associated it with the ratification of this pledge. Thus, Moses sprinkled it with the blood that ratified this covenant, and called it the "book of the covenant." Thus, the book of the law obligates Hebrew Israel even as the Decalogue does. Thus, when they walk in gospel obedience to its ordinances, they "keep God's covenant."

✦ Additions to the Book at Sinai from the Tabernacle (Leviticus)

> And Jehovah called unto Moses, and spoke unto him out of the tent of meeting, saying (Lev. 1:1); If ye walk in my statutes, and keep my commandments, and do them; then I will give your rains in their season, and the land shall yield its increase (Lev. 26:3–4); But if ye will not hearken unto me, and will not do all these commandments; and if ye shall reject my statutes, and if your soul abhor mine ordinances, so that ye will not do all my commandments, but break my covenant; I also will do this unto you: I will appoint terror over you, even consumption and fever, that shall consume the eyes, and make the soul to pine away; and ye shall sow your seed in vain, for your enemies shall eat it (Lev. 26:14–16); These are the statutes and ordinances and laws, which Jehovah made between him and

the children of Israel in mount Sinai by Moses (Lev. 26:46); These are the commandments, which Jehovah commanded Moses for the children of Israel in mount Sinai (Lev. 27:34).

These additions include: (1) The law of sacrifices (Lev. 1:2–7:38); (2) the consecration (Lev. 8:1–9:24) and law (Lev. 10:1–20) of the priesthood; (3) the law of clean and unclean foods (Lev. 11:1–47); (4) the law of childbirth (Lev. 12:1–8); (5) the law of leprosy (Lev. 13:1–14:57); (6) the law of a bodily issue (Lev. 15:1–33); (7) the law of the day of atonement (Lev. 16:1–34); (8) the law of blood (Lev. 17:1–16); (9) the law of purity and sanctity: of the people (Lev. 18:1–30, Lev. 19:1–20:27), of the priests (Lev. 21:1–22:16), and of the offerings, (Lev. 22:17–33); (10) the law of the set feasts (Lev. 23:1–44); (11) the law of continual accessories, lamp oil and showbread (Lev. 24:1–9); (12) the law of a case of blasphemy (Lev. 24:10–23); (13) the law of the possession of the land (Lev. 25:1–55); (14) the blessings of gospel obedience and judgments for breaking the covenant (Lev. 26:1–46); and (15) the law of vows and dedicated things (Lev. 27:1–34).

✦ Additions to the Book of the Law in the Wilderness (Numbers)
God also amended his Book of the Law as they journeyed throughout the wilderness for forty years. Numbers records these additions.[22]

✦ The Completed Book of the Law at Moab (Deut. 12:1–26:15)

> And it came to pass, when Moses had made an end of writing the words of this law in a book, until they were finished, that Moses commanded the Levites, that bare the ark of the covenant of Jehovah, saying, Take this book of the law, and put it by the side of the ark of the covenant of Jehovah your God, that it may be there for a witness against thee (Deut. 31:24–26).

God told Moses to put the completed book of the law next to the tables of stone in the most holy place as an additional witness to this covenant. God called for evangelical obedience to this entire body of theocratic law. This body of law was superior to the law of any other nation on earth: "And what great nation is there, that has statutes and ordinances so righteous as all this law, which I set before you this day?" (Deut. 4:8).

---

22. Num. 3:1–51, 4:1–49, 5:1–31, 6:1–27, 8:1–26, 9:1–14, 10:1–10, 15:1–41, 16:37–40, 17:10, 18:1–32, 19:1–22, 27:1–11, 28:1–31, 29:1–40, 30:1–16, 34:1–29, 35:1–34, 36:1–13.

The Ratification or Dedication of the Mosaic Covenant

Introduction: Overview of Dedication: When? Where? How?

God first ratified or dedicated this covenant at Sinai, when the redeemed generation of Israel entered the wilderness. He concluded its dedication when the inheritance generation entered Canaan. At Sinai he ratified it with blood, affirmation, a communion meal, and attestation. At Moab he added two additional witnesses and completed its dedication with a prophecy. Then he consummated its ratification in Canaan with a commemoration ceremony and monument and with divine sanctions. We now consider these seven aspects of ratification.

Blood (Exod. 24:4–8; Heb. 9:17–20)

> And Moses wrote all the words of Jehovah, and rose up early in the morning, and built an altar under the mount, and twelve pillars, according to the twelve tribes of Israel. And he sent young men of the children of Israel, who offered burnt-offerings, and sacrificed peace-offerings of oxen unto Jehovah. And Moses took half of the blood, and put it in basins; and half of the blood he sprinkled on the altar. And he took the book of the covenant, and read in the audience of the people: and they said, All that Jehovah hath spoken will we do, and be obedient. And Moses took the blood, and sprinkled it on the people, and said, Behold the blood of the covenant, which Jehovah hath made with you concerning all these words (Exod. 24:4–8).

> For a testament is of force where there has been death: for it never avails while he that made it lives. Wherefore even the first covenant has not been dedicated without blood. For when every commandment had been spoken by Moses unto all the people according to the law, he took the blood of the calves and the goats, with water and scarlet wool and hyssop, and sprinkled both the book itself and all the people, saying, This is the blood of the covenant which God commanded to you-ward (Heb. 9:17–20).

At Sinai Moses ratified this covenant with the blood of sacrificed animals. Blood represents death. Living men can change their wills; dead men can't. This signifies that the participants are saying: "I will no more go back on my commitment than a dead man will change his last will. My commitment to this covenant is as final as a dead man's last will." The connection of Hebrews 9:17 with 9:18 supports this construction: "for it never avails while he that made it lives. *Wherefore* even the first covenant has not been dedicated without blood." Moses sprinkled with blood the people and the book. Thus, both God and Israel signify that this covenant is as permanent as the commitment of a dead man to his last will.

Affirmation (Exod. 24:7; 19:7–8, 24:3; Deut. 26:17–19)

At Sinai the redemption generation of Israel solemnly affirmed their commitment to the Mosaic covenant. While Moses sprinkled them with the blood of the covenant they said: "all that Jehovah has spoken we will do."[23] They vowed to obey the voice of God that spoke the Ten Commandments and to obey all the ordinances in the book of the covenant. At Moab the inheritance generation of Israel also solemnly affirmed their commitment to the Mosaic covenant. They promised that Jehovah would be their God and Jehovah promised that they would be his people. Their commitment reached its zenith after they entered Canaan and added their affirmation of "Amen" to the covenant sanctions uttered by the Levites (Deut. 27:14–26).[24]

Communion Meal

> Then went up Moses, and Aaron, Nadab, and Abihu, and seventy of the elders of Israel. And they saw the God of Israel; and there was under his feet as it were a paved work of sapphire stone, and as it were the very heaven for clearness. And upon the nobles of the children of Israel he laid not his hand: and they beheld God, and did eat and drink (Exod. 24:9–11).

The elders of the redemption generation communed with God in a special meal that indicated their unique relation to him as his people. God thus dedicated his pledge with the entire nation.

---

23. "And Moses came and called for the elders of the people, and set before them all these words which Jehovah commanded him. And all the people answered together, and said, All that Jehovah hath spoken we will do. And Moses reported the words of the people unto Jehovah" (Exod. 19:7–8); "And Moses came and told the people all the words of Jehovah, and all the ordinances: and all the people answered with one voice, and said, All the words which Jehovah hath spoken will we do" (Exod. 24:3); "And he took the book of the covenant, and read in the audience of the people: and they said, All that Jehovah has spoken will we do, and be obedient" (Exod. 24:7).

24. "Thou hast avouched Jehovah this day to be thy God, and that thou wouldest walk in his ways, and keep his statutes, and his commandments, and his ordinances, and hearken unto his voice: and Jehovah hath avouched thee this day to be a people for his own possession, as he hath promised thee, and that thou shouldest keep all his commandments; and to make thee high above all nations that he hath made, in praise, and in name, and in honor; and that thou mayest be a holy people unto Jehovah thy God, as he hath spoken" (Deut. 26:17–19); "Cursed be he that confirms not the words of this law to do them. And all the people shall say, Amen" (Deut. 27:26).

Attestation: Witnesses, Testimony[25]

God attested this covenant with permanent witnesses at Sinai and at Moab. At Sinai he attested it with the tables of stone, at Moab with the book of the law. At Moab he supplied an additional attestation. He prepared a song that Israel was to learn as an abiding personal testimony to this covenant.

✦ The Tables of Stone at Sinai[26]

At Sinai God completes the inauguration in Exodus 24:12 when he tells Moses that he will supply the tables of stone. On those tables God himself engraved the very words that his voice spoke to Israel. Moses calls them the *"tables of the testimony."* This indicates that they are an attestation. They are a permanent witness, engraved in stone, to the voice that spoke at Sinai. God calls his attestation: "the law and the commandment," a hendiadys. The Decalogue is God's moral code and requirement. Paul uses these terms in Rom. 7:7–12.

✦ The Book of the Law at Moab[27]

At Moab God further attests this covenant with the completed book of the law. Moses tells the Levites to place the book next to the witness he supplied at Sinai. Thus, God provides two witnesses, side by side, of this covenant. The tables and book of the law permanently serve as concrete attestations of the Mosaic covenant.

✦ The Song of Moses: Personal and Perpetual Witness[28]

> Now therefore write ye this song for you, and teach thou it the children of Israel: put it in their mouths, that this song may be a witness for me against the children of Israel (Deut. 31:19).

The final witness is not an inanimate object like tables and a book. It is a song that God tells Moses to put in their mouths. God commanded

---

25. Exod. 24:12, 31:18; Deut. 31:26; Deut. 31:19, 32:1–44.

26. "And Jehovah said unto Moses, Come up to me into the mount, and be there: and I will give thee the tables of stone, and the law and the commandment, which I have written, that thou mayest teach them" (Exod. 24:12); "And he gave unto Moses, when he had made an end of communing with him upon mount Sinai, the two tables of the testimony, tables of stone, written with the finger of God" (Exod. 31:18).

27. "Take this book of the law, and put it by the side of the ark of the covenant of Jehovah your God, that it may be there for a witness against thee" (Deut. 31:26).

28. Deut. 31:19, 22, 30, 32:44; Deut. 32:1–43.

Israel to learn this song and teach it to their children throughout their generations. The song was to be a living witness, from their own mouths, of their commitment to the Mosaic covenant. Scripture records this song of attestation (Deut. 32:1–43). It affirms repeatedly that if they serve other gods, they have broken this covenant and brought its judgments and curses upon themselves.

Prediction: Prophecy (Deut. 30:1–10)

At Moab God adds a prophecy to the ratification process, just as he did with Abraham. He predicts that in the land of Canaan Israel will experience first the blessings then the curses of the covenant. After God restores them to Canaan, he will "circumcise their hearts" and the hearts of their children. God's people will become a nation circumcised in heart throughout their generations. What a remarkable prediction! At the beginning, when they enter Canaan, he foretells the end, the gospel transformation of Israel by the Messiah. This gives them hope throughout their entire history as God's theocratic nation.

> And it shall come to pass, when all these things are come upon thee, the blessing and the curse, which I have set before thee, and thou shalt call them to mind among all the nations, whither Jehovah thy God hath driven thee, and shalt return unto Jehovah thy God, and shalt obey his voice according to all that I command thee this day, thou and thy children, with all thy heart, and with all thy soul; that then Jehovah thy God will turn thy captivity, and have compassion upon thee, and will return and gather thee from all the peoples, whither Jehovah thy God hath scattered thee.... And Jehovah thy God will circumcise thy heart, and the heart of thy seed, to love Jehovah thy God with all thy heart, and with all thy soul, that thou mayest live (Deut. 30:1–3, 6).

Commemoration: Ceremony and Monument[29]

God completes the ratification in Canaan when the inheritance generation crosses the Jordan. He prescribes a ceremony of commemoration. He commands them to write the words of the book of the law on large stones as a

---

29. Deut. 11:29–31, 27:2–8, 11–13; Josh. 8:30–35.

monument to the Mosaic covenant.[30] They are to offer sacrifices.[31] Half are to stand on mount Ebal for the curses and half on mount Gerizim for the blessing.[32] Scripture records how Joshua performed this ceremony (Josh. 8:30–35).

Divine Sanction (Deut. 27:14–26; Gal. 3:10)

The last element of the ratification of the Mosaic covenant appears to be associated with the monument ceremony. God commanded the Levites to declare divine sanctions. These sanctions affirm divine wrath and punishment for anyone who despises and breaks this covenant. He commanded the inheritance generation to affirm these sanctions with "Amen." He commanded twelve sanctions. The last sanction pronounced the judgment of God on anyone who would not affirm all the words of his theocratic law. The very last word of its ratification was "Amen":

> And the Levites shall answer, and say unto all the men of Israel with a loud voice, Cursed be the man that makes a graven or molten image, an abomination unto Jehovah, the work of the hands of the craftsman, and sets it up in secret. And all the people shall answer and say, Amen.... Cursed be he that confirms not the words of this law to do them. And all the people shall say, Amen (Deut. 27:14–15, 26).

The apostle Paul declares the evangelical application of these sanctions. They herald the superiority of the new covenant and the necessity of justification by grace, Christ, and faith alone:

> For as many as are of the works of the law are under a curse: for it is written, Cursed is every one who continues not in all things that are written in the book of the law, to do them (Gal. 3:10).

The Religious Service of the Mosaic Covenant: Tabernacle and Priesthood

In Hebrews 9:1 Scripture speaks of the *"ordinances of religious service"* associated with the Mosaic covenant. God ordained the means by which he would

---

30. "And it shall be on the day when ye shall pass over the Jordan unto the land which Jehovah thy God gives thee, that thou shalt set thee up great stones, and plaster them with plaster: and thou shalt write upon them all the words of this law" (Deut. 27:2–3).

31. "Thou shalt build the altar of Jehovah thy God of unhewn stones; and thou shalt offer burnt-offerings thereon unto Jehovah thy God: and thou shalt sacrifice peace-offerings, and shalt eat there; and thou shalt rejoice before Jehovah thy God" (Deut. 27:6–7).

32. And it shall come to pass, when Jehovah thy God shall bring thee into the land whither thou goest to possess it, that thou shalt set the blessing upon mount Gerizim, and the curse upon mount Ebal (Deut. 11:29); see also Deut. 27:11–13.

commune and fellowship with his people. He established religious institutions and ordinances by which his people would draw near to him to show him homage and devotion. As he institutes this covenant, he defines the foundations of its religious service, the tabernacle and Aaronic priesthood (Exod. 25–30). At Sinai God speaks from the tabernacle of sacrifices, set feasts, and other ordinances through which his people draw near to him. He adds additional ordinances in the wilderness. At Moab he completes the entire set of ordinances for his religious service.

The Tabernacle: God's Dwelling (Exod. 25–27; Heb. 9:1–5)

First, Scripture introduces the tabernacle (Exod. 25:1–9). It explains God's *provision* for the tabernacle, a freewill offering (25:1–7). It identifies God's *purpose* for the tabernacle, his special presence, dwelling, and communion with his people (25:8). It affirms God's *regulation* of his tabernacle by special revelation (25:9, also 25:40, 26:30). Then Scripture unfolds God's *blueprint* for his tabernacle (Exod. 25:10–27:21). His blueprint specifies these ten features:

(1) The ark: 25:10–16: *The ark contains the tables of stone, the testimony or witness*

(2) The mercy seat with cherubim: 25:17–22: *Where God speaks with them*

(3) The table: 25:23–30: *Where the showbread was placed continually*

(4) The candlestick with its lamps: 25:31–39

(5) The tabernacle with its curtains and boards: 26:1–30

(6) The veil: 26:31–35: *to separate the most holy place from the holy place*

(7) The screen for the tabernacle door: 26:36–37

(8) The altar: 27:1–8

(9) The court of the tabernacle: 27:9–18

(10) The accessories: 27:19–21: *instruments and olive oil for the tabernacle light*

On this foundation, Scripture records how Moses provided for and fabricated the tabernacle according to this blueprint (Exod. 35:4–38:31). It records how he erected it (Exod. 40:16–33) and how God blessed it with his special presence (Exod. 40:34–38).

◆ God Dwelt in the Tabernacle in the Wilderness

Scripture records various names for the tabernacle: the "tent of meeting" (Exod. 33:7, 40:34); "the tent of the testimony" (Num. 9:15); "the tabernacle of witness" (Num. 17:7–8); and the "tabernacle of the congregation" (Num. 17:4; Deut. 31:14). Moses set it up outside the camp because they were stiff-necked. God warned that if he dwelt in the midst of them he would consume them. When anyone sought the Lord, they went outside the camp to the tabernacle (Exod. 33:7–10). God manifested his presence with his people at the tabernacle with a cloud and fire (Num. 9:15–16). He guided them through the wilderness by this cloud (Exod. 40:34–38). When they were about to enter Canaan, he spoke to Moses and Joshua from the tabernacle (Deut. 31:14–15). He charged Joshua to bring them to their inheritance in Canaan (Deut. 31:23).

◆ God Dwelt in the Tabernacle in Canaan until Solomon's Temple

When they entered Canaan they set up the tabernacle in Shiloh, not far from Mount Ebal and Mount Gerizim (Josh. 18:1). There they divided the land (Josh. 19:51). There it remained until the days of Samuel (1 Sam. 2:22). God continued to dwell there until the building of the temple (2 Sam. 7:6; 1 Chron. 6:32). The ark was temporarily separated from the tabernacle, captured by the Philistines, and returned (1 Sam. 4:3–4). Then David brought the ark to Jerusalem (1 Chron. 16:1; 2 Chron. 1:4). In the days of David and Solomon the tabernacle moved to the high place in Gibeon, where God appeared to Solomon (1 Chron. 21:29; 2 Chron. 1:3, 7). Then Solomon brought all its furnishings, including the ark, into the temple (1 Kings 8:4; 1 Chron. 17:5). God continued his special presence with his people in his temple until their captivity. After a remnant returned to Canaan, God rebuilt a temple that lasted until the days of Messiah, when it was destroyed. Under the new covenant Christ builds his spiritual temple.

The Aaronic Priesthood (Exod. 28–30)

In conjunction with his tabernacle, God also ordained a priesthood to foster his fellowship with his people, to lead divine worship, and to portray Christ and his redemptive work. God ordained in detail all the features and functions of this priesthood. Scripture outlines seven aspects of God's blueprint for the priesthood (Exod. 28–30):

(1) The identity or order of the priesthood: 28:1: *Aaron, his sons: Aaronic order*

(2) The garments of the priesthood: 28:2–43: *breastplate, ephod, robe, coat, mitre, girdle*

(3) The consecration of the priesthood: 29:1–46: *washing, clothing, anointing, offerings, eating, week of cleansing, result*

(4) The most holy service of the priesthood: 30:1–10: *the altar of incense, burn daily incense, make annual atonement*

(5) The stewardship of the priesthood: 30:11–16: *maintain sanctuary, half shekel*

(6) The washing of the priesthood: 30:17–21: *the daily washing in the laver*

(7) The accessories of the priesthood: 30:22–38: *anointing oil and incense*

After Moses set up the tabernacle, God ordered him to consecrate Aaron and his sons as priests. Scripture records how Moses consecrated them (Lev. 8:1–9:23) and how God openly displayed his approval before the whole congregation (Lev. 9:24). In the book of the law God reveals the complete set of ordinances for their priestly service. Soon after their consecration, God consumed two of Aaron's sons who drew near to God contrary to his ordinance (Lev. 10:1–7). In the wilderness God blessed Phinehas, Aaron's grandson, because he turned away God's wrath from Israel. God perpetuated the Aaronic priesthood to his posterity (Num. 25:11–13). God kept this covenant with Phinehas. His descendants continued to serve as priests in the temple until the days of the captivity (1 Chron. 6:4–15). After the captivity God continued faithful to this pledge to Phinehas. He gave the priesthood to Ezra, the descendant of Phinehas (Ezra 7:1–5). When Christ came God transformed the priesthood and its ordinances (Heb. 7:11–12). In Christ God makes his people a society of royal priests, in accord with his promise of theocracy (1 Pet. 2:9).

The Token of the Mosaic Covenant: The Hebrew Sabbath

> Speak thou also unto the children of Israel, saying, Verily ye shall keep my sabbaths: for it is a sign between me and you throughout your generations; that ye may know that I am Jehovah who sanctifies you.... Wherefore the children of Israel shall keep the sabbath, to observe the sabbath throughout their generations, for a perpetual covenant. It is a sign between me and the children of Israel for ever:

for in six days Jehovah made heaven and earth, and on the seventh day he rested, and was refreshed (Exod. 31:13, 16–17).

God told Moses to tell the children of Israel that keeping the Sabbath was a token of God's pledge to them throughout their generations (31:13, 16, 17). Like circumcision, this sign requires human compliance. Like circumcision, those who break the Sabbath must be cut off from God's people (31:14). If God sees Israel keeping the Sabbath, it reminds him of his pledge to preserve and bless them as his people. If he sees them keeping his Sabbath, it reminds him of his pledge that when Messiah comes he will make them a society of royal priests. Conversely, if he sees them profaning the Sabbath, it reminds him of his pledge to punish and judge them with all the curses of his covenant.

Thus, what was a creation ordinance, gracious provision, and moral obligation became a sign of the Mosaic covenant. This introduces tension. When the Mosaic covenant transitions to the new covenant, so also this token is transformed. Then the observance of the Hebrew Sabbath, Saturday, will no longer distinguish the people of God. Yet under the new covenant his people must have a Sabbath day, because God engraves on their hearts the very law he engraved on tables of stone (Jer. 31:33). The Lord's Day resolves this tension.

The Historical Fruition of the Mosaic Covenant

The prophecy recorded in Deuteronomy 30:1–10 provides the framework for understanding the outcome of this conditional pledge. As predicted, God first blessed Israel unto the days of David and Solomon as they lived in compliance with his law. Then followed an era marked by disobedience and rebellion that culminated in the captivity of Israel and Judah. Then God restored a remnant to Canaan and rebuilt the temple. In the fullness of time, God sent his Son, the Messiah. Although Hebrew Israel rejected him, he transformed God's people into a visible society of Abraham's spiritual posterity circumcised in heart. We consider now five aspects of its outcome: blessedness, accursedness, restoration, rejection, and transformation.

The Mosaic Covenant Resulted in Blessedness
Scripture records God's promise of blessing upon gospel obedience (Lev. 26:3–13; Deut. 28:1–14). It unfolds two general aspects of blessedness, the

blessedness of individual believers and the blessedness of Israel as a society. This national blessedness was especially experienced under the judges, under David and Solomon, and under David's dynasty in Judah.

The Blessedness of Individual Believers

Throughout their history, individual Hebrew believers walked in gospel obedience to God's law and kept his covenant. These knew the Lord and experienced his favor and blessing: "All the paths of Jehovah are lovingkindness and truth Unto such as keep his covenant and his testimonies" (Ps. 25:10); "But the lovingkindness of Jehovah is from everlasting to everlasting upon them that fear him, And his righteousness unto children's children; To such as keep his covenant, And to those that remember his precepts to do them" (Ps. 103:17–18).

The Blessedness of Hebrew Israel under the Judges

During the period of the judges, God blessed his people through judges who delivered them from their enemies that oppressed them. Yet, the blessing was intermingled with judgment. After the judge was dead, they followed other gods and brought divine punishment on themselves (Judg. 2:18–23).

The Blessedness of Hebrew Israel under David and Solomon

> Judah and Israel were many as the sand which is by the sea in multitude, eating and drinking and making merry.... And Judah and Israel dwelt safely, every man under his vine and under his fig-tree, from Dan even to Beer-sheba, all the days of Solomon" (1 Kings 4:20, 25).

God brought his people to the experience of blessedness when he made David their king. He put the fear of David on the nations, cut off all his enemies, and gave him victory wherever he went (1 Chron. 14:14–17, 17:7–9, 18:13–14). David subdued all the land that God promised to Abraham (1 Kings 4:24–25; 1 Chron. 22:18). He led people to serve only the Lord (1 Chron. 29:20–22). Then God blessed Solomon to reign over all that land in peace and great prosperity. In his days God fulfilled his pledge to bless their bodies, livestock, crops, and labor (1 Kings 4:20, 5:4, 10:23–27). In these days their blessing reached its zenith. After this the predominant trend was spiritual decline and judgment, especially in the northern kingdom of Israel.

The Blessedness of Hebrew Israel under David's Dynasty

> And Asa did that which was good and right in the eyes of Jehovah his God.... And he built fortified cities in Judah; for the land was quiet, and he had no war in those years, because Jehovah had given him rest (2 Chron. 14:2, 6).

> And the fear of God was on all the kingdoms of the countries, when they heard that Jehovah fought against the enemies of Israel. So the realm of Jehoshaphat was quiet; for his God gave him rest round about (2 Chron. 20:29–30).

While Israel was in great spiritual decline, God blessed Judah with deliverance and victory under the dynasty of kings descended from David. When they trusted and called on him, he heard their cry and delivered them. This blessedness marked the reign of Asa (2 Chron. 14:2–16:14), Jehoshaphat (2 Chron. 17:1–20:37), Hezekiah (2 Chron. 29:1–32:33), and Josiah (2 Chron. 34:1–35:27). God blessed Asa with peace and rest (2 Chron. 14:6). He put the fear of God on Jehoshaphat's enemies so that they did not fight with him, so that Judah enjoyed rest and peace (2 Chron. 17:10, 20:29–30). He blessed Hezekiah with prosperity, delivered him from Assyria, and exalted him in the sight of the nations (2 Chron. 31:20–21, 32:20–23). He postponed the judgment of Judah until after Josiah's death (2 Chron. 34:23–28).

The Mosaic Covenant Resulted in Accursedness

Scripture records the curses that God pledges to inflict on those who break his covenant (Lev. 26:14–39; Deut. 28:15–68). Even in the wilderness Israel rebelled against God. He inflicted his wrath on them repeatedly until at last the generation of adult men that he redeemed from Egypt died in the wilderness. During the period of the judges he also repeatedly afflicted them for their rebellion. Even while their blessing was at its zenith, their steep decline to ruin began even in the days of Solomon. God rent most of the kingdom from Solomon because he made provision for his many foreign wives to sacrifice to their gods (1 Kings 11:11). We look more closely at the accursedness of Israel that led to captivity in Assyria, and the accursedness of Judah that led to captivity in Babylon.

The Accursedness of Israel: Captivity in Assyria

> And the king of Assyria carried Israel away unto Assyria, and put them in Halah, and on the Habor, the river of Gozan, and in the cities of the Medes, because they obeyed not the voice of Jehovah their God, but transgressed his covenant, even all that Moses the servant of Jehovah commanded, and would not hear it, nor do it (2 Kings 18:11–12).

Jeroboam incited Israel to great sin that ultimately resulted in their judgment and captivity in Assyria. Before God inflicted that ultimate judgment, he punished them with increasing severity for their rebellion. Although prophets called them repeatedly to repent, their rebellion increased until God evicted them (2 Kings 17:15–23).

The Accursedness of Judah: Captivity in Babylon

> And Jehovah, the God of their fathers, sent to them by his messengers, rising up early and sending, because he had compassion on his people, and on his dwelling-place: but they mocked the messengers of God, and despised his words, and scoffed at his prophets, until the wrath of Jehovah arose against his people, till there was no remedy. Therefore he brought upon them the king of the Chaldeans (2 Chron. 36:15–17).

> The house of Israel and the house of Judah have broken my covenant which I made with their fathers. Therefore thus says Jehovah, Behold, I will bring evil upon them, which they shall not be able to escape (Jer. 11:10–11).

Similarly, Judah walked in the ways of Israel until God finally evicted them from Canaan. God sent prophets who warned them repeatedly, but they would not listen. God punished them with increased severity, but they continued in their rebellion until at last he sent them into captivity in Babylon (Jer. 11:9–11, 22:8–9). Those prominent in provoking this judgment on Judah were: Jehoram (2 Chron. 21:5–20), Ahaziah and his mother Athaliah (2 Chron. 22:1–23:21), Ahaz (2 Chron. 28:1–27), Manassah, Amon (2 Chron. 33:1–25), Jehoiakim, Jehoiachin, and Zedekiah (2 Chron. 36:5–17).

The Mosaic Covenant Resulted in Restoration

> And yet for all that, when they are in the land of their enemies, I will
> not reject them, neither will I abhor them, to destroy them utterly,
> and to break my covenant with them; for I am Jehovah their God;
> but I will for their sakes remember the covenant of their ancestors,
> whom I brought forth out of the land of Egypt in the sight of the
> nations, that I might be their God: I am Jehovah (Lev. 26:44–45).

As God promised, he did not make a full end of Israel. He restored them to
Canaan after seventy years of captivity in Babylon. In the days of Ezra and
Nehemiah they rebuilt the temple and the wall of Jerusalem (Ezra 1:2–4).
They remained in Canaan until the coming of Messiah and the institution
of the new covenant.

The Mosaic Covenant Resulted in Rejection

> Therefore say I unto you, The kingdom of God shall be taken away
> from you, and shall be given to a nation bringing forth the fruits thereof
> (Matt. 21:43).

Israel never returned to physical idolatry after their restoration. Nevertheless, they rejected Jehovah when God the Son became human and dwelt
among them. For this he removed unbelieving Hebrews from Christian
Israel and revoked the theocracy from Hebrew Israel.

When Jehovah came into his own theocratic society, they received him
not (John 1:11–12). Like their fathers, they were a society stiff-necked and
uncircumcised in heart and ears (Acts 7:51–53). They refused to receive his
Word. They rejected his claim to be their God and King. They demanded his
crucifixion. They put on themselves and their children liability for shedding
his blood (Matt. 27:25, 37). They opposed his gospel and persecuted those
who proclaimed it. Thus, the vengeance of the Mosaic covenant came on them
to the uttermost (Matt. 23:34–38; 1 Thess. 2:14–16). When Hebrew Israel
rejected and killed their King, Jehovah Jesus, God took the theocracy away
from them (Matt. 21:43). Ironically, when they shed the blood of their King,
they unwittingly shed the very blood by which he ratified the new covenant.

The Mosaic Covenant Resulted in Transformation

> What then is the law? It was added because of transgressions, till
> the seed should come to whom the promise has been made (Gal.
> 3:19); For the priesthood being changed, there is made of necessity

a change also of the law (Heb. 7:12); being only (with meats and drinks and divers washings) carnal ordinances, imposed until a time of reformation (Heb. 9:10).

The Mosaic covenant ultimately resulted in the spiritual transformation of Israel. God intended this covenant to endure only until the Messiah came (Gal. 3:19). Christ's appointment as royal priest required an alteration of the law governing his people (Heb. 7:11–12). The ordinances of divine service, the tabernacle, temple, and the Aaronic priesthood, were only set up until the gospel reformation accomplished by Messiah (Heb. 9:10). Under the new covenant, the book of the law no longer serves as the constitution of God's people. Only the general equity of its civil statutes still pertains to them (1 Cor. 9:8–10). Yet, under the new covenant, he writes his moral law, the Decalogue, on the hearts of his people (Heb. 8:8, 10).

The Conditional Form of the Mosaic Covenant

The conditionality of this pledge exposes the heart of fallen man and commends God's grace. Yet it produces tension. This tension occasions much discussion and debate over its nature and characteristics. Some suggest that it promotes salvation from sin by man's works as a republication of a covenant of works. I have actually heard someone teach that the Hebrews should have rejected it! Further, the fact that it resulted in disobedience and rejection occasions further disparagement of the Decalogue as useless or harmful. While others, at the opposite extreme, suggest that even the new covenant is conditional, just like the Mosaic, so that even now Christian Israel is still under the blessing if they comply and the curse if they rebel, just like Hebrew Israel used to be. What do we say to such things?

Such suggestions fail to grasp, on one hand, its evangelical nature, and on the other, its limitation and inferiority to the new covenant. Positively, even though it was conditional, this divine covenant was evangelical and beneficial. Negatively, because it was conditional, this divine covenant was weak and limited, and as such, was provisional and inferior to the new covenant. We now unfold both of these implications, first the negative, then the positive.

Since it was Conditional, it was Limited, Temporary, and Inferior

Since it was Conditional, it was Limited and Weak

First, the Mosaic covenant is limited because the Decalogue cannot break the power of reigning sin.[33] Sin reigns in the hearts of all men by nature, even in the hearts of Abraham's patriarchal posterity circumcised in body. Natively, without regenerating grace that circumcises the heart, no man ever can or will comply with God's law. This is because the carnal mind is enmity against God and can never be subject to his law. No man in the flesh with sin reigning in his heart can ever please God, or obey his law evangelically. Only the law of the Spirit, the Decalogue written on the heart by the Spirit, can set us free from reigning sin. The Decalogue, written on stone, is external to sinners, and thus can never circumcise their hearts or break the power of their reigning sin. In the Mosaic covenant, God called the society of Hebrew Israel to evangelical obedience to the Decalogue. Yet he gave them no guarantee that he would write his law on their hearts. He did not circumcise most of their hearts. They were a community composed largely of unconverted men at enmity with God. This is why the Mosaic covenant was weak. This is why it produced wrath (Rom. 4:15). This is why it stirred up sin in the hearts of sinners who lived under it.[34]

Second, the Mosaic covenant is limited because the Decalogue condemns sin but can never forgive it.[35] It focuses on the duty of man to obey God, "*You* shall not kill. *You* shall not commit adultery.... *You* shall not covet." The law focuses on "you." This is why Paul says the law is "not of faith" (Gal. 3:12). Faith focuses on Christ, the law on you. This does not make the law evil, but it does make it weak. It teaches Christians how to love, for love is the fulfillment of the law (Rom. 13:8–10). Yet it can never

---

33. "For what the law could not do, in that it was weak through the flesh, God, sending his own Son in the likeness of sinful flesh and for sin, condemned sin in the flesh: that the ordinance of the law might be fulfilled in us, who walk not after the flesh, but after the Spirit...because the mind of the flesh is enmity against God; for it is not subject to the law of God, neither indeed can it be: and they that are in the flesh cannot please God" (Rom. 8:3–4, 7–8).

34. "For when we were in the flesh, the sinful passions, which were through the law, wrought in our members to bring forth fruit unto death" (Rom. 7:5).

35. "Be it known unto you therefore, brethren, that through this man is proclaimed unto you remission of sins: and by him every one that believeth is justified from all things, from which ye could not be justified by the law of Moses" (Acts 13:38–39); "Now we know that what things soever the law says, it speaks to them that are under the law; that every mouth may be stopped, and all the world may be brought under the judgment of God: because by the works of the law shall no flesh be justified in his sight; for through the law cometh the knowledge of sin" (Rom. 3:19–20).

produce love. Further, it has no power to atone for the lack of love. It has no power to pay the price of sin. It has no power to pardon the sinner. Only Christ can do that. No man can get right with God by keeping his law. Men get right with God only by faith in Christ.

Thus, the Mosaic covenant was limited and weak because the Decalogue cannot regenerate or justify. It can never morally change the heart or pardon wrong. The Holy Spirit regenerates and sanctifies the heart, not man. Christ atones for sin, not man. The Mosaic covenant could teach a community of believers how to please the God they love, but could never convert or pardon a community of sinners:

> For the law having a shadow of the good things to come, not the very image of the things, can never with the same sacrifices year by year, which they offer continually, make perfect them that draw nigh. Else would they not have ceased to be offered? because the worshippers, having been once cleansed, would have had no more consciousness of sins. But in those sacrifices there is a remembrance made of sins year by year. For it is impossible that the blood of bulls and goats should take away sins (Heb. 10:1–4).

Since it was Conditional, it was Temporary and Provisional

God intended it only until Christ came (Gal. 3:19; Heb. 9:10). Christ has done what his law could never do. He has written his law on the hearts of his people by his Spirit. Now they walk in gospel obedience to it (Rom. 8:3–5). He has put away sin by the sacrifice of himself (Heb. 9:26, 10:12–14, 18). Now that Christ has done what the Mosaic covenant could never do, its symbolic institutions are unnecessary.

Since it was Conditional, it is Inferior to the New Covenant[36]

The new covenant has better promises than the old. Its promises are superior precisely because they are unconditional. There is no *"if"* in these better promises. God says: "I will put my laws into their mind," and "all shall know me," and "I will be merciful to their iniquities." God promises to produce a

---

36. "But now has he obtained a more excellent ministry, by how much also he is the mediator of a better covenant, which was established upon better promises" (Heb. 8:6); "For this is the covenant that I will make with the house of Israel after those days, says the Lord; I will put my laws into their mind, and write them in their hearts: and I will be to them a God, and they shall be to me a people: And they shall not teach every man his fellow-citizen, And every man his brother, saying, Know the Lord: For all shall know me, From the least to the greatest of them. For I will be merciful to their iniquities, And their sins will I remember no more" (Heb. 8:10–12).

visible community of believers, composed of Abraham's spiritual children. The community of the new covenant is not under a curse like Hebrew Israel (Gal. 3:10). God certainly will write his law on their hearts. They will all know him. Their sins will be forgiven. Their compliance depends on him alone. He guarantees it.

Although Conditional, it was Good, Gracious, and Evangelical[37]
Paul says the Mosaic covenant made Hebrew Israel privileged, not under-privileged. He says that the gospel does not undermine the law, but rather establishes it. Surely he does not mean that the gospel of grace establishes a scheme of salvation by works! He does not disparage the Decalogue. He says it is holy, righteous, and good. He affirms that the Mosaic covenant is not the enemy of the gospel. First I support its evangelical nature biblically, then explain its conditional form evangelically.

Biblical Support for its Evangelical Nature[38]
We begin with the promise of Deuteronomy 30:6: "Jehovah thy God will circumcise thy heart." Reformed Baptists did not invent the concept of heart circumcision. Neither did Paul. The promise of a community marked by heart circumcision goes all the way back to the ratification of the Mosaic covenant. The fruit of heart circumcision is a society enabled "to love Jehovah" with all its heart. Moses taught Israel that in order to love God it was necessary to have your heart circumcised. Imagine a Hebrew asking Moses, "What is heart circumcision? Why is it needed to love God?" Did Moses preach a different heart circumcision than Paul? Did he preach a different conversion to God? In Paul's words, absolutely not! Moses predicted a society marked by heart circumcision. Paul says that very prediction has been fulfilled (Col. 2:11–13). The heart circumcision Moses preached is "the putting away of the body of the flesh," the moral regeneration of the heart by the Holy Spirit. Thus, Moses taught Israel that they must be born again. This is why Jesus chided Nicodemus for being a leader in Israel ignorant of the new birth (John 3:9–10).

---

37. "What advantage then hath the Jew? or what is the profit of circumcision? Much every way: first of all, that they were entrusted with the oracles of God" (Rom. 3:1–2); "Do we then make the law of none effect through faith? God forbid: nay, we establish the law" (Rom. 3:31); "So that the law is holy, and the commandment holy, and righteous, and good" (Rom. 7:12); "Is the law then against the promises of God? God forbid" (Gal. 3:21).

38. "And Jehovah thy God will circumcise thy heart, and the heart of thy seed, to love Jehovah thy God with all thy heart, and with all thy soul, that thou mayest live" (Deut. 30:6).

Moses calls them to conversion, "if you turn to Jehovah your God with all your heart and all your soul" (Deut. 30:10). This involves repentance toward God and faith in his promised Savior. Moses knew the gospel promise of Genesis 22:18, "in thy seed shall all the families of the earth be blessed." He wrote Genesis 22! In their conversion they were to "call on the name of the Lord" and trust in the Messiah, Abraham's heir, to bless them with every spiritual blessing, including the forgiveness of their sins.

This next observation is crucial. Moses links obedience to God's law with this very gospel conversion: "you shall obey the voice of Jehovah…if you turn unto Jehovah" (Deut. 30:10). Moses called them to gospel obedience to the Decalogue and the book of the law. He called them to an obedience linked to and built on gospel conversion and heart circumcision. Else they never could have experienced the blessings of the Mosaic covenant.

Thus, the Mosaic covenant did not promote legalism. It did not teach that sinners get right with God by the works of the law. It was not a republication of a pre-fall covenant of works. It called Israel as a society to gospel obedience. God built the Mosaic covenant on the foundation of the need for regeneration and of justification by faith.

Many passages in Scripture confirm that Hebrew Israel had evangelical religion, not a legalistic religion built on human merit and salvation by works. Consider two from each Testament:

> Look unto me, and be ye saved, all the ends of the earth; for I am God, and there is none else. By myself have I sworn, the word is gone forth from my mouth in righteousness, and shall not return, that unto me every knee shall bow, every tongue shall swear. Only in Jehovah, it is said of me, is righteousness and strength; even to him shall men come; and all they that were incensed against him shall be put to shame. In Jehovah shall all the seed of Israel be justified, and shall glory (Isa. 45:22–25).

> Surely he hath borne our griefs, and carried our sorrows; yet we did esteem him stricken, smitten of God, and afflicted. But he was wounded for our transgressions, he was bruised for our iniquities; the chastisement of our peace was upon him; and with his stripes we are healed. All we like sheep have gone astray; we have turned every one to his own way; and Jehovah hath laid on him the iniquity of us all.… He shall see of the travail of his soul, and shall be satisfied: by the knowledge of himself shall my righteous servant justify many; and he shall bear their iniquities (Isa. 53:4–6, 11).

> But now apart from the law a righteousness of God hath been manifested, being witnessed by the law and the prophets; even the righteousness of God through faith in Jesus Christ unto all them that believe; for there is no distinction (Rom. 3:21–22).

> But to him that works not, but believeth on him that justifies the ungodly, his faith is reckoned for righteousness. Even as David also pronounces blessing upon the man, unto whom God reckons righteousness apart from works, saying, Blessed are they whose iniquities are forgiven, and whose sins are covered. Blessed is the man to whom the Lord will not reckon sin (Rom. 4:5–8).

Isaiah preached a gospel of salvation by looking to Jehovah, in whom is righteousness and strength. According to Isaiah, Jehovah's righteousness saves us, not our own. Jehovah's strength, power, and work save us, not our own. He said that all Israel's seed are justified in Jehovah, not in themselves. He said that they are justified by the knowledge of Christ. Isaiah also proclaimed pardon for sin based on the suffering of Christ. Paul says that the Old Testament bears witness to the virtue of Christ by which God justifies men. He says that David blessed the man to whom God reckons righteousness apart from works.

I chose support that covers the entire history of the Mosaic covenant, from its ratification through Moses, to the zenith of its blessing in the days of David, to its era of decline and judgment in the days of Isaiah. From beginning to end, the Mosaic covenant promoted evangelical religion, and only gospel religion.

An Evangelical Explanation of its Conditional Form

In this conditional promise God doesn't say: "if you repent and believe, then you will be my special people," but, "if you keep my law, then you will be my special people." God said to Adam, if you eat you will die, implying, if you obey you will retain life and Eden. Similarly, he said to Israel, if you obey, you will retain Canaan, but if you disobey, you will be judged and disinherited. As Adam lost Eden, you will lose Canaan. This similarity explains why some suggest that the Mosaic covenant republished a covenant of works. Evidently, the Mosaic covenant pictures the fall of man and displays how inveterate and ruinous human sin really is. Yet this does not mean it was "a covenant of works."

Clearly, the Mosaic covenant called for evangelical obedience founded on gospel conversion (Deut. 30:10). How then is its conditional form consistent with this evangelical nature? God promised them that if they lived in gospel obedience, then they would become a holy community of royal priests who worship him acceptably and reign with him perpetually. By walking in gospel obedience they would retain their present inheritance and receive the Messianic inheritance at his coming. This teaches the necessity of gospel obedience unto complete salvation. It exposes that none can produce gospel obedience by his own strength. Scripture underscores the necessity of gospel obedience unto complete divine salvation:

> Ye shall therefore keep my statutes, and mine ordinances; which if a man do, he shall live in them: I am Jehovah (Lev. 18:5).

> For I say unto you, that except your righteousness shall exceed the righteousness of the scribes and Pharisees, ye shall in no wise enter into the kingdom of heaven (Matt. 5:20).

> Brethren, we are debtors, not to the flesh, to live after the flesh: for if ye live after the flesh, ye must die; but if by the Spirit ye put to death the deeds of the body, ye shall live. (Rom. 8:12–13).

Jesus warned that evangelical righteousness was necessary to enter heaven. Paul said that unless we walk in a lifestyle of gospel holiness we will die, that is, endure God's wrath. He plainly taught that gospel holiness leads to eternal life, a wicked life to eternal death. This is how the conditional promise of the Mosaic covenant applies to the Christian life. It demonstrates the necessity of perseverance in gospel faith and holiness. It displays that apart from divine regeneration and preservation there can be no perseverance. Thus, Paul sums its substance as: "he that does them shall live in them" (Gal. 3:12). The law is gracious because it teaches us that if we live a holy life, mortify the deeds of the body, and keep evangelically the commandments of God, we will go to heaven, not to hell. We will live. It teaches Christians that the end of gospel holiness is life; of wickedness, death. A holy life does not replace faith in Christ as the alone means of justification. But a holy life is as indispensable as faith in Christ. No man is justified without gospel faith; yet no man is glorified without gospel holiness. Gospel faith justifies. Gospel holiness eventuates in eternal life.

Thus, the Mosaic covenant was not a proclamation of works righteousness, but of gospel sanctification. It proclaimed, not that sinners are justified by human virtue, but that gospel holiness is necessary for heaven. Consider the dynamic created by pressing the necessity of a holy life on a community of unconverted men. In love he redeemed them and by grace gave them a homeland. Yet their hearts were not disposed to be grateful, or to trust him, or to reciprocate his love. They had no ability to comply with his call to gospel holiness. Sin reigned in their hearts. They must first be converted, regenerated, have their hearts circumcised. They must get right with God. Else they will resent his law. They will despise his Sabbaths. They will serve other gods. They will turn his grace to lasciviousness, and his law to legalism.

The Practical Functions of the Mosaic Covenant

This divine pledge serves many beneficial ends. We now unfold the role of the Mosaic covenant in the corporate life of God's people in redemptive history and in their religious experience.

Functions of the Mosaic Covenant in Redemptive History

> Israelites; whose is the adoption, and the glory, and the covenants, and the giving of the law, and the service of God, and the promises; whose are the fathers, and of whom is Christ as concerning the flesh, who is over all, God blessed for ever. Amen (Rom. 9:4–5).

Paul enumerates some of the benefits of this covenant for the society of God's people. We consider seven practical functions: (1) it separates and preserves his people for Messiah, (2) provides the constitution of the theocracy, (3) discloses God's abiding moral law, (4) institutes the ordinances of corporate worship, (5) restores the blessing of sacred rest, (6) bestows the privilege of special revelation, and (7) administers the divine patriarchal inheritance.

It Separated and Preserved his People for Messiah

> What then is the law? It was added because of transgressions, till the seed should come to whom the promise has been made.... So that the law is become our tutor to bring us unto Christ (Gal. 3:19, 24); but when the fullness of the time came, God sent forth his Son, born of a woman, born under the law, that he might redeem them that were under the law, that we might receive the adoption of sons (Gal. 4:4–5).

The Mosaic covenant segregated Abraham's patriarchal posterity from the rest of mankind. It set them apart from the other nations and preserved them until Christ came. God promised that Christ would be the descendant of the Patriarchs and David. By the Mosaic covenant he isolated their posterity and preserved it, in order to fulfill that promise. He kept them intact with his theocratic law. He kept them stable with genealogical records, to attest his faithfulness to his solemn promises.

It Provided the Constitution of the Hebrew Theocracy

> What great nation is there, that has statutes and ordinances so righteous as all this law, which I set before you this day?... And Jehovah commanded me at that time to teach you statutes and ordinances, that ye might do them in the land whither ye go over to possess it (Deut. 4:8, 14).

The book of the law regulated their civil and religious life as a nation living in Canaan. It formed their principles of jurisprudence. God gave them a body of civil law superior to that of every nation contemporary with them. This code of just law gave them a solid foundation for national justice, peace, stability, and prosperity.

It Disclosed God's Abiding Moral Law: The Decalogue

> Now we know that what things soever the law says, it speaks to them that are under the law; that every mouth may be stopped, and all the world may be brought under the judgment of God: because by the works of the law shall no flesh be justified in his sight; for through the law cometh the knowledge of sin.... Do we then make the law of none effect through faith? God forbid: nay, we establish the law (Rom. 3:19–20, 31).

Scripture commends the Ten Commandments as the moral law of God. Thus, God's moral law defines and exposes human sin (Rom. 3:19–20). Therefore, the gospel does not do away with the Decalogue but rather establishes it (Rom. 3:31). Scripture affirms that it is holy, just, and good (Rom. 7:12). God by grace wrote his law in the heart of Hebrew believers under the Mosaic covenant (Ps. 37:31). But this spiritual blessing did not distinguish Hebrew Israel as a community. Thus, the new covenant is superior. It insures evangelical compliance by the society of Christian Israel because God writes the Decalogue on their hearts (Heb. 8:8–10).

God declared in the Ten Commandments what he requires from all men everywhere. The law of God is intimately related to the human conscience (Rom. 2:14–15). Even Gentiles that never had the privilege of exposure to special revelation have *the law's work* in their hearts. The fact that they have the law's work in their hearts means that they *"are the law* for themselves." What is the law's work? What function does it perform? How does this relate to the conscience? First, the law defines right and wrong. Second, it obliges right and forbids wrong. Third, it promises blessing if you do right, and judgment if you do wrong. For example, it promises: "Honor your father and mother that it may be well with you and that your days may be long upon the land." And it threatens: "You shall not take the name of the Lord your God in vain, for the Lord will not hold him guiltless that takes his name in vain." This is precisely the function of conscience. Conscience defines right and wrong. Conscience obliges right and forbids wrong. Conscience excuses you when you think you've done right, and accuses you when you think you've done wrong (Rom. 2:15). After the fall, sin defiles even the conscience (Titus 1:15). Defiled conscience no longer has the proper standard of right and wrong. Men call evil good and good evil (Isa. 5:20). This perverts its function of commending and condemning. Sometimes men excuse what they should condemn (Rom. 1:32) and condemn what they should approve (Matt. 12:7).

On Sinai God codified, amplified, and purified the voice of the human conscience. This is the great moral blessing that the Decalogue bestows, not merely on Hebrew Israel, but on all who hear it.

It Instituted the Blessings of Corporate Worship

> Now even a first covenant had ordinances of divine service, and its
> sanctuary, a sanctuary of this world (Heb. 9:1).

Through the Mosaic covenant God blessed his people with the tabernacle and priesthood, visible institutions of corporate worship and fellowship with himself. When they saw the pillar of cloud and fire they had special evidence that God really exists, hears, and responds. In the priesthood and sacrifices he provided a provisional system to picture Christ's atonement for sin and guilt. He also provided special occasions, the feasts, when his people could draw near to him in his house for corporate worship.

It Restored the Blessing of Sacred Rest: The Sabbath

> Jehovah has given you the sabbath, therefore he gives you on the
> sixth day the bread of two days; abide ye every man in his place, let
> no man go out of his place on the seventh day. So the people rested
> on the seventh day (Exod. 16:29–30).

God restored to his people the creation ordinance of sacred rest (Exod.
16:22–30). Through centuries of slavery this blessing was abridged or
denied. He featured it as the token of this covenant.

It Bestowed the Privilege of Special Revelation: The Scriptures

> What advantage then hath the Jew? or what is the profit of circum-
> cision? Much every way: first of all, that they were entrusted with
> the oracles of God (Rom. 3:1–2).

Paul stresses the tremendous value of this privilege (Rom. 2:17–20).
Before the Mosaic covenant there was no Bible. God revealed the Old Testament over the course of their history and entrusted it to Hebrew Israel.

It Administered the Divine Patriarchal Inheritance: Canaan

> If ye walk in my statutes, and keep my commandments, and do
> them; then I will give your rains in their season, and the land shall
> yield its increase, and the trees of the field shall yield their fruit
> (Lev. 26:3–4).

Through the Mosaic covenant God dispenses and regulates their divine
inheritance in Canaan (Lev. 20:24, 26). His law defines the borders of the
land he allotted to them (Exod. 23:31). His law also regulates their retention
of it. If they walk in gospel obedience to his law, they retain the land and its
blessings (Lev. 26:3–4). If they forsake his law, and do the abominations of
the nations that they drove out of Canaan, then God will also drive them out
of their inheritance (Deut. 4:25–27). The land will "vomit them out":

> Ye therefore shall keep my statutes and mine ordinances, and shall
> not do any of these abominations; neither the home-born, nor the
> stranger that sojourns among you; (for all these abominations have
> the men of the land done, that were before you, and the land is
> defiled); that the land vomit not you out also, when ye defile it, as it
> vomited out the nation that was before you (Lev. 18:26–28).

Functions of the Mosaic Covenant for Morality and Religion

The Mosaic covenant furnishes rich moral and religious instruction. It furnishes a rich depiction of Christ. It furnishes many practical lessons about salvation and godliness. It gives valuable instruction about the principles of justice in family, church, and state.

It Furnishes a Rich and Diverse Portrait of Christ:

> And beginning from Moses and from all the prophets, he interpreted to them in all the scriptures the things concerning himself.... And he said unto them, These are my words which I spoke unto you, while I was yet with you, that all things must needs be fulfilled, which are written in the law of Moses, and the prophets, and the psalms, concerning me (Luke 24:27, 44),

Would that our hearts so burned. Would that our Savior opened our minds to see and rejoice in the rich portrait that the Mosaic covenant paints of him.

♦ God's Righteous Servants Picture Christ and His Work

> Moses indeed said, A prophet shall the Lord God raise up unto you from among your brethren, like unto me (Acts 3:22)

Moses, the mediator of the old covenant, pictures Jesus, the mediator of the new. Moses was God's righteous servant, faithful in all his house, to whom God spoke face to face, who mediates God's covenant with his people, and leads them through their redemption to their inheritance. So also is Jesus.

Similarly, Joshua was God's righteous servant who upon the death of the mediator allotted divine inheritance to his people. So also, Jesus, upon the death of the new covenant mediator, dispensed divine inheritance to his people. How? He did so by resurrection from death! As Joshua dispensed Canaan so Jesus dispenses the Holy Spirit. Similarly, Aaron was a high priest, appointed by God to make atonement for his people. So also is Jesus. Again, Aaron's grandson, Phinehas, was a righteous priest, who turned God's wrath away from his people, to whom God made a covenant of a perpetual priesthood. So also Jesus is God's righteous priest, who turns away God's wrath, with whom God makes a covenant of perpetual priesthood.

✦ Religious Ordinances and Objects Picture Christ and His Work
John says that Moses pictured Christ when he lifted up the serpent in the wilderness and called the dying to look in faith and live (John 3:14–15). Jesus says that he is the living manna who came down from heaven and gives life to those who believe in him (John 6:31–35). Paul says that the sacrifice of the passover lamb pictures the sacrifice of Christ (1 Cor. 5:7–8). Scripture declares that the tabernacle and its ordinances were a "copy and shadow" of Christ's priestly work (Heb. 8:4–5). When the high priest entered the most holy place annually to atone for the people's sins he pictured the atonement of Christ.

It Furnishes Practical Lessons about Salvation and Godliness

We consider five practical lessons that the Mosaic covenant teaches about experiential religion.

✦ It Displays the Need of Grace for Justification (Rom. 3:19–20)
The Decalogue belongs in evangelism. It exposes the futility of salvation by works. It exposes the need of sinners for Christ and salvation in him. It displays the necessity of divine grace for salvation. Since it purifies and amplifies the voice of conscience, it shouts the very truth that conscience whispers. It shuts the mouth of human pride and leaves the entire world guilty before God and in need of salvation.

✦ It Leads Sinners to Christ's Righteousness

> For being ignorant of God's righteousness, and seeking to establish their own, they did not subject themselves to the righteousness of God. For Christ is the end of the law unto righteousness to every one that believeth (Rom. 10:3–4).

Christ is the destination of the Decalogue. It carries men convicted of sin to Jesus for virtue, pardon, and acceptance with God. It brings us to the end of ourselves, and our own virtue, so that we look away from ourselves, by faith to Christ for salvation from our sins.

✦ It Calls Christians to Gospel Holiness (Matt. 5:20; Rom. 8:12–13)
God told Hebrew believers to teach their children the meaning of keeping the law. They were to explain that they kept it for gospel motives, out of gratitude to God for redeeming them in love and giving them Canaan

by grace. Then they were to explain its role in sanctification. To walk in gospel obedience would be their evangelical virtue (Deut. 6:20–25). Jesus said evangelical virtue was necessary for heaven: "For I say unto you, that except your righteousness shall exceed the righteousness of the scribes and Pharisees, ye shall in no wise enter into the kingdom of heaven" (Matt. 5:20). He expounded that virtue in his sermon on the mount. Gospel virtue comes from gospel obedience. Paul underscored its absolute necessity to enter heaven (Rom. 8:12–13). Thus, the Mosaic covenant calls Christians to embrace the necessity of gospel holiness, appreciate its blessedness, and cultivate it by God's grace by the power of the Holy Spirit.

+ It Shows Christians How to Love (Rom. 13:8–10)

> He that loves his neighbor has fulfilled the law.... Love works no ill to his neighbor: love therefore is the fulfillment of the law (Rom. 13:8, 10).

Since the Decalogue educates the conscience, it teaches Christians how to love. Love is the fulfilling of the Decalogue. Love does not murder, commit adultery, steal, or covet. Love does not selfishly harm others. The Decalogue shows Christians how to love others in a way that pleases God.

+ It Warns Christians about the Perils of Hypocrisy (1 Cor. 10:5–14)

> Howbeit with most of them God was not well pleased: for they were overthrown in the wilderness. Now these things were our examples, to the intent we should not lust after evil things, as they also lusted.... Now these things happened unto them by way of example; and they were written for our admonition, upon whom the ends of the ages are come (1 Cor. 10:5–6, 11).

Paul warns the church in Corinth to avoid the tragic experience of the wilderness generation. They experienced divine redemption from Egypt and miraculous divine provisions for their needs. Yet most of them did not make it to Canaan. They perished in the wilderness due to their unbelief and rebellion. So Paul warns the Corinthians that God wrote these things as an example for us. He warns them not to do the things they did. Specifically, he warns them to stay away from Gentile idolatry. He warns them not to make trial of the Lord, or murmur against him, or commit fornication, like they did. He warns them not to be proud, but to walk in humility and dependence on God. In this way, the Mosaic covenant warns Christians and Christian churches about the perils of hypocrisy.

It Gives Valuable Instruction about Equity and Justice

> They say unto him, Why then did Moses command to give a bill of divorcement, and to put her away? He says unto them, Moses for your hardness of heart suffered you to put away your wives: but from the beginning it has not been so (Matt. 19:7–8).

> For it is written in the law of Moses, Thou shalt not muzzle the ox when he treads out the corn. Is it for the oxen that God cares, or says he it assuredly for our sake? Yea, for our sake it was written: because he that plows ought to plow in hope, and he that threshes, to thresh in hope of partaking. If we sowed unto you spiritual things, is it a great matter if we shall reap your carnal things? (1 Cor. 9:9–11).

The Mosaic covenant discloses generic principles of justice for family, church, and state. These passages both reflect on the book of the law. Jesus refers to a civil law regarding marriage (Deut. 24:1–4), Paul to a statute regarding fair treatment of animals (Deut. 25:4). Jesus teaches that the Mosaic civil statute on divorce and remarriage took into account the hardness of men's hearts. The civil legislation did not enforce the full extent of morality required in the seventh commandment. Jesus said that the Pharisaic practice of "divorce on demand" was sinful and violated the seventh commandment, even though the Mosaic civil law permitted it. Moses received that civil law from God. God the Legislator considered the hard hearts of his theocratic citizens when he framed his statute on divorce and remarriage. Surely there is wisdom here from which modern legislators should learn. Civil law has limited effectiveness. The most stringent civil laws are not always the most effective ones. Thus the Mosaic covenant provides a gold mine of wisdom to lawmakers from every nation on earth.

Paul's insight comes from a completely different vantage point. He commends the spirit of the civil law. The statute regarding the ox embodies a general principle of equity. Paul first discovers that principle, then applies it to the issue of just compensation of gospel workers. The principle of justice embodied in this statute applies to the church, the family, and the state. This is true of every civil statute in the book of the law. Thus, the Mosaic covenant furnishes parents, churchmen, and legislators with a wealth of information about ethics, equity, justice, and morality. God gave the Mosaic civil code, not just for Hebrew Israel to live by in Canaan, but so that Christians would learn the general principles of ethics and justice, so that we could apply them to our lives and live by them in our homes and churches.

Conclusion: the Mosaic Covenant and the Covenant of Grace

If the Mosaic covenant cannot regenerate or forgive sinners, how then were sinners saved under its auspices? They had the promise of a Savior and Messiah (Gen. 3:15, 22:18). They had throughout their history ongoing disclosure of the gospel with ever increasing light and fullness. They had in their religious service many pictures of Christ and his work. The Holy Spirit blessed these gospel promises and pictures of Christ as means of grace. Through them he fulfilled the covenant of grace and created spiritual children of Eve and Abraham. Through those means he regenerated and circumcised their hearts. Thus he created faith and repentance in their hearts. Thus he blessed Hebrew believers with the spiritual blessings of the new covenant. They had the law written on their hearts, knew the Lord, and had their sins forgiven on the ground of Christ's coming atonement. Many of the witnesses of faith enumerated in Hebrews 11 lived under the Mosaic covenant: "Gideon, Barak, Samson, Jephthah; David and Samuel and the prophets, who through faith subdued kingdoms, wrought righteousness, obtained promises, stopped the mouths of lions" (Heb. 11:32–33). These all had faith in Christ. They were justified by faith and lived by faith. They died in faith and sat down with Abraham, Isaac, and Jacob in heaven and glory.

Hebrew Israel was not a visible society of a spiritual posterity. It was a visible society of Abraham's patriarchal posterity, circumcised in body. But within that nation there was a "remnant that did not bow their knees to Baal." This remnant was composed of Abraham's spiritual children, circumcised in heart. Under the old covenant this remnant had no unique ordinances that organized them into a visible community. Christ organized the gospel remnant of Hebrew Israel into a visible community when he instituted the new covenant.

Finally, we should not disparage the Mosaic covenant. To do so would despise God's wisdom and goodness. We should appreciate its manifold display of divine glory. Yet, its limits, weakness, and inferiority give us even more cause to bless God for our privilege of living under the new covenant and its better promises. Finally, let us pray that God would give us grace to take to heart the moral lessons, gospel exhortations, and spiritual warnings that the Mosaic covenant presses on our consciences.

— 13 —

The Davidic Covenant

"I have made a covenant with my chosen, I have sworn unto David my servant:
Thy seed will I establish forever, And build up thy throne to all generations."

—PSALM 89:3–4

Introduction: Survey of the Biblical Testimony

Psalm 89:3–4 epitomizes the biblical testimony. This text establishes the fact of the Davidic covenant and identifies its essential features. It establishes the fact: "I have made a covenant.... I have sworn." It defines two features. It identifies its partakers, David and his royal posterity: "David my servant... thy seed." It articulates its central promise: "thy seed will I establish forever, And build up thy throne to all generations." Scripture records this promise to David (2 Sam. 7:8–16; 1 Chron. 17:10–14). Yet this record does not either say explicitly that God made a covenant, or use terms for an oath. Inspired reflections reveal its covenantal nature (Ps. 89:26–36; Acts 2:30).

Scripture also discloses the historical fulfillment of this pledge through Solomon, the kings of Judah, and Christ:

> Howbeit Jehovah would not destroy the house of David, because of the covenant that he had made with David, and as he promised to give a lamp to him and to his children always (2 Chron. 21:7).

> Brethren, I may say unto you freely of the patriarch David, that he both died and was buried, and his tomb is with us unto this day. Being therefore a prophet, and knowing that God had sworn with an oath to him, that of the fruit of his loins he would set one upon his throne; he foreseeing this spoke of the resurrection of the Christ (Acts 2:29–31).

Scripture also discloses the practical function of this pledge to supply peace, justice, and stability for God's people (Isa. 9:6–7):

Accordingly, we consider its essential features, historical fulfillment, and practical functions.

The Essential Features of the Davidic Covenant

Like God's covenant with his righteous servant Noah, this divine pledge is very basic. Scripture explicitly discloses simply its partakers and promises, no token or other ritual trappings.

The Partakers of the Davidic Covenant

The principle partaker is King David, God's righteous servant. As with the Noahic servant covenant, his royal posterity participates as beneficiaries of this pledge. As with the covenant with his righteous servant Abraham, Christ is its ultimate heir and partaker.

The Principal Partaker: King David[1]

> Now therefore thus shall you say unto my servant David.... I will make you a name, like unto the name of the great ones that are in the earth. And I will appoint a place for my people Israel, and will plant them, that they may dwell in their own place, and be moved no more; neither shall the children of wickedness waste them any more, as at the first, and as from the day that I commanded judges to be over my people Israel; and I will subdue all your enemies. Moreover I tell you that Jehovah will build you a house (1 Chron. 17:7–10; also 2 Sam. 7:8–11).

> Verily my house is not so with God; Yet he has made with me an everlasting covenant, Ordered in all things, and sure: For it is all my salvation, and all my desire, Although he makes it not to grow (2 Sam. 23:5).

> My covenant will I not break, Nor alter the thing that is gone out of my lips. Once have I sworn by my holiness: I will not lie unto David: His seed shall endure forever, And his throne as the sun before me (Ps. 89:34–36).

---

1. 2 Sam. 7:8–11, 23:5; 1 Chron. 17:7–10; Ps. 89:3, 34–36, 132:11; Acts 2:29–30.

Scripture records the reign of David (1 Chron. 11:1–29:30). After God delivered David from Saul, brought him to the throne, and gave him victory and rest, David expressed to Nathan his concern to build a house for God (2 Sam. 7:1–3). God responds to David's concern with this solemn commitment to build David a house (2 Sam. 7:4–11). This establishes a close connection between this divine pledge and God's house. David's house is his posterity, his royal descendants. God's house is the place of his special presence. Christ merges these.

David's Royal Posterity[2]

> Thy seed will I establish forever, And build up thy throne to all generations…. His seed also will I make to endure forever, And his throne as the days of heaven. If his children forsake my law, And walk not in mine ordinances; If they break my statutes, And keep not my commandments; Then will I visit their transgression with the rod, And their iniquity with stripes. But my lovingkindness will I not utterly take from him, Nor suffer my faithfulness to fail (Ps. 89:4, 29–33).

As with God's pledges with his righteous servants Noah and Abraham, his covenant with David focuses on and blesses his posterity. For this reason David's royal posterity partake in this divine pledge as its beneficiaries. David's royal posterity begins with his immediate heir who will arise to his throne after his death. It includes the dynasty of kings of Judah, descended from David and his heir, who reign in Jerusalem until its destruction and the Babylonian captivity.

David's Ultimate Heir: Christ Jesus[3]

> Your house and your kingdom shall be made sure forever before you: your throne shall be established forever (2 Sam. 7:16); and his throne shall be established forever (1 Chron. 17:14).

> And behold, you shall conceive in your womb, and bring forth a son, and shall call his name JESUS. He shall be great, and shall be called the Son of the Most High: and the Lord God shall give unto him the throne of his father David: and he shall reign over the house

---

2. 2 Sam. 7:12–15; 1 Chron. 17:11–13; Ps. 89:4, 29–33.
3. 2 Sam. 7:16; 1 Chron. 17:14; Ps. 89:36; Luke 1:31–33; Acts 2:29–31.

of Jacob for ever; and of his kingdom there shall be no end (Luke 1:31–33).

Brethren, I may say unto you freely of the patriarch David, that he both died and was buried, and his tomb is with us unto this day. Being therefore a prophet, and knowing that God had sworn with an oath to him, that of the fruit of his loins he would set one upon his throne; he foreseeing this spoke of the resurrection of the Christ (Acts 2:29–31).

David's dynasty of Judean kings does not exhaust the partakers of this pledge. David's ultimate heir is the Messiah, who rules on David's throne as the beneficiary and ultimate heir of this pledge.

The Promises of the Davidic Covenant

God pledged permanent rule to David. He swore to him that his dynasty and kingdom would abide in perpetuity. His pledge focuses first on his immediate heir who will sit on his throne and fulfill his vision for the house of God. Next it focuses on his dynasty of royal heirs who reign on his throne in Jerusalem. He promises to treat them as sons and perpetuate their kingdom. His pledge concludes with David's ultimate heir, the Christ, who will reign on his throne forever.

Promises to David's Immediate Heir: the King of Israel

When thy days are fulfilled, and you shall sleep with thy fathers, I will set up thy seed after thee, that shall proceed out of thy bowels, and I will establish his kingdom. He shall build a house for my name, and I will establish the throne of his kingdom for ever. I will be his father, and he shall be my son: if he commit iniquity, I will chasten him with the rod of men, and with the stripes of the children of men; but my lovingkindness shall not depart from him, as I took it from Saul, whom I put away before thee (2 Sam. 7:12–15 also 1 Chron. 17:11–13).

These promises focus on David's son and immediate heir. God promises to establish his kingdom (7:12). God promises that he will fulfill David's vision and build God's house (7:13). God promises to perpetuate his throne (7:13). God promises to regard and treat him as a son (7:14–15). This means that he will chasten him if he forsakes God's law. However, even though he judges him, he will never take the kingdom from him as he took it from Saul.

Promises to David's Royal Heirs: the Kings of Judah[4]

> If his children forsake my law, And walk not in mine ordinances; If they break my statutes, And keep not my commandments; Then will I visit their transgression with the rod, And their iniquity with stripes. But my lovingkindness will I not utterly take from him, Nor suffer my faithfulness to fail. My covenant will I not break, Nor alter the thing that is gone out of my lips. Once have I sworn by my holiness: I will not lie unto David (Ps. 89:30–35).

God's promise to perpetuate the kingdom of David's immediate heir includes his royal heirs as beneficiaries. Since they participate in this promise they are also regarded and treated as a son. Though God will punish and chasten them for their sin, he will not take the kingdom from them. As long as the kingdom of David and Judah remains, their royal heirs will rule over it.

Promises to David's Ultimate Heir: the Christ[5]

God pledges to perpetuate the rule of David (2 Sam. 7:16) and his immediate heir (1 Chron. 17:14). This promise goes beyond the destruction of Jerusalem and the collapse of the dynasty of the kings of Judah (Ps. 89:36, 38–39, 49). It envisions the coming of Christ and his perpetual reign on David's throne (Isa. 9:6–7).

The Historical Fulfillment of the Davidic Covenant

We consider the fulfillment of this divine pledge through Solomon, the dynasty of kings in Judah, and Christ.

David's Immediate Heir: Solomon, the King of Israel

> And David said to Solomon his son, As for me, it was in my heart to build a house unto the name of Jehovah my God. But the word of Jehovah came to me, saying, You have shed blood abundantly, and have made great wars: you shall not build a house unto my name, because you have shed much blood upon the earth in my sight.

---

4. 2 Sam. 7:14–15; 1 Chron. 17:11–13; Ps. 89:30–35.
5. 2 Sam. 7:16; 1 Chron. 17:14; Ps. 89:38–39, 49; Isa. 9:6–7.

> Behold, a son shall be born to you, who shall be a man of rest; and
> I will give him rest from all his enemies round about; for his name
> shall be Solomon, and I will give peace and quietness unto Israel
> in his days: he shall build a house for my name; and he shall be my
> son, and I will be his father; and I will establish the throne of his
> kingdom over Israel for ever (1 Chron. 22:7–10).

David's immediate heir is Solomon. God promised to establish his kingdom. He promised that he would fulfill David's vision and build the house
of God. He promised to perpetuate his throne and regard and treat him as
a son. Scripture records how God fulfilled these promises in Solomon's life.

God Established Solomon's Kingdom

> Solomon sat on the throne of Jehovah as king instead of David his
> father, and prospered; and all Israel obeyed him (1 Chron. 29:23).

> And Solomon sat upon the throne of David his father; and his king-
> dom was established greatly (1 Kings 2:12).

> But king Solomon shall be blessed, and the throne of David shall be
> established before Jehovah forever. So the king commanded Bena-
> iah the son of Jehoiada; and he went out, and fell upon him, so that
> he died. And the kingdom was established in the hand of Solomon
> (1 Kings 2:45–46).

Solomon Built God's House

> And, behold, I purpose to build a house for the name of Jehovah
> my God, as Jehovah spoke unto David my father, saying, Your son,
> whom I will set upon your throne in your room, he shall build the
> house for my name (1 Kings 5:5).

> Jehovah said unto David my father, Whereas it was in your heart to
> build a house for my name, you did well that it was in your heart:
> nevertheless you shall not build the house; but your son that shall
> come forth out of thy loins, he shall build the house for my name.
> And Jehovah has established his word that he spoke; for I am risen
> up in the room of David my father, and sit on the throne of Israel,
> as Jehovah promised, and have built the house for the name of Jeho-
> vah, the God of Israel (1 Kings 8:18–20).

God Treated Solomon as a Son and Perpetuated his Kingdom

Wherefore Jehovah said unto Solomon, Forasmuch as this is done of you, and you have not kept my covenant and my statutes, which I have commanded you, I will surely rend the kingdom from you, and will give it to your servant. Notwithstanding in your days I will not do it, for David your father's sake: but I will rend it out of the hand of your son. Howbeit I will not rend away all the kingdom; but I will give one tribe to your son, for David my servant's sake, and for Jerusalem's sake which I have chosen (1 Kings 11:11–13).

God promised Solomon perpetual rule over all Israel if he would obey his law (2 Chron. 7:17–18). Tragically, Solomon did not comply because his many foreign wives turned his heart away. Solomon sinned against the Lord God by building high places for the gods of his foreign wives (1 Kings 11:7–10). God chastened him by rending most of the kingdom from him (1 Kings 11:11). He said he would postpone this judgment until after Solomon's death (1 Kings 11:12). He left him rule over Judah (1 Kings 11:13). Thus God kept his promise. He punished Solomon for sin and yet perpetuated his kingdom. God also revealed this to Jeroboam (1 Kings 11:31–36).

David's Royal Heirs: the Dynasty of Kings in Judah[6]
Scripture features the promise to perpetuate David's throne by a succession of royal descendants. Due to Solomon's sin God fulfills this promise with a dynasty of kings in Judah that ruled in Jerusalem for over four hundred years. Scripture certifies this remarkable dynasty (1 Chron. 3:10–16). This dynasty includes twenty kings descended from David who ruled successively in Jerusalem until the captivity in Babylon. Their names are listed below:

1. Solomon: 2 Chron. 1:1–9:31
2. Rehoboam: 2 Chron. 10:1–12:16
3. Abijah: 2 Chron. 13:1–22
4. Asa: 2 Chron. 14:1–16:14
5. Jehoshaphat: 2 Chron. 17:1–20:37
6. Joram (Jehoram): 2 Chron. 21:1–20
7. Ahaziah (Athaliah, his mother): 2 Chron. 22:1–12, 23:1–21

---

6. "So shall their blood return upon the head of Joab, and upon the head of his seed forever: but unto David, and unto his seed, and unto his house, and unto his throne, shall there be peace forever from Jehovah" (1 Kings 2:33); "Great deliverance gives he to his king, And shows loving-kindness to his anointed, To David and to his seed, for evermore" (Ps. 18:50).

8. Joash: 2 Chron. 24:1–27
9. Amaziah: 2 Chron. 25:1–28
10. Azariah (Uzziah): 2 Chron. 26:1–23
11. Jotham: 2 Chron. 27:1–9
12. Ahaz: 2 Chron. 28:1–27
13. Hezekiah: 2 Chron. 29:1–32:33
14. Manasseh: 2 Chron. 33:1–20
15. Amon: 2 Chron. 33:21–25
16. Josiah: 2 Chron. 34:1–35:27
17. Johanan (Jehoahaz): 2 Chron. 36:1–4
18. Jehoiakim (Eliakim): 2 Chron. 36:5–8
19. Jehoiachin (Jeconiah): 2 Chron. 36:9–10
20. Zedekiah: 2 Chron. 36:11–21

Scripture reflects on the fact that God fulfills his pledge to David through this dynasty.[7] God thus displayed his great faithfulness to this pledge to David. He kept his promise in spite of sin. He kept it as long as the temple remained in Jerusalem. While Judah remained in Canaan, David's royal heirs ruled over them. When they walked in the ways of the kings of Israel, he chastened them. He kept the dynasty intact in spite of the sins and plots of evil men and women. Eventually the dynasty came to an end when God judged Judah for their sin. This created a tension that the psalmist laments:

> But thou hast cast off and rejected, Thou hast been wroth with your anointed. You have abhorred the covenant of your servant: You have profaned his crown by casting it to the ground.... Lord, where are your former lovingkindnesses, Which you swore unto David in your faithfulness? (Ps. 89:38–39, 49).

This created expectation and hope. God's people waited for the day when God would keep his pledge to David. They hoped for the coming of

---

7. "Ought ye not to know that Jehovah, the God of Israel, gave the kingdom over Israel to David for ever, even to him and to his sons by a covenant of salt?" (2 Chron. 13:5); "Jehoram was thirty and two years old when he began to reign; and he reigned eight years in Jerusalem. And he walked in the way of the kings of Israel, as did the house of Ahab; for he had the daughter of Ahab to wife: and he did that which was evil in the sight of Jehovah. Howbeit Jehovah would not destroy the house of David, because of the covenant that he had made with David, and as he promised to give a lamp to him and to his children always" (2 Chron. 21:5–7); "And all the assembly made a covenant with the king in the house of God. And he said unto them, Behold, the king's son shall reign, as Jehovah has spoken concerning the sons of David" (2 Chron. 23:3); "thus says Jehovah concerning the king that sits upon the throne of David" (Jer. 29:16).

Christ, the King, who would sit on the throne of David. This explains why their Messianic hope focused on Christ's identity as David's heir who would restore his kingdom.

David's Ultimate Heir, the Christ: Jesus' Perpetual Reign
During the dynasty and the captivity the prophets enhance the promise of David's ultimate heir. They unfold with greater clarity and detail the coming of the Messiah and his reign over Israel on David's throne. The New Testament identifies the Messiah as Jesus of Nazareth. It certifies his identity as the son and heir of David. It confirms God's faithfulness to this pledge. It affirms its fulfillment in the coronation of Christ on the throne of David by his resurrection and session at God's right hand. We consider first the prophetic witness and then the witness of the New Testament.

Prophetic Testimony that Christ is David's Ultimate Heir
Isaiah reveals the deity and reign of the Messiah. When he comes he will re-establish David's throne and reign on it (Isa. 9:6–7). Jeremiah affirms that after the captivity David's son will reign over Israel. He will reign when he comes to the remnant that returned from captivity. He will reign when he accomplishes righteousness and salvation from sin (Jer. 33:15–17, 20–21).[8] Ezekiel confirms the coming and reign of the Messiah. Ezekiel speaks of the blessings and realities of the new covenant in terms of the concrete realities of the old. The organic and symbolic connection of Abraham's patriarchal and Messianic posterities supports this imagery. He speaks of the Messiah as "David," for he shall reign in the likeness of his father David on his throne. Like David, the Messiah will reign over a united kingdom of Israel. Like David, the Messiah will shepherd God's sheep. When Messiah comes to reign over Israel, God will make with them a new covenant, the covenant of peace (Ezek. 34:23–25, 37:21–28). Zechariah confirms the coming and reign of Messiah. He discloses that, unlike the kings of Judah, he will also be a priest. He will be a "priest on his throne." Like David's immediate heir,

---

8. "In those days, and at that time, will I cause a Branch of righteousness to grow up unto David; and he shall execute justice and righteousness in the land. In those days shall Judah be saved, and Jerusalem shall dwell safely; and this is the name whereby she shall be called: Jehovah our righteousness. For thus says Jehovah: David shall never want a man to sit upon the throne of the house of Israel.… Thus says Jehovah: If ye can break my covenant of the day, and my covenant of the night, so that there shall not be day and night in their season; then may also my covenant be broken with David my servant, that he shall not have a son to reign upon his throne" (Jer. 33:15–17, 20–21).

Solomon, the Messiah, his ultimate heir, will also build God's temple. He will thus display his glory.[9]

New Testament Testimony that Jesus is David's Ultimate Heir
The New Testament features the identity of Christ as the heir of Abraham and David (Matt. 1:1; Luke 1:31–33). It documents and certifies his descent from David. His legal father, Joseph, was a royal descendant of David (Matt. 1:1–16). His biological mother, Mary, was a physical descendant of David (Luke 3:23–31). Paul confirms this: "who was born of the seed of David according to the flesh" (Rom. 1:3). Jesus himself affirmed that the Messiah was both David's descendant and his Lord (Matt. 22:41–46). Nathanael testified that Jesus was the Christ, David's heir, the king of Israel, the Son of God (John 1:49). Hebrew Israel rejected Christ and crucified their king. Yet that did not eviscerate God's pledge. God raised Jesus from the dead. He seated him in heaven on David's throne. He crowned him king over his people, Christian Israel (Acts 2:29–33; 13:34–37).[10] Now, in fulfillment of this pledge, Jesus reigns on David's throne. He builds God's spiritual temple. He rules with justice over God's people. He fights God's enemies. He will continue to reign until he subdues every enemy. He will utterly defeat Satan, sin, and death. He will consummate his reign when he returns to judge all men. Then he will reign forever and ever in fulfillment of this pledge.

Practical Functions of the Davidic Covenant
It Gives Peace, Security, and Stability to God's people

> For unto us a child is born, unto us a son is given; and the government shall be upon his shoulder: and his name shall be called

---

9. "Thus speaks Jehovah of hosts, saying, Behold, the man whose name is the Branch: and he shall grow up out of his place; and he shall build the temple of Jehovah; even he shall build the temple of Jehovah; and he shall bear the glory, and shall sit and rule upon his throne; and he shall be a priest upon his throne; and the counsel of peace shall be between them both" (Zech. 6:12–13).

10. "And we bring you good tidings of the promise made unto the fathers, that God has fulfilled the same unto our children, in that he raised up Jesus; as also it is written in the second psalm, You are my Son, this day have I begotten you. And as concerning that he raised him up from the dead, now no more to return to corruption, he has spoken on this wise, I will give you the holy and sure blessings of David. Because he says also in another psalm, You will not give Your Holy One to see corruption. For David, after he had in his own generation served the counsel of God, fell asleep, and was laid unto his fathers, and saw corruption: but he whom God raised up saw no corruption" (Acts 13:32–37).

Wonderful, Counselor, Mighty God, Everlasting Father, Prince of Peace. Of the increase of his government and of peace there shall be no end, upon the throne of David, and upon his kingdom, to establish it, and to uphold it with justice and with righteousness from henceforth even forever (Isa. 9:6–7).

Through this pledge to David God blessed his people with peace and stability. David ruled over Israel with justice and integrity. His royal sons who walked in righteousness also brought blessing and peace to his people through their rule. Ultimately, through the rule of Christ, God blesses his people with peace. When Jesus reigns in righteousness forever, his rule gives stability, peace, justice, and victory to Christian Israel under the new covenant.

It Portrays and Displays Christ's Rule and Kingdom

David my servant shall be their prince forever. Moreover I will make a covenant of peace with them; it shall be an everlasting covenant with them (Ezek. 37:25–26).

The man whose name is the Branch: and he shall grow up out of his place; and he shall build the temple of Jehovah; even he shall build the temple of Jehovah; and he shall bear the glory, and shall sit and rule upon his throne (Zech. 6:12–13).

David and Solomon portray Christ and his rule. Like David, Christ is the shepherd King who rules in justice over God's people and subdues all their enemies. Like Solomon, Jesus is David's royal heir who builds God's temple and rules over his people in peace and prosperity.

It Perpetuates God's Mediatorial Theocracy

He shall be great, and shall be called the Son of the Most High: and the Lord God shall give unto him the throne of his father David: and he shall reign over the house of Jacob for ever; and of his kingdom there shall be no end (Luke 1:32–33).

Through this pledge Christ, the God-man, rules over God's people forever. This calls us to thank and bless the Lord for his great goodness to his people.

Conclusion

We have considered the features, fulfillment, and functions of God's covenant with David. All now stands in readiness. The table is set. God's people wait in expectation for Christ, the son of David, to revive his throne and reign on it over God's people under a new covenant forever.

— 14 —

The New Covenant

"I will make a new covenant with the house of Israel";
"this cup is the new covenant in my blood."
—JEREMIAH 31:31; LUKE 22:20

The biblical witness to this divine pledge has three focal points: the pro-phetic prediction,[1] Christ's testimony,[2] and the apostolic teaching.[3] This witness highlights five categories of thought: the biblical foundations, essen-tial features, historical fulfillment, superior form, and practical functions of the new covenant.

The Biblical Foundations of the New Covenant

The prophets predict that God will make a new covenant when he restores a remnant of Israel from captivity. He makes the new covenant in fulfillment of his pledge to Abraham to bless the nations through his heir with spiritual

---

1. The prediction of the prophets: ten texts: (1) Isa. 42:1–7; (2) Isa. 49:5–13; (3) Isa. 54:9, 10; (4) Isa. 59:20, 21; (5) Jer. 31:31–34; (6) Jer. 32:36–42; (7) Ezek. 16:60–63; (8) Ezek. 34:23–31; (9) Ezek. 36:24–28; (10) Ezek. 37:21–28.

2. The testimony of Christ: ten texts: (1) Matt. 16:18; (2) Matt. 21:42–44; (3) Matt. 26:26–29; (4) Matt. 28:18–20; (5) Mark 1:15; (6) Mark 14:22–24; (7) Luke 22:19, 20; (8) John 4:1; (9) John 8:37–44; (10) John 14:26.

3. The teaching of the apostles: thirty texts: (1) Acts 2:32, 33; (2) Acts 2:38–42; (3) Acts 3:22–26; (4) Acts 20:28; (5) Rom. 2:28, 29; (6) Rom. 8:3, 4; (7) Rom. 9:6, 7; (8) Rom. 11:5–7; (9) Rom. 11:19–23; (10) 1 Cor. 11:23–26; (11) 2 Cor. 3:6–8; (12) Gal. 4:4–9; (13) Gal. 6:14–16; (14) Eph. 1:3, 7; (15) Eph. 2:11–13, (16) Eph. 2:19–22; (17) Eph. 3:20, 21; (18) Phil. 3:3; (19) Heb. 7:20–22; (20) Heb. 8:6–13; (21) Heb. 9:1, 6–12; (22) Heb. 9:15–18; (23) Heb. 9:23, 24; (24) Heb. 10:14–25; (25) Heb. 10:26–31; (26) Heb. 12:22–24; (27) Heb. 13:15, 16; (28) Heb. 13:20; (29) 1 Pet. 1:3–5; (30) 1 Pet. 2:9, 10.

blessing. To that end he sends Christ from heaven. John and Jesus reform Israel with the gospel. Jesus redeems Christian Israel from sin through his blood and gives them the earnest of their Messianic inheritance. In this setting God makes the new covenant with his people.

Restoration of a Remnant of Hebrew Israel from Captivity[4]

Jeremiah and Ezekiel foretell the coming of Christ and God's new covenant. They associate it with the return to Canaan of a remnant of Hebrew Israel. This restoration serves as the foundation of the new covenant with Messianic Israel. The remnant of Hebrew Israel rescued from Babylon pictures the remnant of Hebrew Israel that Messiah rescues from sin.

Messianic Fulfillment of the Abrahamic Covenant[5]

God fulfills his pledge to Abraham through patriarchal and Messianic posterities. Abraham's spiritual children possess the spiritual blessings of the gospel by means of repentance and faith. To fulfill his pledge to Abraham, God, after Pentecost, blesses Gentiles through Christ with gospel blessing. He justifies Gentiles by faith and gives them his Holy Spirit. Thus, the Abrahamic covenant is foundational to the new covenant.

The Incarnation of the Messiah and Redeemer[6]

When God fulfills his promise to Abraham, he also fulfills his covenant with David. Isaiah, Jeremiah, and Ezekiel foretell that when the Messiah comes, God will enter a new covenant with his people, a covenant of peace. Ezekiel calls the Messiah, "David," because he is David's descendant, who walks in his ways, as a righteous ruler and shepherd of God's people. Ezekiel speaks in metaphors. He pictures the realities of the new covenant era in concrete terms drawn from the era of the old covenant.

The Gospel Reformation of Israel by John and Jesus

Isaiah says that the Redeemer will come unto "those that turn from transgression" (Isa. 59:20). Malachi adds that God will send Elijah to turn his people from sin (Mal. 4:5, 6). Jesus taught his disciples that John the Baptist was the promised "Elijah" (Matt. 11:12–15). Jesus identified John the

---

4. Jer. 32:36, 37; Ezek. 36:24, 37:21, 22.
5. Luke 1:68–75; Acts 3:25, 26; Gal. 3:6–9, 13, 14, 29.
6. Isa. 59:20, 21; Jer. 33:14–17; Ezek. 34:23, 24, 27:24–26.

Baptist as Elijah because John ministered in the spirit and power of Elijah (Luke 1:16, 17). In fulfillment of these prophecies John and Jesus reformed Israel by preaching the gospel. They preached repentance and faith (Mark 1:15). Like John, Jesus formed a visible society of disciples, Christian Israel (John 4:1). This gospel reformation is the foundation of the new covenant with Christian Israel.

Messianic Redemption Accomplished[7] and Inheritance Supplied[8]
Isaiah predicted that God would make a new covenant when a Redeemer came to Zion. Christ redeemed his people from their sins with the blood of his cross. As the old covenant rested on divine redemption from Egypt, even so, the new covenant rests on divine redemption from sin. Again, as ratification of the old covenant coincided with the down payment of their inheritance in Canaan, even so, ratification of the new covenant coincides with receiving the Holy Spirit as down payment of the Messianic inheritance.

The Essential Features of the New Covenant

Several passages of Scripture epitomize the biblical witness to the essential features of the new covenant.[9] These passages reveal seven distinctive features: (1) its Author and Mediator: *Jehovah Jesus*; (2) its partakers: *Christ's disciples and the spirits of just men made perfect*; (3) its promises: *every spiritual blessing, permanent Messianic theocracy*; (4) its guarantee and surety: *Christ's person and work*; (5) its ratification: *Christ's blood*; (6) its religious service: *heavenly tabernacle and royal priesthood*; (7) and its token: *the Lord's Supper*. These features correspond with the features of the old covenant. The chief difference is that where the old covenant has a condition, the new has a surety and guarantee. This highlights their similarity and distinction.

The Author and Mediator of the New Covenant[10]
Moses mediated the old covenant through the angel of Jehovah. So also, Jesus, Jehovah incarnate, mediates the new covenant. Since Jesus is Jehovah, God the Son, he is both the Author and Mediator of this superior divine pledge. It is his personal pledge. When God makes this final covenant with

---

7. Isa. 59:20, 21; Eph. 1:7; Heb. 9:12, 15.
8. John 14:26; Acts 2:32, 33; Gal. 3:13, 14; Eph. 1:13, 14.
9. Matt. 26:26, 27; Luke 22:19, 20; Heb. 7:22, 8:6–13, 9:1, 11, 12, 15–24, 12:22–24.
10. Matt. 26:26–28; Luke 22:19, 20; Heb. 8:6, 9:15, 12:24.

his people, he does not mediate it through a mere man. He institutes it through the God-man.

The Partakers of the New Covenant[11]

Its partakers are Jesus' posterity. They are the community saved from sin, Christian Israel, heavenly Zion. They are comprised of Christ's disciples on earth and of the glorified spirits in heaven. This new covenant community has original, successive, and final generations.

The Original Generation of Partakers

On earth, by his death, Jesus instituted the new covenant with his disciples. When Jesus ratified the new covenant he specified its partakers: "gave *it* to the disciples.... Drink from it, all of you" (Matt. 26:26, 27). Jesus told his disciples, his spiritual children, to partake in the token of the new covenant. Yet Scripture identifies the partakers of the new covenant as the house of Israel (Heb. 8:8, 9) and as heavenly Zion (Heb. 12:22–24). How can the visible community of Jesus' disciples be Israel and Zion? The answer lies in Christ's gospel reformation. His disciples are Israel because Christ had removed unbelieving Hebrews from God's people (Acts 3:22, 23). His disciples are the evangelical remnant of Hebrew Israel. In Romans 9:1–11:36 Paul expounds the concept of this gospel remnant according to the election of grace. He says that this remnant obtained the Messianic blessing that Hebrew Israel awaited for centuries (Rom. 11:5–7). This gospel remnant includes all true local churches of Christ on earth.[12] Thus Paul called the church in Corinth, composed largely of Gentile disciples, rightly to observe the Lord's Supper, the token of the new covenant (1 Cor. 11:23–26).

In heaven upon his ascension Jesus instituted the new covenant with glorified spirits.[13] When Jesus ascended into heaven the glorified saints for the first time beheld the glorified God-man. What a day, what a sight, that must have been in heaven! Thus, heavenly Zion includes all the churches on earth, "the church of the firstborn," and the "spirits of just men made perfect"

---

11. Matt. 26:26, 27; Heb. 8:8, 12:22, 23.

12. Rom. 2:28, 29, 9:6, 7, 11:19–23; Gal. 6:14–16; Eph. 2:11–13, 19–22; Phil. 3:3.

13. "But, you are come to Zion Mountain: and to a living God's city, celestial Jerusalem; and to myriads of angels joyfully gathered; and to a church of firstborn, of those registered in heaven; and to a Judge, God of all; and to spirits of just men perfected; and to a mediator of a new covenant, Jesus; and to blood of sprinkling that speaks something better than Abel" (Heb. 12:22–24). This translation follows verse divisions used in the Greek New Testament of the United Bible Societies (UBS).

in heaven. All these partake in the new covenant. Jesus, the mediator of the new covenant, abides with the heavenly partakers. His Spirit abides with the earthly partakers. Every glorified soul from every era is now united in the heavenly community of the new covenant. Eve, Abel, Noah, Melchizedek, Abraham, Sarah, Isaac, Jacob, Joseph, Moses, Joshua, Caleb, Samuel, Deborah, Gideon, Ruth, David, Isaiah, Jeremiah, Daniel—and every other Old Testament believer—now stand united in heaven with Paul, Peter, John, James, Timothy—and every New Testament believer. Through Christ and his Spirit all true churches on earth are united with these heavenly partakers. When those Hebrew Christians entered the church some two thousand years ago, they entered heavenly Zion. So do Christians today. What a privilege to enter this glorious city. What a privilege to belong to this blessed community of Jesus' spiritual posterity in heaven and on earth.

Successive Generations of Partakers

Isaiah envisions divine perpetuation of Zion's spiritual posterity in every generation by his Word and Spirit (Isa. 59:20, 21). God creates Jesus' spiritual posterity by his Word joined to his Spirit, not by rationalism, his Word without his Spirit, or by mysticism, his Spirit without his Word. Isaiah speaks of Zion's *spiritual* children. He cannot refer to all Zion's physical descendants. If he does, then God promises to save all the physical children and grandchildren of every Christian in every church in every generation. Even Abraham, the father of believers, did not experience such blessing: "Esau I hated." Rather, God promises to perpetuate Jesus' seed so that the church on earth will have spiritual children in every generation.[14]

Accordingly, Christ stands committed to build his church in every generation until he returns (Matt. 16:18). The church of Christ is the visible society of his spiritual posterity. Thus it perpetuates and grows by spiritual generation. This happens when God creates spiritual children through the gospel and adds to his church those "being saved" (Acts 2:38–42, 47). Thus, the survival of the church rests on fulfillment of the covenant of grace. Thus, the church should admit only Eve's spiritual children, at enmity with the devil. Men look on credible confessions of faith. Thus it is always possible for hypocrites to infiltrate the earthly chapter of the new covenant community. The heavenly chapter of Zion grows in every generation when genuine Christians die and join the glorified spirits in heaven.

---

14. The Psalms underscore this promise: Pss. 102:28, 103:17, 18.

The Final Generation of Partakers[15]

This new covenant community in heaven and on earth will remain as long as the era of Christ's heavenly reign continues. It will endure until the second coming of Christ. When Jesus returns he will unite the heavenly and earthly branches of his new covenant community. Then he will remove from the church on earth all sin and every hypocrite. Then he will consummate the new covenant. Then his people will live and reign with him forever in the new heavens and earth in which dwells righteousness.

Practical Application: Moral Tension in the Church

The church on earth, composed of the churches, partakes in the new covenant in every generation until Jesus comes. The church on earth is a visible society of Christ's spiritual posterity. It should, by right, de jure, receive and retain only genuine believers. Yet in fact, de facto, it receives professing Christians with a credible testimony. Thus it may potentially receive hypocrites and apostates. Even the most conscientious churchmen can only discern a credible confession of faith. Only God infallibly sees a circumcised heart. When Christ formed this visible community of his spiritual posterity, he ordained this moral tension until he returns. Regarding this struggle Bavinck cogently observes:[16]

> Inasmuch as the covenant of grace enters into the human race in this historical and organic manner, it cannot here on earth appear in a form which fully answers to its essence. Not only does there remain much in the true believers which is diametrically opposed to a life in harmony with the demand of the covenant.... But there can also be persons who are taken up into the covenant of grace as it manifests itself to our eyes and who nevertheless on account of their unbelieving and unrepentant heart are devoid of all the spiritual benefits of the covenant. That is the case now not only, but has been so throughout all the ages....

---

15. "But we do not want you to be uninformed, brethren, about those who are asleep, that you may not grieve, as do the rest who have no hope. For if we believe that Jesus died and rose again, even so God will bring with Him those who have fallen asleep in Jesus. For this we say to you by the word of the Lord, that we who are alive, and remain until the coming of the Lord, shall not precede those who have fallen asleep. For the Lord Himself will descend from heaven with a shout, with the voice of the archangel, and with the trumpet of God; and the dead in Christ shall rise first. Then we who are alive and remain shall be caught up together with them in the clouds to meet the Lord in the air, and thus we shall always be with the Lord. Therefore comfort one another with these words" (1 Thess. 4:13–18).

16. Herman Bavinck, *Our Reasonable Faith*, 278–79.

On the basis of this conflict between essence and appearance, some have tried to make a distinction and a separation between an internal covenant, which was made exclusively with the true believers, and an external covenant, comprehending the external confessors. But such a separation and difference cannot stand in the light of the Scriptural teaching. What God has joined together, no man may put asunder. No one may take away from the demand that being and appearance answer to each other and from the demand that confessing with the mouth and believing with the heart shall correspond (Rom. 10:9). But, even though there are not two covenants standing loosely alongside each other, it can be said that there are two sides to the one covenant of grace. One of these is visible to us; the other also is perfectly visible to God, and to Him alone. We have to keep to the rule that we cannot judge of the heart, but only of the external conduct, and even of that defectively.

Accordingly, on the night Jesus instituted the new covenant, Judas, a hypocrite, was included in the visible society of his disciples (Luke 22:20–22). Jesus could have removed him so that he never could have betrayed him, but that was not his plan. Christ knows every false brother that infiltrates his church in every generation. He could kill them all with lightning bolts, but ordinarily he doesn't. Rather, he charges his church to watch carefully. If the church discovers hypocrites, he calls her to remove them from her communion (Matt. 18:15–18). Judas held the office of apostle, had access to church funds, robbed the church, and accepted bribe money. Similarly, in every generation evil men like Diotrephes can infiltrate the spiritual leadership of the church. When they infect elderships and pulpits they sow discord and abuse church discipline. Only eternity will unveil how much harm wolves, disguised as sheep, have done to the church over the centuries from its parsonages and pulpits (3 John 9, 10). Paul reveals how dangerous false brothers really are. As he enumerates the serious perils he faced in his ministry, he includes false brothers, along with robbers and persecutors, in his list of dangerous persons (2 Cor. 11:26). He reiterates Christ's charge to remove wicked persons from the church (1 Cor. 5:1–13). He pronounces the curse, not on the churches of Galatia, but on any man who teaches a heretical gospel (Gal. 1:9).

Apostasy, falling away, is another way in which false brothers plague the church in every generation. Jesus warned that some would confess faith temporarily, and in a time of temptation fall away (Luke 8:13). The writer of Hebrews enlarges this warning. He calls the churches to watch lest any member is a false brother with an evil heart of unbelief who falls away from the living God (Heb. 3:12–14). Temporary faith looks like saving faith for a while. Thus, apostates confess what appears to be genuine faith in Christ. They are baptized and join the church. The church recognizes them as Christian brothers and receives them into its membership and privileges. They partake in the Lord's Supper. In this sense they are sanctified *ecclesiastically*, separated from the world and identified with the visible society of believers (Heb. 10:29). How did the blood of the new covenant effect this ecclesiastical sanctification? Through his blood Jesus ratified the new covenant and formed the visible society of his spiritual posterity. Thus, when apostates join that society, his blood sanctifies them ecclesiastically. This does not mean that Jesus died to save reprobates from sin. Further, when apostates return to the world, they insult the Messianic inheritance, the Holy Spirit. They sin with a high hand and trample under foot Christ and the gospel. Their future is bleak. They face divine punishment more severe than that meted out on those who despised the old covenant (Heb. 10:26–31). However, the peril of apostasy does not mean that Christian Israel breaks the new covenant. To the contrary, God's curse abides on apostates and hypocrites, not on the church. The substance and surety of the new covenant make it absolutely certain that Christian Israel never can or will turn away from the Lord.

The Promises of the New Covenant

God reveals the substance of his new covenant promises through the prophets. The writer of Hebrews quotes Jeremiah 31:31–34.[17] This preeminent text defines the content of the new covenant as comprehensive spiritual blessing. In the new covenant God pledges the *root, substance,* and *fruit* of comprehensive spiritual blessing.

The Root of Comprehensive Spiritual Blessing[18]

The foundational blessing of the new covenant with heavenly Zion is the promise that the gospel Word will come in the saving power of the Spirit.

---

17. "For this is the covenant that I will make with the house of Israel after those days, says the Lord: I will put my laws into their minds, and I will write them upon their hearts. And I will be their God, and they shall be my people. And they shall not teach everyone his fellow citizen, and everyone his brother, saying, Know the LORD, for all shall know me, from the least to the greatest of them. For I will be merciful to their iniquities, and I will remember their sins no more" (Heb. 8:10–12).

18. "And as for me, this is my covenant with them, says the LORD: my Spirit which is upon you, and my words which I have put in your mouth, shall not depart from your mouth, nor from

This occurs when God couples the general and effectual call of the gospel. God creates faith and repentance in the heart of sinners and imparts his Spirit to new believers. This is the root of every spiritual blessing that God lavishes on Christian Israel.

The Substance of Comprehensive Spiritual Blessing[19]

First, God promises moral blessing: "I will put my laws into their minds, and I will write them upon their hearts." In the new covenant God writes his law on the hearts of Christian Israel. This fulfills his promise to circumcise their hearts (Deut. 30:6). Ezekiel describes this blessing as regeneration: "I will give you a new heart;" and as gospel sanctification: "I will put my Spirit within you, and cause you to walk in my statutes."[20]

Second, God promises experiential blessing: "for all shall know me." He promises that Christian Israel will experience saving fellowship with him in Christ. They will love, fear, and serve the Lord throughout their lives. Jeremiah confirms this: "I will put the fear of me in their hearts" (Jer. 32:40). God's people experience this blessing because God puts his Spirit within them (Ezek. 36:27).

Third, God promises legal blessing: "For I will be merciful to their iniquities, and I will remember their sins no more." God justifies Christian Israel through Christ's virtue. By means of their faith, he accepts them as righteous and pardons all their sins on the ground of Christ's obedience and blood.

The Fruit of Comprehensive Spiritual Blessing[21]

God promises that his favor will never depart from heavenly Zion. His church will always be the object of his redeeming love (Isa. 54:10). He pledges to bless heavenly Zion with spiritual children in every generation. By means of gospel success the church will endure until Christ returns (Isa. 59:21). He pledges to watch over his people, to bless them, and do them good always. He pledges to insure their perseverance as a society in faith and

---

the mouth of your offspring, nor from the mouth of your offspring's offspring, says the LORD, from now and forever" (Isa. 59:21).

19. Jer. 31:33, 34; Ezek. 36:25–28.

20. "Then I will sprinkle clean water on you, and you will be clean; I will cleanse you from all your filthiness and from all your idols. Moreover, I will give you a new heart and put a new spirit within you; and I will remove the heart of stone from your flesh and give you a heart of flesh. And I will put my Spirit within you and cause you to walk in my statutes, and you will be careful to observe my ordinances" (Ezek. 36:25–27).

21. Isa. 54:9, 10, 59:21; Jer. 32:40; Ezek. 37:23–27.

gospel fear of God. This is why the church must and will remain faithful to God in every generation (Jer. 32:40). God also pledges never to remove his special presence and fellowship from Christian Israel (Ezek. 37:26, 27). He also pledges perpetual Messianic theocracy to Christian Israel (Ezek. 37:23, 25). In sum, in the new covenant God pledges permanent redeeming grace, permanent evangelical fellowship, and permanent theocracy.

The Surety and Guarantee of the New Covenant[22]

This feature captures the distinctive genius of the new covenant. It emphasizes its superiority to the old covenant. The promised blessing of the old covenant was conditional, and without guarantee. In stark contrast, God insures and guarantees that Christian Israel will perpetually receive the promise of comprehensive spiritual blessing and perpetual divine favor. The substance of this guarantee is Christ: "by so much also has Jesus become the surety of a better covenant" (Heb. 7:22). The word translated "surety" is ἔγγυος. This word occurs nowhere else in the New Testament. It conveys the idea of "guarantee, someone or something given as a pledge."[23] The verb form, ἐγγυαω, which means, "to give as a pledge," occurs in the LXX. In Prov. 6:1 it translates the Hebrew עָרַב, which has identical meaning.[24] David asks God to be his surety (עֲרֹב) for good (Ps. 119:122). God warns his people not to become surety (עָרַב) for strangers (Prov. 11:15). God also discloses this idea when he says that he gave Christ as his pledge for his people (Isa. 42:6, 49:8). Thus, Christ himself is God's guarantee that the promises of the new covenant can never fail. Christ himself is God's pledge that Christian Israel can never break the new covenant like Hebrew Israel broke the old. Christ makes certain that Christian Israel will never depart from God because he has purchased them with his blood (Acts 20:28). On behalf of Christ God grants them faith (Phil. 1:29). Christ died in order that they would walk in gospel obedience (Rom. 8:3, 4). Christ died to redeem them from all sin and to purify them as a people zealous of good works (Titus 2:14). Every spiritual blessing flows to Christian Israel through Christ, because of Christ, and in Christ (Eph. 1:3). Christ also prays for his people to secure their perseverance in faith and holiness in every generation (Heb. 7:25). Thus, because of Christ Christian Israel can never break the new covenant.

---

22. Isa. 42:6, 49:7; Heb. 7:20–22.
23. BAG, 213.
24. BDB, 786, defines עָרַב as: "take on pledge," "give in pledge," "exchange."

The Ratification of the New Covenant[25]
God dedicated even the old covenant with blood, signifying a commitment as permanent as a last will and testament (Heb. 9:15–18). God dedicated the old covenant with animal blood to symbolize his solemn commitment to his pledge to Hebrew Israel. Yet Jehovah Jesus dedicated the new covenant, not with animal blood, but with his own blood. God incarnate shed his blood on the cross to ratify this solemn pledge. Jesus' blood cries out for pardon and blessing. Jesus' blood certifies all the promises of the new covenant. The death of Jehovah Jesus on the cross confirms that his pledge to Christian Israel is his last will and testament. Therefore, God will never revoke or modify the new covenant. Christ's heirs must receive their Messianic inheritance forever. Further, Jesus ratified the new covenant, not in eternity past, nor just after the fall, but when he accomplished eternal redemption. Soon after the fall God ratified the covenant of grace. He ratifies the new covenant when he sends the Redeemer. Accordingly, he collects God's elect, the partakers of the covenant of grace, into a visible society and ratifies the new covenant with that visible society. This highlights the distinction between the ratification of the new covenant and the ratification of the covenant of grace.

The Religious Service of the New Covenant[26]
The old ordinances of divine service were copies and shadows. The new covenant community draws near to God with a better *tabernacle* and *priesthood*.

The Tabernacle or Temple of the New Covenant
The community of the new covenant has branches in heaven and on earth. Accordingly, the new covenant has heavenly and earthly tabernacles. Christ and the glorified spirits of believers inhabit its heavenly tabernacle. Christ entered not into a holy place made with hands, but into heaven itself. There he appears in the presence of God for his people. There he intercedes and pleads the merit of his blood. The glorified spirits of believers reign with Christ on his throne in glory. They live in the presence of God in fullness of joy and worship in the heavenly temple of the new covenant. The earthly temple of the new covenant is the Christian heart and church. God's new covenant temple is not a building. It is no longer restricted to one location.

---

25. Luke 22:20; Heb. 12:24, 13:20.
26. Heb. 9:1, 6, 7, 11, 12, 23, 24.

Rather, his people are his temple on earth. It is hard to express adequately the mammoth significance of this advancement over the religious service of the old covenant. God gives his Spirit to each Christian consecrating each as his temple (1 Cor. 6:19, 20). Thus Christians live in the presence of God every day. They never depart from his temple, for they are his temples. Further, God gives his Spirit to each church consecrating each as his temple (1 Cor. 3:16, 17; Eph. 2:20–22). Not merely three times a year, but every Sunday, the new covenant community is privileged to enter God's special presence in his ecclesiastical temple. Then God communes with them by his Word and Spirit. Thus the Spirit's power and presence characterize corporate Christian worship (Phil. 3:3).

The Royal Priesthood of the New Covenant

The royal high priest of the new covenant is Jesus Christ. He made atonement for his people in his earthly life, now intercedes for them in heaven, and will eradicate all sin from them when he returns in glory (Heb. 9:11, 28, 10:21). Christ's priesthood is superior to Aaron's (Heb. 7:20–22). His priesthood required a change in the law that regulated religious service (Heb. 7:12–14). Christians, Jesus' children, are the royal priests of the new covenant. Thus, Christian Israel is a nation of royal priests. This highlights the intimate connection of the Messianic and new covenants. Every Christian enjoys the privilege of entering the holy place to offer spiritual sacrifices acceptable to God through Jesus Christ (1 Pet. 2:5, 9–10). Christians offer the spiritual sacrifice of contrition for remaining sin (Ps. 51:18). They offer themselves to God as living sacrifices (Rom. 12:1, 2). They offer the spiritual sacrifices of singing and giving (Heb. 13:15–16).

The Token of the New Covenant[27]

When Christ says, "this cup is the new covenant," he clearly displays the commemorative nature of the Lord's Supper as the visible reminder of this divine pledge. As God equated circumcision with his pledge to Abraham, so he equates the Lord's Table with his new covenant with Christian Israel. As with the Hebrew Sabbath and circumcision, this divine token comes into existence through human compliance. When God sees true churches observing this token in gospel faith, he remembers his pledge to bless them

27. Luke 22:19, 20; 1 Cor. 11:23–26.

with every spiritual blessing, to preserve them in every generation by gospel conversions, and to dwell with them forever as his Messianic theocracy.

Christian baptism implicitly depicts the new covenant because the partakers of the new covenant are the visible community of Jesus' spiritual children. Thus, heart circumcision and Christian baptism mark the partakers of the new covenant, like circumcision marked the partakers of the Mosaic covenant.

The Historical Fulfillment of the New Covenant

Scripture records the fulfillment of the old covenant over some fourteen hundred years, from Joshua's conquest of Canaan to the coming of Christ. The New Testament only records the historical fulfillment of the new covenant in the apostolic generation. Nevertheless, it promises its certain fulfillment in every subsequent generation on earth. Further, Scripture predicts that when Christ returns God will fulfill the new covenant in the consummation in glory in new heavens and earth forever.[28]

The Fulfillment of the New Covenant in the Apostolic Generation
Scripture testifies that the church in Ephesus received all the spiritual blessings promised in the new covenant (Eph. 1:3). This was also true of every genuine church. In fulfillment of the new covenant, the apostolic churches received saving gospel grace, every moral, experiential, and legal blessing, and Messianic favor and theocracy.

First, God blessed the apostolic churches with saving gospel grace. The churches in Ephesus and Thessalonica heard and believed the gospel. The gospel came to them in power through the Holy Spirit (Eph. 1:13; 1 Thess. 1:4, 5). God put his Spirit in them when they believed the gospel. This blessing marked not only those two churches; it marked every true church of Christ. In this way he fulfilled his promise, recorded in Isaiah 59:20, 21, of saving gospel grace through God's Word and Spirit.

Second, God blessed the apostolic churches with moral blessing. In the new covenant God promises his people that he will write his law on their hearts, take out their hearts of stone, and circumcise their hearts. He promises to put his Spirit within them and cause them to live in gospel obedience to his law. Thus, the church in Rome walked in gospel obedience to the law

---

28. Rom. 8:3, 4, 8, 9; Gal. 4:9; Eph. 1:7, 3:21, 5:25–27; Col. 3:11; Rev. 14:13, 21:1–7.

by the power of the Spirit who lived in them (Rom. 8:4, 8, 9, 13). God sanctified the Corinthian church when the Spirit wrote his law on the soft tablets
of their hearts (1 Cor. 6:11; 2 Cor. 3:3). God morally re-created the church in
Ephesus unto good works that he prepared for them to do (Eph. 2:10). The
church of the Philippians walked in gospel obedience because God worked
in them the resolve and effort to please him (Phil. 2:12, 13). The church of
Colossian Christians was circumcised in heart by the power of Christ (Col.
2:11). Paul taught Titus that God saved the churches of Crete by the moral
blessing of regeneration and renewal by the Holy Spirit (Titus 3:5, 6). These
churches all experienced the moral blessing promised in the new covenant.
The church is a morally renewed society with hearts that are regenerated,
spiritually circumcised, made soft and teachable, and on which the Spirit
has written the Decalogue. The Spirit also dwells in their hearts and works
in them to keep God's law in gospel obedience. He makes their hearts holy,
dedicated to God's glory. He produces the resolution and effort by which
they please the Lord through a life rich in good works.

Third, God blessed the apostolic churches with experiential blessing. In
the new covenant God promises that all his people will know him and commune with him in gospel fear in his special presence by the Holy Spirit. The
churches in Judea walked in the fear of God and the comfort of the Holy
Spirit (Acts 9:31). The church in Rome had hope, joy, and peace in the power
of the Holy Spirit (Rom. 15:13). The churches of Galatia communed with
God as sons in the presence and power of the Spirit of adoption who dwelt
in them (Gal. 4:6). They had come to know God in personal fellowship,
even as he had come to know them (Gal. 4:9). They experienced the blessed
fruits of the Spirit who dwelt in them and blessed them with love, joy, peace
and every grace (Gal. 5:22, 23). Plainly then, God fulfilled his new covenant
promise when he poured out on the apostolic churches the Holy Spirit and
the manifold experiential blessings that they enjoyed through his power and
presence. As he promised, he put his fear in their hearts and enabled them
to know him personally.

Fourth, God blessed the apostolic churches with legal blessing. In the
new covenant God promises to forgive all the sins of his people and remember them no more. The church in Rome was justified by faith (Rom. 5:1,
2). They were right with God on the ground of Christ's virtue and blood.
God pardoned their sins and accepted them as righteous by means of faith.
God blessed the churches of Galatia spiritually by faith, just like their spiritual father, Abraham (Gal. 3:7–9). The church in Ephesus had their sins

forgiven through the blood of Christ (Eph. 1:6, 7). Clearly God fulfilled the new covenant when he justified the apostolic society of Christians and forgave their sins.

Fifth, God blessed the apostolic churches with Messianic favor and theocracy. In the new covenant God promises to preserve his people forever in his love, fellowship, and rule. He promises that he will work in them so that they will never depart from him. God began a good work of grace in the Philippians and was committed to complete it until the second coming of Christ (Phil. 1:6). Peter wrote to churches of Gentile Christians that God was committed to preserve them by faith unto a heavenly inheritance, the second coming of Christ, and the revelation of complete salvation (1 Pet. 1:3–5). Again, Peter told them that they were now God's people, his theocratic nation, who had obtained his mercy, grace, compassion, and love (1 Pet. 2:9, 10). Similarly, Paul told the Colossian church that God had translated them into the Messianic theocracy (Col. 1:12–14). Thus, God fulfilled his new covenant promise when he blessed the apostolic churches with permanent favor, love, and theocracy under the rule of Christ.

The Fulfillment of the New Covenant in Subsequent Generations

God promises and predicts the fulfillment of the new covenant in successive generations, both in the church on earth and among the spirits of just men made perfect in heaven.

Its Fulfillment in Subsequent Generations on Earth

When a Christian dies, he no longer belongs to the church on earth or participates in its life. Therefore, either God creates spiritual children of Jesus, Abraham, and Eve in every generation, or death will decimate the church and exterminate it. Paul views the church as continuing on earth and glorifying God in every generation (Eph. 3:20, 21). He affirms that the church will be here on earth when Jesus returns to present it to himself as a glorious church (Eph. 5:25–27). Again, when Jesus called the church to spread the gospel to all the nations, he promised to be present with his church in her mission of evangelism until the end of the world (Matt. 28:18–20). Therefore, God stands committed to save sinners in every generation until Jesus returns. Death will never destroy the church. The church will have victory in its spiritual war with the devil, sin, and death (Matt. 16:18). It will prevail and endure through gospel success in every generation. God will see to it in fulfillment of the new covenant. Further, in every generation the church will continue to enjoy all the spiritual blessings of the gospel. In every generation the churches will experience its moral, experiential, and legal blessings. In every generation God will preserve them in his love and fellowship. In every generation they will be God's people, the Messianic theocracy. God will fulfill his new covenant pledge in this way in every generation on earth until Jesus comes again.

God's promise to preserve the church universal does not mean that every local church will persevere from its origination until the second coming. Rather, Scripture predicts that through heresy some will fall away from the faith (1 Tim. 4:1). Nevertheless, in spite of persecution, death, and apostasy, the church universal, composed of the churches, will persevere in every generation until Christ returns.

Its Fulfillment in Subsequent Generations in Heaven

When a Christian dies, his glorified soul joins the spirits of just men made perfect in heaven. He does not leave the new covenant community. He merely transfers to its heavenly chapter of partakers. Jesus says that the fulfillment of the new covenant will continue beyond the apostolic generation. Many from all around the world will sit down with Abraham in heaven. They will hear the gospel, believe it, live the Christian life in the church on earth, and will die in Christ. Then they will enter the heavenly branch of the new covenant community (Matt. 8:11). John affirms the blessedness of those that die in Christ from the apostolic generation onward (Rev. 14:13). As long as Christians die in the Lord, their souls will enter the rest of the glorified spirits in heaven. There they will reign with Christ until he returns to finish salvation (Rev. 20:4). In this way God continues to fulfill the new covenant among the glorified spirits in heaven in every generation. Thus the heavenly chapter of the new covenant community continues to grow larger and larger. It now includes all the Old Testament saints and all the Christians who have died in the Lord over some two thousand years since Christ began his heavenly reign. It will continue to grow until he returns in glory.

The Fulfillment of the New Covenant in the Final Generation

When Jesus returns, God will complete the fulfillment of the new covenant. He will dwell with his people in love, fellowship, and peace. They will reign with Christ forever. Scripture tells us how God will fulfill this promise when Christ comes again. The glorified spirits in heaven will return with Christ. The dead in Christ will rise first. God will resurrect their bodies.

Then he will glorify the church living on earth. They will never experience death. They will be changed in a moment. He will remove every vestige of sin from their souls. He will glorify their bodies. At that very moment he will forever rid the church of every hypocrite. Then God will translate his glorified church into heaven, to meet Christ and his resurrected saints in the air (1 Cor. 15:51–58; 1 Thess. 4:13–18). Then they will see the wrath of God destroy the wicked. The earth and atmosphere will be burned up and destroyed with fire (2 Pet. 3:10–13). Then all will stand before the throne of Christ for judgment. Christ will condemn the wicked. They will go away into everlasting shame and contempt. They will suffer torment forever in body and soul in the lake of fire with the devil and the demons. Then the resurrected community of the new covenant will live with the Lord in new heavens and earth without sin or suffering forever. They will receive fully the Messianic inheritance (Rev. 21:1–7).

The Superior Form of the New Covenant

Scripture highlights the superiority of the new covenant: "But now has he obtained a ministry the more excellent, by so much as he is also the mediator of a better covenant, which has been enacted upon better promises" (Heb. 8:6). In contrast with the old covenant, this new pledge is better. Its promises are better because they are unconditional, guaranteed, and spiritual.

The Superior Promises of the New Covenant are Unconditional
The covenant of grace is God's unconditional pledge to accomplish salvation in Christ and to apply it to his elect. God applies this salvation to his elect by the general and effectual call of the gospel. God accomplishes it in Christ in the historical framework of covenant communities of his people. The old and new covenants directly relate to these visible communities of God's people. The old covenant promises relate to the organized society of Abraham's physical descendants circumcised in body. The new covenant promises relate to the organized society of Abraham's spiritual children circumcised in heart. This is the environment in which Scripture presents the superiority of the new covenant promises. Thus, consideration of the conditional form and substance of the old covenant promises fosters better appreciation of this superiority.

The old covenant promises were evangelical. The Mosaic covenant was gracious and good.[29] Yet God presented this pledge as a *conditional* promise of perpetual favor and blessing.[30] Scripture insists that God required gospel obedience, not legalistic works righteousness (Deut. 30:6–10). God says, "*If* you will indeed obey my voice and keep my covenant." His voice personally spoke from heaven the Ten Commandments to the entire nation. He promised them, on condition of evangelical obedience to the Ten Commandments, perpetual favor as God's special people and sustained theocracy: "*then* you shall be my own possession from among all peoples." In addition, God required gospel compliance with his statutes in the book of the law[31] as the condition for receiving the manifold blessings of the old covenant.[32] Conversely, God connects the curses of the old covenant to disobedience in unbelief to the book of the law.[33] God addressed these conditions to Israel as a community. Gospel obedience to the Decalogue is how Hebrew Israel sustains theocracy as a society (Exod. 19:6), not how individual sinners get right with God. Gospel compliance to the book of the law is how Hebrew Israel as a community sustains the blessings of national prosperity and avoids bringing the curses of the covenant on their society.

In stark contrast with these old covenant promises, the promises of the new covenant contain no "if." God fulfills the new covenant promises by his own supernatural power without dependence on human compliance. He does not require his people to do any work as the condition of

---

29. Rom. 3:1, 2, 31, 7:12; Gal. 3:21.

30. "Now then, if you will indeed obey My voice and keep My covenant, then you shall be My own possession among all the peoples, for all the earth is Mine" (Exod. 19:5); "So He declared to you His covenant which He commanded you to perform, *that is*, the Ten Commandments; and He wrote them on two tablets of stone" (Deut. 4:13).

31. Exod. 24:7, 8; Deut. 4:14.

32. "Now it shall be, if you will diligently obey the LORD your God, being careful to do all his commandments which I command you today, the LORD your God will set you high above all the nations of the earth. And all these blessings shall come upon you and overtake you, if you will obey the LORD your God. Blessed shall you be in the city, and blessed shall you be in the country" (Deut. 28:1–3); also Lev. 26:3–5.

33. "But if you do not obey me and do not carry out all these commandments, if, instead, you reject my statutes, and if your soul abhors my ordinances so as not to carry out all my commandments, *and* so break my covenant, I, in turn, will do this to you: I will appoint over you a sudden terror, consumption and fever that shall waste away the eyes and cause the soul to pine away; also, you shall sow your seed uselessly, for your enemies shall eat it up. And I will set my face against you so that you shall be struck down before your enemies; and those who hate you shall rule over you, and you shall flee when no one is pursuing you" (Lev. 26:14–17); also Deut. 28:15–18.

their fulfillment. God unconditionally pledges to heavenly Zion that his love will never depart from her and that his pledge to dwell in perpetual peace with her will never be revoked.[34] God also unconditionally promises heavenly Zion that his Spirit and Word will never depart from her, or from her spiritual children, or from her spiritual grandchildren, forever.[35] God unconditionally pledges to write the Decalogue on the hearts of the partakers of the new covenant, to fellowship personally with them, and to forgive all their sins.[36] God unconditionally promises Christian Israel that he will never turn away from following them to do them good, and that he will put his fear in their hearts so that they will never depart from him.[37] Again, he promises unconditionally to replace their heart of stone with a new heart that is soft and compliant, and to put his Spirit in them and cause them to keep his statutes.[38]

These unconditional promises of the new covenant comport with the unconditional promise of the covenant of grace to apply redemption to God's elect: "I will put enmity between you and the woman, and between your seed and her seed" (Gen. 3:15). When God in history forms through Christ an organized society of his elect, then he makes these unconditional promises of the new covenant with them. This highlights the intimate connection between the new covenant and the covenant of grace. It underscores that the spiritual children of Christ are the partakers of the covenant of grace and of the new covenant. The covenant of grace views them as individuals to whom God applies redemption with the gospel. The new covenant views them as an organized community formed by Jesus in history.

This underscores the superiority of the new covenant promises. Although the church may receive some unconverted persons unwittingly, it will always remain the organized society of those saved from sin. In virtue of God's faithfulness to his new covenant promises, it will always be the organized community of those who have regenerate hearts, who know the Lord, who have their sins forgiven, and who have God's Spirit in their hearts to produce evangelical obedience in them. It will always be the society that God preserves in faith and holiness by putting his fear in their hearts. The fulfillment of the new covenant promises does not depend on the church. It

---

34. Isa. 54:9–10.
35. Isa. 59:21.
36. Jer. 31:33–34.
37. Jer. 32:40.
38. Ezek. 36:26–27.

depends on God alone. This uncovers the connection of the new covenant promises with divine fulfillment of the covenant of grace. Unless God saves sinners in every generation, death will destroy the church. Yet in the new covenant God unconditionally promises to preserve the church. This mandates that God must in every generation fulfill the covenant of grace and apply redemption to sinners with the gospel.

The Superior Promises of the New Covenant are Guaranteed
The old covenant had a condition, but no guarantee or surety. God never guaranteed their gospel compliance as a community with its conditions. He could have sent his Spirit and saved from sin the vast majority of Hebrew Israel in every generation. They had sufficient means of grace. Yet he did not circumcise most of their hearts. Throughout their generations most of them remained uncircumcised in hearts and ears. Only a remnant of them knew the Lord. Thus Hebrew Israel broke the old covenant (Heb. 7:7–9). In his inscrutable wisdom, he shut up even his people to disobedience, in order that he might have mercy on men from every kindred, tribe, and tongue (Rom. 11:32–36). Instead of a condition the new covenant has a guarantee and surety. Christ personally insures that Christian Israel will never break the new covenant like Hebrew Israel broke the old (Heb. 7:22). This shouts its superiority. It calls for praise and thanksgiving to God. It elicits great confidence and hope in God.

The Superior Promises of the New Covenant are Spiritual
The promises of the new covenant are also superior in their content and focus to the promises of the old covenant. The old covenant promises focused primarily on material blessings related to living temporally in Canaan.[39] The new covenant promises focus on spiritual blessings, moral, experiential, and

---

39. "If you walk in my statutes and keep my commandments so as to carry them out, then I shall give you rains in their season, so that the land will yield its produce and the trees of the field will bear their fruit. Indeed, your threshing will last for you until grape gathering, and grape gathering will last until sowing time. You will thus eat your food to the full and live securely in your land. I shall also grant peace in the land, so that you may lie down with no one making *you* tremble. I shall also eliminate harmful beasts from the land, and no sword will pass through your land. But you will chase your enemies, and they will fall before you by the sword; five of you will chase a hundred, and a hundred of you will chase ten thousand, and your enemies will fall before you by the sword. So I will turn toward you and make you fruitful and multiply you, and I will confirm my covenant with you. And you will eat the old supply and clear out the old because of the new. Moreover, I will make my dwelling among you, and my soul will not reject you. I will also walk among you and be your God, and you shall be my people" (Lev. 26:3–12).

legal, related to living eternally in new heavens and earth (Heb. 8:10–12). This is because the new covenant community is composed of a spiritual posterity. This creates tension. The church is a society of Christ's spiritual children marked by spiritual blessings. Yet the church lives on earth, with bodily needs. Church members need rains, increase from their land, fruit, and bread (Lev. 26:4–5). They desire to live in safety, security, and peace (Lev. 26:5–6). They are citizens of nations that at times must fight to defend their freedom, homeland, and way of life. Then they need courage and victory (Lev. 26:7–8). Yet the new covenant does not feature these material and earthly blessings. How then is it superior? When God provides for the eternal needs of the soul, he presupposes his provision for the temporal needs of the body. Thus, he provides for the bodily needs of Christians as long as they live in the body and for the temporal needs of the church as long as it lives in this world.[40] At times God calls his people to suffer trials and persecutions in this life. He uses these to conform his people to Christ. Through such sufferings Christians and the church are conquerors through Christ. Thus, in fulfillment of the new covenant God even uses the afflictions of his people for their good (Rom. 8:28, 32–39).

The Practical Functions of the New Covenant

Scripture commends the practical functions of the new covenant in redemptive history and for experiential religion.

Seven Functions of the New Covenant in Redemptive History

First, the new covenant organizes the Messiah's posterity and preserves them until he returns. As the old covenant organized the patriarchs' posterity, the new organizes Christ's posterity. Jesus' posterity includes Christians on earth and the spirits of just men made perfect in heaven. As the old covenant preserved his people for the first coming of Messiah, so the new covenant preserves them until his second coming.

Second, the new covenant provides the constitution of the Messianic theocracy, the New Testament. The old covenant in the book of the law provided statutes for Hebrew Israel in Canaan. Similarly, the new covenant provides regulations for the church on earth. Jesus appointed apostles to

---

40. Matt. 6:25–33; Rom. 15:26–27; Phil. 4:18–19.

govern his church and set its permanent polity until he returns. The New Testament records these inspired policies.

Third, the new covenant establishes God's abiding moral law. The old covenant disclosed God's abiding moral law, the Decalogue. The new covenant establishes the Decalogue by writing it by the power of the Holy Spirit on the hearts of God's people.

Fourth, the new covenant enhances the blessing of corporate worship. The old covenant instituted the privilege of corporate worship for God's people through the tabernacle and Aaronic priesthood. The new covenant greatly enhances corporate worship. The church is God's spiritual temple. Heavenly Zion has Christ as high priest. Christians are royal priests appointed to offer spiritual sacrifices. The new covenant community worships in Spirit and truth in a manner pleasing to the triune God.

Fifth, the new covenant transforms the blessing of sacred rest. The old covenant restored the blessing of the day of sacred rest. The new covenant transforms it. God takes his people from the Hebrew Sabbath to the Christian Sabbath, the Lord's Day.

Sixth, the new covenant completes the privilege of special revelation. The old covenant initiated and bestowed the privilege of special revelation. Under the old covenant God gave Hebrew Israel the Old Testament. Under the new covenant he enhances and completes special revelation. He reveals the New Testament and gives his people the Bible, the finished body of Scripture.

Seventh, the new covenant administers the Messianic inheritance. Under the old covenant God administered to Hebrew Israel their patriarchal inheritance, Canaan. Under the new covenant he dispenses to Christian Israel their Messianic inheritance. He gives them the Holy Spirit as its down payment. He unites them at death with the glorified spirits in heaven. He will bring them at Christ's second coming to the new heavens and earth, where they will live forever with him in righteousness, peace, and joy.

Seven Functions of the New Covenant for Experiential Religion
First, under the new covenant God fulfills all of the types and shadows of Christ and his work. Under the old covenant God furnished his people with many pictures of Christ (Heb. 9:23–24). Under the new covenant he provides Christ himself. Christ himself mediates the new covenant and founds it on the accomplishment of his redemptive work (Heb. 9:28, 10:1).

Second, under the new covenant God provides a complete exposition of salvation from sin. Under the old covenant God disclosed gospel promises and pictures. He limited this disclosure mostly to Hebrew Israel. Under the new covenant he provides the apostolic gospel. He dispenses this gospel indiscriminately among all the nations of the earth. The apostles proclaim the message of salvation from sin fully, plainly, and indiscriminately (Rom. 1:14–17). The apostles explicitly identify the promised Christ as Jesus of Nazareth. They fully expound his person and his saving work.

Third, under the new covenant God provides all the grace necessary for salvation and godliness. The old covenant pointed Hebrew Israel to its need of grace and godliness. The new covenant provides all the grace that its partakers need. God conveys the grace needed for conversion.[41] He makes sinners right with God through Christ.[42] He enables Christians to practice gospel holiness and love.[43] He warns and preserves Christians from the perils of hypocrisy. Under the old covenant he warns his people; under the new he warns and preserves them.[44]

Fourth, the new covenant calls Christians to worship and serve God with confidence. Since the new covenant provides remission of sin, Christians should draw near to God through Christ with boldness and confidence (Heb. 10:18–23).

Fifth, the new covenant calls Christians to live in humility.[45] The forgiveness experienced by the partakers of the new covenant calls Christians, not only to confidence, but also to humility. Christians should walk softly because God has forgiven the sins of which they are now ashamed. When God, on the ground of Christ's blood, removes a person's liability to punishment for sin, that person should respond in lifelong gratitude and humility. The partakers of the new covenant should always remember with gospel shame their former wickedness. Thus, the new covenant engenders humility.

Sixth, the new covenant calls Christians to thank God for the riches of his grace: "Blessed *be* the God and Father of our Lord Jesus Christ, who has blessed us with every spiritual blessing in the heavenly *places* in Christ" (Eph. 1:3). Beholding the spiritual blessings of the new covenant calls Christians to lifelong thankfulness and devotion. The partakers of the new covenant

---

41. Isa. 59:20–21; 1 Thess. 1:4, 5; Heb. 8:10.
42. Rom. 5:1; Heb. 8:12.
43. Ezek. 36:36–37; Gal. 5:22; Heb. 8:11.
44. Jer. 32:40; Heb. 3:12–14, 6:9; 1 Pet. 1:3–5.
45. "Thus I will establish my covenant with you, and you shall know that I am the LORD, in order that you may remember and be ashamed, and never open your mouth anymore because of your humiliation, when I have forgiven you for all that you have done, the Lord God declares" (Ezek. 16:62–63).

should contemplate their spiritual blessings until their hearts are lost in wonder, love, and praise. They should thank God for his moral blessings, experiential blessings, and legal blessings. They should thank him for gospel conversion and for divine preservation throughout life. They should bless God for the Holy Spirit who dwells in them as the earnest of their Messianic inheritance. They should bless God for eternal election and glorification.

Seventh, the new covenant calls Christians to live in hope of their full inheritance: the coming of Christ and eternal glory: "Wherefore girding up the loins of your mind, be sober and set your hope perfectly on the grace that is to be brought unto you at the revelation of Jesus Christ" (1 Pet. 1:13). The new covenant calls Christians to wait for and earnestly desire the full measure of their Messianic inheritance. It calls them to order their lives on earth in the light of their blessed hope, knowing that it is certain, because God will assuredly fulfill every aspect of the new covenant.

Conclusion

In the new covenant God implements the final earthly phase of his plan to save. The promised Redeemer accomplishes redemption in fulfillment of the covenant of grace. God completes his written Word. He forms the visible society of the spiritual children of Eve, Abraham, and Jesus. They are the ultimate society of his people, heavenly Zion. By his Spirit he connects Christ's spiritual children on earth and in heaven as partakers of the new covenant. As things are now, so they shall remain until the second coming. Now his people wait in anticipation of the great day when Christ will descend from heaven and consummate the new covenant. Even so, come Lord Jesus.

—15—

The Messianic Covenant

"Jehovah has sworn, and will not repent: You are a priest forever after the order of Melchizedek"; "the word of the oath, which came after the Law, appoints a Son, made perfect forever."
—PSALM 110:4; HEBREWS 7:28

Scripture establishes the fact of the Messianic covenant (Ps. 110:1–4; Heb. 7:21–28). It declares that God swore a pledge to Christ: "Jehovah has sworn," "the word of the oath." Scripture never explicitly calls this pledge a covenant, but it has the distinguishing traits of one. It is a promise confirmed with an oath. It expresses God's goodwill to its principal partaker, his righteous servant Jesus. It is ratified in history with Christ upon his coronation. It implicitly includes Jesus' spiritual children as beneficiaries. It is associated with God's redemptive favor to his people. Hodge endorses this way of discerning a covenant:[1]

> That the plan of salvation is presented in the Bible under the form of a covenant is proved not only from the significance and usage of the words above mentioned, but also and more decisively from the fact that the elements of a covenant are included in this plan.

Peter supports Hodge's principle of interpretation (Gen. 22:16, 18; Acts 3:25, 26). The Psalmist also endorses his hermeneutical method (2 Sam. 7:8–16; Ps. 89:3–4, 26–36). Since God ratifies this covenant with Jesus in history, it seems prudent to call it the "*Messianic*" covenant, to distinguish

---

1. Charles Hodge, *Systematic Theology*, 2: 355.

it from the eternal counsel of redemption.[2] These passages uncover the biblical foundations of the Messianic covenant: "the word of oath *appoints* a Son made perfect." They define its essential features. They identify its partaker and promise: "you are priest forever after the order of Melchizedek." They specify its ratification: "the word of the oath, which came after the Law, *appoints* a Son made perfect." They describe its historical fulfillment in Christ's endless life: "because He abides forever, holds His priesthood permanently" (Heb. 7:24). They extol its practical function in redemptive history "so much the more also Jesus has become the guarantee of a better covenant" and for experiential religion "He is able to save forever" (Heb. 7:22, 25). Accordingly, we expound the biblical foundations, essential features, historical fulfillment, and practical functions of the Messianic covenant.

The Biblical Foundations of the Messianic Covenant

In the fullness of time (Gal. 4:4) God fulfills his covenants with Abraham and David by sending his Son, Jesus Christ, as their son and heir (Matt. 1:1). As Abraham's heir, Christ blesses men from every kindred, tribe, and tongue with spiritual blessing through the gospel. As David's heir Christ rules over God's people on David's throne. This fulfillment begins at his incarnation (Luke 1:31–33, 69, 72–75), heightens in his anointing with the Holy Spirit at his baptism, and consummates at his resurrection and session at God's right hand (Acts 2:29–36). Then God makes this covenant with Jesus at his coronation. Thus, the Messianic covenant rests on God the Son's incarnate life in fulfillment of his covenant faithfulness to Abraham and David. God does all this in fulfillment of his covenant of grace and of his eternal predestination of the Redeemer.

It Rests on God's Pledges to Abraham and David
God emphatically fulfills his pledge to the patriarchs when he raises Christ from the dead and seats him in glory. Then he receives and bestows the blessing of Abraham, the promise of the Holy Spirit (Gal. 3:8, 14). Thus the Messianic covenant rests on the foundation of God's faithfulness to his promise to bless Jew and Gentile alike with spiritual blessing through the gospel (Acts 2:33, 3:25, 26).

---

2. For the sake of emphasis Pink uses "Messianic covenant" for the new covenant. Arthur W. Pink, *The Divine Covenants* (Grand Rapids: Baker Book House, 1983), 259.

The Messianic covenant also rests on God's pledge to David. God fulfills his pledge to David when he sends Christ into the world in the family of David (Matt. 22:42–45; Luke 1:31–33). God further fulfills this pledge to David when he anoints Christ with his Spirit to authorize him to rule God's people as their king (John 1:32, 33, 49). Ultimately, God fulfills his pledge to David when he raises Christ from the dead and seats him on David's throne (Acts 2:29–31).

It Rests on God the Son's Incarnate Life
In one sense the Messianic covenant rests on Christ's incarnate life in its entirety. Yet this pledge especially focuses on his royal identity as God's Son, *"appoints* a Son," and on his priestly commission, "you are priest forever." Thus, the Messianic covenant especially rests on key events in Christ's life closely connected with his royal identity and his priestly work. These events are his incarnation, baptism, transfiguration, crucifixion, and perfection. His perfection denotes his resurrection and session in glory.

The Messianic Covenant Rests on Christ's Incarnation
As David's heir, the king of Israel, Jesus enters the world as the royal Son of God (John 1:49). Further, his miraculous conception without a human father marks him uniquely as God's Son (Luke 1:35; John 1:1, 14, 18).

The Messianic Covenant Rests on Christ's Baptism
God used John the Baptist to identify his Son. At Jesus' baptism God anointed him with the Holy Spirit to fulfill his Messianic commission. God also called him his Son and expressed his delight in him (Luke 3:21–22).

The Messianic Covenant Rests on Christ's Transfiguration
Again, at his transfiguration God spoke out of heaven to Jesus. He again designated him as his Son, the Lord's anointed Messiah and king of Israel. As Israel heard the voice of God speak the Decalogue, so the apostles heard God identify their Messiah and king: "this is my Son, my chosen, hear him." Peter remembered this experience. It confirmed his conviction that Jesus is the Messiah and King of God's people.[3]

---

3. Luke 9:34–35; 2 Pet. 1:16–18.

The Messianic Covenant Rests on Christ's Crucifixion[4]

Although this pledge perpetuated his priestly commission, it did not commence it. When God anointed Christ with the Spirit, he anointed him not only as king, but also as a priest. Christ fulfilled his priestly commission when he shed his blood as a propitiatory sacrifice to atone for the sins of his people. After Christ offered this sacrifice, he sat at God's right hand. He entered into the most holy place in heaven. Thus, the Messianic covenant rests on his completed work of atonement. It perpetuates his priestly office.

The Messianic Covenant Rests on Christ's Perfection[5]

The coronation of Christ in heaven is its occasion. God swore this pledge to the glorified God-man seated on David's throne. In Hebrews 5:5–6, Scripture associates Psalm 2:6–8 and Psalm 110:1–4 with Christ's perpetual appointment as high priest. In Psalm 2:6–8 Scripture describes the coronation of Messiah. In Acts 13:33 Scripture states explicitly that this coronation occurs in conjunction with Christ's bodily resurrection. Thus, the import of Hebrews 5:5 is that Jesus did not presume to make himself high priest. Rather, his Father, the very Person who made him king, made him high priest. When the Father seated Jesus as king, he pledged perpetual priesthood to him: "a Son made perfect forever."

It Rests on God's Covenant of Grace and Counsel of Redemption

God sends Christ in history in fulfillment of his pledge of a Redeemer. This in turn rests on God's eternal counsel of redemption. LCF 7:3 affirms this.

The Essential Features of the Messianic Covenant

Like God's covenants with Noah and David, this pledge is very basic. Scripture highlights three features: its partakers, promise, and ratification. As in the case of God's pledge to David, Scripture associates neither a ceremonial

---

4. Heb. 2:17; 10:11–13.

5. "So Christ also glorified not himself to be made a high priest, but he that spoke unto him, You are my Son, This day have I begotten you: as he says also in another place, You are a priest for ever after the order of Melchizedek" (Heb. 5:5, 6); "Yet I have set my king upon my holy hill of Zion. I will tell of the decree: Jehovah said unto me, You are my son; this day have I begotten you. Ask of me, and I will give you the nations for your inheritance, and the uttermost parts of the earth for your possession" (Ps. 2:6–8); "that God has fulfilled the same unto our children, in that he raised up Jesus; as also it is written in the second psalm, You are my Son, this day have I begotten you" (Acts 13:33).

ritual with its ratification nor an explicit token with its substance. Nevertheless, Scripture connects it implicitly with heart circumcision and baptism and with the Lord's Supper.

The Partakers of the Messianic Covenant

In God's covenantal relation to Noah, Abraham, and David, their posterities benefit from and partake in God's pledges with them. This is also true of God's pledge to Messiah. Jesus' children participate in and benefit from God's pledge with him. Thus they partake dependently in the Messianic covenant. They are implicitly its beneficiaries.

The Principal Partaker: Jesus the Messiah[6]

The principal partaker of this pledge is Jesus, the God-man. Scripture explicitly asserts that Psalm 110:1–4 refers to Jesus (Matt. 22:42–45; Heb. 5:6, 7:21). Thus, God perpetuates Jesus the Messiah as high priest with the oath of this covenant.

The Dependent Partakers: Jesus' Spiritual Posterity[7]

The Bible testifies that Jesus' spiritual descendants also partake in this pledge. Scripture affirms the *existence* of Jesus' spiritual posterity, defines their *identity*, and discloses their implicit *participation* in this pledge.

✦ The Existence of Jesus' Spiritual Children

Isaiah predicts that the Messiah will "see his seed" (Isa. 53:10, 11). After God makes his soul an offering for sin, the Messiah prolongs his days. He lives after his death. In his resurrection life he begets children. Plainly, Isaiah is not talking about physical children. He refers to the spiritual children that Christ begets by spiritual generation. Christ begets spiritual children through the gospel when God implements the covenant of grace through the general and effectual call. Thus, Jesus generates spiritual children when God circumcises hearts. Christ's spiritual children are spiritual children of Eve and Abraham (Gal. 3:29). In Hebrews 2:13 Scripture confirms that God gives the Messiah children. Again, these cannot be physical children.

---

6. Matt. 22:42–45; Ps. 110:1, 4; Heb. 5:5, 6, 10, 6:20, 7:20–22, 28.
7. Isa. 53:10, 11; Heb. 2:13; 1 Pet. 2:9, 10; Rev. 1:5, 6, 2:26, 27, 3:21.

+ The Identity of Jesus' Spiritual Children

Scripture identifies Christ's children as Christians, his disciples, God's elect. Scripture discloses their distinguishing traits in Hebrews 2:10–17. They are sons of God brought to glory (2:10). Christ is the author of their salvation from sin (2:10). They are consecrated to God's glory as holy ones (2:11). Christ calls them his brothers, his spiritual family (2:11, 12, 17). They are human, since they share in flesh and blood (2:14). Christ delivers them from death itself. He will raise them from the dead (2:15). They are spiritual children of Abraham (2:16). Christ makes propitiation for their sins through his blood (2:17). They are God's people under the new covenant, ratified in the blood of Christ (2:17). Plainly, Jesus' spiritual children are all God's elect, who trust in Christ alone for salvation. Jesus collects his spiritual posterity into an organized society, the new covenant community. Its visible chapter is the community of his disciples on earth, the church. For this reason Jesus called his disciples his "children" and "little ones."[8] Warfield shows that "these little ones" in Mark 9:42 are Christ's disciples:[9]

> We think we should not go wrong, therefore, if, neglecting everything else, we should say that our Savior calls his disciples "these little ones" because he thinks of them as the particular objects of his protecting care and gives in this designation of them a supreme expression to the depth and tenderness of his love for them. It is thus the diminutive of endearment by way of eminence; the purest expression, among all his affectionate names for his disciples, of the fondness of his love for them. They were his friends and his children: his sheep and his lambs: but, above all these, they were "his little ones"—"his little ones" who needed him and whom he would never fail in their times of need, even though their times of need be all times as indeed they are.

+ The Participation of Jesus' Spiritual Children in this Pledge[10]

Christians are implicit beneficiaries of this pledge because they are sons of God, kings, and royal priests. God makes this covenant with Christ as his Son. Christ's children, Christians, are also sons of God (Gal. 3:26). This pledge perpetuates Christ's royal high priesthood. Christ's children too are royal priests (1 Pet. 2:9; Rev. 1:5–6). Christ receives this pledge as the king

---

8. Mark 9:42, 10:24: John 13:33–35, 21:4–5.
9. B. B. Warfield, "Christ's 'Little Ones,'" in *Selected Shorter Writings*, 1: 252.
10. Gal. 3:26; 1 Pet. 2:9; Rev. 1:5, 6, 2:26, 27, 3:21.

reigning on David's throne. Christ's children also reign with Christ and rule the nations on his throne (Rev. 2:26, 27, 3:21). Thus, implicitly, Jesus' children partake with him in this covenant.

The Promise of the Messianic Covenant[11]
God makes this covenant with Christ as the Son of God, the King of Israel, ruling on the throne of David. God promises Christ perpetual priesthood: "you are priest *forever.*" He also promises him royal priesthood: "you are priest forever *after the order of Melchizedek.*" In sum, the substance of this pledge is perpetual royal priesthood.

God Promises His Perfected Son Perpetual Priesthood
This promise rests on Christ's endless resurrection life. It stands in stark contrast with the Aaronic priesthood. Each Aaronic priest ministered on earth only until death ended his priestly service.[12]

God Promises His Perfected Son Royal Priesthood[13]
Melchizedek was king of Salem and priest of God most high (Gen. 14:18– 20). He had a royal priesthood. The phrase in Psalm 110:4, "after the order," conveys similarity and analogy. In the Hebrew the nuance is "upon the manner of Melchizedek." In Hebrews 7:11, the nuance of the Greek is "according to the arrangement of Melchizedek." The priesthood of Melchizedek thus establishes the pattern for Christ's priesthood. The manner of Christ's priesthood is analogous to that of Melchizedek. Since Melchizedek was simultaneously a king and a priest, so also is Christ. Thus, Christ's priesthood, like that of Melchizedek, is a royal priesthood. Observe the stark contrast with the Aaronic priesthood. The kings of Judah were strictly forbidden to serve as priests. When King Uzziah defied this restriction, God inflicted leprosy upon him.[14] Similarly, the Aaronic priests never reigned as kings over God's people. God instituted and enforced a strict separation between the kings and the priests of his people under the old covenant. In Christ God has abolished this separation of powers. It does not pertain to Christ, like it did not pertain to Melchizedek. God promised Christ a royal priesthood that reflected the manner and arrangement of Melchizedek's.

---

11. Ps. 110:4; Heb. 7:20–22, 28.
12. Heb. 7:23–24.
13. Gen. 14:18–20; Ps. 110:4; Heb. 7:1–4, 11–14.
14. 2 Chron. 26:16–21.

The Ratification of the Messianic Covenant

God ratified the Messianic covenant in history in conjunction with the coronation of Jesus of Nazareth as Christ and King.[15] God enters this pledge with Christ at his coronation on David's throne at his right hand: "the word of the oath, which came after the Law, *appoints* a Son, made perfect forever." Therefore, it is prudent carefully to distinguish the eternal counsel of redemption, which the Trinity resolved before the foundation of the world, from this Messianic covenant made in history with the Lord Jesus Christ. This conserves the element of truth recognized both by those Reformed theologians who include the Holy Spirit in God's eternal counsel of redemption,[16] and by those who affirm that the Father and Son have a special relationship that is covenantal.[17] All three Persons of the Trinity resolve the eternal counsel of redemption. Yet the partaker of the Messianic covenant is God the Son incarnate. This is because the Son alone, not the Holy Spirit, became human and because God swears this pledge in history to Jesus as the God-man. Therefore, Scripture does in fact feature a divine covenant in which the principal partaker is the incarnate Son. However, God ratified this covenant, not in eternity, but in history, at Christ's coronation, when he ascended into heaven and sat on David's throne in glory.

Conclusion: Implicit Emblems of the Messianic Covenant

Although this divine pledge has no explicit token, Scripture implicitly associates sacred symbols with it. Scripture implicitly connects it with heart circumcision, Christian baptism, and the Lord's Supper.

First, Scripture implicitly connects the Messianic covenant with heart circumcision and Christian baptism. The organization of Jesus' spiritual posterity into a visible society displays this connection. Jesus' spiritual children are Abraham's spiritual children (Gal. 3:29; Heb. 2:13–16). The spiritual children of Abraham and Jesus are all circumcised in heart (Col. 2:11–12). Christ organizes his spiritual children into a visible society of his disciples (John 4:1–2). Only his spiritual children have the right to join that society. Christ instituted Christian baptism as a solemn rite of identification with this visible society of his spiritual children.[18] This closely ties baptism to heart circumcision.

---

15. Ps. 110:1–2, 4; Acts 2:29–31, 36; Heb. 7:21, 28.

16. For example, John Gill, *Body of Divinity*, 1: 350–54.

17. For example, Louis Berkhof, *Systematic Theology*, 267–71.

18. Thus in an article, "The Polemics of Infant Baptism," B. B. Warfield concedes: "All Protestants should easily agree that only Christ's children have a right to the ordinance of

Second, Scripture implicitly connects the Messianic covenant with the Lord's Supper. The priesthood of Melchizedek displays this connection. Scripture says little of Melchizedek. Yet it tells us that this prototype royal priest ministered to Abraham with bread and wine (Gen. 14:18). Thus, when Christ institutes the new covenant, he uses these very elements, the bread and the cup, to establish its token. Surely this is not a mere coincidence! This points, at least implicitly, to the fact that God appoints his arrangement with Melchizedek as the pattern of Christ's priesthood. In this way Scripture implicitly connects the Lord's Supper, the token of the new covenant, with the Messianic covenant.

The Historical Fulfillment of the Messianic Covenant

God fulfills this covenant both in the life of Christ and in the lives of Jesus' spiritual children.

Its Fulfillment in Christ's Life[19]

Through God's faithfulness to this pledge, Christ has reigned as high priest in heaven for the last two thousand years (Ps. 110:1). God continues to fulfill this pledge today. While Christ now reigns in heaven and intercedes as high priest for Christian Israel, he pleads the merit of his blood before God (Heb. 7:24–25). In this way God will continue to fulfill this pledge until Christ emerges from the heavenly tabernacle to eradicate sin permanently from those who wait for him (Heb. 9:24, 28). Then Christ will forever enjoy the glory of his finished priestly work by which he made atonement for sin on the cross, made intercession for his people in heaven, and eradicated their sin at his second coming. Then Christ will give his kingdom to God for an eternal sacrifice of consecration and praise (1 Cor. 15:24).

Its Fulfillment in the Lives of Christ's Posterity[20]

God begins to fulfill this covenant in the Christian life on earth. He makes Christians sons of God by faith in Christ (Gal. 3:26). He makes them a royal priesthood (1 Pet. 2:9; Rev. 1:5–6). They offer to God spiritual sacrifices acceptable through Jesus Christ. God also fulfills this covenant in

---

baptism." In *The Works of Benjamin B. Warfield* (10 Vols.; Grand Rapids: Baker Book House, 1981), 9: 389.

19. Ps. 110:1–2; Heb. 7:24–25, 9:24, 28.

20. 1 Pet. 2:9; Rev. 1:5, 6, 2:26, 27, 3:21, 5:6, 21:7.

heaven. After death the glorified spirits of Christians reign with Christ in heaven as sons of God and royal priests.[21] With perfect hearts they offer to God spiritual sacrifices of consecration and praise. Ultimately, God will fulfill this covenant in the new heavens and earth. When Christ comes again Christians will receive glorified bodies as God's sons (Rom. 8:23). Then they will reign forever with Christ as royal priests. With impeccable hearts in immortal bodies they will offer to God spiritual sacrifices of consecration and praise forever.[22]

The Practical Functions of the Messianic Covenant

Like the new covenant, the Messianic covenant has practical functions both in redemptive history and for experiential religion.

Three Practical Functions in Redemptive History
First, the Messianic covenant establishes Christ's superior priesthood.[23] God's solemn pledge to Christ demonstrates that Christ's priesthood is superior to the priesthood of Aaron. Aaron's priesthood was not confirmed with an oath as a solemn pledge. Thus it was temporary. Christ's priesthood is superior precisely because God confirmed it with this divine pledge. Thus, it is permanent because God is ever faithful to this pledge.

Second, the Messianic covenant guarantees God's new covenant with Christian Israel: "so much the more also Jesus has become the guarantee of a better covenant" (Heb. 7:22). The blood of Christ's atoning sacrifice secures every spiritual blessing for the community of the new covenant.

Third, the Messianic covenant certifies every Christian's complete salvation.[24] In faithfulness to this pledge God perpetuates Christ's priestly intercession on behalf of each of his spiritual children. Christ's intercession is effectual to accomplish deliverance from sin and death for every Christian.

Five Practical Functions for Experiential Religion
First, the Messianic covenant calls Christians to appreciate and honor their royal priesthood: "But you are a chosen race, a royal priesthood, a holy nation, a people for God's own possession, that you may proclaim the

---

21. Rev. 2:26, 27, 3:21, 21:7.
22. Rom. 8:19, 21, 23; Phil. 3:21; Rev. 5:10, 22:5.
23. Heb. 7:20–21.
24. Heb. 7:24–25.

excellences of him who has called you out of darkness into his marvelous light" (1 Pet. 2:9). As Christ's spiritual children Christians enjoy the great privilege of royal priesthood. They should appreciate this privilege and bless God for it. They should honor this privilege by living holy lives rich in good works that reflect God's glory.

Second, the Messianic covenant calls Christians to offer acceptable spiritual sacrifices to God: "You also, as living stones, are being built up as a spiritual house, for a holy priesthood, to offer up spiritual sacrifices, acceptable to God through Jesus Christ" (1 Pet. 2:5). God conferred on Jesus' children royal priesthood so that they would offer to him through Christ spiritual sacrifices that please him. He calls them to offer to him spiritual sacrifices of contrition for sin (Ps. 51:18) and consecration of their lives (Rom. 12:1). On this foundation, he calls them to draw near in faith with spiritual sacrifices of praise and giving (Heb. 13:15–16).

Third, the Messianic covenant calls Christians to draw near to God with confidence.[25] God's covenant with Christ should instill in Christians confidence in God and Christianity. It assures Jesus' children of their certain hope. It motivates them to remain steadfast in the Christian religion. It encourages them to draw near by faith to the throne where their royal high priest reigns and intercedes for them. It encourages them to expect on Christ's behalf God's favor, blessing, and help.

Fourth, the Messianic covenant calls Christians to steadfast faith, holiness, and hope.[26] God's covenant with Christ calls Christ's children to overcome the world, mortify remaining sin, and resist the devil. It motivates them to perseverance in faith and hope with a view to reigning with Jesus in glory in fulfillment of this covenant.

Fifth, the Messianic covenant calls Christians to wait and pray for Christ's appearing: "so Christ also, having been once offered to bear the sins of many, shall appear a second time, apart from sin, to them that wait for him, unto salvation" (Heb. 9:28). God's covenant with Christ calls his posterity to wait for him to appear from heaven in order to eradicate their sin in fulfillment of this pledge. It thus calls Christ's children to hope, wait, and pray for his second coming.

---

25. Heb. 4:14–16.
26. Rev. 3:21, 26–27.

Finally, God's covenant with Jesus the Messiah furnishes solid ground for Christ's spiritual children to thank God for his goodness and faithfulness. It furnishes much fuel for them to praise God and rejoice in him.

Conclusion: The Christian Covenantal Economy

We now conclude this study of the Messianic covenant with an overview of the Christian covenantal economy and its relation to the covenant of grace.

An Overview of the Christian Covenantal Economy

The Christian covenantal economy is the ultimate set of God's covenants with his people. It is comprised of the Messianic and new covenants. Jesus reforms and transforms Hebrew Israel into Christian Israel, accomplishes their redemption from sin, and mediates God's new covenant with them in his blood. They are his children, his spiritual posterity. Upon Christ's resurrection and coronation, God perpetuates his royal priesthood by means of the Messianic covenant. Thus, the Messianic covenant relates to the new covenant in a remarkable way. In one sense, it reflects the relation of the Abrahamic covenant to the old covenant. In another sense, it reflects the relation of the Davidic covenant to the old covenant. Jesus is both the patriarch and the king of Christian Israel. The new covenant community is both his spiritual posterity and his theocratic kingdom. The diagram to the right illustrates the Christian covenantal economy:

The Covenant of Grace and the Christian Covenantal Economy

God's covenants rest on the covenant of grace. They fulfill God's pledge to accomplish redemption through the Redeemer. How does the Christian covenantal economy relate to God's pledge to apply redemption through the gospel?

Let's reminisce for a minute. Eve's spiritual children form a remnant within Noah's posterity. Most partakers in the old covenant community were the devil's spiritual children (Ps. 95:8–11; Jer. 9:25–26; Acts 7:51; Rom. 10:20–21). Yet within Hebrew Israel was an elect remnant of Abraham's spiritual children (Rom. 11:4–5). As individuals they possessed every spiritual blessing in Christ. They experienced forgiveness of sins (Ps. 32:1–2), had God's law written in their hearts (Pss. 37:31, 40:8), and knew the Lord (Ps. 36:10; 1 Sam. 2:12, 3:7). Yet that remnant was "invisible," without unique ordinances. When Christ came he collected this invisible society. He

SERVANT
COVENANT:
Messianic

God's Righteous
Servant

*Jesus the Patriarch
and King*

POSTERITY
BENEFICIARIES:
*Jesus' Spiritual
Children*

JESUS'
POSTERITY

IMPLICITLY

INCLUDED

DIVINE
SALVATION:
*Redemption
From Sin*

FOUNDATONAL GENERATION

SAVED COMMUNITY

SAVED
COMMUNITY
COVENANT:
New Covenant

*Apostolic Generation
Christian Israel
Heavenly Zion*

Messianic Theocracy

ORGANIC
PERPETUITY:
*Successive
Generations
of Jesus'
Spiritual
Children*

*Successive Generations
of Christian Israel,
Zion's Spiritual Children*

formed them into a visible body of believers. He made the new covenant with this organized community. He gave them their own ordinances of baptism and the Lord's Supper. He engrafted Gentile believers into that community. Thus he transformed his people. The distinguishing trait of this community is that God has applied redemption to them (1 Thess. 1:1, 4–5). Thus, the devil's children have no right to belong to this visible society (Matt. 18:15–18; 1 Cor. 5:13). Only Eve's seed, the partakers of the covenant of grace, have that right. Nevertheless, some of the wicked, false disciples and hypocrites, still manage to infiltrate it (Heb. 10:29). The Lord will end this anomaly when he presents his church to himself (Eph. 5:26–27).

Therefore, the community of the Messianic and new covenants on earth includes by right only the partakers of the covenant of grace. It is the very image of the glorified society of God's elect in the new heavens and earth. This is because this covenantal community is a visible and organized society of Christ's spiritual children. What a blessing, what a privilege, to belong to such a society on earth!

CONCLUSION:
Practical Application of God's Covenants

"God…interposed with an oath…that we may have a strong encouragement."
—HEBREWS 6:18

God's covenants have a profound impact on revelation, redemption, and religion. We have already considered some practical implications of God's covenants for redemptive history. We have seen that God's covenants configure the Bible and Christ's person and work. We have seen that God's covenants certify, display, and disclose God's plan of salvation. We have considered various practical implications of specific divine covenants for redemptive history and gospel living. Now we conclude by highlighting the profound impact of God's covenant love and faithfulness on the practical religion of his people. God's covenants incite Christians to walk in evangelical obedience, to extol his love and faithfulness, to pray, to proclaim his gospel, and to trust him in all their afflictions.

God's Covenants Motivate Christians to Gospel Obedience

> Know therefore that Jehovah thy God, he is God, the faithful God, who keeps covenant and lovingkindness with them that love him and keep his commandments to a thousand generations, and repays them that hate him to their face, to destroy them: he will not be slack to him that hates him, he will repay him to his face. Thou shalt therefore keep the commandment, and the statutes, and the ordinances, which I command thee this day, to do them. And it shall come to pass, because ye hearken to these ordinances, and keep and do them, that Jehovah thy God will keep with thee the covenant and the lovingkindness which he swore unto thy fathers (Deut. 7:9–12).

What man is he that fears Jehovah? Him shall he instruct in the way that he shall choose. His soul shall dwell at ease; And his seed shall inherit the land. The friendship of Jehovah is with them that fear him; And he will show them his covenant (Ps. 25:12–14).

This motivation pertains to Christians under the new covenant even more than it pertained to Hebrews living under the old covenant. God's people should walk in gospel obedience precisely because he is the faithful God who keeps covenant with those who love him and keep his commandments. Those who walk in gospel fear receive his instruction, dwell at ease, and see his covenant love and faithfulness. Christians should love one another because God loves them in covenant love. Christians should keep their word because God keeps his covenant promises. Christians should imitate the love and faithfulness of our covenant keeping God.

God's Covenants Incite Christians to Extol His Love and Faithfulness

I will sing of the lovingkindness of Jehovah forever: With my mouth will I make known thy faithfulness to all generations (Ps. 89:1).

Blessed be the Lord, the God of Israel; For he has visited and wrought redemption for his people, And has raised up a horn of salvation for us In the house of his servant David (As he spoke by the mouth of his holy prophets that have been from of old), Salvation from our enemies, and from the hand of all that hate us; To show mercy towards, our fathers, And to remember his holy covenant; The oath which he spoke unto Abraham our father (Luke 1:68–73).

The psalmist extols God's love and faithfulness displayed in his covenant with David. He declares to all generations God's faithfulness to these promises. Zacharias blesses God for his faithfulness to his solemn pledge to Abraham. He declares the glorious redemption that God accomplished in covenant love and faithfulness.

Christians should do likewise. In Christ and because of Christ we are the heirs of these very covenant promises to Abraham and David. Therefore we should sing his praise. We should bless his name for his covenant love and faithfulness to David, Abraham, Jesus, Hebrew Israel, and Christian Israel. In covenant love and faithfulness God has given to Christians Christ's virtue and Spirit. He has blessed Christians with every spiritual blessing in Christ. This calls Christians to praise him and declare his great goodness and reliability.

God's Covenants Motivate Christians to Pray

> O Jehovah, the God of Israel, there is no God like you, in heaven above, or on earth beneath; who keeps covenant and lovingkindness with your servants, that walk before you with all their heart; who has kept with your servant David my father that which you did promise him (1 Kings 8:23–24).

> I beseech you, O Jehovah, the God of heaven, the great and terrible God, that keeps covenant and lovingkindness with them that love him and keep his commandments (Neh. 1:5).

> Lord, where are thy former lovingkindnesses, which you swore unto David in thy faithfulness? Remember, Lord, the reproach of thy servants (Ps. 89:49–50).

> I prayed unto Jehovah my God, and made confession, and said, Oh, Lord, the great and dreadful God, who keeps covenant and lovingkindness with them that love him and keep his commandments (Dan. 9:4).

God's covenants make known his will for the future. They make history predictable. They disclose what to hope for, and thus, what to plead before him. In this way, God's covenant love and faithfulness motivated Solomon, Nehemiah, Ethan the Psalmist, and Daniel to pour out their hearts to God in prayer.[1] Covenant promises to Abraham, Israel, and David called them to prayer and taught them what to pray. Similarly, covenant promises to Abraham, David, Jesus, and Christian Israel call Christians to plead with God that he would in faithfulness keep these covenant commitments. These blessed divine pledges call Christians to plead for the very blessings he has promised to bestow in Christ on all who believe.

Thus, the new covenant promises of spiritual blessing through the gospel fueled Paul's prayers. He regularly blessed God for those spiritual blessings.[2] He pleaded with God to give Christians deeper understanding and experience of their spiritual blessings.[3] He exhorted and entreated Christians to pray for the success of the gospel in fulfillment of the covenant of grace (Eph. 6:18–19; 2 Thess. 3:1; 1 Tim. 2:1–8). Even so, let us pray.

---

1. 1 Kings 8:23–24; 2 Chron. 6:14–15; Neh. 1:5, 9:32–33; Ps. 89:47–50; Dan. 9:4– 5.
2. 1 Cor. 1:4–7; 2 Cor. 1:3–4; Eph. 1:3; Phil. 1:3–6; Col. 1:3–5; 1 Thess. 1:2–3.
3. Eph. 1:15–19, 3:14–19.

God's Covenants Motivate Christians to Proclaim His Gospel

> And the scripture, foreseeing that God would justify the Gentiles by faith, preached the gospel beforehand unto Abraham, saying, In thee shall all the nations be blessed (Gal. 3:8).

In virtue of his covenant of grace, his covenants with David and Abraham, and the Messianic and new covenants, God stands committed to save sinners indiscriminately from every branch of the human race in each generation until Jesus comes again.[4] God certainly will fulfill these solemn pledges. Precisely because God is faithful to his covenant promises, the gospel always has and ever will come in power in every generation among all the nations. Jesus will see of the travail of his soul and will be satisfied. God's Word and Spirit will never depart from Christian Israel. With supernatural power by the Holy Spirit, through the gospel, God will create spiritual children for Jesus, Eve, and Abraham in every generation. Preaching the gospel is not a fool's errand precisely because God keeps his covenant commitments. This furnishes great incentive to Christians to proclaim Christ among all the nations. It offers much comfort and hope to Christians in the face of opposition and rejection.

God's Covenants Motivate Christians to Trust Him in Affliction

> Wherein God, being minded to show more abundantly unto the heirs of the promise the immutability of his counsel, interposed with an oath; that by two immutable things, in which it is impossible for God to lie, we may have a strong encouragement, who have fled for refuge to lay hold of the hope set before us (Heb. 6:17–18).

The author of Hebrews writes to Christians suffering affliction in this life and persecution for their faith in Christ. Christ is their refuge from the wrath of God upon human sin. They live in hope, not merely of a better earthly lot, but of eternal life. God's faithfulness to his redemptive pledges provides solid ground for Christians to trust God. His covenants bolster confidence in God. They assure Christians that their hope of eternal glory is not empty, but certain. The faithful God, who can never lie, stoops in kindness to confirm with an oath his promise of spiritual blessing. He does so to give much encouragement and comfort to those who believe in Christ. Thus, God's

---

4. Gen. 3:15, 22:18; Gal. 3:7–9; Eph. 2:12–13, 3:6–9, 20–21.

covenants assure believers that heaven is certain, the new heavens and earth are sure, and hell is inevitable for unbelievers who live and die in their sins.

In closing, I once heard the late D. James Kennedy say something in a sermon that epitomizes the thrust of this practical application. He said in essence that divine promise distinguishes our God from every pagan god. He said that men have made many promises to their idols, but that idols never made any promises to men. He said this was not surprising, since idols don't really exist. The living and true God not only makes promises, he solemnizes his redemptive promises with an oath, so that those who have fled to Christ for refuge would have strong encouragement.

Oh that God would bless his people with greater faith so that Christians would trust him more and commit to him our every need and care. Oh that he would give Christians greater grace to face every earthly trial with peace and comfort, knowing that we have an inheritance in heaven. His covenant love has reserved this eternal inheritance for us. His covenant faithfulness will bestow it on us when Jesus comes again. Even so come, Lord Jesus.

APPENDICES

APPENDIX 1
The Eternal Counsel of Redemption

"Christ who was foreknown indeed before the foundation of the world."
—1 PETER 1:19–20

God's covenant with the Redeemer in history, the Messianic covenant, rests on and fulfills his predestination of the Redeemer in eternity, the eternal counsel of redemption. LCF depicts Christ's predestination as an eternal covenant transaction between the Father and the Son.[1] Gill defines this covenant as a compact that consists in stipulation and restipulation: "In this compact there are mutual engagements each party enters into, stipulate and restipulate about, which make a proper formal covenant."[2] Concerning the participation of the Spirit in this eternal counsel, he adds: "The Spirit, gave his approbation of, and assent unto, every article in the covenant.... There are many things which the Holy Spirit himself undertook and engaged in covenant to do; and nothing more strongly proves this than his doing them; for had he not agreed to do them, they would not have been done by him."[3] Dabney calls this eternal decree "a free and optional compact between two equals, containing a stipulation which turns on a proper, causative condition."[4] To avoid error he concedes that there is no "holding the purposes of either party suspended in doubt on the promisings or doings of the other party. But it has always been certain from eternity, that the conditions would be performed; and the consequent reward would be bestowed, because there has always been an ineffable and perfect accord in the persons

---

1. LCF:7:3, 8:1.
2. Gill, *Body of Divinity*, 1: 309.
3. Ibid., 350–52.
4. Dabney, *Lectures in Systematic Theology*, 432.

of the Trinity, on those points: an accord possessing all the absoluteness of the other parts of the decree."[5] This model of the eternal counsel of redemption portrays the Persons of the Trinity as "contracting parties." To its credit, it aims to honor the equality of the Father, Son, and Spirit.

Does Scripture reveal the predestination of Christ the Redeemer? Does it portray God's eternal decree about the Redeemer as covenantal? Does it support a contract model of this eternal covenantal resolution and relation? Reformed theologians have labored to find scriptural support for an eternal compact between the Father and the Son. Hodge first supports it generically. He affirms that God's remedial decree possesses the distinctive elements of a covenant: contracting parties, promise, and condition.[6] He then cogently cites John 17:4.[7] Gill cites Isaiah 49:1–6, 53:10–12, Psalm 40:6–8, and John 17:4, 5. Dabney, for explicit support, appeals especially to Psalm 40:7–8.[8] He also cites Isaiah 42:6, 49:8, and Malachi 3:1.[9] Flavel exposits Isaiah 53:12.[10] Boston cites Psalm 89:3.[11] Yet, careful examination of this testimony shows that it does not affirm an eternal compact between the Father and the Son with mutual stipulations. In Psalm 89:3–4, Scripture refers to David and the Davidic covenant. In Isaiah 42:1–4 and 49:6, Scripture foretells the ministry of the Messiah as God's chosen servant. In Psalm 40:7–8, Scripture presents the Messiah as coming from heaven to earth to do God's will. In Isaiah 53:12, Scripture describes the Messiah as God's servant in his experience of exaltation that follows his humiliation and death. In John 17:4, as Hodge rightly observes, Scripture says that Christ fulfills the redemptive work that the Father gave him in eternity.

Thus, Scripture does indeed reveal God's eternal predestination of the Redeemer. Peter peers at this mystery in 1 Peter 1:17–20. He calls God's children to walk in gospel fear: "conduct yourselves in fear during the time of your stay *upon earth*, knowing that you were not redeemed with perishable things…but with precious blood." Gospel fear of God flows from a solid

---

5. Ibid., 431.

6. Charles Hodge, *Systematic Theology*, 2: 360.

7. Ibid., 361.

8. Dabney, *Lectures in Systematic Theology*, 432.

9. "And the Lord, whom you seek, will suddenly come to His temple; and the messenger of the covenant, in whom you delight, behold, He is coming, says the LORD of hosts" (Mal. 3:1).

10. John Flavel, "The Covenant of Redemption between the Father and the Redeemer," in *The Works of John Flavel* (6 Vols.; London: The Banner of Truth Trust, 1968), 1: 52–53.

11. Thomas Boston, "Of the Covenant of Grace," in *The Complete Works of Thomas Boston* (12 Vols.; Wheaton, IL: Richard Owen Roberts Publishers, 1980), 1: 314–16.

assurance of salvation. This assurance and gospel fear rest on the high price of redemption. God redeems his people, not with money, but with precious blood. Peter identifies this blood: "as of a lamb unblemished and spotless, *the blood* of Christ." On that foundation he launches into the mystery of Christ's predestination. Speaking of the Lamb whose blood redeemed his people, he says: "who was foreknown before the foundation of the world, but has appeared in these last times for the sake of you" (1 Pet. 1:20). When Paul says, "whom He foreknew" (Rom. 8:29), he refers to God's intimate affection and love for his elect. Thus, when Peter says that Christ the Lamb was "foreknown," he means that God the Father loved him with eternal affection. Then Peter says that Christ "has appeared." He means that the Father sent him into the world to rescue his people from their sins. Thus, Peter unveils God's eternal decree regarding the Redeemer. This decree involves the Trinity interrelating in the work of redemption. These redemptive relations of the Trinity involve mystery so profound as to evoke great reverence. This commends great care to adhere closely to the words of Scripture.

Accordingly, Scripture provides an inspired shepherd to guide his people to grasp the deep biblical roots that support this eternal decree of redemption. This guide is Ephesians 1:11: "who works all things after the counsel (βουλη) of His will." The word βουλη, translated "counsel," signifies "purpose," "resolution," "decision."[12] This makes "counsel" a term well suited to depict the predestination of the Redeemer. This inspired guide says that what God does in history is exactly what he decided to do in eternity. When Scripture describes Christ's ministry in history, it portrays exactly what God predetermined about Christ in eternity. First, in history God the Father sent God the Son to accomplish redemption through his incarnation, public ministry, perfect life, and atoning death on the cross. Second, in history God raised him from the dead and glorified him with coronation. He enthroned him with the oath of the Messianic covenant to apply to redemption to his people by the Holy Spirit. Third, in history God the Father will send Christ a second time to complete redemption. This is what happens in history. Therefore, this is exactly what God resolved in eternity. In this way Scripture uncovers the pervasive and solid biblical support for the eternal counsel of redemption. Accordingly, we survey the biblical testimony and then summarize the biblical teaching on this eternal counsel of redemption.

---

12. BAG, 145.

Survey of the Biblical Testimony

The witness of Scripture rests on the deity and incarnation of God the Son. Before he came to earth to rescue his people, Christ was with God the Father in heaven. Christ is the Supreme Being, God the Word: "In the beginning was the Word, and the Word was with God, and the Word was God" (John 1:1). God the Word created the universe: "All things came into being by Him" (John 1:2). This Person became human: "And the Word became flesh, and dwelt among us" (John 1:14). He took to himself a real human body and a true human soul. As a result, he became, at one and the same time, both human and divine. All this happened in history, because this is exactly what God in eternity decided would happen. The incarnation of Christ is a redemptive mission in history that grows out of a redemptive commission in eternity. Scripture features the words of the Son incarnate regarding his mission and commission. Since he experiences this personally, his testimony deserves the preeminence. Inspired predictions by prophets and inspired reflection by apostles round out this testimony.

The Personal Testimony of God the Son Incarnate

Christ speaks about his rescue mission that brought him from heaven to earth. He also speaks about his personal involvement with the redemptive mission and commission of the Holy Spirit. Finally, he describes his second coming to save and judge.

Christ Testifies of His Redemptive Commission and Mission

First, in John 3:17,[13] Christ calls his incarnation a rescue mission to save from their sins sinners from every branch of the human family. He says his Father sent him on this rescue mission. His Father implemented in history the very commission he resolved in eternity.

Second, in John 5:22, 23, 26, 27,[14] Jesus says the Father gave him, as the God-man, all authority, including authority to judge all men. Further, the Father granted that he, the God-man, would have "life in himself." What the

---

13. "For God did not send the Son into the world to judge the world, but that the world should be saved through him" (John 3:17).

14. "For not even the Father judges anyone, but he has given all judgment to the Son, in order that all may honor the Son, even as they honor the Father. He who does not honor the Son does not honor the Father who sent him.... For just as the Father has life in himself, even so he gave to the Son also to have life in himself; and he gave him authority to execute judgment, because he is the son of man" (John 5:22–23, 26–27).

Father actually gave Jesus in history is exactly what the Father in eternity resolved to give him. Jesus is God the Son, the very Person the Father loved in eternity. The Son always was the exact Representation of the Father. There never was the Pattern, the Father, without his Representation, the Son. As the Father is the Supreme Being, so is the Son. As the Father is eternal, so is the Son. Thus the Son incarnate unveils the mysteries of the counsel of redemption. The Father endows the incarnate Son with all authority and life in himself. God does this so that men would honor the Son incarnate even as they honor the Father. This all happens in history, because it is exactly what God resolved in eternity.

Third, in John 6:37–39,[15] the Son says the Father has given him a people. The Father gave his people to the Son before the foundation of the world (Eph. 1:4; 2 Tim. 1:9). In eternity, the Father chose a people in union with his Son, to whom he entrusted them. In eternity, he appointed the Son, his equal and beloved, as their Mediator, Redeemer, Savior, and Representative. In eternity, the Father decided to send the Son to earth to rescue his elect from sin. In eternity, he decided that this rescue mission would effectively redeem every person he entrusted to his Son. In eternity, the Father decided that all his elect would be saved to the uttermost and would forever enjoy everlasting life in a glorified body. Here Jesus lays out the substance of his Father's eternal decision. He says plainly that he came to earth to implement this decision in every detail. Here is mystery indeed. The Son is equal with the Father in power and glory. Yet, God the Father resolves decisively to redeem the elect, while God the Son resolves it deferentially. He calls this eternal decree his Father's decision: "not to implement my own decision, but the decision of him that sent me. And this is the decision of him that sent me." Before the Son had a human will, the Father sent him from heaven. The Son descended from heaven to implement the decision of his Father. This cannot possibly mean that the Son is unequal with the Father, or that the Son is a separate divine Being with a separate faculty of will. Rather, Jesus means that his Father related to this redemptive decree decisively. He says that was not his own decision because he resolved it deferentially. Thus the Son defers as his Father selects his people and unites them to him. He defers as his Father appoints him the Lamb to endure humiliation and suffer the

---

15. "For I have come down from heaven, not to do my own will, but the will of him who sent me. And this is the will of him who sent me, that of all that he has given me I lose nothing, but raise it up on the last day" (John 6:38–39).

wrath of God for his people's sins. Oh the depth of the deference and grace of God the Son. Oh the depth of the Father's love, to select and commission his own Son to be the propitiation for the sins of his people (1 John 4:9, 10). Who can fathom it? Blessed be his Name.

Fourth, in John 8:16, 18,[16] Christ said things that not surprisingly made him a controversial figure. The Pharisees accused him of hypocrisy and tried to turn his own words against him. When he spoke of his Father sending him they did not understand him. Further, God the Father sent Christ from heaven in history, because the Father commissioned him in eternity.

Fifth, in John 8:42,[17] Jesus again says plainly that he came to earth on a mission, with a commission from God his Father. The Father sent his Son to earth in history, because in eternity he decided to send him to earth to save his people from their sins.

Sixth, in John 10:27–30,[18] Jesus alludes to the eternal decree in which the Father gave and entrusted his people to him. He appointed him as their Savior and Shepherd. Jesus says that he will give his sheep eternal life, and that no one is powerful enough to wrest them from his protection. He asserts that this rests on his deity: "I and the Father are one." They got the point. They picked up stones to kill him for blasphemy, for claiming to be equal with God. Indeed, if he were a mere man as they supposed, it would have been blasphemy. This declares that the Son's deference to his Father's will in this eternal resolution is not ontological subordination. It does not connote inequality with the Father. Rather, the Son participates in this eternal counsel as the Supreme Being, equal to the Father in power and glory.

Seventh, in John 10:36,[19] Jesus engages these leaders in controversy about his identity. He says that the Father "sanctified and sent" him into the world. He does not mean that the Father "morally renewed" him, for he is and always was an impeccable Person, God the Son. Rather, his meaning relates

---

16. "But even if I do judge, my judgment is true; for I am not alone *in it*, but I and he who sent me.... I am he who bears witness of myself, and the Father who sent me bears witness of me" (John 8:16, 18).

17. "Jesus said to them, If God were your Father, you would love me; for I proceeded forth and have come from God, for I have not even come on my own initiative, but He sent me" (John 8:42).

18. "My sheep hear my voice, and I know them, and they follow me; and I give eternal life to them, and they shall never perish; and no one shall snatch them out of my hand. My Father, who has given them to me, is greater than all; and no one is able to snatch them out of the Father's hand. I and the Father are one" (John 10:27–30).

19. "Do you say of him, whom the Father sanctified and sent into the world, You are blaspheming, because I said, I am the Son of God?" (John 10:36).

to the general significance of the verb. To sanctify someone or something is to dedicate him or it for a sacred purpose. Thus, Christ means that the Father consecrated and selected him for a sacred purpose. Then the Father sent him to earth to accomplish it. Thus, the Father sent the Son on this mission in history, because he selected him in eternity for this very purpose.

Eighth, in John 11:42,[20] as the Son addresses his Father, he mentions his Messianic commission as a fact. The Father sent him from heaven to earth in history, because in eternity he decided to do so.

Ninth, in John 12:48, 49,[21] the Son unfolds his identity as God the Word. He says that the Father who sent him also gave him his words. Since the Father ordains the words of the Son, the Son is God the Word, whose words are the Word of God. In this respect Jesus, the God-man, functions as God's prophet, who speaks words that the Lord has put in his mouth. The Father sent the Son in history on a mission that was redemptive and revelatory, because he resolved in eternity to do so.

Tenth, in John 17:5, 7–8, 24,[22] the Son pulls back the veil of time and speaks of the mysteries of God's remedial decree. He reminisces with his Father about their eternal relations and experiences. He remembers his eternal glory as God the Son before he created the universe. He remembers God's eternal decree of election: "yours they were." He remembers his eternal commission as Redeemer: "you gave them to me." He remembers leaving heaven in history when his Father sent him on his rescue mission: "I came forth from thee." Here is a comprehensive display of the eternal counsel of redemption in its formulation and execution. The Father loved him as the Lamb, the Redeemer of God's elect, before the foundation of the world.

---

20. "And I knew that thou hearest me always; but because of the people standing around I said it, that they may believe that thou didst send me" (John 11:42).

21. "He who rejects me, and does not receive my sayings, has one who judges him; the word I spoke is what will judge him at the last day. For I did not speak on my own initiative, but the Father himself who sent me has given me commandment, what to say, and what to speak" (John 12:48–49).

22. "I glorified you on the earth, having accomplished the work which you have given me to do. And now, glorify me together with yourself, Father, with the glory which I had with you before the world was. I manifested your name to the men whom you gave me out of the world; yours they were, and you gave them to me, and they have kept your word. Now they have come to know that everything you have given me is from you; for the words which you gave me I have given to them; and they received *them*, and truly understood that I came forth from you, and they believed that you sent me.... Father, I desire that they also, whom you have given me, be with me where I am, in order that they may behold my glory, which you have given me; for you loved me before the foundation of the world" (John 17:4–8, 24).

Christ Testifies of the Spirit's Redemptive Commission

John records Christ's promise to send the Holy Spirit to his people. After his death, resurrection, and coronation, Christ fulfilled his promise (Acts 2:33).

First, in John 14:16–17,[23] the Son says that the Father will send the Spirit to his people in answer to his prayers. He describes the coming of the Spirit as a "gift." The Father sends his Spirit in history because he decided before the foundation of the world to give his Spirit to his people. This unveils the Spirit's involvement in God's eternal decree as the Comforter and Spirit of Truth.

Second, in John 14:25–26,[24] Christ promises that the Father will send the Spirit in his name. The Father sent the Spirit in Christ's name on a redemptive mission in history, precisely because he decided in eternity to do so. Thus, the Spirit deferentially resolves this eternal counsel.

Third, in John 15:26,[25] Jesus promises that he too will send them the Spirit. This unveils the remarkable truth that in eternity the Son resolved to send the Spirit in history. Thus, the eternal decision to send the Spirit was the decision of the Father and of the Son. The Father and Son resolved the mission of the Spirit decisively, the Spirit, deferentially and receptively.

Fourth, in John 16:7,[26] Jesus repeats that he sends the Spirit on his redemptive mission. This underscores that in eternity the Father and Son commissioned the Spirit.

Fifth, in John 16:13–15,[27] Jesus declares that when God the Spirit comes he does not speak from himself. He speaks what he hears. The Spirit inspires the apostles in history. In history the Spirit declares the truth that

---

23. "And I will ask the Father, and He will give you another Helper, that he may be with you forever; *that is* the Spirit of truth, whom the world cannot receive, because it does not behold him or know him, *but* you know him because he abides with you, and will be in you" (John 14:16–17).

24. "These things I have spoken to you, while abiding with you. But the Helper, the Holy Spirit, whom the Father will send in my name, he will teach you all things, and bring to your remembrance all that I said to you" (John 14:25, 26).

25. "When the Helper comes, whom I will send to you from the Father, *that is* the Spirit of truth, who proceeds from the Father, he will bear witness of me" (John 15:26).

26. "But I tell you the truth, it is to your advantage that I go away; for if I do not go away, the Helper shall not come to you; but if I go, I will send him to you" (John 16:7).

27. "But when he, the Spirit of truth, comes, he will guide you into all the truth; for he will not speak on his own initiative, but whatever he hears, he will speak; and he will disclose to you what is to come. He shall glorify me; for he shall take of mine, and shall disclose *it* to you. All things that the Father has are mine; therefore I said, that he takes of mine, and will disclose *it* to you" (John 16:13–15).

he hears from the Father and the Son. As the living Breath of the Father and of the Son, he conveys God's Words to men. He works redemption in history in accord with his relation to the Father and Son experienced from all eternity. He declares their words in history because they resolved in eternity that their living Breath would declare their words to men.

In sum, the Father and Son send the Spirit to apply redemption to his people individually and corporately. When he comes he dwells in every true Christian and in every true church. He comes as the Spirit of truth to illumine them. He comes as the Comforter to encourage them with hope, peace, and joy in believing. He comes as the Holy Spirit to sanctify them and conform them to Christ. He comes as the Spirit of the Father and of the Son, the Spirit of Adoption, to give them filial fellowship with the triune God. The Father and Son do this in history because this is exactly what the Father and Son resolved in eternity, in the counsel of redemption.

Christ Testifies of His Return to Save and Judge

In John 5:26–29,[28] Jesus says that the Father has given him authority to judge all men on the last day. This even includes the right and power to speak to the dead to summon them to the throne of God to give account. In Matthew 25:31–46 the Son describes how he will carry out this authority. He says that he will divide the righteous from the wicked, condemn and curse the wicked, and commend and bless the righteous. He also says that his Father will decide the exact timing of his second coming (Matt. 24:36). Thus, the Father will send the Son to judge the world, even as he sent him to rescue the world. God does in history exactly what he planned in eternity. Therefore, the Father decided in this eternal counsel of redemption to send the Son back to earth on the last day to consummate redemption and judge the world.

Corroborating Testimony from Prophets and Apostles

Several texts in the Old and New Testaments also shed light on this profound mystery. We consider passages that Reformed theologians have typically cited to support the covenant of redemption.

---

28. "He gave him authority to execute judgment, because he is *the* son of man. Do not marvel at this; for an hour is coming, in which all who are in the tombs shall hear his voice, and shall come forth" (John 5:27–29).

First, the prophet Isaiah predicts the ministry of the Messiah as God's righteous servant. God loves his servant, delights in him, upholds him, anoints him with his Spirit, and blesses him. God promises to make the ministry of his servant effective to the ends of the earth. Thus, Christ redeems Gentile and Jew alike (Isa. 42:1–4, 49:6).[29] Yet Isaiah further predicts that God bruises his servant for sin. In his humiliation God's servant bears the sins of his people and suffers the wrath of God. Thus he makes atonement and pays the price of sin. After his death, God highly exalts and glorifies his servant. Then he shall see his seed. This predicts Christ's resurrection and his exaltation in glory (Isa. 53:4, 10–12).[30]

God does all this with Christ in history, because it is precisely what the Father decided in eternity in the counsel of redemption to do for and with Christ. These texts present the God-man as God's servant. The Son incarnate does the will of the Father as his servant. Thus, in the counsel of redemption the Father decided to constitute his Son his servant through his incarnation. These passages do not endorse an eternal compact with mutual stipulations between the Father and Son. Neither does the psalmist: "Then I said, behold, I come; in the scroll of the book it is written of me; I delight to do your will, O my God; your law is within my heart" (Ps. 40:7–8). This text oft cited to support an eternal compact also presents the Messiah as God's servant, who loves to do God's will.

Second, the apostle Paul describes the incarnation of God the Son. When the Son descended from heaven, and took a human body and soul, he

---

29. "Behold, my servant, whom I uphold; my chosen one *in whom* my soul delights. I have put my Spirit upon him; he will bring forth justice to the nations. He will not cry out or raise *his voice*, nor make his voice heard in the street. A bruised reed he will not break, and a dimly burning wick he will not extinguish; he will faithfully bring forth justice. He will not be disheartened or crushed, until he has established justice in the earth; and the coastlands will wait expectantly for his law" (Isa. 42:1–4); "It is too small a thing that you should be my servant to raise up the tribes of Jacob, and to restore the preserved ones of Israel; I will also make you a light of the nations so that my salvation may reach to the end of the earth" (Isa. 49:6).

30. "Surely our griefs he himself bore, and our sorrows he carried…. But the LORD was pleased to crush him, putting *him* to grief; if he would render himself *as* a guilt offering, he will see *his* offspring, he will prolong *his* days, and the good pleasure of the LORD will prosper in his hand. As a result of the anguish of his soul, he will see *it* and be satisfied; by his knowledge the Righteous One, my servant, will justify the many, as he will bear their iniquities. Therefore, I will allot him a portion with the great, and he will divide the booty with the strong; because he poured out himself to death, and was numbered with the transgressors; yet he himself bore the sin of many, and interceded for the transgressors" (Isa. 53:4, 10–12).

assumed the form of a servant (Phil. 2:5–7, 9).[31] He thus displayed grace and deference that every Christian should imitate. He regarded equality with the Father as his rightful possession, not as robbery or stolen property. As the Supreme Being the Son was co-eternal with the Father, equal to him in power and glory. In the Father's form, the Son too dwelt in light unapproachable. His special presence was in heaven. He ruled in glory. Angels worshipped him. He was invisible, invulnerable, dwelling in light unapproachable. Nevertheless, he divested himself of the outward appearance of his glory. He took on the outward appearance of a mere man and became visible. Without ceasing to possess the attributes of the Supreme Being, he became human, in the form of a servant. The Lawgiver was born under his own law. As God's righteous servant he subjected his human will to the will of his Father. What deference the Son showed when he came from heaven to earth. Thus the Father highly exalted him, with the highest name in the universe. God raised him from the dead, invested him with all authority, and seated him in heaven. The Father did this in history, because he decided to do so in eternity in the counsel of redemption. God the Son in history at his incarnation displayed the very deference expressed in eternity in the counsel of redemption.

Third, in Hebrews 7:28,[32] the writer affirms that the Father in history entered the solemn pledge of the Messianic covenant with Christ. Thus, God the Father resolved in eternity to ratify this pledge with Christ in history at his coronation.

Fourth, in Acts 20:28,[33] Luke describes the redemptive mission of the Spirit in which he ordains elders in the church. The Spirit appointed those elders in history, because he resolved in eternity to ordain them in the eternal counsel of redemption.

---

31. "Have this attitude in yourselves which was also in Christ Jesus, who, although he existed in the form of God, did not regard equality with God as robbery but emptied himself, taking the form of a bond-servant, and being made in the likeness of men.... Therefore also God highly exalted him, and bestowed on him the name which is above every name" (Phil. 2:5-7, 9).

32. "For the Law appoints men as high priests who are weak, but the word of the oath, which came after the Law, *appoints* a Son, made perfect forever" (Heb. 7:28).

33. "Be on guard for yourselves and for all the flock, among which the Holy Spirit has made you overseers, to shepherd the church of God which he purchased with His own blood" (Acts 20:28).

Fifth, in 1 Corinthians 12:11,[34] Paul writes that the Spirit dispenses spiritual gifts as he sees fit. The Spirit dispenses gifts in history at his discretion because in eternity the Spirit resolved the measure and moment of the application of salvation in the eternal counsel of redemption.

Summary of the Biblical Teaching

This biblical testimony features the general nature, essential substance, interpersonal relations, messianic focus, and practical benefits of the eternal counsel of redemption.

The General Nature of the Eternal Counsel of Redemption

Generically this eternal counsel of redemption is an aspect of God's eternal decree. Therefore, it has its distinguishing traits. It is unconditional (Eph. 1:5), immutable (Job 23:13–14), invincible (Isa. 14:27), immaculate (Eph. 1:3), and incomprehensible (Rom. 11:33–36). Gill and Dabney affirm these characteristics.[35]

The Essential Substance of the Eternal Counsel of Redemption

God determines this eternal counsel in the decretive function of his faculty of will (Eph. 1:11). I offer this definition of its substance:

> The eternal counsel of redemption is an aspect of God's eternal decree, an eternal decision and resolution of the will of the Trinity:[1]
>
> In which God the Father selects God the Son as Redeemer and Representative of his elect people, thus giving and entrusting them to him,[2] and resolves and determines (1) to send him to earth to accomplish their redemption from sin by his incarnation, anointing, perfect life, and atoning death,[3] (2) to resurrect him and seat him permanently, with the oath of an everlasting covenant, at his right hand to apply their redemption,[4] and (3) to send him to earth a second time, on the last day, to complete their redemption and judge the world;[5] and God the Son relates receptively and deferentially to this eternal determination, resolution, and selection of his sovereign will:[6]

---

34. "But one and the same Spirit works all these things, distributing to each one individually just as he wills" (1 Cor. 12:11).

35. Gill, *Body of Divinity*, 1: 354–359; Dabney, *Lectures in Systematic Theology*, 430.

And in which, God the Father[7] and God the Son[8] resolve and determine to send God the Holy Spirit to earth to effect the application of redemption to their elect people: individually, in their conversion, life as saints, and death;[9] corporately in the Christian church;[10] and completely in resurrection glory;[11] and God the Spirit relates receptively and deferentially to this eternal determination of his sovereign will:[12]

And in which, God the Spirit, as the Spirit of the Father and of the Son,[13] resolves and determines the measure, manner, and moment of his individual and corporate application of redemption.[14]

Testimony in support of each aspect of this eternal counsel is collated below:

1. Eph. 1:3, 11; 2 Tim. 1:9; 1 Pet. 1:19, 20
2. Isa. 42:1; John 6:37–39, 10:27, 28, 17:7, 24; Rom. 5:12–19
3. John 3:17, 8:16, 8:42, 10:36, 11:42, 12:48, 49, 17:7, 8; Luke 4:14, 18
4. Eph. 1:20–22; Phil. 2:9; Heb. 7:21, 28
5. John 5:26–29
6. John 6:37–39
7. John 14:16, 17, 25
8. John 15:26, 16:7; Acts 2:33
9. Titus 3:5, 6
10. John 16:7, 13–15
11. Rom. 8:11
12. John 14:16, 17, 25, 15:26, 16:7; Acts 2:33
13. Acts 16:7
14. Acts 13:2, 20:28; 1 Cor. 12:11.

The Interpersonal Relations of the Eternal Counsel of Redemption

This eternal counsel of redemption portrays redemptive relations of the Persons of the Trinity in eternity. Scripture features their ontological foundation, manifold description, crucial distinction, and specific identification.

Their Ontological Foundation: Divine Singularity and Trinity

These redemptive relations rest on the singularity and Trinity of the Supreme Being. There is only one divine nature, one divine mind, and one divine faculty of will. There are not three distinct but equal Supreme Beings, only One, the Father, and the Son, and the Holy Spirit. There are not three infinite minds, only one. Yet that omniscient mind is the mind of the Father, of the Son, and of the Spirit. There are not three divine wills, only one. Yet that sovereign will is the will of the Father, of the Son, and of the Spirit. How do three Persons with one faculty of will resolve decisions? How did they interrelate in their eternal decree to save? Only the Supreme Being himself can answer such questions. There are no other Tri-Personal Beings. Nothing can illustrate such mystery. It summons all with reverent awe to gaze at glory divine. The Trinity resolves this decree in a manner most remarkable.

The Manifold Description of these Interpersonal Relations

The Trinity is incomprehensible and unique. This mandates special care to honor the terms and categories in which Scripture defines the eternal decree of redemption. Seven ideas emerge as prominent. Some depict its eternal resolution, others its historical implementation: (1) equality,[36] (2) unity,[37] (3) giving,[38] (4) sending and sanctifying (John 10:36),[39] (5) doing the will of, deferring (John 6:39), (6) serving,[40] and (7) covenanting with an oath (Ps. 110:4; Heb. 7:21, 28). The eternal decree about the Redeemer is consonant with the decree about the redeemed, election. In his eternal decision to save sinners the Father selected his people in Christ, gave them grace in Christ, and determined to conform them to the image of Christ (Rom. 8:29; Eph. 1:4–5; 2 Tim. 1:9). These terms for the resolution and execution of this decree do not portray the Persons of the Trinity as contracting parties agreeing to a formal compact. The notion of contracting parties fails to do justice to the biblical depictions of *giving, sending,* and *deferring.* It also imperils the singularity of the Supreme Being on which these redemptive relations rest. In eternity the Father and Son are not separate Beings, with separate natures, and separate faculties of will. They do not bring separate faculties of will into agreement with a formal compact. Again, the Spirit is not a separate Being, with a separate faculty of will, who brings his will into agreement with the will of the Father and of the Son. Definition of this eternal counsel should take as much care to honor the unity and singularity of the Supreme Being as it takes to honor the equality of the Father, Son, and Spirit. This requires sticking closely to the language of Scripture.

---

36. John 1:1, 5:18, 8:58, 10:27, 28, 10:36; Phil. 2:5–7.
37. John 8:16, 10:27, 28, 16:13–15.
38. John 5:22, 23, 26, 27, 6:37, 39, 10:27, 28, 14:16, 17:5, 7, 8, 24.
39. John 3:17, 6:39, 8:16, 18, 42, 10:36, 11:42, 12:48, 49, 17:5, 8; John 14:25, 26, 15:26, 16:7.
40. Isa. 42:1, 49:6, 53:10–12; Phil. 2:5–7.

The Crucial Distinction in these Interpersonal Relations

Jesus makes remarkable disclosures concerning these eternal relations. He says that the Father gave him a people and sent him from heaven to earth to save them. He associates sanctifying with this sending. His words convey donation, allocation, commission, and consecration. The Father donated, entrusted, or allocated his elect to the Son. The Father consecrated for a sacred purpose (sanctified) the Son and commissioned (sent) him. Not vice versa. These terms ascribe *donation* to the Father, *reception* and *acceptance* to the Son. The Father willingly gave and entrusted his elect to the Son. The Son willingly received and accepted his elect as their Representative and Redeemer. Thus grace was given in Christ before the foundation of the world. They also ascribe *decisiveness* to the Father and *deference* to the Son. This deference is not eternal subordination of the Son's will to the Father's will. In eternity the Father and Son did not have separate faculties of will, but the same faculty of will. The Son reveals that when the Trinity resolves the counsel of redemption, each Person does not relate to each decision in the same way. When the Supreme Being determines a Redeemer, the Father relates to this decision decisively, the Son deferentially. In John 6:39 Jesus expresses this so bluntly that it is almost shocking. It is important carefully to distinguish this decision in eternity from the submissiveness in history of the human will of the Son incarnate. The incarnate Son has two wills, a human will and the divine will, for he has two natures, human and divine. Thus when he says "not my will, but your will be done," he subordinates his human will to the divine will. Yet, when he subjected his human will to his divine will, he says "*your* will be done," not *our* will be done. The submission of his human will in history harmonizes with his deference in this decision of his divine will in eternity. The Son did not have two wills in eternity, because he did not have a human nature in eternity. Who can fathom it?

The Specific Identification of these Interpersonal Relations

God the Father relates decisively to every aspect of this eternal counsel of redemption (John 17:5, 7, 8, 25; 14:25, 26). God the Son relates deferentially and receptively to this eternal resolution of his will as it pertains to his mission as Redeemer (John 6:37–39, 17:5, 24; Phil. 2:5–7). Yet, he relates decisively to this decree as it pertains to the mission of the Holy Spirit (John 16:7). God the Spirit relates deferentially and receptively to this eternal decision about his redemptive mission (John 16:13–15). Yet, the Spirit also relates decisively to this eternal determination about his redemptive mission as far as the manner, measure, and moment of his ministry and influence are concerned (Acts 13:2, 20:28; 1 Cor. 12:11). How does the Spirit relate to this decision as it pertains to the mission of the Son? Scripture says nothing explicitly. Yet, he relates as he relates because he is who he is. He is the Spirit of the Father and of the Son. As the Spirit of the Father, he relates decisively, as the Spirit of the Son, deferentially. How can the Spirit relate both decisively and deferentially to the same decision of his will? Should there be shock at incomprehensible mystery? How can he be the Spirit of the Father and of the Son? If the Trinity cannot be fully comprehended or explained, how can these redemptive relations? Oh the depth of God's Being and wisdom.

The Messianic Focus of the Eternal Counsel of Redemption
This eternal counsel consists of decisions, determinations, or resolutions of God's decretive will. Its provisions are all grace from God given in Christ Jesus before times eternal. They include every blessing of the work of redemption and every redemptive action of each divine Person. Their special focus is the Messiah and his work. The predestination of the Redeemer is the core and focus of the eternal counsel of redemption. In this decision the Father resolves to ratify the Messianic covenant with the incarnate Son upon his session and coronation. He determines in eternity to swear this oath to the Son incarnate in history. Surely for this reason there is warrant for LCF to speak of this decision of God's will as an eternal *"covenant transaction"* (7:3). This explains why covenant theologians have featured the role of the Father and Son in this eternal counsel, and why they have appropriately labored to depict this eternal decree in covenantal terms. This explains why some contemporary Reformed theologians refer to the predestination of the Redeemer as God's eternal counsel[41] and why others still call it his eternal covenant.[42] Since Scripture is silent on whether an oath was sworn in eternity, flexibility is preferable to dogmatism. Rather than quibble over such terminology, it is better to display the mind that was in Christ, and count others better than self.

---

41. For example, Morton Smith, *Systematic Theology*, 1: 329–331. Smith calls it the "counsel of peace."
42. For example, Louis Berkhof, *Systematic Theology*, 265–271.

Conclusion: Practical and Experiential Benefits

First, the eternal counsel of redemption is a solid foundation for all Christian confidence. This eternal decree unites and secures all God's promises and actions that relate to salvation. It unifies every promise framed in mercy and fulfilled in faithfulness. It founds the covenant of grace, the gospel of Christ, and redemption accomplished, applied, and completed. It secures the eternal welfare of all God's elect. It makes absolutely certain the final salvation of everyone the Father entrusted to Christ before the foundation of the world. Thus no one will ever pluck Christ's sheep from his Father's hand. He remains permanently committed to save to the uttermost all who believe in him and wait for him. No power in earth or hell can overthrow any aspect of this eternal decree about the Redeemer.

Second, the eternal counsel of redemption affords much fuel for grateful praise to the Trinity. The Father so loved his people that he entrusted them to his Son, and sent him to earth to endure his own wrath for those who believe in him. Here is love indeed (1 John 4:9, 10). Christians should dwell on this love and bless God for his unspeakable gift.

Third, the eternal counsel of redemption calls Christians to imitate Christ's gracious deference. Paul exhorts Christians to have that mind in them that was in Christ when, with infinite deference, he became human (Phil. 2:5). Christ's example beckons all his followers to imitate him. Christians should put away all selfishness and carnal self-promotion from their lives and churches. Christians should put away the carnal pride that thinks very highly of self and of personal prerogatives, but that thinks little of the concerns, rights, or prerogatives of others. Christians should put away carnal squabbling over influence, role, or profile. They should imitate Christ's grace displayed in his redemptive mission and his deference expressed in the eternal counsel of redemption.

APPENDIX 2
The Adamic Covenant

"And Jehovah God commanded the man saying, Of every tree of the garden you may freely eat; but of the tree of the knowledge of good and evil, you shall not eat of it; for in the day that you eat thereof you shall surely die."

—GENESIS 2:16–17

Dogmatic theology is the vestibule of systematic theology. Our treatment of God's representative prohibition reflects this. I present this prohibition (which I call the *"Adamic covenant"*) from dogmatic and exegetical perspectives. Familiarity with dogmatic theology fosters better analysis of the biblical data. Thus, I present the Reformed theology of this prohibition, "the covenant of works," then attempt a biblical exposition. I conclude with practical applications.

The Reformed Theology of the Adamic Covenant
"The first covenant made with man was a covenant of works" (WCF 7:2)

The *covenant of works* is a doctrine, teaching, belief, tenet, viewpoint, scheme, hypothesis, perspective, motif, or model. It reflects an attempt by Reformed theologians to explain and account for the biblical data associated with this prohibition to Adam. We consider the development, definition, defense, critique, and modification of the covenant of works.

Development of the Covenant of Works
We consider its development through the early church, the Reformation, and the Reformed creeds. We conclude with subsequent development of the covenant of works by Reformed theologians.

The Early Church

The use of covenant to describe the original relation between God and Adam is of ancient origin. In unpublished anthropology handouts, Anthony Hoekema names Augustine (354–430) as the first Christian theologian to depict this prohibition as a covenant. He cites Augustine: "The first covenant which was made with the first man is just this, In the day thou eatest thereof thou shalt surely die (City of God: Book 16: Chapter 27)." Then he adds: "Although Augustine did not use the expression *covenant of works*, this is the first time the relationship between God and Adam in Paradise before the fall was spoken of as a covenant."[1]

According to Warfield, the Western Church, following Jerome (342–420) and the Vulgate, translated Hosea 6:7: "They like Adam transgressed the covenant." While the Eastern Church, following the LXX and the Syriac, translated it: "they like men."[2] Warfield further notes that Cyril of Alexandria (c. 376–444), bishop from 412–444, was an exception who translated it "they like Adam." He cites Cyril as saying that Adam "might have had communion with God and attained immortality and enjoyed the delights of paradise, yet neglected the divine command and fell from his pristine glory."[3] Thus, throughout church history, some have translated Hosea 6:7 "they like Adam," and accordingly, have spoken of God's covenant with Adam; others have not.

The Reformation

Regarding its development at the time of the Reformation, Anthony Hoekema observes: (1) Franciscus Junius (1545–1602) "worked out the doctrine of the covenant of works into its more developed form"; (2) Amandus Polanus (1561–1610), a teacher at Basel, "was the first to give the name *foedus operum* (covenant of works) to this covenant made with Adam before the fall"; and (3) Johannes Coccejus (1603–1669) "made the covenant of works the starting point of his covenant theology."[4]

Calvin translates Hosea 6:7 "they like men." He acknowledges that some translate it "they like Adam," but calls their exposition "frigid" and

---

1. Anthony Hoekema, Handouts: The Doctrine of Man (ST 421), (Grand Rapids: Calvin Seminary, 1977), 12.

2. Warfield, "Hosea VI.7: Adam or Man," in *Selected Shorter Writings*, 1:116.

3. Ibid., 117.

4. Hoekema, Doctrine of Man Handouts, 13–14.

"diluted." Then he says he can't pause to refute it because it is "vapid."[5] Yet, in his exposition of the sacraments in his *Institutes* (4:14:18), he named the tree of life and the rainbow as "proofs" and "seals" of God's *covenants* with Adam and Noah:

> He gave Adam and Eve the tree of life as a guarantee of immortal-ity, that they might assure themselves of it as long as they should eat of its fruit [Gen. 2:9; 3:22]. Another, when he set the rainbow for Noah and his descendants, as a token that he would not destroy the earth with a flood [Gen. 9:13–16]. These, Adam and Noah regarded as sacraments. Not that the tree provided them with an immortality which it could not give to itself; nor that the rainbow (which is but a reflection of the sun's rays upon the clouds opposite) could be effective in holding back the waters; but because they had a mark engraved upon them by God's Word, so that they were proofs and seals of his covenants.[6]

Although Calvin translates Hosea 6:7 "they like men," he affirms a divine covenant with Adam before the fall, which God sealed by the tree of life. Further, in his comments on Genesis 2:16, he acknowledges that man would have lived on earth only temporarily:[7]

> His earthly life truly would have been temporal; yet he would have passed into heaven without death, and without injury.

Calvin does not overtly formulate a covenant of works doctrine. Yet he affirms a divine covenant with Adam before the fall, and that God would have translated sinless Adam into heavenly life.

Luther, according to Warfield, translated Hosea 6:7 "they like Adam."[8] Luther also confessed that Adam would eventually have been translated into a heavenly existence without death.[9]

---

5. John Calvin, *Commentaries on the Minor Prophets: Hosea*, in *Calvin's Commentaries* (22 Vols.; Grand Rapids: Baker Book House, 1979) 13: 235.

6. John Calvin, *Institutes of the Christian Religion*, Edited by John T. McNeill, Translated by Ford Lewis Battles (2 Vols.; Philadelphia: The Westminster Press, 1967), 2: 1294.

7. John Calvin, *Commentaries on the First Book of Moses called Genesis*, in *Calvin's Commentaries* (22 Vols.; Grand Rapids: Baker Book House, 1979), 1:127.

8. Warfield, "Hosea 6:7: Adam or Men," in *Selected Shorter Writings*, 1: 119, 129.

9. Martin Luther, *Luther's Works*, edited by Jaroslav Pelikan, translated by George V. Schick (56 Vols.; Saint Louis: Concordia Publishing House, 1958) 1: 110–111.

The Reformed Confessions
In the middle of the 17th Century the covenant of works ascended to confessional prominence. We consider its place in the Westminster Standards, LCF, and the Triple Knowledge.

◆ The Westminster Standards
The Westminster Standards, and the Savoy Declaration, confess a pre-fall covenant. They call it a "covenant of works," or "covenant of life," terms they use as synonyms. WCF defines it in WCF 7:2, 19:1; the Catechisms in WLC 20 and WSC 12 as follows:

> Q. 20. What was the providence of God toward man in the estate in which he was created?
>
> A. The providence of God toward man in the estate in which he was created, was the placing him in paradise, appointing him to dress it, giving him liberty to eat of the fruit of the earth; putting the creatures under his dominion, and ordaining marriage for his help; affording him communion with himself; instituting the Sabbath; entering into a covenant of life with him, upon condition of personal, perfect, and perpetual obedience, of which the tree of life was a pledge; and forbidding to eat of the tree of the knowledge of good and evil, upon the pain of death.
>
> A. When God had created man, he entered into a covenant of life with him, upon condition of perfect obedience; forbidding him to eat of the tree of the knowledge of good and evil, upon the pain of death (WSC 12).

◆ LCF
LCF completely omits WCF 7:2 without defining a pre-fall covenant. It also deletes "covenant of works" from LCF 19:1:

> God gave to Adam a law of universal obedience written in his heart, and a particular precept of not eating the fruit of the tree of knowledge of good and evil; by which he bound him and all his posterity to personal, entire, exact, and perpetual obedience; promised life upon the fulfilling, and threatened death upon the breach of it, and endued him with power and ability to keep it.

Further, LCF deleted the doctrine of the covenant of works from LCF 6:1, which was based in part on Paragraph 4 of the First London Confession of 1644 and in part on the Savoy Declaration:

> God having made a covenant of works and life, thereupon, with our first parents and all their posterity in them, they being seduced by the subtlety and temptation of Satan did wilfully transgress the law of their creation, and break the covenant in eating the forbidden fruit (SD 6:1).

> Although God created man upright and perfect, and gave him a righteous law, which had been unto life had he kept it, and threatened death upon the breach thereof, yet he did not long abide in this honor; Satan using the subtlety of the serpent to subdue Eve, then by her seducing Adam, who, without any compulsion, did wilfully transgress the law of their creation, and the command given unto them, in eating the forbidden fruit, which God was pleased, according to his wise and holy counsel to permit, having purposed to order it to his own glory (LCF 6:1).

Thus, LCF intentionally deleted WCF 7:2 entirely and revised LCF 7:2 to accommodate this deletion. It also intentionally deletes the phrase "covenant of works" when employing WCF 19:1 and SD 6:1. However, it does not remove every vestige of this doctrine.[10] Nevertheless, these deletions are significant and strategic. They express distance. The Baptist fathers do not deny a pre-fall covenant with Adam. Yet, at the very least, they decline to confess a covenant of works, as defined in WCF 7:2, 19:1 and in SD 6:1. Thus, the covenant of works doctrine does not have the same prominence in LCF that it has in the Westminster Standards and Savoy Declaration.

✦ The Triple Knowledge

These standards do not mention a pre-fall covenant. Hoekema acknowledges this. He also observes that the Triple Knowledge differs from the Westminster Creeds in this respect:[11]

> By the middle of the 17th century, therefore, the doctrine of the covenant of works was firmly embedded in Reformed theology. Because the Heidelberg Catechism and the Belgic Confession are

---

10. LCF 20:1 begins: "The covenant of works being broken by sin," a verbatim quote of SD 20:1. The correct explanation for this inconsistency is not clear to me.
11. Anthony Hoekema, Doctrine of Man Handouts, 14.

16th-century creeds, the doctrine of the covenant of works is not found in them. Neither do we find any reference to the covenant of works in the Canons of Dort, though they were drawn up in the early 17th century. The covenant of works does, however, occupy a prominent place in the Westminster Creeds.

Its absence from CSD could be explained by their more limited focus, namely, refuting Arminian error. Although they never explicitly mention a pre-fall covenant, they do affirm that total depravity is rooted in original sin, which stems from Adam's first sin. They trace depravity to its roots when they unfold the "Effect of the Fall on Human Nature" (CSD 3:1) and the "Spread of Corruption" (CSD 3:2). They also affirm solidarity in Adam when they refute the error that his first sin was not sufficient to condemn the human race or to warrant eternal punishment (CSD 3:P1). Still, the Triple Knowledge doesn't explicitly confess a pre-fall covenant, Kersten's valiant effort to find it there notwithstanding.[12]

Subsequent Development

In the Westminster stream, note the work of Thomas Boston,[13] W. G. T. Shedd,[14] Charles Hodge,[15] R. L. Dabney,[16] Geerhardus Vos,[17] Morton Smith,[18] and Professor John Murray.[19]

In the stream of Dutch Calvinism: Brakel,[20] Kersten,[21] Bavinck,[22] Berkhof,[23] and especially Herman Hoeksema. He confesses a pre-fall covenant yet critiques the covenant of works.[24]

---

12. G. H. Kersten, *Reformed Dogmatics*, 193, 202–03.
13. Thomas Boston, "Man's Fourfold State," in *Complete Works*, 8: 16–19.
14. W. G. T. Shedd, *Dogmatic Theology*, 2: 152–167.
15. Hodge, *Systematic Theology*, 2: 117–122, 124–125.
16. Dabney, *Lectures in Systematic Theology*, 302–305.
17. Geerhardus Vos, *Biblical Theology*, (Grand Rapids: Wm. B. Eerdmans Publishing Co., 1948), 27–40.
18. Morton Smith, *Systematic Theology*, 1: 278–286.
19. John Murray, *Collected Writings*, 2: 47–59.
20. Wilhelmus à Brakel, *Reasonable Service*, 1: 355–367.
21. G. H. Kersten, *Reformed Dogmatics*, 1: 192–208.
22. Bavinck, Volume 3 of *Reformed Dogmatics*, 224–228.
23. Berkhof, *Systematic Theology*, 215–218.
24. Herman Hoeksema, *Reformed Dogmatics*, 214–226.

In the stream of LCF: Gill,[25] Dagg,[26] and Boyce.[27]

Definition of the Covenant of Works

Introduction: The Generic Concept

What is the general idea? The Westminster Standards define the general concept in WCF 7:2, 19:1 and WLC 20:

> A covenant of works wherein life was promised to Adam and in him to his posterity, upon condition of perfect and personal obedience (WCF 7:2); God gave to Adam a law, as a covenant of works, by which he bound him and all his posterity to personal, entire, exact, and perpetual obedience, promised life upon the fulfilling, and threatened death upon the breach of it, and endued him with power and ability to keep it (WCF 19:1); entering into a covenant of life with him, upon condition of personal, perfect, and perpetual obedience, of which the tree of life was a pledge; and forbidding to eat of the tree of the knowledge of good and evil, upon the pain of death (WLC 20).

Their covenant of works has five essential features: (1) *its partakers*, Adam and his posterity, "Adam and in him to his posterity"; (2) *its promise*, permanent life, "promised life upon the fulfilling"; (3) *its condition*, obedience, "upon condition of personal, perfect, and perpetual obedience"; (4) *its penalty*, death, "and threatened death upon the breach of it"; and (5) *its pledge*, the tree of life, "of which the tree of life was a pledge." They also address the fulfillment of the covenant of works, "promised life *upon the fulfilling.*" This intimates that after a successful probation period, Adam would have received immutable life. The Westminster Standards also affirm its outcome, namely, that Adam broke it: "Man, by his fall, having made himself incapable of life by that covenant" (WCF 7:3). Thus, we consider its *features, fulfillment,* and *fruition.* I use as guides the expositions just noted and the critique of Herman Hoeksema.

---

25. John Gill, *Body of Divinity*, 1: 444–451.
26. John Dagg, *A Manual of Theology* (Harrisonburg: Gano Books, 1982), 144–150.
27. James Boyce, *Abstract of Systematic Theology* (Christian Gospel Foundation, reprint, n. d.), 234–239.

The Essential Features of the Covenant of Works
We now unfold its five essential features. We consider its partakers, promise, condition, penalty, and pledge.

• Its Partakers or Parties: Adam and His Posterity
They affirm that Adam and his posterity partake in this covenant. God condescends to man's level to establish a covenant with him (WCF 7:1). Adam acts as the representative head of the human race. The covenant of works is a legal contract. It establishes a legal relationship between God and Adam and his posterity.

• Its Promise: Permanent Life
Neither WLC nor WSC explicitly defines any promise of this covenant. WCF defines its promise in WCF 7:2, "life was promised," and WCF 19:1, "promised life upon the fulfilling." They say that the life promised would follow *upon the fulfilling.* Thus, they cannot intend the life Adam already had. Plainly, Adam was already alive physically and spiritually, but his life was mutable. Thus, they must have in mind a quality of life superior to the life he possessed. They envision the life Christians experience in the world to come. They refer to immutable life, impervious to sin and death. Thus, they mean that God promises permanent life to Adam if and when he fulfills the condition. Thus, the promise is impeccable life, without the possibility of sin, which is immortal life, without the possibility of death.

• Its Condition: Perfect and Perpetual Obedience
They say that the condition is "perfect and perpetual" obedience to all God's commandments. The special focus of this condition is God's prohibition regarding the tree of the knowledge of good and evil.

• Its Penalty: Death
God threatens death as the penalty to be inflicted for disobedience. As history tragically displays, death includes spiritual death, physical death, and eternal death.

• Its Pledge or Sacrament: The Tree of Life
WCF calls the tree of life the "pledge" of this covenant. Calvin uses "sacrament." Berkhof says that Adam could eat from the tree of life as long as

he remained righteous.[28] Hodge says that Adam would only have access to the tree of life upon completion of a successful probation.[29] WCF does not address that issue.

The Fulfillment of the Covenant of Works: A Probation Period
WCF intimates a probation period when it says: *"upon the fulfilling."* Some probation period is essential to this entire scheme. Otherwise, how could Adam ever fulfill it? He would have to keep it *forever* before God gave him *permanent* life, which makes no sense. Thus, WCF confesses that after a period of "perfect and perpetual obedience," God would have bestowed immutable life on Adam. Possibly only I feel this tension, but I find it difficult to reconcile a probation period with "perpetual" obedience. Perpetual signifies continual, constant, enduring, lasting indefinitely, permanent, or unending. Its antonym is temporary. Let me put it as a question. Why wouldn't *perpetual* last indefinitely for sinless Adam? Why wouldn't it last as long as creation? Why wouldn't it last until Adam fulfilled the creation mandate with which his Creator blessed and commissioned him: "be fruitful and multiply and replenish the earth and subdue it"? Someone could answer that perpetual can also signify uninterrupted or occurring repeatedly. Possibly, the best approach is to resolve this tension by taking perpetual in this context to mean *uninterrupted.* Another approach, of course, would be to scrap the speculative notion of a probation period, since Scripture says nothing whatsoever about it, and since God actually did require from Adam "perpetual" obedience of indefinite duration. This obedience would last until he fulfilled the creation mandate. Then, when sinless man finished the work God gave him to do in this creation, God would have translated him without death to a new mandate in a new creation. Surely Calvin and Luther correctly affirmed Adam's hope. So that even sinless Adam worked on his creation mandate in hope of entering God's rest when his work on earth was done. The Sabbath day was God's token and pledge of this hope.

The Fruition or Outcome of the Covenant of Works: Broken
All agree that Adam broke this covenant. Yet some disagreement exists among Reformed theologians about the upshot of this outcome. Hodge and Professor Murray correctly affirm that it is abrogated totally. Some,

---

28. Berkhof, *Systematic Theology,* 217.
29. Hodge, *Systematic Theology,* 2: 125.

however, allege that it is still in force "hypothetically." They say that men could still merit eternal life by works, if they could perform perfect and perpetual obedience. This idea is self-contradictory. The requirement of "perpetual" obedience exposes this. Suppose, hypothetically, that someone keeps God's law perfectly his *entire life*. Then, by this hypothesis, he would merit eternal life and never die. So, how would he ever receive its promise? He would spend his endless life fulfilling its requirement. Should we invent a probation period, as with Adam? Where does Scripture encourage such a contrivance? If it weren't for death, which provides a convenient "probation period," none would ever even conceive of such a scheme. Yet they forget that if men actually did keep it, they wouldn't die. Thus, this whole scheme of hypothetical potency is nonsense.

Defense of the Covenant of Works
Reformed theologians offer several arguments to support this covenant of works formula. Let's consider four.

First, they affirm that God's prohibition (Gen. 2:16–17) has all the elements of a covenant. Hodge presents this argument.[30] He regards promise, condition, and penalty as the essential elements. He also argues that since gaining eternal life by faith is called a covenant, gaining eternal life by works must have also been a covenant.

Second, they say that the threat of death necessarily implies a promise of immutable life and heavenly reward. Even Professor Murray reasons this way.[31]

Third, they argue that the parallel between Adam and Christ supports the covenant of works. They say that what Christ actually gained, immutable life, is exactly what Adam would have gained. A period of obedience successfully completed by Christ results in permanent life for everyone Christ represents; therefore they say, by analogy, a period of obedience successfully completed by Adam would have resulted in immutable life for everyone Adam represents. Professor Murray also uses this argument:[32]

> Analogy is drawn in Scripture between Adam and Christ. They stand in unique relations to mankind; there is none before Adam— he's the first man. There is none between—Christ is the second man.

---

30. Hodge, *Systematic Theology*, 117.
31. Murray, *Collected Writings*, 2: 54.
32. Ibid., 49.

There is none after Christ—he is the last Adam (1 Cor. 15:44–49). Here we have an embracive construction of human relationships. We know also that in Christ there is representative relationship and that obedience successfully completed has its issue in righteousness, justification, life for all he represents (1 Cor. 15:22). So, a period of obedience successfully completed by Adam would have secured eternal life for all represented by him.

Fourth, some allege that Hosea 6:7 explicitly affirms the covenant of works. For example, Berkhof and Kersten cite this text. Hodge, however, admits that Scripture does not explicitly assert a covenant of works. Warfield presents a thorough analysis of the translation and use of this text in church history.[33] In any case, even if it does assert a pre-fall covenant, it says nothing whatsoever about probation or immutable life or heavenly reward. It merely says that Adam broke this pre-fall covenant. So at best, this text proves an Adamic covenant that was conditional and broken. It does not prove the covenant of works doctrine.

Critique of the Covenant of Works
The Reformed Critique

Every Reformed theologian has not embraced the covenant of works doctrine. Some, for example Herman Hoeksema, critique it. He confesses a pre-fall covenant, but rejects the covenant of works model. He affirms that the Triple Knowledge does not teach a covenant of works. He defines the covenant of works as follows:[34]

> We may summarize its various elements as follows: (1) The covenant of works was an arrangement between God and Adam entered into by God and established by him after man's creation. It was not given with creation, but was an additional arrangement. (2) It was a means to an end. Adam had life, but did not possess the highest, that is, eternal life. He was free, but his state was not that of highest freedom. He was lapsable. And the covenant of works was arranged as a means for Adam to attain to that highest state of freedom in eternal life. (3) The specific elements of the covenant were a promise (eternal life), a penalty (eternal death) and a condition (perfect obedience). (4) In this covenant, Adam was placed on probation. There would come a time when the period of probation was ended and

---

33. Warfield, "Hosea 6:7: Adam or Men," in *Selected Shorter Writings*, 1:116–129.
34. Hoeksema, *Reformed Dogmatics*, 216.

when the promise would be fulfilled. (5) At the end of the period of probation Adam would have been translated into a state of glory analogous to the change of believers that shall live at the time of Christ's second advent. (6) The fruit of this obedience of Adam would have been reaped by all Adam's posterity.

This doesn't sound like a straw man to me. Rather, Hoeksema accurately presents the features and fulfillment of the covenant of works as the Westminster Standards define it. Now we consider three of his critiques of the covenant of works doctrine.

First, Hoeksema argues that the covenant of works is based on speculation, not mandated by Scripture. He says that God's threat of death for disobedience does not necessarily imply a promise of immutable life or of heavenly translation. He says that this threat necessarily implies only that by obedience Adam would continue to live and never die, no more. Clearly, this critique is cogent.

Second, Hoeksema argues that no mere man could ever merit any special reward from God. All Adam could ever have said was: "I am an unprofitable servant." Adam could not by obedience have merited anything more than what he already had. This is true enough. However, God condescends to commend and reward the sincere obedience of his people, although they do not merit such a reward: "you shall be recompensed at the resurrection of the just," etc.

Third, Hoeksema argues that the supposed promise of heavenly life is "inconceivable" without violating the design of creation. He says the covenant of works devalues creation and pits Genesis 2:17 against the creation mandate in Genesis 1:28: "be fruitful, and multiply, and replenish the earth, and subdue it." How would translation to heavenly life after a probation period comport with Adam's vocation? Hoeksema has a vital insight and valid concern.

The Neo-Orthodox Critique

In recent years it has become fashionable to denounce the covenant of works. Neo-Orthodox teachers especially despise it. The gist of the Neo-Orthodox attack is as follows. They say that the covenant of works doctrine errs because it affirms the priority of law. They say that Reformed theologians err because they construe Adam's relation to God a legal one, and thus make law prior to grace. They assert that the opposite is true. They say that grace is always prior to law. To support this they appeal to the fact that God gave the Mosaic Law to a redeemed covenant community. Ultimately, they aim to undermine the relation between Christ's atonement and God's law. They are averse to the idea that Christ suffered the penalty of a broken law in our place. Their attacks on the idea that God required Adam to obey in our place serve as back door attacks on a penal vicarious atonement. There is an element of truth in their critique. Yet we must beware of their agenda. Don't throw out the baby with the bath water.

Modification of the Covenant of Works

John Murray and others recast the covenant of works motif. We focus now on amendments he proposes. He retains the core concept, which he calls the "Adamic administration." He says it is

> construed as an administration in which God, by a special act of providence, established for man the provision whereby he might pass from the status of contingency to one of confirmed and indefectible holiness and blessedness, that is, from posse peccare and posse non-peccare to non-posse peccare. The way instituted was that of an intensified and concentrated probation, the alternative issues being dependent upon the issues of obedience or disobedience (*Collected Writings*, 2: 49).

Nevertheless, he reconstructs its presentation. He stresses the gracious character of Adam's relation to God. First, he replaces both "covenant" and "works." Second, he rejects the idea that the covenant of works is presently in force hypothetically.[35] Third, he rejects using the Adamic Administration to define the Mosaic covenant. He says we should not use texts that say: "this do and you shall live," to support a covenant of works.[36] Fourth, with Hoeksema, he rejects the notion that any mere man, even a sinless one, could ever merit any reward from God.[37] He says that if Adam received any added blessing through this probation, it would have been all of grace.

Conclusion to the Reformed Theology

We must subject every pronouncement of dogmatic theology to the scrutiny of Scripture. Dogmatic theology is the protective fence around systematic

---

35. Murray, *Collected Writings*, 2: 50, 57.
36. Ibid., 50, 55.
37. Ibid., 56.

theology. Scripture is the final judge of men's dogma. The final question is always, "What says the Scripture?" Thus, I now attempt a scriptural analysis and exposition of God's representative prohibition to Adam.

A Biblical Exposition: The Adamic Covenant
Introduction: Principles of Interpretation

I introduce this exposition by uncovering the principles of interpretation on which it rests. We should overtly state hermeneutical principles because they are the eyeglasses with which we examine every bit of data. I acknowledge three relevant perspectives.

The Relationship Between Genesis 1 and 2
In Genesis 1:26–27 Scripture presents an embracive overview of the original relation between God and Adam. The text surveys the entire panorama of Genesis 2:5–25. The prohibition of Genesis 2:16–17 does not define a separate relationship between Adam and God superimposed on a relation defined in Genesis 1:26–27. Rather, it is an integral aspect of that personal relationship.

The Relationship Between Adam and Christ
The relationship between Adam and Christ involves a twofold parallel or typology. Scripture intimates the first analogy in Romans 5:12–21. Adam and Christ are both representative heads in solidarity with an entire humanity. Adam represents the original humanity, Christ the new humanity. Scripture intimates the second parallel in 1 Corinthians 15:45. Adam and Christ both inaugurate a mode of human life. Adam inaugurates earthly life, Christ resurrection life. That passage affirms that since man has a body in his earthly life in Adam, he also has a body in his resurrection life in Christ. It further affirms that as we have borne the image of Adam in earthly life, so we who believe will bear the image of Christ in resurrection life.

I stress this to underscore the propriety of using this analogy between Adam and Christ and also the need to discern its biblical limits. If we extrapolate and press it beyond these limits, the result will be unreliable. The contrasts Paul uses in Romans 5:12–21 underscore this warning. So does the fact that God the Son, Jesus Christ, is and always was a divine Person, Adam a human person. Adam did not exist before his creation. Christ always existed. He is God the Son, infinite, eternal, and impeccable.

The Relationship Between Creation and Redemption

The relationship between creation and redemption exhibits both continuity and discontinuity. The gulf of sin separates creation from redemption. The relationship also exhibits harmony. Redemption is not against creation. It is against sin. Furthermore, there is progress and advancement. Creation was "very good." Redemption is superior to very good. The restoration achieved in redemption is not retrogressive. It doesn't take man back to pre-fall Eden. It produces something better than Eden. God restores sinless hearts, but not pre-fall innocence. The end result of redemption is greater than original creation minus sin. In sum, the relation between creation and redemption displays harmony and improvement.

To unravel arguments for and against the covenant of works, we must first identify the assumptions on which they rest. We can evaluate them more accurately when we see that some wear a different set of interpretive eyeglasses. It is important to establish biblical principles of interpretation with which to examine what men teach on any topic, especially this one. Now consider with me the *foundations*, *features*, *function*, *form*, and *fruition* of the Adamic covenant.

The Foundations of the Adamic Covenant

The Adamic covenant rests on Adam's filial relation with God, on his blessed vocation, and on his eternal hope. WLC 20 rightly couches the representative prohibition in its biblical context. These foundations determine its tone and design.

Adam's Filial Relation to God

Scripture defines this relation in Genesis 1:26–27. Adam's original relation to God was filial on Adam's part, parental on God's part. We now unfold its *substance*, *privileges*, and *obligations*.

✦ The Substance of Adam's Sonship: Royal and Representative

We consider its dual substance. It was *royal* and *representative* sonship. As an introduction, I unfold biblical testimony from three witnesses in support of Adam's sonship to God.

First, in Genesis 5:1–3[38] Scripture affirms man's identity as the image of God. It repeats Genesis 1:26–27 almost verbatim. The text explicitly connects image and likeness with parenthood and sonship. Seth, Adam's son, is his image and likeness. He has a filial relationship with Adam. Adam has a parental relationship with Seth. Similarly, Adam has a filial relationship with God because he is God's image and likeness. Thus, God has a parental relationship with Adam.

Second, in Luke 3:23, 37–38,[39] Scripture completes the genealogy of Jesus. Luke identifies Adam as "the *son* of God." Adam procreated Seth in his own image. Seth was Adam's son. God created Adam in his own image. Adam was God's son. Luke's genealogy instructs us that the relation of a father to the son he procreated pictures the relation of God to the son he created, Adam.

Third, in Hebrews 1:3, Scripture calls the Son incarnate "the very image (χαρακτηρ)" of his Father.[40] Again, it depicts Christ, the Son of his Father's love, as the "image (εἰκων) of the invisible God" (Col. 1:13, 15). This confirms that Christ, God's Son incarnate, is God's image. Even so, God created his son Adam as his image, the living visible representation of the invisible God.

In this original relationship Adam was God's son both by creation, *naturally*, and by moral likeness, *spiritually*. After the fall, sinners continue to be God's offspring naturally (Acts 17:28). Fallen man retains this aspect of his identity as God's living representation (James 3:9). But man in sin no longer represents God accurately. Rather, he misrepresents God morally and spiritually. Thus, a lost sinner is no longer God's son or image spiritually. Thus, Jesus said to his unconverted countrymen: "You are of your father, the devil" (John 8:37, 39, 42, 44). Men in the state of sin are no longer God's spiritual children but spiritual children of the devil. Thus sin grievously distorted and

---

38. "This is the book of the generation of Adam. In the day that God created man, in the likeness of God made he him; male and female created he them, and blessed them, and called their name Adam, in the day when they were created. And Adam lived an hundred and thirty years, and begat a son in his own likeness, after his image; and called his name Seth" (Gen. 5:1–3).

39. "And Jesus himself, when he began to teach, was about thirty years of age, being the son (as was supposed) of Joseph, the *son* of Eli…the *son* of Enoch…the *son* of Seth, the *son* of Adam, the *son* of God" (Luke 3:23, 37–38).

40. "Has at the end of these days spoken unto us in *his* Son, whom he appointed heir of all things, through whom also he made the worlds; who being the effulgence of his glory, and the very image of his substance, and upholding all things by the word of his power, when he had made purification of sins, sat down on the right hand of the Majesty on high" (Heb. 1:2–3).

spiritually abrogated man's filial relation with God. The tragedy of the fall is personal and relational, not just moral and legal.

In sum, Adam's original relation to God was familial and filial-parental. Thus it was warm and affectionate, not cold or distant. It was not an impersonal relationship between "contracting parties." It was not between a disinterested judge and an unrelated defendant, or a ruler to an unknown subject. Thus, a "covenant of works" model simply doesn't comport with its filial-parental framework. Categories like "contracting parties," "stipulations," and "penalties" are foreign to this familial relation. Such categories might suitably define a contract between corporations forging a business venture through their lawyers. They seem woefully inadequate to define a *parental* prohibition. In Genesis 2:16–17 God addresses Adam, not as a lawyer, but as a Father. This prohibition is an integral part of Adam's filial relation to God. Thus, the covenant of works model wrenches this prohibition from its filial foundation. This is my primary objection to imposing this motif and its categories on this prohibition.

First, Adam's sonship was *royal*. Sonship does not negate the fact that God was also Adam's Ruler, Master, and Judge. Rather, Adam's Father ruled over him and judged him. Adam's sonship was like the relation of a prince to a king. A king, at one and the same time, is a father, master, ruler, and judge to a prince. Adam was not just anybody's son. He was the King's son. He was the prince of the original creation. God intimates Adam's royalty when he gives him dominion over creation: "let them have dominion." The Creator is King. Creation belongs to him. He rules over it and judges it. The King gave his son, Adam, dominion over his works (Ps. 8:3–9).

It is important to grasp the impact of this. Royal sonship has familial and legal aspects. A prince is his father's subject and servant. Even so Adam was his Father's subject and servant. A king is a prince's father and judge. So God was Adam's Father and Judge. A prince is capable, as Absalom was, of leading a revolt against his father's kingdom. Even so, Adam was capable of treason against his Father's government. As a prince is liable to civil punishment if he commits treason, so also Adam, if he chose to rebel against his Father's authority, was liable to his Father's condemnation. God's family is the royal family of the universe. Thus, Scripture stresses equally that God was Adam's Father and King.

Second, Adam's sonship was *representative*. Adam, God's son, stood before his Father in a representative capacity. God made Adam the representative head of all his posterity. Scripture teaches this plainly (Rom.

5:12–21). In this respect Paul calls Adam a "type" of Christ. Thus Adam acted in the room and stead of all his posterity in this prohibition. God established solidarity. This solidarity does not diminish Adam's filial relation to God. Rather, as God's son Adam represented his natural posterity. Similarly, Jesus did not cease to be God's Son because God made him the representative head of his spiritual posterity. Christ's relation to God the Father did not cease to be filial because it is representative. So it was with Adam. This underscores that we should use categories consonant with a filial relationship to define this prohibition.

♦ The Privileges of Adam's Sonship: Life and Paradise

We observe two filial privileges, or a twofold privilege, life and the enjoyment of paradise in Eden.

First, Adam enjoyed the unmerited privilege of physical and spiritual life. He enjoyed communion with God. He knew God. He had affectionate fellowship with him. Scripture calls such knowledge and fellowship with God "life" (John 17:3). Thus Adam had life, physical and spiritual. Thus, he had the right to eat from the tree of life (Gen. 2:16). Yet, it is also true that Adam's life was mutable.

Second, Adam enjoyed the unmerited privilege of home in paradise, the Garden of Eden. Adam lived in blessing and delight. The Garden of Eden was beautiful and comfortable. God abundantly supplied their every need.

Now, consider carefully the source and ground of these privileges. Adam did not merit life in paradise. He never earned it. God gave all this to him from the beginning, freely, out of paternal favor. Adam enjoyed blessing from his Father that was unmixed and unmerited. God established Adam's filial relationship and its privileges wholly from his *creative paternal favor.* He founded it on unmerited favor to the son he created upright (Eccles. 7:29). Adam enjoyed every privilege and blessing freely from the generous love of his Creator Father. Again, categories like "contracting parties," and "stipulations," misrepresent God's unmerited favor from which he freely gave every privilege and blessing to his son Adam.

♦ The Obligations of Adam's Sonship: Imitation and Obedience

Adam's sonship entails filial privilege and filial obligation. The two go hand in hand. Parental law doesn't eviscerate a filial relation; it regulates it. A human father freely gives privileges to a son. He may give additional privileges to a son who walks in obedience. A son is obligated to obey his father's will. This is even true of Adam's royal sonship to God. Adam's Father did not withhold all privilege from Adam until he merited it. Rather, he gave privilege freely, prior to obedience (Gen. 2:16). Yet, disobedience to his Father's law forfeited filial privilege and provoked his punishment (Gen. 2:16–17). Thus, in Eden, neither privilege nor law had ultimate priority. They were correlative. Law was neither ultimate nor irrelevant. Privilege was neither irrevocable nor merited. Privilege and responsibility both motivated Adam's obedience. Adam's heavenly Father regulated his sonship by parental *example* and by parental *commandment*.

First, Adam was obliged to imitate God's parental example. God regulates Adam's sonship by setting an example for his son to follow. This remains true for God's redeemed children: "be ye therefore imitators of God, as beloved children; and walk in love" (Eph. 5:1–2). Therefore, Adam's obligation as God's son was to imitate God within the framework he had instituted. God intended Adam to imitate him, not in the abstract, but within his created order. Four creation ordinances constitute this framework. These are: (1) *procreation*, marriage and the family (Gen. 1:28, 2:18–25), (2) *vocation*, labor and economy (Gen. 1:28, 2:15), (3) *dominion*, rule and government (Gen. 1:26, 28), and (4) *religion*, the Sabbath and worship (Gen. 1:1–31; 2:1–3; Exod. 20:11).

How was Adam to imitate God? In all his actions the Creator has and manifests love to himself and to his creatures. Thus, Adam's moral obligation was to imitate this love. He was responsible to love God and his fellow creatures. Thus imitating God coincides with keeping his moral law, obeying his revealed will. Thus, Adam's obligation included implicitly every sanction that God codified in the Ten Commandments. Adam should reverence what God reverenced. The Ten Commandments uphold the sanctity of God's being, nature, name, designated day, instituted authority, life, marriage, personal property, truth, and the inner life. When Adam reverenced these things he imitated his heavenly Father.

Further, all of us who bear the image of God in Adam have that same responsibility. The revelation of permanent moral obligation displays continuity and development. From the beginning God wrote it on Adam's conscience. Then he verbalized and codified it at Sinai. Then Christ fulfilled it in his earthly life. God writes it in the covenant of grace on the hearts of his elect and in the new covenant on the hearts of the community he redeemed from sin in Christ.

Second, Adam was obliged to obey God's parental commandments. Adam must not only imitate his Father's ways, but he must also obey his Father's commandment. The Creator imposed a prohibition as a Royal Parent on his son, the prince of creation.

Adam's Blessed Vocation: The Creation Mandate

Scripture defines Adam's blessed vocation in Genesis 1:28–30. His vocation forms the foundation and framework of this prohibition. Thus, what we posit about the Adamic covenant must be congruous with the creation blessing and mandate that define his vocation:

> And God blessed them and God said to them: Produce fruit and grow numerous, and fill the earth and subdue it. And rule over the fish in the sea and over the birds in the heavens and over every living creature that moves on the earth (Gen. 1:28).

This is God's blessed prescription for mankind on earth. Everything God prescribes for human life flows from his goodness and favor. He communicates this blessedness personally and verbally to Adam and Eve: "and God blessed them and God said to them." In this blessing God prescribes for man activities and occupations that define his vocation on earth. By this blessing God prescribes how man should occupy his time and energy. God begins Adam's earthly vocation with procreation of numerous offspring. He tells Adam and Eve to "produce fruit and grow numerous." He blesses procreation within marriage, which he instituted to convey the blessing of family and society. He designed the human family to grow numerous. Next, God defines Adam's vocation in relation to his environment, the earth: "fill the earth and subdue it." By his labor man subdues his environment and expands his habitat to encompass the globe. Thus, God blessed Adam and his offspring with the mammoth vocation of populating and harnessing the entire earth.

Therefore, whatever we posit about the content, duration, and fruition of this prohibition must comport with this creation blessing and mammoth mandate. Therefore, Hoeksema wisely warns that the covenant of works motif pits the representative prohibition against the creation mandate. This we must avoid. Otherwise, we devalue creation and wrench the Adamic covenant from its biblical foundation.

Adam's Eternal Hope: Enter God's Rest

Scripture intimates Adam's eternal hope in Genesis 2:1–3. On the seventh day God rested from all his creative work (Gen. 2:2). Then God set that day apart as sacred (Gen. 2:3). Its focus was on physical refreshment and spiritual nourishment. On this sacred day of rest Adam could lay aside his labor, fellowship with God, and focus on his works. This sacred day was an emblem of the eternal rest that he hoped to enter after he finished his work on earth. By *eternal hope* I refer to this expectation of divine blessing once he fulfilled his mammoth vocation. When he had populated and subdued the earth, he would have entered his rest. He would have entered his rest in God's heavenly presence without death. What would have followed the fulfillment of his hope is a matter of pure speculation. Possibly God would have blessed Adam and his posterity with a new creation mandate in a new universe.

God freely blessed Adam with the Sabbath and with the hope it symbolized. Adam did not earn the Sabbath by works. Thus, Adam did not merit his hope by works—but he could sin and forfeit his hope. The covenant of works motif seems to say that Adam had to earn the hope of eternal rest that God gave him freely as a privilege.

The Features of the Adamic Covenant

We expound three features of the Adamic Covenant: its partakers, substance, and implicit token.

The Partakers: Adam and His Posterity

Scripture plainly says, "And Jehovah God commanded the man, saying" (Gen. 2:16). Adam is the principal partaker. Paul's inspired interpretation reveals that God addressed this parental pledge to his son Adam in his *representative capacity* (Rom. 5:12–21). This prohibition does not define a higher relationship to which Adam's sonship was a stepping-stone. Rather, in this matter God established solidarity between his son Adam and his posterity. Adam acts, not as a private person, for himself alone, but as a representative of his natural descendants. God imputes what Adam does to them. Thus, Paul affirms: "by the one man's disobedience the many were made sinners" (Rom. 5:19).

The Substance: God's Permission, Prohibition, and Pledge
Its substance consists in three things: (1) God's permission or provision, "of every tree of the garden you may freely eat," (2) his prohibition or restriction, "but of the tree of the knowledge of good and evil, you shall not eat of it," and (3) his pledge or solemn explanation, "for in the day you eat thereof, you shall surely die."

✦ God's Permission: Generous Provision
God says to Adam: "Of every tree of the garden you may freely eat." The Father couches his prohibition and pledge in generosity. God gave Adam permission to eat from every tree in the garden except one, the tree of the knowledge of good and evil. Generous provision of food to sustain life corresponds with his privilege of life. It flatly contradicts Genesis 2:16 to assert that God forbade Adam to eat from the tree of life. He could eat from every tree but one—not all but two!

Speculation has set a snare here for good men. That snare goes something like this. Adam parallels Christ. Christ by obedience gained for his posterity permanent life in immutable holiness. Therefore, Adam would by obedience have gained immutable life for his posterity. The tree of life symbolized what Adam would have gained. Therefore, Adam had to obey in order to earn the right to eat from the tree of life. Therefore, Adam did not have the right to eat from the tree of life during his probation. All very logical—but the text flatly contradicts the conclusion. Thus, the reasoning, no matter how logical, is not biblical, but flawed. Where are its flaws? For one thing, Christ obtained by obedience far more than Adam ever could have merited. For another, the tree of life symbolized the life Adam already had and stood to lose. Nevertheless, even the godly and erudite have been taken in this snare.[41] Thankfully, not all Reformed theologians have been caught in this quagmire.[42]

✦ God's Prohibition: Sovereign Restriction
God sovereignly restricts his son Adam: "but of the tree of the knowledge of good and evil, you shall not eat of it" (Gen. 2:17). God locates this tree in the

---

41. Murray, *Collected Writings*, 2: 48; Hodge, *Systematic Theology*, 2: 124–125.
42. Berkhof observes: "When Adam forfeited the promise he was debarred from the sign," *Systematic Theology*, 217. And Calvin says that after the fall Adam was "excommunicated" from the tree of life, *Commentaries*, 1: 184.

middle of the Garden of Eden next to the tree of life (Gen. 2:9). The proximity of these two trees portrays the proximity of obedience and life. The tree of knowledge was good for food, not poisonous (Gen. 3:6). Thus, by this restriction God asserts his sovereign right to control Adam's life. This prohibition constitutes *the condition* of the Adamic covenant. Its fruition hinges on whether Adam complies with this restriction or violates it.

• God's Pledge: Solemn Warning and Implicit Promise
God gives Adam a parental explanation. This explanation contains a solemn warning of severe penalty that he will inflict on his son for disobedience. Implicit in that pledge of punishment is his promise of continual life, happiness, and hope.

First, God's pledge contains his solemn warning: "for in the day you eat thereof, you shall surely die" (Gen. 2:17). The King gave his royal son good reason for not eating from that tree. At times parents give children an explanation that children cannot fully comprehend due to limited experience. In such a case, a child must trust its parent. So too, this explanation required Adam to trust his Father. Adam has never seen human death, and cannot comprehend it experientially. He must believe his Father knows best, tells him the truth, and has his best interest at heart. God warns Adam that if he disobeys he forfeits his life, not merely physical life, but also spiritual life. The day he eats will be the day he dies.

Second, God's pledge contains his implicit promise. Adam could properly conclude that as long as he obeyed God and refrained from the forbidden fruit he would continue to live. He would continue to enjoy the life, physical and spiritual, which he received from God as an unmerited gift. He would continue to enjoy the privileges and blessings that his Father lavished on him freely. He would continue to have hope of entering God's rest after he completed his earthly work. Boyce unfolds in detail the implicit promise of continual life with all its attendant blessings. He says reading more into it is speculative.[43] Dagg and Hoeksema echo Boyce.[44] Yet some read much more into this divine pledge. We should not extrapolate beyond Scripture.

---

43. Boyce, *Abstract of Systematic Theology*, 236–237.
44. Hoeksema, *Reformed Dogmatics*, 217; Dagg, *Manuel of Theology*, 145.

The Implicit Token: The Tree of Life

In Genesis 3:22–23 Scripture connects the tree of life implicitly with the Adamic covenant. Thus, when Adam ate from the tree of life, it was a reminder of God's implicit promise that he would never die as long as he refrained from the tree of knowledge. Thus, when he broke the Adamic covenant, he was "debarred," as Berkhof says, or "excommunicated," as Calvin says, from the tree of life.

The Functions of the Adamic Covenant: Symbolic and Educational

God's fatherly purpose was benevolent. He intended it for good. No text tells us explicitly or exactly why God commanded Adam not to eat from this tree. Yet Scripture provides three lamps to guide us: (1) the name of the tree, (2) the parental and royal nature of the prohibition, and (3) the analogy between Adam and Christ. We should stay on the path illumined by these divinely lit lamps.

To begin with, its filial framework regulates its intent. This prohibition is not a legal contract between unrelated parties. Its design is *parental* rather than *probationary*. Probation is a period of testing someone's suitability. It is a test to see if someone will work out all right. When someone lands a new job they usually face a period of about six months during which they are on probation. The employer watches them carefully to see whether they will perform acceptably. At the end of six months, if they perform up to snuff, they are hired permanently. If they fail to make the grade, they are fired. Consider the analogy between Adam and Christ. Did the Father put Jesus on probation? That thought is repulsive. Christ's earthly life wasn't a test period to see whether he would measure up. Adam too was God's son. Therefore, even though he was mutable, it doesn't follow that this prohibition had a probationary design. What then was God's purpose? Scripture intimates at least a twofold design in this parental restriction. It was both *symbolic* and *educational*.

This Prohibition was Symbolic

We receive an inkling of its significance from the strategic place Paul assigns to it in Romans 5:12–21. God imputes only this one sin of Adam to his posterity. He does not impute Adam's subsequent sinning. This discloses its strategic role in their relationship. It serves as the badge of familial love and loyalty. It epitomizes all that Adam was as God's son. It symbolizes his obligation to honor his Father's authority and submit to the rule of his King. That lone restriction, sovereignly imposed, underscores that only God's will controls the royal house. Sonship reaches its apex in obedience to a father's will. As Jesus in agony said to his Father: "not my will, but your will be done." In this Adam represents all in him. When he violated the restriction that symbolized his Father's rule, God imputed that sin to his posterity.

This Prohibition was Pedagogical or Educational
This restriction was about learning the difference between right and wrong. The name of the tree guides us to this: "the knowledge of good and evil." So does the analogy with Christ. Christ, by suffering temptation, learned to comfort those who are tempted (Heb. 2:18). He learned obedience, experientially, through what he suffered (Heb. 5:8). Thus, this tree was about learning, education, and knowledge. Specifically, it was about experiential knowledge of good and evil.

Thus, Adam's God and Father intended this restriction, and even the temptation associated with it, for Adam's good. Through it he intended that his son Adam would learn about right and wrong experientially. Adam was to learn obedience through enduring temptation. Before the fall, Adam lacked experiential knowledge of good and evil; by the fall he attained it (Gen. 3:22). But he attained it as one who chose evil. Would he also have learned it experientially if he had resisted temptation and chosen good? Regarding this Geerhardus Vos observes:[45]

> To attain to a knowledge of good and evil is not necessarily an unde-
> sirable and culpable thing. It could happen in a good way.... Because
> man was forbidden to eat of the tree associated with the knowledge
> of good and evil, it has been rashly assumed that the knowledge of
> good and evil was forbidden him.... Man was to attain something
> he had not attained before. He was to learn the good in its clear
> opposition to the evil.

If Vos is correct, then Adam would also have gained this experiential knowledge of right and wrong by resisting temptation. In that case, however, by choosing good, he would have learned experientially to obey through suffering temptation, just as Christ did. He would have learned experientially to encourage those that are tempted, just as Christ did. He would have learned

---

45. Geerhardos Vos, *Biblical Theology* (Grand Rapids: Wm. B. Eerdmans Publishing Company, 1975), 31.

experientially the difference between right and wrong from the standpoint of proven commitment to God and moral integrity.

This fits the filial-parental relationship. It portrays a loving Father training his son Adam, to teach him obedience by an ordeal of temptation. God intends to develop mature moral discernment in Adam in a world beset with evil. This also fits a King-prince relationship. It is well known that a crown prince is often subjected to rigorous and difficult training. This is because a prince must reign and judge. He must learn loyalty to authority to exercise authority well. The best king will not be easily enticed by evil persons. The best king is a loyal prince, trained to withstand all opposition to his father's throne. Even so, God the King prepared prince Adam. He subjected his crown prince to rigorous discipline. He gave him schooling designed to work in his heart moral discernment, so that Adam could exercise just and wise dominion. The King proved the character of the crown prince, so he could demonstrate loyalty, even at great personal cost. The King swore no oath to his son, to insure his continued fidelity during his education in moral discernment. Nor did he promise him any special reward. He merely warned him that disloyalty was treason, a capital offense, and gave him more-than-adequate armor to withstand any satanic onslaught.

The Form of the Adamic Covenant

This covenant or divine pledge is *conditional* in form. God's pledge, which contains his solemn warning and implicit promise, is conditioned on the prohibition. If Adam complies with the prohibition, then God fulfills the implicit promises. If Adam violates the prohibition, then God fulfills his solemn warning to punish Adam with death. The table below pictures this conditionality:

The Condition: God's Prohibition: Refrain from tree of knowledge	God's Pledge: Solemn warning and Implicit promise	The Fruition: Life or Death
Compliance with condition	Fulfill Implicit Promise	Continued Life
Violation of condition	Fulfill Solemn Warning:	Death

This conditional form is similar to the conditional form of the Mosaic covenant. This similarity has led some astray. Although the form is similar, the design and substance are very diverse.

Observe that Adam had the moral power to comply with the condition. God created him morally upright and perfect. He had no trace or taint of sin. His violation of this condition poses a spiritual mystery that human wisdom can never fathom. Observe that if he had complied with the condition, he would simply have done what was required. He would not have merited or earned anything—because he merely gave what he owed, trust and compliance.

The Fruition of the Adamic Covenant

So much of the discussion surrounds the "hypothetical," that we must consider the question, "What would have happened if?" Yet I begin with what actually happened in history and fact.

Its Actual and Historical Outcome

Consider with me five aspects of what actually happened.

First, Adam disobeyed God's commandment. He violated this prohibition. He sinned against God (Gen. 3:7). First Eve ate the forbidden fruit, then Adam (Gen. 3:6).

Second, Adam lost his privilege of life. He lost both spiritual life (Gen. 3:8) and physical life (Gen. 5:5). The very moment he sinned he lost spiritual life. He was alienated from the life of God. He hid from the Father with whom he once walked. Eventually, after living for 930 years, he died physically. God fulfilled his solemn warning. He punished Adam with death in fulfillment of his pledge.

Third, God revoked his privileges of living in the Garden of Eden and eating from the tree of life (Gen. 3:22).[46] Thus Berkhof rightly observes that God "debarred" him from the tree of life:[47]

> We should not think of the fruit of this tree as magically or medically working immortality in Adam's frame. Yet it was in some way connected with the gift of life. In all probability it must be conceived of as an appointed symbol or seal of life. Consequently, when Adam forfeited the promise, he was debarred from the sign. So conceived the words of Gen. 3:22 must be understood sacramentally.

---

46. "And now, lest he put forth his hand, and take also of the tree of life, and eat, and live forever—therefore Jehovah God sent him forth from the garden of Eden" (Gen. 3:22–23).

47. Berkhof, *Systematic Theology*, 217.

This does not necessarily imply that Adam never ate from the tree of life before the fall. Nor does it mean that if Adam after the fall ate from that tree even once, he would have been incapable of physical death. Calvin makes this point with irony:[48]

> It is indeed certain that man would not have been able, had he even devoured the whole tree, to enjoy life against the will of God.

Thus, this text simply says that after the fall God sent Adam out of Eden and restricted the way to the tree of life. It simply implies that if, after the fall, Adam continued to eat from the tree of life, he would continue to live. Was God's concern purely sacramental? Only God knows for certain. Yet eating from the tree of knowledge had an impact that was more than symbolic (Gen. 3:7). Probably eating from the tree of life would have also. Yet Calvin sees divine benevolence even in Adam's "excommunication":[49]

> In short, God resolved to wrest out of the hands of man that which was the occasion or grounds of confidence, lest he should form for himself a vain hope of the perpetuity of the life which he had lost.

Fourth, eventually God destroyed the Garden of Eden, the tree of life, and the tree of knowledge. In all probability this happened through the flood. The cherubim once guarded the path to the tree of life (Gen. 3:24). In those days men could journey to Eden and behold with their own eyes the flaming sword of God. But when God sent the flood, the garden was buried in the depths of the seas, and brought down to the nether parts of the earth.[50] Even if Ezekiel 31:18 does not refer explicitly to the flood, it nevertheless affirms that those trees and that garden are gone forever. Thus, this prohibition about the tree of knowledge could not possibly be a means of attaining heaven for anyone living on earth today, even hypothetically. No one alive today has ever even seen this tree, let alone refrained from it.

Fifth, all Adam's natural posterity sinned in Adam. By his first sin they were made sinners (Rom. 5:12–21). Thus all his natural children are conceived in sin, with a polluted heart and a guilty record. All his natural posterity are conceived dead in sin and alienated from the life of God (Eph. 2:1–3). This is what has happened with respect to this prohibition. This is

---

48. Calvin, *Commentaries*, 1: 184.
49. Ibid.
50. "Yet shalt thou be brought down with the trees of Eden unto the nether parts of the earth" (Ezek. 31:18).

not hypothetical speculation. It is human history. Thus, this prohibition is still in force *representatively*. It shall ever remain in force, while the earth lasts. Adam's disobedience is, and shall ever be, imputed to all his descendants at their conception.

Hypothetical Questions and Speculations about its Outcome
Most Christian parents in family devotion have probably heard a question like, "What would have happened if Adam never ate from the tree of knowledge?" Another question our children ask is, "What if Eve had sinned, but not Adam?" Such questions can never be answered absolutely, because Scripture doesn't tell us. It is natural and innocent for our children to ask such questions, but we shouldn't build our theology on speculative reasoning. We should root theology in *the facts* of biblical revelation, not in *hypothetical extrapolations*. Nor should we condemn our brothers for reluctance to engage in such speculations. Sadly, this topic leaves us quite vulnerable to "vain and unprofitable" questions that engender strife. Thus, with due caution, let's consider four questions commonly associated with this topic.

First: If Adam had never sinned, would Adam's posterity have been accepted with God on the basis of Adam's virtue or their own? Consider Professor Murray's use of the parallel between Adam and Christ. Christ's obedience was imputed to those in solidarity with him. Adam's disobedience was imputed to those in solidarity with him. These are undeniable facts of revelation. Would Adam's obedience have been imputed to his posterity? This parallel prompts us to say, yes. Thus far, we may go with Murray. All that necessarily follows is that Adam's righteousness would have been imputed to his posterity. With that righteousness they would continue to possess the life that God granted to Adam freely as a privilege. Adam's posterity would have known nothing of condemnation, depravity, or death. They would have experienced only acceptance, righteousness, and life.

Someone may reply, what if only Eve had eaten from the tree of knowledge? What if one of their children had sinned? Which would have prevailed, their individual responsibility or Adam's representative headship? The Bible says very little about this. It says that Eve knew that she should not eat from the tree of knowledge. It says that what she did was sinful, and that God held her accountable for it (Gen. 3:3, 13). It says that their eyes were both opened when Adam ate (Gen. 3:7). The Bible says no more about such speculations.

It simply says that Adam, not Eve, was the representative head of his posterity and that God held Eve personally accountable for her sin.

Second: How long would this representative prohibition have lasted? Scripture does not answer this question either. It never asserts, implies, or intimates that God would have rescinded this prohibition as long as Adam lived in Eden and fulfilled his vocation to populate and subjugate the earth. The notion of a "probation period" is pure speculation. It is utterly without biblical ground or support. However, in light of the parallel with Christ, it is plausible and probable that Adam's concentrated period of temptation would have ended, just as it did with Jesus. This leads to the next question.

Third: How long would Adam have remained morally mutable and able to sin? Would he have become impeccable by resisting a period of temptation? It is highly probable that by resisting temptation Adam would have gained experiential knowledge of good and become impeccably good. Just as eating when tempted actually confirmed his soul in moral evil, even so not eating when tempted would have confirmed his soul in moral good. Yet, this is a matter of speculation, not something to be dogmatic about. The parallel with Christ points in a different direction. Christ did not pass, by resisting temptation, from peccability to impeccability. Christ was impeccable before and after he was tempted. Yet, if Adam would have attained impeccability by resisting temptation, it's hard to avoid the inference that Christ actually did, which we know is not the case.

Further, some want to extrapolate from the fall of angels to answer this question. These point out that when the concentrated period of temptation ceased, angels were no longer mutable. So, they conclude, it would have been with Adam. Probably this is true. Yet the angelic situation is so divergent that it is precarious to draw hard and fast conclusions. For example, angels apparently fell as individuals, not by the act of a representative angel; but I say *apparently*. If there was an angelic prohibition in some way analogous to this representative prohibition, Scripture tells us nothing about it. Thus, this extrapolation from the case of angels is also inconclusive.

Therefore, Adam probably would have become impeccable by resisting temptation. Yet Scripture neither affirms nor necessarily implies this. Thus, we shouldn't be dogmatic about this conclusion or build covenant theology on it.

Fourth: How long would life in Eden have continued? Would God have translated Adam into heavenly existence right after he successfully endured a period of training and temptation? Calvin and Luther rightly affirmed Adam's eventual translation to heavenly life. The Sabbath emblem of eternal rest confirms this (Gen. 2:3; Heb. 4:3–10). Nevertheless, this translation would have occurred in harmony with Adam's vocation (Gen. 1:28). God wouldn't have scrapped the creation ordinances he just instituted and blessed. Adam would have fulfilled his creation mandate in hope of entering God's eternal rest after he had completed his earthly vocation. Adam would have entered this eternal rest without death.

As to the duration of Adam's earthly vocation, it would have continued long after the period of temptation ended and he attained impeccability. The call to fill the earth and to harness its potential is an enormous mandate. It would have occupied the labors of multitudes of humans over many millennia. God wouldn't say to Adam: If you obey me through a period of temptation, then I will immediately take you from this new earth to heaven and scrap everything I put you here to do. Possibly, when the innocent myriads of pristine mankind in a sinless Adam had finished adorning and harnessing this universe, and had entered God's eternal rest, God would have created another universe and pronounced another mandate for that new universe. If so, it would have happened in the path of obedience to God's prohibition, but not as a meritorious reward. We can never know for sure what would have happened. All we know for certain is that God fulfills all hope of resurrection life and eternal glory in a new universe in Christ, not in Adam.

These last two questions focus on the heart of the covenant of works. In that model God holds out gain or reward for Adam. He says, in essence, if you obey me through a period of temptation, you will gain a better life, one of impeccability, in a better place, either a heavenly abode or a better heavens and earth. Yet the focus of the prohibition is not on what Adam stood to gain, but rather on what he stood to lose. That seems to be missed. That doctrine paints Adam as a man with everything to gain and little to lose. That dilutes the force of God's words. He warns Adam as if he has everything to lose. He doesn't say, obey me and you'll gain a better life. He says, disobey me and you'll forfeit your wonderful and blessed life. Again, he doesn't say, obey me to attain a place better than paradise. He says, disobey me and you will die spiritually and lose the privilege of being with me in paradise. Adam indeed had much to lose—and he lost it.

Conclusion to the Biblical Exposition

To conclude this exposition, I evaluate the covenantal nature of this prohibition, then summarize what Scripture teaches.

The Covenantal Nature of this Prohibition

Was this prohibition covenantal? If so, is covenant of works the best way to describe it? We consider *works* first, then *covenant*.

We should use caution with the term covenant "*of works.*" It could give the false impression that God condemns or justifies every human on the basis of his own personal deeds. In fact, the representative deeds of Adam and Christ are the basis of condemnation and justification. This has fostered the error that the Mosaic covenant calls every human to earn eternal life by keeping God's commandments. For this reason, at least in part, Professor Murray prefers *Adamic Administration*. Yet, this term has over three-hundred years of confessional prominence. If we just jettison it, we could give the false impression that we reject Adam's representative headship. So, if we use this term, we should use caution, qualification, and explanation.

We should also evaluate carefully whether it is covenantal.[51] If a covenant is a "compact between equals," then plainly this prohibition was not covenantal. God and Adam made no compact. God issued this prohibition unilaterally and sovereignly. Yet Robertson, Murray, and Gonzales have shown that the essential substance of divine covenant is not a compact between equals. Robertson observes that divine covenant involves a personal bond of love and commitment.[52] Gonzales sums its generic substance as a "formal obligation, self-imposed or imposed upon another."[53] Murray captures its essence as "sworn fidelity," expressed in "an oath-certified assurance of irrevocable grace and promise."[54] How do their insights apply to this prohibition? Did it establish a bond of love and commitment between God and Adam? Yes, it did cement a filial-parental bond of love and commitment. Did it impose a formal obligation on God or another? Yes, in this conditional pledge God imposed a formal obligation both on himself and on

---

51. Robert Gonzales concludes affirmatively upon scholarly and cogent analysis in "The Covenantal Context of the Fall: Did God Make a Primeval Covenant with Adam?" in *Reformed Baptist Theological Review* (IV:2 July 2007), 5–32.

52. Robertson, *The Christ of the Covenants*, 3–15.

53. Gonzales, "The Covenantal Context of the Fall," 8.

54. Murray, *The Covenant of Grace*, 25, 28–30.

Adam. Was it an "implicit promise"? Yes, it conveyed implicitly a promise of continued life and happiness. That prompts a key question.

Was this implicit promise confirmed by divine oath? Consider four things. First, in one sense all God's promises have covenantal force. God can't lie. All his promises are absolutely reliable. Yet God doesn't solemnize all his promises with oaths. If we dub every implicit promise a "covenant," we water down the powerful message God sends us when he solemnizes a promise.

Second, sometimes Scripture says that a divine promise was confirmed by oath, even when its immediate context does not say so explicitly (Gen. 9:12–17; Isa. 54:9–10). Possibly Hosea 6:7 is such a reflection. Yet, as Warfield demonstrates, that text alone is insufficient evidence to warrant a dogmatic conclusion.

Third, the parallel with Christ also points in a covenantal direction, but not conclusively. God clearly entered covenant with Christ (Ps. 110:4). This suggests that God's relation with Adam was also covenantal. Yet, God's relation with Christ could be better than his relation with Adam, like Christ's priesthood is superior to Aaron's. They were made priests without an oath, but Christ with an oath (Heb. 7:21). However, God's covenant with Adam could be conditional, his covenant with Christ unconditional, like the new covenant is a "better covenant, built on better promises."

Fourth, the text itself strongly supports confirmation by oath. The phrase translated, *"you shall surely die,"* literally says: "to die (מוֹת) you(s) will die (תָּמוּת)." This idiom, an absolute infinitive with the imperfect, is emphatic. It intimates the force of an oath in Genesis 32:12 and Numbers 26:65. In Numbers 26:65 this very idiom describes God's pledge to kill a rebel generation in the wilderness: "For the LORD had said of them, they shall surely (מוֹת) die (יָמֻתוּ) in the wilderness." In Psalm 95:11 Scripture says this commitment was an oath: "Wherefore I swore in my wrath, that they should not enter into my rest." In Genesis 32:12 Jacob depicts God's covenant (Gen. 28:14) with this idiom: "you said, I will surely do you good, and make your seed as the sand of the sea." Thus, "you shall surely die," does have the force of an oath. God did indeed solemnize this prohibition.

What is the upshot? The evidence supports the conclusion that this prohibition was covenantal. It conveys implicitly to Adam God's solemn pledge or covenant. Thus, I prefer to call it the *"Adamic covenant."* The Westminster Standards also used *"covenant of life,"* which is preferable to covenant of works. Pastor Robert Fisher called it the *"Creation Bond,"* Robertson, the *"Covenant of Creation,"* and Murray, the *"Adamic Administration."* I have no objection to any of these. Each expresses an aspect of truth. It seems prudent to me not to insist on only one term for this representative prohibition.

Summary of the Biblical Teaching

First, we uncovered *the foundations* of the Adamic covenant. Adam before the fall was God's son, prince of creation, with representative and royal sonship (Gen. 1:26–27). He had the filial privilege of spiritual and physical life, and access to the tree of life (Gen. 1:31, 2:16). He lived and labored in special communion with God, in a sacred place, the Garden of Eden (Gen. 2:15). All this unmerited privilege and happiness carried with it filial obligation. He was obliged as God's image to imitate God, to reverence what God reverenced and to love what God loved. He had a blessed vocation, defined in creation ordinances, endorsed by divine favor. He had the prospect of long-term fulfillment and joy in populating and harnessing the earth (Gen. 1:28). On every Sabbath day he could rest from his labor, spend the day with God in the garden, and eat from the tree of life (Gen. 2:1–3). Every Sabbath was an emblem of God's rest. Thus, Adam labored in hope that when he fulfilled his work on earth, the creation mandate, he would enter God's rest. God would translate him, without death, into his heavenly presence.

On this foundation, we unfolded *the features* of the Adamic covenant. His Father and King spoke this covenant to Adam, in his representative capacity. This covenant consisted in his permission, prohibition, and pledge (Gen. 2:16–17). God permitted him access to every tree in the Garden of Eden except one. God prohibited him from eating from the tree of knowledge. His pledge consisted in a solemn warning and implicit promise. God solemnly warned him that he had much to lose. If he disobeyed, he would destroy his life and forfeit his privileges. Thus his Father implicitly promised that if he trusted and obeyed him, he would retain his life, maintain his privileges, fulfill his vocation, and realize his hope. He implicitly associated the tree of life with this pledge.

After unfolding its features, we discovered *the functions* of the Adamic covenant. God meant it for his good. It was symbolic and pedagogical. It was about education, about the knowledge of right and wrong. God designed it to teach his son Adam right and wrong experientially. Through it Adam was to attain a proven commitment to God and to good by enduring temptation.

We then analyzed the *conditional form* of the Adamic covenant. It was a conditional pledge, which would have its fruition in continued life upon compliance with the prohibition, or in death upon its violation.

That led us to consider *the fruition* of the Adamic covenant. Tragically, Adam ate from the tree of knowledge. He violated the prohibition. He lost his life, his home in paradise, and his hope. He brought God's wrath on himself and his posterity.

Conclusion: Practical Application of the Adamic Covenant

Dagg and Brakel commend the importance of taking to heart the experiential application of each biblical truth. Accordingly, Dagg introduces this prohibition with a call to repentance.[55] Brakel concludes with an exhortation to reflect on the covenant of works.[56] Thus, we unfold its practical lessons about God, man, sin, and Christ.

The Adamic Covenant Furnishes Practical Lessons about God
It calls us to behold and embrace by faith God's sovereignty, generosity, pedagogy, and severity.

It Calls us to Behold and Submit to God's Sovereignty
It begins on this note: "And Jehovah God commanded the man, saying." God speaks with authority. He imposes his will unilaterally on Adam, his creature, son, and prince. He has the right to do what he wills in his creation. His will defines right and good, because he is God. His Word defines his revealed will. The Adamic covenant calls us to submit by faith to God's revealed will, expressed in his Word.

It Calls us to Behold and Appreciate God's Generosity
God lavished generous provision: "Of every tree of the garden you may freely eat." He is good and generous. He provided for Adam a life of comfort, pleasure, and joy. He granted him unmerited privilege and favor. Adam didn't have to earn a home in paradise. He didn't have to merit the privilege of eating from the tree of life. This calls us to appreciate how gracious and generous God really is toward his creatures. It calls us to praise and adore God our Creator.

It Calls us to Behold and Endure God's Pedagogy
God subjected Adam to his moral training: "but of the tree of the knowledge of good and evil, you shall not eat of it." As God trained Adam, so he trains Christians:

---

55. Dagg, *Manuel of Theology*, 138–141.
56. Brakel, *Reasonable Service*, 367.

For whom the Lord loves he chastens, And scourges every son whom he receives. It is for chastening that you endure; God deals with you as with sons; for what son is there whom *his* father chastens not? (Heb. 12:6–7).

God's moral training of innocent Adam was not "chastening," like our moral training. Nevertheless, it calls us to endure by faith our moral training as sons of God.

It Calls us to Behold and Fear God's Severity

God's solemn warning displays his severity: "for in the day that you eat thereof you shall surely die." As God's gospel plan of redemption reveals his goodness and severity (Rom. 11:22), so does his plan for creation in the Adamic covenant. God's severity stems from his holiness and justice. Thus Paul exhorts:

"Well; by their unbelief they were broken off, and you stand by thy faith. Be not highminded, but fear: for if God spared not the natural branches, neither will he spare you. Behold then the goodness and severity of God (Rom. 11:20–22).

Similarly, the Adamic covenant calls us to behold the severity of a holy God and walk humbly with him by faith in gospel fear. If God didn't spare prince Adam, but punished him with death, neither will he spare hypocrites who live wicked lives but say they know God.

The Adamic Covenant Furnishes Practical Lessons about Man

It calls us to behold and embrace by faith man's responsibility, mutability, and solidarity.

It Calls us Submissively to Embrace Man's Responsibility

As it displays God's authority, so it displays man's responsibility: "and Jehovah God *commanded the man*." God is not accountable to man. Man is accountable to God. God, in his Word, defines man's priority and duty: "Fear God, and keep his commandments: for this is the whole duty of man" (Eccles. 12:13). God's Word should define our behavior, values, feelings, and choices. This calls us to submission to our lot as creatures accountable to God.

It Calls us Humbly to Embrace Man's Mutability

Unlike God, man was not impeccable inherently and essentially: "for in the day that you eat thereof you shall surely die." The origin of human sin always was an insoluble mystery.[57] Moral mutability involved choice. Adam could, and did, choose evil (Eccles. 7:29). Conversely, in the gospel God calls fallen men to forsake evil and choose to do what is good. No fallen man can, or ever will, choose to do what is morally good in his own strength.[58] Man could fall, but he cannot redeem himself or renew himself morally. In the covenant of grace God supplies the moral power to choose the good, turn from sin, and come to Christ. Thus, we should embrace with humility man's moral mutability in the state of innocence and moral inability in the state of sin. We should praise God for moral immutability in Christ, experienced in a germinal way in regeneration, and consummately in glorification.[59]

It Calls us Trustfully to Embrace Man's Solidarity

When Paul reflects on the Adamic covenant, he affirms human solidarity in Adam. He affirms that Adam represented his posterity:

> Therefore, as through one man sin entered into the world and through sin death, even in this way death spread unto all men, because all sinned…by the trespass of the one the many died…the judgment from one unto condemnation…by the one trespass of the one death ruled through the one…through one wrongdoing, unto all men, unto condemnation…through the disobedience of the one man the many have been made sinners (Rom. 5:12, 15, 17, 18, 19).

This calls us to respond trustfully. We must define justice by God's Word. We must acknowledge by faith that God's Word reveals the truth about human solidarity. Failure to embrace solidarity in Adam leads to error regarding justification by faith, since justification is based on solidarity in Christ.

The Adamic Covenant Teaches a Practical Lesson about Sin
It displays the enormity of sin:

---

57. I commend Murray's expose of this mystery associated with man's fall, which he dubs the "psychogenetic" problem, in *Collected Writings*, 2: 72–75.

58. "Can the Ethiopian change his skin, or the leopard his spots? then may ye also do good, that are accustomed to do evil" (Jer. 13:23); "No man can come to me, except the Father that sent me draw him: and I will raise him up in the last day" (John 6:44); "because the mind of the flesh is enmity against God; for it is not subject to the law of God, neither indeed can it be: and they that are in the flesh cannot please God" (Rom. 8:7–8).

59. "Whosoever is begotten of God does no sin, because his seed abides in him: and he cannot sin, because he is begotten of God" (1 John 3:9); "on this side of the river and on that was the tree of life…. And there shall be no curse any more…and his servants shall serve him…and they shall reign for ever and ever" (Rev. 22:2–3, 5).

> By the trespass of the one the many died...the judgment from one
> unto condemnation...by the one trespass of the one death ruled
> through the one (Rom. 5:15, 16, 17).

Sin is spiritual treason. It is a betrayal, a personal affront to his God and
Father. Regarding this Gonzales cogently observes:[60]

> An appreciation of the covenantal context of the fall...helps to pre-
> serve a biblical theology of sin. There is a sense in which all human
> sin is tied to that primeval covenant.... Sin is not merely a lack of
> conformity to or transgression of an abstract impersonal law-code;
> it is a betrayal of trust, a breach of friendship, and an affront to a
> benevolent and loving Sovereign who from the beginning had man's
> highest joy in view.

Thus, one sin has occasioned all the suffering and death in the world.
This displays its enormity. This displays the exceeding evil of sin as harmful,
culpable, and destructive.

The Adamic Covenant Teaches a Practical Lesson about Christ

> Adam: who is a pattern of the one who is coming.... Therefore then,
> as through one wrongdoing, unto all men, unto condemnation; so
> also, through one right-doing, unto all men, unto justification of
> life. For just as through the disobedience of the one man the many
> have been made sinners; so also, by the obedience of the one the
> many shall be made righteous (Rom. 5:14, 18, 19).

Paul says that Adam, as representative head of humanity, was a type or
pattern of Christ. Thus the Adamic covenant portrays salvation in Christ.
It points to the need for Christ. It displays the way of salvation in Christ. It
displays the glory and value of the virtue of Christ. Thus, it calls sinners in
Adam to look to Christ alone for salvation. May God be pleased so to bless
our study of the Adamic covenant.

---

60. Gonzales, "The Covenantal Context of the Fall," 32.

Bibliography

Armitage, Thomas. *The History of the Baptists.* Volume 2. Minneapolis: James and Klock Christian Publishing Company, 1977.

Barrett, Michael P. V. *Beginning At Moses: A Guide to Finding Christ in the Old Testament.* Greenville and Belfast: Ambassador-Emerald International and Ambassador Productions, 2001.

Bass, Clarence B. *Backgrounds to Dispensationalism.* Grand Rapids: Baker Book House, 1978.

Bavinck, Herman. *Reformed Dogmatics.* Volume 3. Edited by John Bolt; Translated by John Vriend. Grand Rapids: Baker Publishing Group, 2006.

———. *Our Reasonable Faith.* Translated by Henry Zylstra. Grand Rapids: Baker Book House, 1977.

Berkhof, Louis. *Systematic Theology.* Grand Rapids: Wm. B. Eerdmans Publishing Company, 1972.

Boston, Thomas. "Of the Covenant of Grace." In Volume 1 of *The Complete Works of Thomas Boston.* Wheaton, IL: Richard Owen Roberts Publishers, 1980.

Brakel, Wilhelmus. "The Covenant of Grace." In Volume 1 of *The Christian's Reasonable Service.* Translated by Bartel Elshout. Ligonier, PA: Soli Deo Gloria Publications, 1992.

Brooks, Thomas. "Paradise Opened." In Volume 5 of *The Works of Thomas Brooks.* Edited by Alexander R. Grosart. Edinburgh: The Banner of Truth Trust, 1980.

Brown, John. *Analytical Exposition of the Epistle of Paul the Apostle to the Romans*. Grand Rapids: Baker Book House, 1981.

———. *An Exposition of the Epistle to the Galatians*. Evansville, IN: The Sovereign Grace Book Club, 1957.

———. *Hebrews*. Edinburgh: The Banner of Truth Trust, 1976.

Brown, John. *The Systematic Theology of John Brown of Haddington*. Grand Rapids: Reformation Heritage Books, 2002.

Bruce, F. F. *The Epistle to the Hebrews*. Grand Rapids: Wm. B. Eerdmans Publishing Company, 1977.

Bunyan, John. "The Doctrine of Law and Grace Unfolded." In Volume 1 of *The Works of John Bunyan*. Grand Rapids: Baker Book House, 1977.

———. "An Exposition of the First Ten Chapters of Genesis." In Volume 2 of *The Works of John Bunyan*. Grand Rapids: Baker Book House, 1977.

Calvin, John. *Commentaries on the First Book of Moses called Genesis*. Translated by John King. Grand Rapids: Baker Book House, 1979.

———. *The Epistles of Paul to the Galatians, Ephesians, Philippians, and Colossians*. Edited by David and Thomas Torrance; Translated by T. H. L. Parker. Grand Rapids: Wm. B. Eerdmans Publishing Company, 1974.

———. *Institutes of the Christian Religion*. Volume 1. Edited by John T. McNeill; Translated by Ford Lewis Battles. Philadelphia: The Westminster Press, 1967.

Campbell, K. M. *God's Covenant*. Nutley, NJ: Presbyterian and Reformed Publishing Company, 1974.

Chafer, Lewis Sperry. *Systematic Theology*. Volumes 4, 5, and 7. Dallas: Dallas Seminary Press, 1969.

Dabney, Robert Louis. *Lectures in Systematic Theology*. Grand Rapids: Zondervan Publishing House, 1976.

Dagg, John L. *A Manual of Theology*. Harrisonburg, VA: Gano Books, 1982.

Dick, John. *Lectures on Theology*. Xenia, OH: The Board of Calvinistic Book Concern, 1846.

Eadie, John. *Commentary on the Epistle to the Ephesians.* Grand Rapids: Zondervan Publishing House, 1977.

Edwards, Jonathan. "A History of the Work of Redemption." In Volume 1 of *The Works of Jonathan Edwards.* Edinburgh: The Banner of Truth Trust, 1976.

Flavel, John. "The Covenant of Redemption between the Father and the Redeemer." In Volume 1 of *The Works of John Flavel.* London: The Banner of Truth Trust, 1968.

Gill, John. *Complete Body of Doctrinal and Practical Divinity.* Volume 1. Grand Rapids: Baker Book House, 1978.

Gonzales, Robert. "The Covenantal Context of the Fall: Did God Make a Primeval Covenant with Adam?" in *Reformed Baptist Theological Review,* IV:2 (July 2007).

Gouge, William. *Commentary on Hebrews.* Grand Rapids: Kregel Publications, 1980.

Haldane, Robert. *An Exposition of the Epistle to the Romans.* Mac Dill AFB, FL: Mac Donald Publishing Company, n. d.

Hendriksen, William. *The Covenant of Grace.* Grand Rapids: Wm. B. Eerdmans Publishing Company, 1932.

―――. *Exposition of Paul's Epistle to the Romans.* Grand Rapids: Baker Book House, 1984.

―――. *Exposition of Galatians.* Grand Rapids: Baker Book House, 1975.

―――. *Exposition of Ephesians.* Grand Rapids: Baker Book House, 1976.

Henry, Matthew. *Commentary on the Whole Bible.* Volumes 1 and 6. Old Tappan, NJ: Fleming H. Revell Company, n. d.

Hillers, Delbert. *Covenant: The History of a Biblical Idea.* Baltimore: John Hopkins University Press, 1969.

Hodge, Charles. *Systematic Theology.* Volume 2. Grand Rapids: Wm. B. Eerdmans Publishing Company, 1989.

―――. *A Commentary on Romans.* Edinburgh: The Banner of Truth Trust, 1975.

———. *A Commentary on the Epistle to the Ephesians*. Grand Rapids: Wm. B. Eerdmans Publishing Company, 1966.

Hoeksema, Herman. *Reformed Dogmatics*. Grand Rapids: Reformed Free Publishing Association, 1976.

———. *Believers and Their Seed*. Grand Rapids: Reformed Free Publishing Association, 1977.

Hughes, Philip E. *A Commentary on the Epistle to the Hebrews*. Grand Rapids: Wm. B. Eerdmans Publishing Company, 1977.

Jewett, Paul K. *Infant Baptism and the Covenant of Grace*. Grand Rapids: Wm. B. Eerdmans Publishing Company, 1978.

Jocz, Jacob. *The Covenant: A Theology of Human Destiny*. Grand Rapids: Wm. B. Eerdmans Publishing Company, 1968.

Keil, C. F. and Delitzsch, F. *Commentary on the Old Testament*. Volume 1. Translated by James Martin. Grand Rapids: Wm. B. Eerdmans Publishing Company, 1973.

Kersten, G. H. *Reformed Dogmatics*. Volume 1. Translated by Joel R. Beeke. Netherlands Reformed Book and Publishing Committee, 1980.

Kingdon, David. *Children of Abraham*. Worthing and Haywards Heath: Henry Walter Ltd. and Carey Publications Ltd., 1973.

Kline, Meredith G. *By Oath Consigned: A Reinterpretation of the Covenant Signs of Circumcision and Baptism*. Grand Rapids: Wm. B. Eerdmans Publishing Company, 1975.

———. *Treaty of the Great King: The Covenant Structure of Deuteronomy*. Grand Rapids: Wm. B. Eerdmans Publishing Company, 1963.

Lenski, R. C. H. *The Interpretation of St. Paul's Epistle to the Romans*. Minneapolis: Augsburg Publishing House, 1961.

———. *The Interpretation of St. Paul's Epistles to the Galatians, to the Ephesians, and to the Philippians*. Minneapolis: Augsburg Publishing House, 1961.

———. *The Interpretation of the Epistle to the Hebrews and the Epistle of James*. Minneapolis: Augsburg Publishing House, 1966.

Leupold, H. C. *Exposition of Genesis*, Volume 1. Grand Rapids: Baker Book House, 1974.

Luther, Martin. *Luther's Works*. Volume 1. Edited by Jaroslav Pelikan; Translated by George V. Schick. Saint Louis: Concordia Publishing House, 1958.

Malone, Fred A. *The Baptism of Disciples Alone*. Cape Coral, FL: Founders Press, 2003.

Martin, Hugh. *The Atonement*. Edinburgh: Knox Press, 1976.

McCarthy, D. J. *Old Testament Covenant*. Atlanta: John Knox Press, 1978.

Melanchthon, Philip. *Melanchthon on Christian Doctrine: Loci Communes 1555*. Clyde L. Manschreck, Editor and Translator. New York: Oxford University Press, 1965.

Mendenhall, George E. *Law and Covenant in Israel and The Ancient Near East*. Pittsburgh: The Biblical Colloquium, 1955.

Moule, Handley C. G. *The Epistle to the Romans*. Grand Rapids: Zondervan Publishing House, by special arrangement with Pickering and Inglis Ltd., n. d.

Murray, John. *The Covenant of Grace*. London: The Tyndale Press, 1954.

———. *The Epistle to the Romans*. Volumes 1 and 2. Grand Rapids: Wm. B. Eerdmans Publishing Company, one volume edition, 1979.

———. "Covenant Theology." In Volume 4 of *The Collected Writings of John Murray*. Edinburgh: The Banner of Truth Trust, 1982.

——— and Stonehouse, Ned B. *The Free Offer of the Gospel*. Phillipsburg, NJ: Presbyterian and Reformed Publishing Company, 1979.

Owen, John. *An Exposition of the Epistle to the Hebrews*. Volumes 6 and 7. Edited by W. H. Goold. Grand Rapids: Baker Book House, 1980.

Pink, Arthur W. *The Divine Covenants*. Grand Rapids: Baker Book House, 1983.

Poole, Matthew. *A Commentary on the Holy Bible*. Volumes 1 and 3. London: The Banner of Truth Trust, 1968.

Reisinger, John G. *But I Say Unto You*. Southbridge, MA: Crown Publications, 1989.

Robertson, O. Palmer. *The Christ of the Covenants*. Grand Rapids: Baker Book House, 1980.

———. "Current Reformed Thinking on the Nature of the Divine Covenants." In *The Westminster Theological Journal*, XL:1 (Fall 1977).

Shedd, William G. T. *Dogmatic Theology*. Volume 2. Grand Rapids: Zondervan Publishing House, n. d.

Sibbes, Richard. "The Faithful Covenanter." In Volume 6 of *Works of Richard Sibbes*. Edited by Alexander B. Grosart. Edinburgh: The Banner of Truth Trust, 1983.

Smith, Morton. *Systematic Theology*. 2 Volumes. Greenville: Greenville Seminary Press, 1994.

Spurgeon, Charles H. "Christ the Conqueror of Satan." In *The Metropolitan Tabernacle Pulpit*. Volume 22. Pasadena, TX: Pilgrim Publications, 1971.

Thornwell, James Henley. "Outline of the Covenant of Grace and Testimony to Sublapsarianism." In *The Collected Writings of James Henley Thornwell*, Volume 2. Edinburgh: The Banner of Truth Trust, 1974.

Turretin, Francis. *Institutes of Elenctic Theology*. Volume 2. Edited by James T. Dennison; Translated by George M. Giger. Phillipsburg, NJ: Presbyterian and Reformed Publishing Company, 1993.

Vos, Geerhardus. *Biblical Theology*. Grand Rapids: Wm. B. Eerdmans Publishing Company, 1975.

Waldron, Samuel E. *A Modern Exposition of the 1689 Baptist Confession of Faith*. Darlington: Evangelical Press, 1989.

———. *Biblical Baptism*. Grand Rapids: Truth for Eternity Ministries, 1998.

Warfield, B. B. "Christ's 'Little Ones.'" In Volume 1 of *Selected Shorter Writings of Benjamin B. Warfield*. Edited by John E. Meeter. Nutley, NJ: Presbyterian and Reformed Publishing Company, 1970.

———. "Abraham the Father of the Faithful." In Volume 2 of *Selected Shorter Writings of Benjamin B. Warfield*. Edited by John E. Meeter. Nutley, NJ: Presbyterian and Reformed Publishing Company, 1973.

―――. "The Polemics of Infant Baptism." In Volume 9 of *The Works of Benjamin B. Warfield*. Grand Rapids: Baker Book House, 1981.

―――. *The Plan of Salvation*. Grand Rapids: Wm. B. Eerdmans Publishing Company, 1977.

Wells, Tom and Zaspel, Fred G. *New Covenant Theology*. Frederick, MD: New Covenant Media, 2002.

Witsius, Herman. *The Economy of the Covenants Between God and Man*. 2 Volumes. Phillipsburg, NJ: Presbyterian and Reformed Publishing Company, 1990.

Solid Ground Christian Books is a publishing company committed to the preservation and presentation of the cardinal doctrines of Holy Scripture. Our goal is to spread the fame of the Name of the Lord by finding, uncovering and restoring the best Christian literature from the past and bringing it into the modern world.

We believe that there are many treasured works from the past that the Lord has used in mighty ways, and yet are unavailable to the modern reader. We are always searching for works that have been used by the Holy Spirit in converting sinners, sanctifying saints and preserving them unto the end.

Our desire is to serve pastors, churches, missionaries, chaplains, the military, professors and students of the 21st century. We will seek to keep our prices fair, and our service prompt, personal and courteous.

Our prayer is that the God of sovereign grace will be pleased to smile upon our efforts to further His kingdom and that multitudes throughout the world will be forever changed by reading the books we produce.

Soli Deo Gloria — To God Alone Be The Glory!

Call Us at **205-443-0311**
Visit us on-line at **www.solid-ground-books.com**

OTHER RELATED TITLES FROM SOLID GROUND

In addition to the book COVENANT THEOLOGY by Greg Nichols, we have published more than 300 titles since 2001. Some are as follows:

———————❖———————

The Complete Works of Thomas Manton
Deluxe Leather Edition of the *1689 Baptist Confession of Faith*
Deluxe Leather Edition of the *Three Forms of Unity*
Robert Hawker's *Poor Man's Commentaries*
Scriptural Exposition of the Baptist Catechism by Benjamin Beddome
The Marrow of True Justification by Benjamin Keach
The Travels of True Godliness by Benjamin Keach
Gospel Sonnets by Ralph Erskine
A Body of Divinity by Archbishop James Ussher
Heaven Upon Earth by James Janeway
A Short Explanation of Hebrews by David Dickson
Commentary on Hebrews by William Gouge
Commentary on Jude by Thomas Jenkyn
Commentary on Second Peter by Thomas Adams
Commentary on the New Testament by John Trapp
The Christian Warfare by John Downame
An Exposition of the Ten Commandments by Ezekiel Hopkins
The Harmony of the Divine Attributes by William Bates
The Communicant's Companion by Matthew Henry
The Secret of Communion with God by Matthew Henry
The Redeemer's Tears Wept Over Lost Souls by John Howe

———————❖———————

Call 205-443-0311 for a Free Catalogue

CPSIA information can be obtained
at www.ICGtesting.com
Printed in the USA
LVHW041241090522
718253LV00001B/58